ZONDERVAN
Charts

CHARTS OF

WORLD
RELIGIONS

Books in the Zondervan*Charts* Series

CHARTS OF

WORLD RELIGIONS

H. Wayne House

RESEARCH ASSISTANCE - MATT POWER

ZONDERVAN™

GRAND RAPIDS, MICHIGAN 49530 USA

ZONDERVAN.COM/
AUTHORTRACKER

We want to hear from you. Please send your comments about this
book to us in care of zreview@zondervan.com. Thank you.

ZONDERVAN™

Charts of World Religions
Copyright © 2006 by H. Wayne House

Requests for information should be addressed to:

Zondervan, *Grand Rapids, Michigan 49530*

Library of Congress Cataloging-in-Publication Data

House, H. Wayne.
      Charts of world religions / H. Wayne House.
          p. cm. (ZondervanCharts)
      Includes bibliographical references and index.
      Summary: This collection of charts shows what the major religions of the world have in common and how they
differ in terms of beliefs, practices, and understanding of human nature and the supernatural—Provided by publisher.
      ISBN: 978-0-310-20495-4 (softcover)

      1. Religions—Charts, diagrams, etc. I. Title. II. Series.
      BL82.H68 2005
      200'.22'3—dc22

                                                 2005016025

Interior design by Angela Eberlein

Printed in the United States of America

To Ray and Betty Arnold
In appreciation for the way in which they have cared about
people of different cultures,
and how they have expressed friendship to me
over the last several years.

Contents

Preface

The number and variety of religious faiths and traditions in the world staggers the mind of those who take time to study them. These myriad views of spiritual reality generally share the strong desire of human souls to commune with someone or something that is beyond them. Yet the ways of expressing this communion are as varied as are the religious traditions themselves. The religions of the world have many areas of common concern: the nature of deity, the source of understanding spiritual truth (often in written form), the problem of human failure, the need for achieving a proper relationship or spiritual connection with a higher being (at least theistic religions do), rituals that put us in communion with this being, and matters relating to what happens after death. These are all points of similarity.

Yet for all of this common concern, there is tremendous diversity of views among the world's religions, views that clash repeatedly outside a superficial veneer of agreement. Eastern and Western religions speak of God, but philosophically and theologically they are as different as day and night. Eastern religion often identifies God with the world, whereas Western religion does not. The views of salvation, evil, and the nature of humanity, and more, often are dramatic opposites among these various religions. All of this can become very complicated. It is because of the need to look at similarity and difference, common views and opposites, that this book of charts was written.

Charts of World Religions provides the reader with a general but substantive summary of a wide range of living religious traditions in an easy-to-use format. The book is divided into six major sections: Prolegomena to World Religions, Comparison of World Religions, Ancient Mediterranean Religions, Western Religions, Eastern Religions, and Indigenous Religions. A word of explanation is in order about these divisions. The section on Prolegomena includes charts of a general nature about religion itself apart from any particular religious tradition. The purpose of the Comparison of World Religions is to give an overall look at the various world religions before analyzing each one individually. The Ancient Mediterranean Religions section explains the ancient religions of the Egyptians, the Greeks, and the Romans. The major religions in the section on Western Religions—Judaism, Christianity, and Islam—all had their origins in the Middle East. Eastern Religions usually refers to religious faiths that had their origin in the Far East and share a world religious view uniquely different from that of the West, generally monistic and pantheistic. The last division, Indigenous Religions, includes religious faiths that are diverse, but represent groups in Africa, the Caribbean islands (often from

Africa but with a syncretism of African tradition and Christianity), and Native Americans in North America.

Each of the sections of Western, Eastern, and Indigenous religions contains a chart that displays the historical relationships between the various religions that fall under its heading as well as a chart that compares basic beliefs of these religions. Each major religion has a corresponding timeline; some have a chart that compares their various branches or sects. Each religion's chart contains information on the current data, history, fundamental beliefs, and distinctive beliefs and practices. In some cases further information is given regarding the scriptures, holy days, and/or calendars of the religion.

In a reference work like this, a certain degree of generalization is necessary, and sometimes classifying a religion under a broader religious tradition does not exactly fit. Those interested in pursuing any of this book's topics in greater depth should consult the Sources and the Recommended Reading List. *Charts of World Religions* is primarily concerned with the basic elements of each religion's history, beliefs, and practices. Those desiring to obtain more information about other aspects of the religions covered in this work would be well served to consult additional sources.

Finally, some may object that the topics selected for the charts of religions (Creation, Scripture and Authority, God, Mankind, Sin, Salvation, and Afterlife) are essentially "Western" and thus have a tendency to require that some of the religions be presented in ways that are out of sync with the religions' own distinctive frames of reference. Although this is certainly true to some extent, the author nevertheless believes that the categories employed, when construed in a sufficiently broad manner, capture important features that are common to nearly all religious traditions. In no case is the use of these categories intended to commit a kind of intellectual imperialism by forcing non-Western religions into descriptions that are alien to their own unique perspectives. Rather, it is hoped that these categories (as used in the corresponding charts) will provide the reader with a convenient way to compare and contrast the central doctrines and practices of the various religions described in this book.

Acknowledgments

Many have helped me over the last several years in the accumulation and research on *Charts of World Religions*.

First, to my students at Michigan Theological Seminary, I owe gratitude for their patience as I began to teach the topic of world religions. They taught me much through their questions and research and writing, possibly as much I taught them. I wish also to thank Western Seminary in Portland, Oregon, particularly Dr. Enoch Wan and Dr. Galen Currah, and the students in the course World Religions and Ideologies for the opportunity to teach the doctoral seminar. Unfortunately, I do not have the names of all of these students at MTS and Western, and attempting to list them would inevitably leave some out. But each of them should know that they stirred me toward the writing of the book and contributed much to me. I owe them and appreciate them for this.

In the earlier stages of the book I am especially grateful to Nick Keehus, Dan Tarabek, Bob and Tracy Liichow, Todd Garner, and Lynn Henry for providing resources and organization of materials.

I owe special thanks to Dr. Stan Gundry at Zondervan for his belief in this project and his encouragement throughout, particularly at the final stages. He forever remains a friend. I also wish to express appreciation to two editors who worked on the book, Jim Ruark for his overall guidance and for seeing the work through the final stages before publication and Jane Haradine for her tenaciousness and cheerful manner as she worked closely with me in the final weeks of editing, first from her boat in Florida and then from her home in Michigan. I owe a great debt to her attention to detail and excellent editing.

My researcher, Matt Power, put in many hours collecting materials and helping in writing portions of the book in the preliminary and final stages of the project. I would have found it difficult to do the book without his help.

I owe my wife Leta a great debt of gratitude for the way she took care of me the last several weeks of very difficult work in getting the book to the publisher. She was kind, understanding, and truly served me. I deeply thank her. A word of appreciation also goes to my daughter Carrie, who was always checking on me and concerned about me as I was finishing the project. It is great to have children around when things are tough.

If I have been remiss in mentioning someone, I offer my apologies.

I have endeavored to avoid errors, and many of those named here have assisted me in doing so, but if the reader discovers any mistake, I will be most happy to make adjustments in a future edition.

PART 1
PROLEGOMENA
TO
WORLD RELIGIONS

What Is Religion?

Friedrich Schleiermacher (1768–1834)	"The essence of religion consists in the feeling of absolute dependence."
James Martineau (1805–1900)	"Religion is the belief in … a Divine mind and will ruling the universe and holding moral relations with mankind."
C. P. Tiele (1830–1902)	"Religion is … that pure and reverential disposition or frame of mind which we call piety."
F. H. Bradley (1846–1924)	"Religion is … the attempt to express the complete reality of goodness through every aspect of our being."
James Frazier (1854–1941)	"[Religion is] … a propitiation or conciliation of powers superior to man."
Emile Durkheim (1858–1917)	"[Religion is] … a unified system of beliefs and practices relative to sacred things, … which unite into one single moral community."
Rudolf Otto (1869–1937)	"Religion is that which grows out of, and gives expression to, experience of the holy in its various aspects."
Paul Tillich (1886–1965)	"Religion is the state of being grasped by an ultimate concern, a concern which qualifies all other concerns as preliminary and which itself contains the answer to the question of the meaning of our life."
J. Milton Yinger (1916–)	"Religion is a system of beliefs and practices by means of which a group of people struggle with the ultimate problem of human life."
John Hick (1922–)	"Religion constitutes our varied human response to transcendent Reality."
Ninian Smart (1927–2001)	Six characteristics or dimensions of religion: "the ritual, the mythological, the doctrinal, the ethical, the social, and the experiential."
Peter Berger (1929–)	"[Religion is] … the establishment through human activity of an all-embracing sacred order, that is, of a sacred cosmos that will be capable of maintaining itself in the ever-present face of chaos."
James C. Livingston (1930–)	"Religion is that system of activities and beliefs directed toward that which is perceived to be of sacred value and transforming power."
Roy A. Clouser (1937–)	"A religious belief is any belief in something or other as divine. 'Divine' means having the status of not depending on anything else."
Roland Robertson (1938–)	"[Religion pertains] to a distinction between an empirical and a super-empirical, transcendent reality: the affairs of the empirical being subordinated in significance to the non-empirical."

Chart 1

Four Functional Modes of Religion

Existential	Faith and religious experience
Intellectual	Formal statements of belief (a religion's central beliefs or truth claims)
Institutional	Organizations advocating and transmitting beliefs
Ethical	Teachings and beliefs that relate to moral conduct

Three Basic Views on Faith and Reason

Strong Rationalism	In order for a religious belief system to be properly and rationally accepted, conclusive evidence must be provided that proves the belief system in question to be true.
Fideism (Faith-ism)	Religious belief systems cannot (or ought not) be subjected to rational evaluation.
Critical Rationalism	Religious belief systems can and should be rationally criticized and evaluated, even though conclusive proof of such systems is impossible.

Terms Relating to Religion

Belief	A statement that is taken to be true; a truth claim.
Experience	An event one lives through (either as a participant or as an observer) and about which one is conscious or aware. Such events are not merely emotional states; rather, they involve concepts and beliefs about the Being or Reality that is experienced.
Religious Statement	A truth claim about God or Ultimate Reality and his or its relationship to the world.
Miracle	An event that is (1) contrary to ordinary human experience, and (2) the result of divine activity. On one view, this divine activity "breaks," "suspends," or "counteracts via a supernatural force" the laws of nature. On another, this divine activity causes occurrences that do not conform to the way in which reality is normally experienced.

Charts 2, 3, 4

Six Dimensions of Religion

Experiential	Personal spiritual experiences
Ritual	Sacred activities expressed in worship, sacrifice, and other formalized practices
Myth	Stories that encapsulate fundamental beliefs of a group
Social	Institutional forms of religion
Ethics	Moral codes and guides to behavior
Doctrine	Systematization of beliefs

Do All Religions Lead to God?

Position	Viewpoint	Advocates[1]
Religious Exclusivism	There are elements of truth in other religions, but only one religion is comprehensively and fundamentally true. One religion alone provides the way of salvation.	Old Testament Judaism Historic Christianity Orthodox Islam
Religious Inclusivism	God might reveal himself and acts graciously in various ways and in diverse places. At the same time, it is affirmed that religious claims are either objectively true or objectively false.	Conservative Judaism Post-Vatican II Roman Catholicism Modern Hindism (Sarvapalli Radhakrishnan)[2]
Religious Pluralism	There are many valid religions and life-transforming religious experiences. Different religions embody varying responses to the same divine reality. Most religions can successfully facilitate salvation, liberation, or self-fulfillment.	Liberal Protestantism John Hick[3] Vajrayana Buddhism

[1] The list of advocates is only representative, not complete.
[2] Sarvapalli Radhakrishnan (1888–1975) was a professor at Oxford University who later became the second president of India.
[3] Dr. John Hick (1922–) is a philosopher of religion and theology, who taught at Claremont Graduate University in California and at the University of Birmingham in England.

Comparison of Foundational Religious Worldviews

Atheistic	Monotheistic	Pantheistic	Polytheistic
• From the Greek *atheos* (*a* = none; *theos* = god). Atheism is a worldview that denies the existence of God and/or gods. • Atheistic religions include secular humanism and some schools of Buddhism. • Since no God (or gods) exists in this worldview, the universe is thought to be self-sustaining. Moreover, it is believed that miracles cannot occur, since they require divine activity. (Some atheistic schools of Buddhism nonetheless claim that miracles of a sort can occur and that certain monks possess magical powers.) • Philosophical views similar to atheism include agnosticism and skepticism: Agnosticism (no knowledge): Since knowledge concerning deities cannot be obtained, one cannot know whether God or gods exist. Skepticism: One should always question the reliability of sense perception, since it may be deceptive; reason also has strict limits.	• From the Greek *mono-theos* (*mono* = only or alone; *theos* = god). Monotheism is the belief that there is one God only and not multiple deities. • Monotheistic religions include Judaism, Christianity, Islam, Baha'i, and Zoroastrianism. • Judaism is the root religion of Christianity and of monotheism generally. The famous Shema of Israel in Deuteronomy 6:4 reads, "Yahweh is our God, Yahweh is one." • Christianity is a major monotheistic religion. Christians believe that God is one in essence, yet also consists of three distinct persons. • Islam grew out of Judaism and Christianity. It claims that Allah is the one and only true God. • Hinduism takes monotheistic and polytheistic (often henotheistic) forms. Henotheism (*heno* = one) is the worship of one god without denying the existence of other gods.	• From the Greek *pantheos* (*pan* = all or entire; *theos* = god). Pantheism claims that God is all and all is God. God is "one in being with the universe," and everything in the universe is a manifestation of the one self-existent and impersonal essence. • With some pantheists, God/the universe is said to operate in a rigid, mechanistic way. With others, God/the universe is thought to possess spiritual or metaphysical properties. • Pantheism is exemplified by some kinds of Buddhism and Hinduism.	• From Greek *politheos* (*poli* = many or more; *theos* = god). Polytheism maintains that many finite deities exist, though some polytheistic religions believe that there is a unity of being among these gods. • Polytheistic religions include some forms of Hinduism, some schools of Taoism, Shinto, and ancient Graeco-Roman religions. • In polytheistic Hinduism, the oneness of reality is personified by many sub-deities. • Taoism teaches that the Tao is the ground of reality and is embodied in various forms. • In Shinto, the spirits are called *kami*. • Polytheism was the prevailing worldview in the ancient Mediterranean world. Egypt, Greece, Rome, Babylonia, Persia, and much of northern Europe adhered to it.

Chart 7

PART 2
COMPARISON
OF
WORLD RELIGIONS

Major World Religions in Order of Founding

Religion	Birthdate of Founder	Founder	Deity	Sacred Writings*
Judaism	c. 2100 BC	Abraham	Yahweh (God)	Law, Prophets, and Writings (Hebrew Bible)
Hinduism	c. 1800 BC (early formation)	None or unknown	Brahma, Vishnu, Shiva, Shakti, Krishna	*Vedas* *Upanishads* *Bhagavad Gita*
Zoroastrianism	c. 1300 BC	Zarathushtra	Ahura Mazda	*Avesta*
Taoism	c. 604 BC	Lao-tzu	The Tao	*Tao-te-ching*
Shinto	c. 600 BC (early formation)	None or unknown	The *Kami*	*Ko-ji-ki* *Nihon-shoki*
Jainism	599 BC	Mahavira	Originally none; later the Tirthankaras	*Angas*
Buddhism	c. 560 BC	Gautama Buddha	Originally none; later the Buddha	Pali Canon (*Tripitaka*)
Confucianism	551 BC	Confucius	T'ien (Heaven)	Analects
Christianity	5–3 BC	Jesus Christ	The Trinity: Father, Son, and Holy Spirit	Hebrew and Christian Scriptures
Islam	AD 570	Muhammad	Allah	Koran (Qur'an)
Sikhism	AD 1469	Nanak Dev	True Name	*Granth Sahib*
Baha'i	AD 1819	The Bab (Mirza Ali Muhammad)	Primal Will Divine Manifestations	Certain writings of the Bab, Baha'u'llah, and 'Abdu'l-Baha
Secular Humanism	c. AD 1850 (early formation)	None; several were influential	None	Humanist Manifesto I, II, III

* Only those most central to the religion are listed.

Chart 8

Comparison of Beliefs Among Religions

	Judaism	Christianity	Islam
Creation*	God created the cosmos *ex nihilo* (out of nothing), and every existing thing depends on him for its preservation in being.	The Trinity created the space-time universe *ex nihilo* (out of nothing). He upholds all things by his power.	Allah is the creator, designer, and sustainer of the universe.
God	God is one. The divine attributes include omniscience, omnipotence, perfect benevolence, eternality, infinity, immanence, self-existence, and sovereignty.	Christianity affirms a monotheism wherein God is one in nature, yet exists in three distinct divine persons: Father, Son, and Holy Spirit. God is omniscient, omnipotent, supremely good, eternal, infinite, immanent, and self-existent, and he exercises providence over the world.	There is only one God, Allah. Allah is omniscient, omnipotent, omnipresent, merciful, eternal, and transcendent, and he possesses aseity (self-existence) and hates evil.
Mankind	Mankind was created in God's image with certain communicable characteristics (attributes he shares to a degree with human beings). In the traditional view, mankind became sinful in rebelling against God and needs God's forgiveness to be restored to a state of fellowship with him. Much of modern Judaism reinterprets these points.	Mankind was created in the image and likeness of God and has communicable attributes (ones he shares to a degree with human beings). Mankind's rebellion against God caused human nature to become fallen. Thus, people are sinners in need of redemption.	Mankind is basically good, not sinful by nature. Human beings can and should live in submission to the will of Allah.
Scripture and Authority	The Hebrew Scriptures (Tanakh) are composed of the Torah (Law), Prophets, and Writings. Also important is the Talmud.	The Bible consists of 66 books written by about 40 authors and includes both the Hebrew Scriptures (Old Testament) and the writings of the apostles and their companions (New Testament). Roman Catholicism and Estern Orthodoxy also include books from the Apocrypha.	The holy book is the Koran (Qur'an), given by revelation to Muhammad.

* Caribbean religions covered in this volume (Santeria, Voudon, Umbanda, and Rastafari) are not included as a group in this chart because it is difficult to make useful generalizations about them.

Chart 9

Comparison of Beliefs Among Religions (continued)

	Judaism	Christianity	Islam
Sin	Sin originated in the heart of a fallen angel known as Satan (traditional view) or as a result of human weakness or limitations (modern view). Sin has both personal and social aspects.	Sin originated in the heart of the Devil. Due to the sin of Adam and Eve, all human beings are sinners by nature and hence need salvation. People are morally responsible for their thoughts, words, and deeds.	Sin consists of rejecting right guidance, yet mankind is deemed basically good. Forgiveness of sin is granted by repentance, but no atonement is necessary for salvation.
Salvation	Traditionally, salvation can be obtained by doing good works and sacrifices of various sorts; one's good works are weighed against one's evil deeds. Most of modern Judaism does not focus on this issue, but concentrates on community and doing good works.	Salvation can be obtained only by placing one's faith in the sacrificial work of Jesus Christ, who died to forgive the sins of fallen human beings who believe in him.	Salvation can be obtained through good deeds. Thus, salvation is based primarily on human effort, though in Sunni Islam a strong doctrine of predestination is also taught.
View of Time	God created time when he created the physical universe. The totality of time—past, present, and future—is finite.	God created time along with space and matter. Time is finite and has past, present, and future aspects. History is headed toward a final consummation.	Time was created by Allah and is finite in nature. Time will end upon the initiation of Doomsday.
View of Other Religions	In general, Judaism allows for Gentiles to pursue their religion as long as they abide by God's minimal requirements for righteous Gentiles.	Although other religions may contain elements of truth, only God's revelation as found in Jesus Christ and the Bible provide sufficient truth for salvation and a proper understanding of God.	Islam is exclusivistic, asserting that it alone is the true religion. Adherents of other religions need to surrender to Allah.

Chart 9

Comparison of Beliefs Among Religions (continued)

	Secular Humanism	Hinduism	Buddhism
Creation	The universe consists solely of matter, energy, space, and time. The universe has always existed or is the result of the Big Bang, the cause of which is either unknown or not needed. Only this world and present life exist.	The universe is an unconscious emanation of divinity and is without beginning. Brahman is the only true and ultimate Reality.	The Buddha himself never described the world. However, Mahayana Buddhists hold that the universe consists of a series of heavens.
God	God does not exist. The concept of God is merely a human-cultural invention. Philosophies such as naturalism and materialism accurately describe reality.	Some types are theistic, some are pantheistic, and some are polytheistic. Various gods undergo incarnations. The three chief gods are Brahma, Shiva, and Vishnu.	Buddhism is atheistic in practice. Buddha never denied the existence of a Supreme Being, but he thought that belief in God was not edifying for the religious life. There are many god-like Buddhas and *bodhisattvas*.
Mankind	Humans are a complex conglomeration of molecules, the end result of an evolutionary process that has progressed from single-celled organisms to higher forms of life.	The "self" is an illusion. Human beings undergo many cycles of reincarnation.	Mankind goes through many cycles of reincarnation, yet many schools of Buddhism maintain that the "self" is an illusion.
Scripture and Authority	No divine revelation exists. Truth is obtained through scientific observation and human reasoning. Major ideological expressions are found in *Humanist Manifesto I*, *Humanist Manifesto II*, and *Humanist Manifesto III*.	Most Hindus consider the *Vedas* and *Upanishads* as their most important sacred texts. The *Puranas* and the *Bhagavad Gita* also are central to many schools.	The first Buddhist scripture was the Pali Canon, commonly called the *Tripitaka* (Triple Basket). Various sects give a prominent place to other scriptures as well, including the *Lotus Sutra* and the *Kanjur*.

Chart 9

Comparison of Beliefs Among Religions (continued)

	Secular Humanism	Hinduism	Buddhism
Sin	Sin or evil has no objective reality, but is a social construct. Moral relativism is the sober truth. Morality is just a human idea that differs from one culture to another.	Evil is chaos, suffering, destruction, or bondage. Sin is moral or ritualistic and is defined as bad karma.	The presence of evil and suffering in the world is evidence against the existence of God. At the same time, evil is not ultimately real. The root of all evil is ignorance.
Salvation	There is no salvation as such.	Liberation consists of escaping the cycle of death and rebirth, and entering into the presence of Brahman.	The achievement of liberation is hindered by ignorance. Nirvana (based etymologically on the act of extinguishing, "blowing out"), or a state of oblivion, can be achieved by meditation and other religious practices.
View of Time	Time is finite (à la Albert Einstein), woven into the fabric of the universe along with space and matter.	Like the universe, time has no beginning.	Time is cyclical and eternal.
View of Other Religions	The right use of reason and empirical science provides a reliable way of knowing things and discerning objective truth. Thus Secular Humanism is exclusivist in that it takes itself to be true and anything contrary to it as false. Religion in general ranges from harmless but delusional to very dangerous.	In most of its forms, Hinduism is pluralistic. Human beings can approach Ultimate Reality in many different ways.	Buddhism teaches that one can learn a limited number of things from other religions. Some schools seek converts, while others eschew proselytizing.

Chart 9

Comparison of Beliefs Among Religions (continued)

	Taoism	Shinto	Confucianism
Creation	The Tao is the Way or Path, the natural order of all things, and is based on the principles of yin and yang. The Tao is the universal life force or the underlying nature of all things that exist in the world.	The universe is spiritual in nature. The natural state of the cosmos is one of harmony in which divine, natural, and human elements are all intimately related.	The cosmos as a whole is experienced in the family, society, and government; heaven is immanent in human affairs.
God	"God" is an impersonal force.	Shinto advocates worship of *kami* (spirits; personal forces that are closely associated with, and have great influence on, human life). There are *kami* related to natural objects and creatures, souls of the dead, abstract creative forces, and guardians, to name just a few.	Confucius affirmed the existence of a supernatural being, T'ien (Heaven). In later Confucianism, Heaven came to be viewed as an impersonal reality.
Mankind	Humans live and function as a part of nature. One can understand mankind's nature and behavior through an adequate grasp of the universe.	Human beings are a part of the spiritual universe in which they exist.	Human beings are morally neutral and can be swayed toward good or evil by persuasive leaders. They can be perfected via wisdom and morality. Human relationships are central to life.
Scripture and Authority	The chief writings are the *Tao-te-ching, Chuang-tzu. I-ching,* and *Lieh-tzu.*	Important books include the *Ko-ji-ki, Nihon-shoki, Rokkokushi,* and *Jinno Shotoki.*	Confucius cited four books and wrote one himself (the five classic *Analects*). Other important texts include the *Book of Mencius* and the *Hsiao Ching.*

Chart 9

Comparison of Beliefs Among Religions (continued)

	Taoism	Shinto	Confucianism
Sin	Only human intervention "upsets" natural events. Possessing virtue is good, but, paradoxically, seeking it indicates a lack of it.	Sin is ritualistic and is called pollution. One can become ritually polluted by contact with the dead or through illicit sexual activity. Sinfulness is not based on strictly moral or ethical considerations.	Human beings are not evil and hence there is no significant sin problem to deal with. Nevertheless, training in wisdom is important. Maintaining proper standards of ethics in personal relationships is crucial.
Salvation	To become "one with the Tao" is the Way or Path.	To be granted protection and good fortune by the *kami* (spirits), one must go through ritual purification before worshiping them.	Tutored self-examination results in being true to one's own inner nature and applying that insight to relationships with others. Social stability is paramount.
View of Time	Time and history are cyclical, though history does not simply repeat itself.	Time has been passing for countless ages. The history of Japan began in 660 BC, when Emperor Jinmu took the throne.	Time is potentially infinite. Time renovates itself. Much can be learned from the past.
View of Other Religions	The Tao alone is the Way, yet other religions are tolerated.	Shinto does not espouse rigid beliefs. However, it maintains that Japan is the only divine land and that its people are divine.	Confucianism has mixed fairly well with some kinds of Buddhism and Taoism, but it has fundamental differences with many Western religions.

	Jainism	Zoroastrianism	Sikhism
Creation	The universe is eternal and exists independently of a Creator. It is multilayered and operates according to cosmic laws.	Ahura Mazda formed the world. The universe is dualistic; there is a continual struggle between good and evil.	*Karta Purukh* created the world through his decree. There is no essential duality between matter and spirit.

Chart 9

Comparison of Beliefs Among Religions (continued)

	Jainism	Zoroastrianism	Sikhism
God	There is no creator God. There are innumerable gods (*Tirthankaras*), the number of which continues to increase as more creatures attain liberation.	Some interpretations are strongly monotheistic, with Ahura Mazda as the supreme deity. Others are henotheistic (worship of one God without denying the existence of other lesser gods).	Sikhism is much closer to monotheism than pantheism, though this point is somewhat ambiguous.
Mankind	Human beings have a body and a soul and undergo death and rebirth. They are equal in value to all other living beings.	Human beings were created by Ahura Mazda with a free will and belong to his kingdom by birthright.	Humans are the most highly evolved beings in the process of creation, and they possess an immortal soul, which is part of God.
Scripture and Authority	Sacred scriptures include the *Angas*, *Upangas*, and *Pakinnakas*.	The central holy book is the *Avesta*.	The most important sacred text is the *Sri Guru Granth Sahib*.
Sin	Sins are actions that cause negative karma to build up, limiting one's ability to achieve liberation.	Sin is misusing one's freedom to do evil instead of doing good.	Sin is whatever disrupts the concord between human beings and God. Evil is temporarily real, but will eventually merge with God.
Salvation	Liberation is attained by freeing oneself from attachments and realizing one's intrinsic purity.	People attain salvation if their good actions outweigh their evil actions.	Several paths, though not all, are efficacious for reaching liberation, which consists of escaping the cycle of reincarnation and merging with God.
View of Time	Time is infinite, consisting of an endless series of epochs.	Time was created by God, is linear, and is progressing toward a final goal. At the end of history, finite time will merge with infinite time.	God created time, which will eventually come to an end.
View of Other Religions	Jainism is inclusivistic and does not make judgments about other religions.	Converts normally are not accepted, but people who choose to do good will be saved from divine judgment.	A fundamental and higher unity underlies all true (and apparently diverse) religions. Non-Sikhs should be afforded liberty of conscience.

Chart 9

Comparison of Beliefs Among Religions (continued)

	African	Native American	Baha'i
Creation	God created the universe, and it is permeated by a mystical energy. There is also an invisible world of spirits and ancestors.	Creation revolves around the tribe's sacred homeland; all of life is interconnected and imbued with spirit.	The universe eternally emanates from God, who has no personal relationship with his creation.
God	A supreme God, unique and transcendent, rules over all, controlling nature and the destinies of men.	God is an almighty creator and the source of all life; the world is pervaded by his Spirit.	God is utterly transcendent and incomprehensible, yet he discloses his divine attributes by means of a series of historical manifestations.
Mankind	Mankind was created by God. Human life is sacred, far more so than animal life.	Human beings have two souls and live in a relationship of mystical interdependence with the land.	The whole of the human race participates in a spiritual oneness. All people possess an immortal soul, but do not have a sinful nature.
Scripture and Authority	There are no sacred writings. Religious teachings are transmitted orally, primarily by the use of myths and stories.	There are no holy books. Sacred stories are preserved through oral tradition.	The writings of the Bab, Baha'u'llah, and 'Abdu'l-Baha comprise the scriptures of the Baha'i faith.
Sin	Sin is primarily the failure to maintain proper social relationships. Evil results from witchcraft or offended spirits.	Sins are any behaviors that diminish the harmony of creation.	Sin results when people fail to bring their lower nature into harmony with their spiritual nature.
Salvation	Believers continually seek to obtain tribal security and protection from harm. Spiritism, amulets, and medicine all aid in acquiring such conditions.	Nearly every act can be viewed as a ritual, and the aim of life should be to act in harmony with the created world and the all-pervading Spirit.	Salvation is obtained by turning toward God, believing in his Manifestations (Great Prophets), and following the instructions of the Manifestations.
View of Time	There are two kinds of time: *sasa* and *zamani*. *Sasa* is located near the present moment; *zamani* takes place at a significant distance from the present moment.	There are two kinds of time: a time before or outside of time (mythic time) and historical time. The Hopi appear to have no concept of historical time.	Time is ultimately an illusion, though it is a provisional reality.
View of Other Religions	African religions tend to view ethical monotheisms positively and polytheism negatively. Within limits, syncretism (combination of diverse beliefs and/or practices) is common.	Native American religions tend to have a lower view of religions not affirmed by the tribe, yet a certain degree of syncretism (combination of diverse beliefs and/or practices) is sometimes allowed.	Baha'i tends to view other religions favorably and as potential vehicles for salvation, though revealed religions (those whose fundamental content was revealed by God or gods) are thought to be superior to ones that lack revelation.

Chart 9

Holy Books of World Religions

Baha'i	*The Most Holy Book* *The Book of Certitude* *Gleanings from the Writings of Baha'u'llah*	**Jainism**	*Angas* *Upangas* *Pakinnakas*
Buddhism	Theravada Buddhism: Pali Canon (*Tripitaka*) Mahayana Buddhism: The *Tripitaka* and various other writings from Indian, Chinese, and Japanese sources, including *Lotus Sutra* and *Perfection of Wisdom.* Vajrayana Buddhism: *Kanjur* and *Tanjur*	**Judaism**	Hebrew scriptures (*Tanakh*): *Torah* (Law) *Prophets* *Writings* *Talmud*
Christianity	The Bible: Old and New Testaments	**Shinto**	*Ko-ji-ki* *Nihon-shoki* *Rokkokushi* *Jinno Shotoki*
Confucianism	*Analects* *Book of Mencius* *Hsiao Ching*	**Sikhism**	*Guru Granth Sahib*
Hinduism	Shruti: *Vedas, Upanishads, Brahmanas* Smriti: *Puranas* (including the *Bhagavad Gita*), *Agamas*	**Taoism**	*Tao-te-ching* *I-ching* *Chuang-tzu* *Lieh-tzu*
Islam	Koran (Qur'an)	**Zoroastrianism**	*Avesta*

Chart 10

PART 3
ANCIENT MEDITERRANEAN RELIGIONS

Religions of the Ancient Mediterranean World

Religion	Deities	Time Period	Location
Egyptian	Scholars debate whether Egyptian religion originally was monotheistic or polytheistic. In the 13th century BC, monotheism was established during the reign of Akhenaten, but Egyptian religion reverted to polytheism afterward. Major gods included Amon, Anubis, Horus, Isis, and Maat.	Egyptian religion can be traced as far back as 3400 BC, when writing and a single central government are known to have existed. Certain amulets, pendants, animal tusks, and earthware figures often associated with religious practices go back an additional 2000 to 3000 years. Egyptian religion came to an end in the late 4th century AD, when Egypt officially endorsed Christianity as its national religion.	Egypt and the Nile region of northeast Africa.
African	Various African tribes strongly affirmed monotheism, yet they also believed that spirits inhabited and affected most objects in the world. The Yoruba name for God was Olorun, the Bantu called God Yangombi, and the Fon referred to God as Nana Buluku. Today most Africans are Muslims or Christians.	The earliest evidence of African traditional religion goes back to c. 1500 BC, but various peoples may have practiced tribal religions for centuries before then. Religious changes in Africa began with the introduction of Christianity during the first centuries after Christ and continued with the spread of Islam in the 7th century. Subsequent Christian missionary activity took Christianity into most regions of the African continent.	The entire African continent. Various tribes, each with their own distinctive beliefs, lived in different regions of Africa.
Babylonian	Marduk was the supreme god and the patron god of Babylon, the capital of Mesopotamia; his consort was Sarpanit. His activities are described in the creation epic *Enuma Elish*. His main rival was Ashur, an Assyrian war god. Other significant gods included Tiamat, goddess of the deep, and Anu, the god of heaven.	Marduk superseded earlier local and regional gods and became head of the assembly of Babylonian gods about the time of Hammurabi in the 18th century BC. Babylonian paganism lasted roughly from 1700 BC to 300 BC.	Central area was the flood plain situated between the Tigris and Euphrates rivers, encompassing portions of modern-day Iraq and Syria. The broader region included the lowlands which stretch as far north as the Caucasus mountains, as far east as the Zagros Mountains, southeast to the Persian Gulf, and as far to the southwest and west as the Arabian Desert.

Chart 11

Religions of the Ancient Mediterranean World (continued)

Religion	Deities	Time Period	Location
Phoenician and Canaanite	The most popular of the pantheon was Ba'al, a storm god and god of the High Places. His consort was Astareth, the goddess of fertility, love, and beauty. Melqart, king of the underworld, was another important god.	The origins of Phoenician religion are unclear and disputed. Most scholars would date its beginning to 1400–1300 BC and its end to c. 300 BC, during the aftermath of Alexander the Great's siege of Tyre.	Though its most extensive geographical boundaries are uncertain, its central area ran along the coastal plains of present-day Lebanon and Syria. The land of Canaan included much of present-day Israel, western Jordan, and the territory extending up to the southern border of modern Turkey.
Graeco-Roman	Greek and Roman religions involved belief in the Olympian gods and some lesser deities. Major gods included Zeus (Jupiter), Poseidon (Neptune), Ares (Mars), and Hades (Pluto). Eventually, more popular religious expressions came to the fore, including mysticism, occultism, and "mystery religions."	In its well-established form it lasted from c. 1000 BC to the 4th century AD. In 313 Constantine ended all government support of paganism, and in 391, when Theodosius I declared Christianity to be the official religion of the empire, the practice of paganism began to publicly disappear.	Mediterranean area.

Chart 11

Ancient Near Eastern Deities (Excluding Egypt)

Deity[1]	Region[2]	Country[3]	Position[4]
Adad (Ishkur)	Mesopotamia	Babylonia	God of storms; symbolized by a bull.
Anat (Antit)	Syria-Canaan	Canaan and Syria	Goddess of sex and war. Symbolized by a serpent. Portrayed standing naked on a lion holding a flower.
Anu (An)	Mesopotamia	Sumer and Babylonia	God of the sky, the heavens, and the constellations; king of all gods. Portrayed as a jackal.
Apsu	Mesopotamia	Sumer	God of sweet waters and freshwater seas. Portrayed as a primordial monster.
Arinna	Syria-Canaan	Canaan and Syria	Hittite sun goddess.
Ashtoreth (Astarte in Egypt, Ishtar in Babylonia)	Syria-Canaan	Canaan	Goddess of fertility, sex, and war. Symbols include a dove, horse, lion, and a star inside a circle.
Ba'al	Syria-Canaan	Canaan	Storm god. Associated with growth of vegetation.
Bel	Mesopotamia	Babylon	Another name for Marduk.
Chemosh	Syria-Canaan	Moab	National god of war. Symbolized by a fish.
Dagon	Syria-Canaan	Philistia	National god of grain and agriculture. Symbolized by a fish.
El	Syria-Canaan	Canaan and Syria	Head of Canaanite pantheon of gods. Symbolized by a bull.
Enki (Ea)	Mesopotamia	Sumeria (also known as Sumer)	God of fresh and subterranean water, intelligence, and creation. Symbolized by a fish and by a goat.
Enlil	Mesopotamia	Babylonia	God of wind, the earth, and plant growth.
Ereshkigal	Mesopotamia	Akkad (ancient Babylonia)	Goddess of dust, death, darkness, and the underworld.
Hannahanna	Syria-Canaan	Canaan and Syria	Hittite mother goddess.
Inanna	Mesopotamia	Sumeria (also known as Sumer)	Goddess of language, syntax, and meaning. Portrayed as a serpent and as a lioness.

Chart 12

Ancient Near Eastern Deities (Excluding Egypt) (continued)

Deity[1]	Region[2]	Country[3]	Position[4]
Ishtar (Inanna)	Mesopotamia	Akkad (ancient Babylonia)	Goddess of sex, fertility, and war. Represents the planet Venus.
Ki	Mesopotamia	Sumeria (also known as Sumer)	Goddess of the earth.
Marduk (Amarutu, Bel)	Mesopotamia	Babylonia	Head of the Babylonian pantheon of gods; storm god.
Molech (Malcam)	Syria-Canaan	Ammon	National god of fire. Symbolized by a star.
Mot	Syria-Canaan	Canaan and Syria	God of death, sterility, drought, and barren places.
Nanna (Sin)	Mesopotamia	Sumeria (also known as Sumer)	Moon god. Symbolized by the crescent moon and a tripod lampstand. Portrayed riding a winged bull.
Nebo (Nabu)	Mesopotamia	Babylonia	Son of Marduk.
Ninurta	Mesopotamia	Babylonia	God of war. Portrayed holding a bow and arrow and a mace, sometimes standing on a griffin-like creature.
Queen of Heaven	Syria-Canaan	Canaan	Same as Ashtoreth (similar to Anat and Ishtar).
Tammuz (Dumuzi)	Mesopotamia	Sumeria (also known as Sumer)	God of agriculture, the cycle of seasons, and death and rebirth.
Teshub (Tarhun)	Syria-Canaan	Canaan and Syria	Hittite god of the sky and storms. Symbolized by a bull. Portrayed holding a triple thunderbolt and a double-headed axe or a mace.
Tiamat	Syria-Canaan	Canaan and Syria	Goddess of the chaos waters, saltwater, and of the deep.

1. Gods and goddesses were often known by different names in different countries. This list is representative and not intended to be exhaustive.
2. Mesopotamia was the area between the Tigris and Euphrates Rivers, from the Persian Gulf north to the mountains of Asia Minor. It included much of the Fertile Crescent. Syria-Canaan included present-day Syria and the land to the south between the Jordan River and the Mediterranean Sea.
3. These countries were known by different names during different periods.
4. The attributes of the various gods and goddesses were not always distinct, but were mingled during different time periods.

Chart 12

Egyptian Paganism

Topic	Facts
Current Data	At the zenith of its geographical influence, Egypt's cult practices (especially those surrounding the goddess Isis) extended throughout the Roman Empire as far as northern Gaul and Britain. Today a number of groups that fall under the banner of Egyptian Reconstructionism advocate a return to the religious beliefs and practices of the ancient Egyptians. Prominent organizations include Akhet Hwt-Hrw, the International Network of Kemetics, and the Kemetic Orthodox Faith. There are approximately 100 existing pyramids in Egypt, including major sites at Abu Rawash, Giza, Zawyet el-Aryan, Abu Sir, Saqqara, Dahshur, Lisht, Meidum, Hawarra, and el-Lahun.
History	Prior to the political unification of Egypt, each local community in the Nile River Valley paid tribute to its own god or gods, many of which were associated with animals of various kinds. As Egypt became politically unified (c. 3400 BC), a national pantheon of deities took form in conjunction with an elaborate priesthood that tended to their needs. This polytheism continued until the reign of Pharaoh Amenhotep IV (c. 1353–36 BC), a committed monotheist. Soon after becoming king of Egypt, he changed his name to Akhenaten, declared the sun god Aten to be Egypt's sole deity, and sought to have the name of Amon (the main deity of Egypt prior to Akhenaten) removed from all official inscriptions. During his reign, Akhenaten relocated the royal court from Thebes to his newly decreed capital city of Tell el Amarna—300 miles south of Thebes—where he oversaw the construction of a massive temple to Aten. However, only a few years after Akhenaten's death (c. 1336 BC), Tell el Amarna was destroyed, the royal court was moved back to Thebes, and pre-Akhenaten polytheism was reestablished. The Assyrians invaded Thebes in 674 BC and conquered the city, thereby diminishing the influence of the cult of Amon. In 539 BC the Persians subjugated Egypt but maintained a policy of religious tolerance, so Egyptian cult practices were largely unaffected. In 331 BC, Alexander the Great made a pilgrimage to a shrine of Amon, thereby bolstering Amon's status within the pantheon. After Ptolemy became ruler of Egypt in 323 BC, many Egyptians began to worship Greek gods in addition to traditional Egyptian ones; the same thing happened in 30 BC when Egypt was defeated by the Romans. In the middle of the 1st century AD, Christian missionary efforts began in Egypt. The conversion of many Egyptians to Christianity, intense persecution of Egyptian Christians by the Roman government (especially by Diocletian in AD 284), and the eventual Christian-friendly edicts of Constantine all led to Christianity being firmly established in Egypt by the beginning of the 5th century. Ancient Egyptian polytheism became all but defunct.
Summary of Beliefs	Egyptian paganism was not a static worldview; its beliefs and practices underwent modification and transformation over a period of 3,400 years (11 major periods and 32 dynasties). Variations in belief and practice existed in different regions of ancient Egypt. Nevertheless, certain things can be said to have characterized Egyptian paganism throughout most of its long history. These include the centrality of various sun gods, the importance of the priesthood for keeping the gods/goddesses content, a tight link between the gods/goddesses and Egyptian national life, and a strong emphasis on the afterlife.

Chart 13

Egyptian Paganism (continued)

Topic	Facts
Summary of Beliefs (continued)	Religion shaped every aspect of ancient Egyptian life. With the exception of the monotheism of Akhenaten, Egyptian paganism was polytheistic. (In one recent scholarly interpretation, Egyptian religion was deemed monotheistic, with many legitimate manifestations of that lone deity.) The Egyptian pantheon was populated by at least 741 gods and goddesses during the reign of Tuthmosis III (1480–1426 BC) and eventually it consisted of around 2,000 deities. Some, such as Amon (later known as Amon-Re), were worshiped throughout the nation, while most had only local followings. It was believed that the gods and goddesses dwelled in temples, and each city supported a temple designed specifically for its patron deity. Priests and priestesses carried out the tasks involved in attending to the needs of the deities who resided in these temples. Because the afterlife was heavily stressed, Egyptians spent considerable time and resources preparing for their existence in the next world.

Topic	Summary of View
Creation	Creation myths varied over time and among regions. The Nile River, with its annual floods, had a central place in the cosmic order of things. Each myth spoke of a primordial mound where the temple of its primary god was located, and all functioned to establish the foundations of Egyptian social order. Three major accounts that developed during the Old Kingdom were the Heliopolitan, Memphite, and Hermopolitan myths. The most popular of the creation accounts, the Heliopolitan, centered around Atum-Re (also known as Khepri), who arose from a watery chaos (Nu) and created the air god Shu, along with the god of moisture, Tefnut. These two deities created the earth god Geb and the sky god Nut, who in turn proceeded to create Isis, Nephthys, Osiris, and Set. According to the Memphite myth, Ptah was the supreme creator god; he produced a daughter who in turn created Atum-Re. (This account never achieved widespread support among the ancient Egyptians.) There were several versions of the Hermopolitan myth, each focusing on Thoth, the god of wisdom. In one, an assembly of eight gods jointly fashioned the creation out of a primordial ocean. Another stated the source of life was a cosmic egg. Yet another related the emergence of Thoth from a lotus flower. Further accounts developed during the New Kingdom: one claimed Amon-Re was the creator of man and the other gods; another maintained that the creator god was Khnum, who fashioned human beings using a potter's wheel.
Scripture and Authority	No canonical scriptures as such, though many sacred texts were used for various purposes. These include the *Pyramid Texts*, which contain funerary inscriptions from the early pyramids; the *Egyptian Book of the Dead*, which describes the journey into the afterlife; the *Book of Am-Tuat*, a treatise describing how the sun god Re navigates the underworld in his boat every night; the *Demotic Magical Papyrus*, which includes an array of magic spells; and the *Burden of Isis*, a collection of hymns to the goddess Isis. Priests and priestesses played a vital role in ancient Egyptian society. Only they were allowed to enter the sacred area of the temple and approach the statue

Chart 13

Egyptian Paganism (continued)

Topic	Summary of View
Scripture and Authority (continued)	representing the god or goddess of that temple. Each priest (or priestess) was expected to serve the god or goddess under their care by means of an elaborate system of rituals centered on the statue of that deity. Two important tasks entrusted to the priests were guarding against encroaching social-political chaos and assisting the dead in making the transition to the next world. The pharaohs of Egypt were rulers over the nation, mediators between the Egyptian people and the deities, and performers of many sacred rituals, having received their authority from the deities. This divine sanction of their supreme political-religious position on earth was given in part to preserve Ma'at (truth, justice, order, and cosmic balance). Each pharaoh held the titles Lord of the Two Lands and High Priest of Every Temple.
God	Some scholars argue that ancient Egyptian religion was a form of monotheism in which the attributes and functions of the one deity were represented by the various gods and goddesses of the pantheon; others maintain that ancient Egyptian religion was a form of true polytheism. Adherents at all times and in all regions had a central place for a sun god of one kind or another. Within the pantheon there were anthropomorphic deities (gods who took the form of animals or appeared as part human, part animal), cosmic deities (gods who represented heavenly bodies or elements of nature), and abstract-ideological deities (gods who represented universal concepts). (See chart 14, Gods of the Egyptian Pantheon.) The gods had many of the same needs and desires as human beings, though they possessed comprehensive control over the life of the Egyptian people. In some cases the pharaohs were viewed as gods.
Mankind	Human beings are composed of nine parts, or aspects: a physical form and eight semi-divine parts that survive death: (1) *khet* (appearance), the body that decayed after death (the corpse was known as *khat*) unless preserved by mummification; (2) *ka* (sustenance), the life force that lingered in the tomb, sometimes inhabiting the dead body or statues of the deceased; (3) *ba* (animation), depicted as a human-headed bird that brought air and food to the deceased during the day, but traveled with Re at night; (4) *khaibit* (shadow), an integral aspect of the personality, it could detach itself from the *khat* to partake of funerary offerings; though it was able to travel afar, it always stayed near the *ba*; (5) *akh* (transfigured spirit), the immortal and radiant being that lived on in the *sahu* (spirit-body), it ascended to the heavens to live with the gods and/or the stars; (6) *sahu* (spirit-body), the incorruptible body that dwelt in the heavens after the judgment of the dead was passed successfully; (7) *sekhem*, the incorporeal (bodyless) personification of the *ka*; (8) *jb* (heart), the center of thought and the ground of moral awareness within a person; after death it would either live with the gods (if it was good) or be eaten by the demoness Ammut (if it was evil); and (9) *Ren* (true name), an essential part of the individual, necessary for one's survival beyond the grave; if it was destroyed, so was the entire person.

Chart 13

Egyptian Paganism (continued)

Topic	Summary of View
Sin	Standards of ethics were based on the moral ideal of Ma'at, which included the concepts of truth, justice, order, and cosmic balance; the balance (or imbalance) of the universe was thought to affect every aspect of Egyptian society. Immoral acts—many of which were crimes—included blasphemy; theft in general and stealing from temple offerings in particular; defiling the purity of a sacred place; tampering with grain measures or the boundaries of fields; murder; exploitation of the weak; depriving orphans of their property; lying; inflicting pain, grief, or injury to others; causing hunger; committing adultery; slandering servants before their master; eavesdropping; losing one's temper; and speaking without thinking. Virtues such as justice, honesty, fairness, mercy, kindness, and generosity reflected Ma'at. Morality was not merely a personal matter that determined one's destiny in the afterlife; it had consequences for the nation as a whole.
Salvation	Once an evil act had been committed, it was difficult for the perpetrator to be cleansed from the transgression. Magic spells could assist in regaining moral purity; good deeds helped to overcome the weight of guilt, so that the individual might survive the judgment intact. Living a good life in this world (which included following the established social order) was necessary, but not sufficient, for obtaining a pleasant afterlife. Much additional preparation for the next life took place before death—by collecting an appropriate assortment of objects to place in the tomb of the deceased—and after death, via prescribed funerary rituals and an extensive mummification process of the corpse. Those who proclaimed themselves enemies of the gods had no hope of resurrection; they were punished and annihilated. Priests and priestesses were entrusted with corporate religious matters. When there was social upheaval, it was an indicator that the gods had not been attended to properly, or that the pharaoh had not been adequately performing the tasks of his royal office.
Afterlife	In one account, all people were judged by a tribunal of 42 gods in the Hall of Two Truths. Anubis used a set of scales to weigh each heart against the feather of Ma'at; Thoth recorded the results. During this time, the deceased would recite a formula called the Negative Confession, indicating their desire to be separated from their sins. If a person's heart was heavier than the feather—indicating an excess of evil deeds—it would be devoured by Amemet (a monster who was part crocodile, part lion, and part hippopotamus), and the person would cease to exist. If the person's heart was as light as the feather—indicating that good deeds outweighed bad—Osiris would welcome that person to the next world and give him a piece of land on which to live. In another account, spiritual renewal could be obtained in the mysterious underworld of the primeval waters. Known as Nu, this underworld was divided into twelve portals. Periodically, Ra would enter Nu, shine sunlight into the darkness, and speak magical utterances from the *Book of Gates*. When this happened, all the mummies in Nu would discard their protective wrappings and begin a new life.

Chart 13

Distinctive Beliefs and Practices

Ka (Sustenance, Life Force)	The *ka* was the essential aspect that differentiated a living person from a dead one. After death, each person's *ka* required the same sort of sustenance as the living person had needed during life; hence the *ka* was provided either with real food offerings or with depictions of food on the walls of the tomb. While not eating these food offerings in a physical fashion, the *ka* would absorb their life-preserving energy. The *ka* would rest while the corpse was being mummified, and it needed to be reactivated before the complete transition to the next world could take place.
Ba (Animation)	The *ba* was the distinctive manifestation of an individual, comprised of the non-bodily attributes unique to each person. It was the job of the *ba* to travel from the deceased person's tomb to rejoin that person's *ka* (life force) before being transformed into an *akh* (immortal spirit). The corpse of the deceased had to be reunited with its *ba* every night if it was to survive into the next world. The *ba* had the same physical needs as the living body once had, including food, drink, and sex.
Cats	In ancient Egypt, many kinds of animals were deemed sacred and were revered. Of these sacred animals, the cat (*miu*) was the most highly esteemed. Around 2000 BC, fully domesticated cats became common in Egyptian households; it is believed that they reduced the threat of snakes and vermin to the inhabitants of those houses. During the New Kingdom (1540–1069 BC), pictures in tombs depicted cats as a normal part of day-to-day life. Cats appeared on everyday objects such as bracelets, pendants, amulets, necklaces, rings, mirrors, and cosmetic pots. Many Egyptian parents named their children after cats, especially their daughters; some girls were named Miut. Statues of cats were placed outside houses to ward off evil spirits. In the later periods of Egyptian history, many bronze cat statuettes were made; most were intended for shrines or funerary purposes and had pierced ears with accompanying earrings. When a cat died, its former owners would mourn and shave their eyebrows as an expression of their grief. Egyptian law stipulated that if a human being killed a cat, even unintentionally, that person was to be executed. Official documents reveal that entire armies sometimes were sent to recapture cats that had been smuggled into other nations. Cats even figured in dream interpretation; it was thought that if a person saw a cat in a dream, that person could expect a plentiful harvest. The first Egyptian feline deity was the goddess Mafdet, though Bastet and Sekhmet were more prominent. In the city of Bubastis, cats lived a lavish life in the temples of Bastet. Here they were served and pampered until they died, at which time their bodies were mummified and offered to Bastet; the remains of more than 300,000 cat mummies were found at the site of ancient Bubastis.
Temples	The ancient Egyptians believed that temples were the earthly abodes of their gods and goddesses. There were two main types of temples: (1) cultus temples were dedicated to the worship of a specific deity; and (2) mortuary temples were built to honor a deceased pharaoh; often he was worshiped posthumously as a god. Many temples grew into complex systems of buildings, expanded by means of construction projects ordered by various pharaohs over hundreds of years. The walls of many of them were painted with depictions of a pharaoh in battle or performing rituals. Most temples had a highly organized structure and floor plan.

Chart 13

Distinctive Beliefs and Practices

Cursing Ceremony	In major temples, priests cursed enemies of the divine order—such as the chaos serpent Apophis—by means of an elaborate ceremony wherein images of a particular enemy were drawn on papyrus or made of wax. These images were spat on, trampled, stabbed, and burned; anything that remained was dissolved in buckets of urine. Destructive magic also had the names of foreign enemies and Egyptian traitors inscribed on clay pots, tablets, or figurines. These objects were then burned, broken, or buried in an effort to weaken or obliterate the enemy.
Magic (Heka)	Magic involved the performance of prescribed symbolic actions that resulted in a particular desired effect. All people were thought to possess this ability in some measure. Magic spells usually consisted of two parts: the words spoken and the actions to be performed. Music, dance, and gestures like pointing and stamping also formed parts of certain spells. Sometimes spells were written on papyrus, which was folded and worn on the body. The most propitious time to perform magic was at daybreak, and the magician had to be in a state of ritual purity. Objects associated with ritual magic included potions, amulets, metal or ivory wands (representing the power of the magician to summon the gods), and figurines (thought to work best when used in conjunction with a fragment from the intended victim's body, such as a strand of hair or nail clippings).
Magicians (Hekau)	Magician-priests were viewed as guardians of a secret knowledge given to humanity by the gods/goddesses. The most respected were the lector priests, who read books of magic housed in temple and palace libraries. These priests practiced magic arts believed to protect the pharaoh, to help the dead make their way into the next world, and to heal people. Lower in rank, scorpion charmers used magic to rid areas of poisonous reptiles and insects.
Special Requirements of Priests	Priests were allowed to wear only linens or garments made of plants; articles of clothing made from animals were not permitted. Priests were required to shave their heads and bodies daily and to take baths with cold water several times each day. They had to practice sexual abstinence while performing their duties at the temple. Their daily rituals often consisted of breaking the seal of the temple, lighting a torch, saying prescribed prayers, offering incense, undressing, washing, and anointing the statue of the god or goddess in the temple, putting clean clothing and jewelry on the statue, placing food and drink offerings near the statue, backing out of the shrine while sweeping away their own footprints, and sealing the sacred area.
Pyramids	Among the largest man-made structures ever built, the Egyptian pyramids were constructed during the Old and Middle Kingdom periods as burial monuments to deceased pharaohs. They were built on the west bank of the Nile River due to that location's association with the setting sun. Their archetype was the sacred Ben-Ben stone that was housed in the temple of Heliopolis, the oldest center of the sun god cult. Their shape represented the primordial mound from which the Egyptians believed the earth was created; it also represented the descending rays of the sun. Architecturally speaking, pyramids can be divided into two main types: step

Chart 13

Distinctive Beliefs and Practices

Pyramids (continued)	pyramids and true (sloping) pyramids. A full-scale pyramid complex consisted of a true pyramid with mortuary and valley temples, a causeway between them, and (typically) a number of smaller, subsidiary pyramids.

The first historically documented Egyptian pyramid is attributed to the architect Imhotep, who designed a tomb for Pharaoh Djozer by stacking several *mastabas* (flat-roofed, rectangular buildings with sloping sides—built with mud bricks—that marked burial sites) on top of one another. This pyramid was intended to serve as a stairway by means of which the deceased pharaoh could ascend to the stars.

The most prolific phase of pyramid construction occurred during the early part of the Old Kingdom, when many of the gigantic stone pyramids (whose main bodies were composed of granite and whose outer casting was limestone) were built over the course of three generations, beginning with Pharaoh Sneferu and ending with his grandson Khafre (2613–2532 BC). Many of the pyramids built later were smaller and hastily constructed. Recently found tombs of men who worked on the pyramids provide evidence that many of them were paid craftsmen, not slaves. |
| **Mummification** | To prepare a person for the journey to the next world, the corpse of the deceased was preserved by a long and expensive process called mummification. The ancient Egyptians believed that mummifying a person's body after death—especially the preserving of the heart—was necessary to ensure that person's continued existence in the afterlife. In anticipation of this process, a person would build a tomb, gather an assortment of essential objects to place in the tomb, and appoint a priest to bring offerings to the tomb. In the Old Kingdom, mummification was reserved primarily for the pharaoh and his top advisers. In the Middle and New Kingdoms the practice was extended to the general population, though the expenses involved limited the full procedure to the very wealthy.

The process of mummification was as follows: After death, the corpse was washed and ritually purified in a special shelter (*ibu*) before being taken to the workshop (*wabet*) of the embalmer, who wore a jackal mask to represent Anubis, the god of the dead. There, oils were rubbed onto the skin of the corpse. Various internal organs were removed from the body through an incision in the left side of the abdomen. The brain was pulled out through the nose using long hooks; it was discarded. The other organs were dried, individually wrapped in strips of linen, and sealed in canopic jars, the lids of which represented the sons of the sky god Horus, each of whom was entrusted with protecting a particular organ. The body was then placed on a slanted embalming table and packed with salt crystals (*natron*) to dry it out. After 40 days, the dried and shrunken body was washed again and subsequently stuffed with linen, sawdust, and spices. The embalming cut was sewn up and covered with a patch that depicted the protective eye of Horus; sometimes cedar oil was injected through the rectum. The body was then wrapped in a layer of linen bandages soaked in resin. A portrait mask was placed over the mummy's face, and the body was wrapped a second time in linen bandages, with gold, jewelry, and protective amulets placed between the layers. Fingers and toes were individually wrapped with linen and covered with gold caps. Arms and legs were also wrapped, then the entire body was wrapped with about twenty layers of bandages. After this the |

Chart 13

Distinctive Beliefs and Practices	
Mummification (continued)	fully-wrapped body (mummy) was put into three differently sized, body-shaped coffins that fit into each other. Typically these coffins were made of clay, wood, or stone, though the coffins of pharaohs were made of gold and decorated with colored glass. Many items the person was thought to need in the afterlife were left with the mummy in its tomb. These included food, wine, clothing, hairdressing supplies, furniture, model boats and houses, writing materials, and assorted tools. Wealthy people often included *shabtis*, little statues believed to perform work for the deceased in the next world. Finally, the tomb was sealed.
Opening of the Mouth Ceremony	Done during the process of mummification, this ceremony was thought to enable the deceased to regain the full use of their bodies, so they could enjoy life in the next world. It was believed that during the ceremony, Ptah and Horus together opened the mouth of the deceased. The officiating priest made offerings and touched the lips of the mummy with various implements. The most commonly used implement was an adze (an arched metal blade fastened across the top of a wooden handle with leather thongs). Other implements often used included a *psh-kef* (blunt knife), sharp blades called *ntjrwy*, and a limestone platter that held two tiny bottles and four tiny cups, each of which were half light and half black.

Chart 13

Gods of the Egyptian Pantheon

Egyptian Deity*	Description/Position
Amon **(Amen, Amun, Amun-Re)**	At different stages in the development of Egyptian paganism, Amon took on different divine roles: god of the air, creator of the cosmos and father of the gods, husband of Mut, king (who treated the poor justly), fertility god, and sun god. Depicted variously as a frog, a man seated on a throne with a tall headpiece, a ram, or the sun.
Anat **(Anath)**	Warrior goddess, especially popular from the 17th to the 11th centuries BC. Daughter of Ra and wife of Set. Depicted as a woman holding a shield and/or any number of weapons, often an axe.
Anhur **(Inhert, Onuris)**	God of war and hunting and (later) of the air; popular in the region of Abydos and Thinis. Husband of Menhit. Depicted as a bearded man wearing a robe and a headdress with four feathers, holding a spear, or as a lion-headed man.
Anubis **(Anpu)**	Originally god of the dead; later gatekeeper to the underworld and god of embalming. Son of Osiris. Depicted as a man with a jackal's head.
Anuket **(Anqet, Anukis)**	Originally goddess of the Nile River; later, goddess of lust. Depicted as a woman with the head of a gazelle, wearing a high feather headdress.
Arsaphes **(Herishef)**	God of water and fertility in the region of Heliopolis. Depicted as a ram or as a man with the head of a ram.
Astarte	Goddess of war often paired with Anat. Associated with fertility and sexuality. Daughter of Ra and wife of Set.
Aten (Aton)	God of the sun; great creator god during the reign of Amenhotep IV (Akhenaten).
Atum **(Temu)**	Originally associated with the earth; later became the sun god of Heliopolis; later yet he was associated with Ra. Depicted seated on a throne, wearing the crowns of upper and lower Egypt, sometimes as an elderly man; also represented as a snake.
Bastet **(Bast, Ubasti)**	Originally the protector of Lower Egypt and defender of the pharaoh, depicted as a lion. Later a goddess of perfumes and patron of mothers, depicted as a domestic cat or a woman with a feline face. Associated with Wadjet.
Bes **(Bisu)**	Guardian of the home, protector against snakes, and helper of women in childbirth. Symbolized pleasurable things like music and dancing. Depicted as a dwarf with various feline body parts. Sometimes associated with Tawaret.

* It should be noted that the names, concepts, roles, and depictions associated with each of these gods evolved significantly over time; they were not static. In some cases the identities of gods are ambiguous or merge with those of other gods. The relationships between gods also changed during the course of Egyptian history. Thus the descriptions given here should be seen as general. Moreover, the reader should understand that the Egyptians had more gods than are presented above. The ones chosen are in the view of the author most prominent.

Chart 14

Gods of the Egyptian Pantheon (continued)

Egyptian Deity	Description/Position
Chnum (Khnemu)	Originally the god who was the source of the Nile River and a divine potter who molded the other gods. Later patron of potters. Husband of Satis, father of Anuket, and consort of Heqet. Popular on the island of Elephantine. Depicted as a man with a ram's head and as a man holding a jar with water flowing out of it.
Geb (Seb)	Earth god; also associated with vegetation. Husband of Nut, son of Tefnut and Shu. Depicted as a reclining man or as a black goose.
Hathor (Mehturt)	Her functions and attributes changed considerably over time. Viewed in different periods as a divine waterway, a goddess of motherhood, a fertility goddess, a musician, or a fierce warrior. Wife of Thoth and daughter of Atum-Re. Depicted as a golden cow (sometimes covered with stars) or a hippopotamus.
Hatmehit	Fish goddess of the city of Mendes in the Nile Delta. Sometimes depicted as a woman with a fish on her head. Sometimes associated with Hathor.
Heqet (Heget)	Goddess of life, fertility, and midwives. Daughter of Ra and wife of Sobek (earlier) and Chnum (later). Her cult was especially strong in the city of Antinopolis. Depicted as a woman with the head of a frog.
Horus (Harmerty, Haroersis, Harpocrates, Kemwer, Nekheny)	His roles changed over time; he was alternately a sky god and a god of the sun. Gained fame for partially castrating Set. Originally son of Ra and Hathor; later brother of Osiris and Isis. Depicted variously as a man with a falcon's head, a heron on a perch, or a naked boy with a finger in his mouth.
Imhotep (Immutef)	God of medicine and healing. Held up Nut to hold back chaos. Son of Sekhmet. Depicted as a seated man holding an open papyrus.
Isis (Aset)	The Divine Mother, queen of the throne, and goddess of resurrection. Served as protector of the pharaoh's dead body and canopic jars used in funerary rites. Wife of Osiris, daughter of Tawaret, and mother of Horus. Depicted variously as a woman wearing a throne-shaped headdress while holding a sycamore tree, a woman with cow's horns on her head, or as a kite flying above the body of Osiris.
Khepri (Khepera)	Scarab beetle god who pushed the sun disk across the sky during the day and through the underworld at night. Associated with Ra.
Khonsu (Chons)	Moon god, invoked to protect people from wild animals and increase male sexual potency; also associated with the placenta and childbirth. Son of Amon and Mut. Depicted variously as a child with a hawk's head, wearing a crescent moon and a full moon; a young man holding a threshing device and wearing a *menat* (necklace with several rows of beads which form a counterweight at the back of the neck); a boy riding a goose, ram, or two crocodiles; and as a baboon.

Chart 14

Gods of the Egyptian Pantheon (continued)

Egyptian Deity	Description/Position
Maat (Ma'at)	Goddess of truth, justice, and order. Wife of Thoth, daughter of Ra, and mother of Ogdoad. Depicted as a woman with wings and an ostrich feather on her head.
Min	Originally a rain god and patron of traveling caravans. Later a god of fertility and male virility. Depicted as a man wearing a feathered crown, with a red ribbon around his forehead, while holding his erect penis in his left hand and grasping a flail in his right hand. Symbols of Min included a bed of lettuce and a white bull.
Munt (Month)	Originally a god of the region near Thebes; later a war god representing the pharaoh. Depicted as a man with the head of a falcon.
Mut (Mutt)	Creator goddess and grandmother of Egypt. Wife of Amon and mother of Khonsu. Originally depicted as a vulture; later as a woman with vulture wings, holding an *ankh*, and wearing the dual crown of Upper and Lower Egypt and a red and blue dress, with Maat's feather next to her feet.
Nefertem (Nefertum)	Originally the young god Atum; later a separate god associated with the blue lotus. Son of Ptah and Sekhmet. Depicted as a handsome young man with lotus flowers encircling his head or as a reclining lion.
Nehebkau (Neheb-kau)	Guardian of the gate to the underworld and protector of Ra during his trips to the underworld. Son of Selkhet (sometimes of Gen and Renenutet, a snake goddess). Depicted as a two-headed snake or as a man holding the eye of Horus.
Neith (Net)	Patron goddess of Sais; originally a goddess of hunting and warfare who made warriors' weapons and guarded their bodies after they were killed in battle. Later she became a goddess of weaving and domestic activities, and eventually was viewed as personifying the primordial waters of creation. Wife of Chnum and mother of Ra and Sobek. Often depicted as a woman with the head of a lioness, snake, or cow. She also is depicted as wearing a weavers' shuttle on top of her head, holding a bow and arrows, and at other times as a woman nursing a baby crocodile.
Nekhbet (Nechbet)	Originally patron goddess of the city of Nekheb; later the guardian of Upper Egypt and the Pharaohs. Associated with Wadjet. Wife of Hapy. Depicted as a white vulture clutching an ankh (a cross with a loop at the top) in her talons.
Nephthys (Nebethet)	Goddess of death and decay and a mourner for those who have died; creator of the Nile River. Accompanied Ra during his nighttime journey through the underworld. Wife of Set, daughter of Geb and Nut, and sister of Isis. Depicted as a hawk with outstretched wings or as a vulture.
Nu (Nun)	God of the primeval chaos waters. Androgynous, his female form was named Naunet. Depicted as a frog or a bearded, frog-headed man with blue-green skin.
Nut (Nuit)	Goddess of the sky and resurrection. Wife of Geb and daughter of Shu and Tefnut. Depicted variously as a naked woman whose body forms the arch of heaven, a woman standing with a water pot on her head, and a sow suckling piglets.

Chart 14

Gods of the Egyptian Pantheon (continued)

Egyptian Deity	Description/Position
Osiris (Asar, Ausare)	God of the dead and the underworld. Afforded protection against snakebites and scorpion stings. Husband of Isis and son of Geb and Nut. Depicted as a centipede, a donkey-headed man, or a ram.
Ptah (Peteh)	Creator god of Memphis who represented the Primordial Mound; patron god of stone craftsmen. Father of Atum and Nefertem. Depicted as a mummy wearing a skullcap and holding an ankh (emblem of life; a cross with a loop at the top in the place of the straight vertical section).
Qadesh (Qetesh)	Goddess of sex. Wife of Resheph (god of war and plague) and mother of Min. Represented as a naked woman standing on the back of a lion with the moon on her head or as a woman holding snakes in her right hand and lotus flowers in her left hand.
Ra (Re)	Sun god who traveled through the underworld each night with Maat, Horus and Thoth. Cult center was Heliopolis. Associated with Heryshaf, a creator and fertility god. Depicted as a golden disc or an eye.
Resheph (Reshpu)	God of war and thunder. Father of Min. Represented by a battle ax, spear, and/or shield.
Satis (Satet)	Goddess of fertility and the Nile floods. Consort of Chnum. Depicted as a woman wearing a white crown with antelope horns.
Sekhmet (Sakhet)	Bloodthirsty goddess of war and menstruation. Usually represented as a woman with a lion's head, dressed in red.
Selkhet (Serket, Selchis)	Goddess who protected people from scorpion stings and snakebites, sometimes associated with the scorching heat of the sun. Associated with Isis and Nephthys. Depicted as a scorpion or as a woman with a scorpion on her head.
Serapis (Userhapy)	Syncretistic god having characteristics of both Egyptian (Osiris) and Greek (Zeus) gods. Depicted as a bearded man with a *modius* (a grain measuring basket) on top of his head.
Seshat	Goddess of wisdom, writing, mathematics, astronomy, and architecture; also a divine record-keeper of the Egyptian kingdom. Wife or daughter of Thoth. Represented as a woman dressed in leopard skin with a papyrus plant above her head.
Set (Seth, Sutekh, Setesh)	God of the desert and sandstorms; associated with donkeys, jackals, and aardvarks. Brother of Osiris. Often depicted as a mysterious unidentified creature with a curved snout, square ears, forked tail, and dog-like body; sometimes depicted as an okapi (in the giraffe family, but with a shorter neck).
Shu	God of the air. Son of Atum, brother of Tefnut, father of Geb and Nut. Often depicted as a man separating Nut (the sky) from Geb (the earth).

Chart 14

Gods of the Egyptian Pantheon (continued)

Egyptian Deity	Description/Position
Sobek (Sochet, Soknopais)	God of the Nile and of the Egyptian army. Son of Neith. Depicted as a crocodile or as a man with a crocodile's head.
Sokaris (Seker)	God of the cemetery; represented in the act of separating the *ba* (animating principle) from the *ka* (life force). Patron of metal workers. Depicted as a mummy with a falcon's head and green skin.
Tawaret (Taueret, Taurt)	Goddess who protects women during pregnancy and childbirth. Counterpart of Apep, the god of evil. Depicted as a creature with the head of a hippopotamus, the arms and legs of a lion, the back and tail of a crocodile, and the breasts and stomach of a pregnant woman.
Tefnut	Goddess of moisture and fertility. Daughter of Atum, twin sister of Nut, sister of Shu, and mother of Geb and Nut. Variously depicted as a lion's head, a lioness, or a woman in white clothing.
Thoth (Djehuty)	The god of knowledge, the inventor of writing and the calendar, and the scribe of Ra. Associated with Seshat. Depicted as a man with the head of an ibis or as a baboon holding up a crescent moon.
Wadjet (Edjo, Uto)	Originally a local goddess of the city of Per-Wadjet; later the patron goddess of Lower Egypt and protector of Ra. Wife of Hapy, god of the Nile. Depicted as a cobra or as a woman wearing a uraeus (symbol of sovereignty; upright asp, or cobra, symbol).
Wepwawet (Ophois, Upuaut)	Originally a war god in the form of a wolf. Also a god of the graveyard and an avenger of Osiris. Depicted variously as a wolf or jackal (with gray or white fur) or as a man with the head of a wolf or jackal.

Chart 14

Greek Paganism

Topic	Facts
Current Data	At its height, geographically, cult practices extended beyond mainland Greece to the islands and coasts of Ionia in Asia Minor, Magna Graecia (Sicily and southern Italy), and scattered Greek colonies in the western Mediterranean. Today an ensemble of loosely related groups known collectively as Hellenic Reconstructionism advocates a return to the religious beliefs and practices of the ancient Greeks. Prominent organizations include the Temple of Demeter, Elaion, and Hellenion.
History	Although there is uncertainty as to its precise origin, Greek paganism dates back approximately to the early 2nd millennium BC. At this time, Indo-European peoples migrated to the region of ancient Greece, where they encountered the Aegeans (Pelasgians) and the Minoans of Crete. This was followed by a fusion of their respective cultures, then further mixing with and assimilation of other regional-indigenous cultures. Over time, belief in a cross-cultural ensemble of deities emerged from this religious-cultural hybridization. Now known as the classical Greek pantheon, it was populated by gods from each of the original cultures that had joined together. By the time Homer's *Illiad* was written (c. 8th century BC), there existed a consensus concerning the identities of the most important Olympian gods, though such beliefs were not static. Later, during the civil strife that encompassed Greece in the 5th century BC, the gods of the classical pantheon were viewed by many Greeks as capricious and unreliable. This led to a rejection of the gods by many urban citizens, most of whom had monotheistic leanings anyway. It also resulted in a shift in the more superstitious, popular religion of rural Greece; a new focus on mystery rites and the afterlife became common. Prominent Greek poets and dramatists (such as Aeschylus, Sophocles, and Euripides) began to question the justice and integrity of the gods. Eventually, this decline in Greek pagan piety allowed for the Roman Empire to absorb and transform Greek paganism into a distinctively Roman paganism.
Summary of Beliefs	Greek paganism is the polytheistic religion that was practiced in ancient Greece, primarily in the form of cultic rites. Greek paganism was highly syncretistic, blending Persian, Anatolian, Egyptian, Etruscan, and other cultural-regional elements within a Hellenistic framework (over a span of many centuries). Religious practice was so varied in ancient Greece that in some respects it is more accurate to speak of a spectrum of Greek religions; Greek paganism never was an official system of doctrines or rituals. Indeed, two of the most defining characteristics of the religions practiced in the ancient Greek city-states were their idiosyncratic nature and their localism. Different cities worshiped different deities in accordance with local needs and customs. In addition to the local cults of the major gods, there were various sacred spaces thought to have their own tutelary (guardian) spirits, and special altars and shrines were erected outside temple precincts. A central function of Greek paganism was validating the culture and group identity of local communities.

Chart 15

Greek Paganism (continued)

Topic	Summary of View
Creation	*Theogony* by the Greek poet Hesiod provides a creation myth focusing on deified abstractions like Night and Time. A once-popular account has Earth (Gaia) emerging from chaotic primordial forces and subsequently mating with Sky (Uranus) and Sea (Poseidon). These unions produced three Hecatonchires (giants with 100 arms and 50 heads), three Cyclopes (one-eyed giants), and the Titans (twelve godlike giants—six male and six female—who personified the forces of nature). The Titans Kronos and Rheia then produced several of the Olympian gods, including Zeus, Demeter, Hades, Hera, and Hestia. Next Zeus and Hera mated to produce the gods Ares, Eileithuia, Hebe, and Hephaestus. However, other conflicting genealogies were also in circulation. Many Greeks regarded these creation myths as history. Hence the myths' competing genealogies were used by various regional groups to establish a divine right to their land as well as by families seeking to legitimate their exalted position in the social order.
Scripture and Authority	Adherents in different localities subscribed to different myths or different versions of the same myth, though some myths were widely held. There was no canonical holy book as such, though various writings were influential, including those of Ovid, Plato, and Virgil. Priests and priestesses possessed authority over localized temples and were authorized by the god or goddess they worshiped to perform specialized sacred rites.
God	No God in the sense of monotheism; the gods were not omnipotent, omniscient, or omnipresent. The superhuman features of the Olympian gods (those who ruled after overthrowing the Titans) were their immortality and ability to know the future. The gods were not revered because of their moral qualities, but for their power, which must be propitiated (appeased). Hence the gods were admired and feared, but usually not loved. Zeus ruled the sky, Poseidon ruled the sea, and Hades ruled the underworld. Other major deities included Aphrodite, Apollo, Ares, Artemis, Asclepius, Athena, Cronus, Demeter, Dike, Dionysus, Eros, Gaia, Hephaestus, Hera, Hermes, Hestia, Hypnos, Ouranos, Pan, Prometheus, and Tyche. By means of a complex arrangement of myths and legends, all members of the Greek pantheon were related to one another, comprising a divine family. The gods and goddesses had supernatural powers, but these powers were substantially limited by Fate (unavoidable destiny). The Olympian gods battled one another and frequently meddled in human affairs; they also played important roles as civic deities, wherein each Greek city-state claimed one of them as its guardian. Heroes were demigods or deified humans who formed an important part of local legends. Many city-states had hero cults as well as temples devoted to particular gods.
Mankind	There is not a sharp ontological distinction between human beings and the gods; heroes (deified human beings) are an example of this. However, the fates of humans are more tragic and pitiable than are those of gods, for humans must endure whatever circumstances the gods send them: unrequited love, the sufferings of illness and old age, and ultimately death. Each person has a physical body and an immortal soul.

Chart 15

Greek Paganism (continued)

Topic	Summary of View
Sin	The chief virtue is respect for the gods. Citizens of each city-state had a duty to revere the god or gods of—and engage in the practices peculiar to—that locale. Those who forsook these sacred obligations became impure.
Salvation	Some views were mainly (or entirely) sociopolitical in nature: the safety, sustenance, and flourishing of particular city-states. Other views focused much more (though rarely exclusively) on the happiness and/or post-mortem fate of individuals.
Afterlife	At death the Dogs of Hades carry the deceased to the Land of Shadows in the underworld, where the person's spirit wanders across the Grove of Persephone until it reaches the Gate of Hades. There it encounters Cerberus, the three-headed watchdog, who must be appeased by honey cakes before permitting the spirit to proceed. Next, before entering Hades (Abode of the Dead), the spirit must cross five underground rivers: Acheron, Cocytus, Lethe, Phlegethon, and Styx. To cross Acheron, the spirit must give Charon, the official ferryman, an *obol* (a small coin) for his service. The River Styx is guarded by Phlegyas, who transports spirits from one side of the river to the other. After crossing the river, spirits face a tribunal that judges them and assigns each one to a permanent abode. This tribunal consists of Hades (the god), Aeacus, Minos, and Rhadamanthus. Most spirits are assigned to a neutral region of Hades. Persons who have committed extremely evil acts are cast into Tartarus, a somber place with gates of bronze, surrounded by a triple wall. Those who have lived pure lives are allowed entrance to the Elysian Fields (Islands of the Blest), where they indulge in earthly pleasures amid sunlight and flower-filled meadows.

Distinctive Beliefs and Practices

Topic	Summary of View
Sacrifices	The most common act of public worship in ancient Greece was the sacrifice of grain or animals. Typically, the blood, bones, and hide of a sacrificed animal would be offered to a god; the rest would be eaten by worshipers.
Temples	Most Greek temples were not public gathering places and usually contained little more than an idol of the deity and votive gifts accumulated by worshipers. In most cases the altar was located in a sacred area (*temenos*) outside the temple.
Votive Gifts	These offerings to the deities included bronze tripods, cauldrons, figurines, terracotta tablets, lamps, vases, armor, weapons, jewelry, and marble statuettes. They were made for benefits already conferred, anticipated divine favors, or as propitiation to the gods and goddesses for crimes involving blood-guilt, impiety, or breach of religious customs.
Public Worship	Public worship was designed to please the gods and goddesses so they would grant worshipers such benefits as rain, a good harvest, economic prosperity, and military victories. Public prayers were highly formulaic and ritualized.

Chart 15

Greek Paganism (continued)

Distinctive Beliefs and Practices

Oracles	In ancient Greece, oracles were a special class of people thought to dispense wise counsel and to possess prophetic abilities. ("Oracle" could also refer to the sites where such announcements were made as well as to the utterances themselves.) The preeminent Greek oracle, the Sibyl (Pythia), worked at the temple of Apollo at Delphi. She exerted considerable influence on Hellenistic culture, as she was consulted by the Greeks before embarking on any major undertaking, such as founding a new colony.
Mystery Religions	An alternative to the public cults of the gods and goddesses, mystery religions offered an opportunity to experience mystical awakening, learn systematic doctrine, and to participate in worship that was less formal and more communal. Some of these mysteries, like those of Eleusis and Samothrace, were localized. Others were enacted in various locations, like the mysteries of Dionysus.
Symbols	**Ears of Corn**: Sacred to the goddess Demeter, ears of corn symbolized fertility and fecundity (fruitful in offspring). **Cornucopia**: The cornucopia (horn of plenty) was said to be fashioned from the horn of the goat Amaltheia, whom Zeus placed in the heavens (as the constellation Capricorn) in gratitude for his help. It represented the inexhaustible flow of energy in the universe and taught the importance of giving and receiving.

Chart 15

Roman Paganism

Topic	Facts
Current Data	At its height, the power of the Roman Empire (and the influence of its various cults) extended across a vast geographical area: as far north as Britain, as far west as Spain, south of the northern coast of Africa, and eastward well into Asia. Today a number of organizations, known collectively as Roman Reconstructionism, advocate a return to the religious beliefs and practices of the ancient Romans while making as few concessions to modern sensibilities as possible. Prominent organizations include Nova Roma, Societatis Viae Romanae, and the Julian Society.
History	The ultimate origins of Roman paganism can be traced back to mid-10th-century BC, when the first known settlement—a farming community—was formed at the future site of Rome. The inhabitants of this early agrarian society held to a form of animism wherein localized spirits, called *numina*, inhabited a wide variety of objects in the world and oversaw various domains, including both the workings of the natural world and cultural activity. These proto-Roman peoples also engaged in the worship of ancestors; each family honored its own deceased relatives via a set of religious rites partly unique to that household. The Greeks began colonizing regions of Italy in the middle of the 8th century BC, and c. 700 BC the Etruscan civilization started to flourish. These events provided the cultural context from which Roman religious beliefs and practices developed. Rome as a major urban center was founded c. 625 BC. Though the Romans had a sizable pantheon of indigenous deities, not long after the establishment of the Roman republic in 510 BC, a large-scale adaptation of foreign deities commenced; this project was undertaken for a number of political-religious reasons. Some of these imported gods were taken from proto-Indo-European, Latin tribal, and/or Etruscan sources; many others were Greek in origin. Most of the Roman gods and goddesses of this time exhibited a mixture of religious influences. As the territorial dominion of the Roman republic expanded, it continued to assimilate the religions of the conquered regions for the political and economic benefits conferred thereby, which further diversified the religious landscape. During the transition of the Roman republic into the imperial system of the Roman Empire in the second half of the 1st century BC, Roman religion took on a new dimension by deifying its emperors, beginning with Julius Caesar. At first this exaltation of human rulers to the level of gods was largely rejected by the Roman populace, but the great popularity of Caesar helped to pave the way for this doctrine to be accepted by later citizens of Rome. However, the power and influence of the Roman imperial cult underwent a gradual decline starting in the late 1st century AD. This weakening was due to such factors as the popularity of the Persian sun god Mythras in the Roman military, the growing influence of Stoicism with its attendant pantheism, and the increasing number of converts to Christianity. Christianity eventually supplanted all other forms of Roman religion: in AD 313 Emperor Constantine issued the Edict of Milan, thereby legally establishing toleration of the Christian religion; and in AD 391, during the reign of Emperor Theodosius, all forms of paganism were outlawed while Christianity was made the official religion of the Roman Empire.

Chart 16

Roman Paganism (continued)

Topic	Facts
Summary of Beliefs	At the peak of its historical development, Roman paganism was an extremely elaborate religious-political system combining a vast pantheon of gods, temples, altars, a priesthood, public and private rituals, taboos, traditional Graeco-Roman religious beliefs, regional idiosyncrasies, and a cult of Roman emperors. Though it was cohesive in terms of its political consequences, Roman paganism was very diverse and eclectic when it came to matters of doctrine and practice. The Romans viewed their religion primarily as a contractual relationship between their empire and divine forces that were in control of the stability and prosperity of that empire. Because of this, Roman paganism was fluid and highly pragmatic in nature, constantly changing in response to prevailing social conditions. The state cult concerned itself with public ceremonies thought to influence political, economic, and military affairs, while the heads of Roman families carried out domestic rituals and prayers thought to affect the well-being of their households. For the Romans, religious observance was fundamentally a public duty rather than a private impulse.

Topic	Summary of View
Creation	Many of the creation myths were borrowed from Greek mythology and modified in various ways. However, the most important myth described not the creation of the cosmos, but the founding of Rome by Romulus and Remus. According to one version, King Amulius of Albagonga forced his niece Rhea Silvia, the future mother of Romulus and Remus, to become a vestal virgin. He did this because Rhea's father, Numitor, had been on the throne before Amulius had overthrown him, and Amulius wanted to prevent Rhea from having any sons who might seek to usurp his kingship. However, Rhea consented to have sexual relations with Mars, thereby violating her vows of chastity. She conceived and subsequently bore twin sons, Romulus and Remus. Amulius ordered one of his servants to kill the newborn twins, but the servant could not bring himself to carry out the order. He put the two babies in a bag and placed the bag in the Tiber River. The river god Tiberinus saw to it that they washed ashore, where they were found and nursed by a female wolf, Lupa. When they were older, Romulus and Remus were discovered by a shepherd named Faustulus, who took them to his wife, Acca Larentia. Together the couple raised the boys as their own, in their own home. Faustulus told Romulus and Remus about their history when they reached adulthood, whereupon the pair returned to Albagonga, killed Amulius, and reinstated Numitor to the throne. Then, on April 21, 753 BC, Romulus and Remus began making plans to construct a new city; they thought it best that one of them would be the primary builder and the other would be his helper. As a way of deciding who would play the leading role in the city's construction, they asked the gods for signs involving the flight patterns of birds. Next Romulus journeyed to the top of Palatine Hill, and Remus traveled to the top of Aventine Hill. Romulus became convinced that he had been selected by the gods, so he threw his lance on the hill to find the exact location of the future city. With the assistance of a cow and a bull (both white), he followed the traditional Etruscan practice of tracing the borders of his town using a plough. When Remus dared to cross the unfinished city wall that stood on this border, thereby invading Romulus's territory, Romulus slew him with

Chart 16

Roman Paganism (continued)

Topic	Summary of View
Creation (continued)	his sword, declaring that anyone who offended the city of Rome would suffer death for such arrogance. Soon remorseful, Romulus named the city Roma, made himself its king, and married Hersilia. He increased the city's population by inviting exiles, refugees, criminals, and runaway slaves to live there.
Scripture and Authority	Though no sacred text or collection of texts held universal authority, there was a complex and extensive system of priestly authority that regulated and performed public religious rites. Included in this system were several priestly *collegia*, lower-ranking priesthoods known as *sodalicia*, and many quasi-independent priests of various cults. There also were a number of well-established cults of foreign origin with their own priesthoods (like those of Serapis and Isis). The Pontifex Maximus (Greatest Pontiff) acted as the speaker for the Collegium Pontificum (College of Pontiffs), and administered the affairs of the vestal virgins (see "Distinctive Beliefs and Practices"). The Rex and Regina Sacrorum (King and Queen of the Sacred) performed various public rites and announced festival days. The Collegium Augurium (College of Auguries) was a group of priests who interpreted the will of the gods by studying the flight of birds, set apart *templum* (sacred space), and advised the Roman Senate. Other types of priests included the Septemviri Epulones (Seven Epulones), who organized public religious feasts; *pontifices*, who kept records of religious procedures and days of special religious significance; *flamines*, who carried out priestly duties to individual gods; Fratres Arvales (Arval Brethren), who offered annual sacrifices in order to guarantee good harvests; Luperci (Brothers of the Wolf), who officiated at purification and fertility rites; the Collegium Fetalium (College of the Fetiales), who represented Rome in matters of foreign diplomacy; and the Quindecemviri Sacris Faciundis (Fifteen Who Make Sacrifices), who guarded and interpreted the *Sibylline Books* (a collection of oracular utterances consulted during crises by the Roman government).
God	Monotheism was strongly rejected; none of the gods were all-powerful, all-knowing, or present everywhere. Although the early Romans barely concerned themselves with the distinct characteristics of the gods and goddesses within their pantheon (whose personal histories, unlike those of their Greek counterparts, lacked marriages and genealogies), there was a rather rigid understanding of what each particular deity was responsible to do. There were two main classes of gods, the *di indigetes* and the *de novensides*. The former were the original gods of the Roman state, and the latter were deities whose cults were introduced later in Rome's history. Jupiter, Mars, and Quirinus were the three most important gods during much of Roman history. Other major deities included Bacchus, Ceres, Cupid, Diana, Janus, Juno, Maia, Mercury, Minerva, Neptune, Pluto, Proserpine, Sol, Saturn, Uranus, Venus, Vesta, and Vulcan. During the Imperial period, the divinity of the emperor was ardently maintained. Many emperors took on the title Kurios (Lord) and called on their subjects to revere them as gods. It was common practice for emperors to accept divine honors before their deaths, sometimes requiring ritual sacrifice as a sign of loyalty.

Chart 16

Roman Paganism (continued)

Topic	Summary of View
Mankind	There is not a sharp ontological distinction between human beings and the gods; the claim of the emperors to deity is an example of this. Each person has a physical body and an immortal soul. There is a strong link between the importance of the individual and the expansion of the Roman Empire. Personal identity is bound up with the state and its politics-religion.
Sin	The primary vice is refusing or failing to fulfill specified obligations: not engaging in proper rituals, not venerating the emperor, criticizing the gods or the Roman government, etc. Refusal to acknowledge the deity of the emperor and the all-encompassing nature of the loyalty demanded by the state is spiritual as well as political treason.
Salvation	Fundamentally sociopolitical in nature; the peace, stability, and expansion of the Roman Empire was of first importance. A comprehensive sacrificial system and numerous festivals, oaths, prayers, libations, and purification rites were employed to ensure the continued flourishing of the empire. The Roman emperor was the Soter (Savior) of the Roman people.
Afterlife	Beliefs are very similar to that of Greek paganism (see Greek Paganism, Afterlife).

Distinctive Beliefs and Practices	
Omens	The Romans tended to be quite superstitious and relied heavily on omens (phenomena thought to portend good or evil) for making major decisions regarding such things as whether or not to embark on a military campaign. In particular, the flight patterns of birds were believed to aid in assessing the feasibility of accomplishing certain goals.
Haruspex	A *haruspex* was someone who practiced divination (sought omens) by inspecting the entrails of sacrificed animals. In particular, the livers of sacrificed sheep were thought to provide the basis for successful prognostication.
Vestal Virgins	The city of Rome sponsored six vestal virgins. Traditionally, these girls were selected from esteemed patrician families at a young age. They lived in a palatial building next to the temple of Vesta at the Roman forum. Their primary duty was to guard the sacred fire in the temple. Other duties included performing prescribed rituals and baking sacred salt cakes.
Religious Festivals	The Romans celebrated a great many festivals throughout the year. Most of these festivals were held in honor of particular gods/goddesses and had their own unique elements. Each February marked the Parentilia, a period of nine days during which families would worship their dead ancestors, and the Lupercalia, a fertility festival.

Chart 16

Roman Paganism (continued)

Distinctive Beliefs and Practices

Caduceus	Sacred to the god Mercury, the caduceus is a wand with two serpents wrapped around it, surmounted by two small wings or a winged helmet. For the Romans it served as a symbol of moral equilibrium and good conduct. The wand represents power, the two snakes represent wisdom, the wings represent diligence, and the helmet represents lofty thoughts.
Lar Familiaris (Guardian Spirit of the Family)	In the privacy of their own homes, Romans worshiped domestic deities known as *lares* and *penates*. It was believed that every household was assigned a guardian spirit known as the Lar Familiaris, who brought about the welfare and prosperity of the wider household (including extended family and slaves). Each Lar Familiaris was associated with a particular place and did not accompany a family that moved. *Penates*, although domestic guardian spirits too, more specifically were protectors of the master of the household and his immediate family. Different spirits were assigned to different, specific responsibilities within a home, such as protecting the door, the threshold, the hinges, or the hearth. All family functions included these household gods in some fashion. Each home had an altar to the Lar Familiaris called a *lararium*, where rites were performed and prayers were said; usually it was located near the hearth or in a corner of the atrium.

Chart 16

Graeco-Roman Deities

Greek Name*	Roman Name	Description/Position
Aphrodite**	Venus	Goddess of love and beauty. Wife of Hephaestus and daughter of Zeus. She often was escorted by the Oreads (mountain fairies). Her cult was centered on the Island of Cythera. Her festival, Aphrodisiac, was held in Athens and Corinth. Often depicted with dolphins, swans, doves, lime trees, and pomegranates.
Apollo	Sol (identified with Helios)	Apollo was a god of youth who oversaw a wide range of human activity, including colonization, medicine and healing, hunting, archery, poetry, music, dance, prophecy, and learning; he was also the patron of shepherds. Son of Zeus and twin of Artemis. Apollo had an oracle in Crete and was leader of the Muses (nine water fairies). He was honored every four years at the Pythian Games at Delphi. Depicted as a swan and as a man with a bow and arrows, a laurel crown, a kithara (similar to a lyre), and a plectrum (small object used to pluck the strings of certain instruments).
Ares	Mars	God of war. Son of Zeus and Hera. Worshiped in Thracia and Sparta. Depicted wearing a helmet and holding a spear. Associated with dogs and vultures.
Artemis	Diana	Goddess of the moon, sexual purity, fertility, childbirth, healing, hunting, wild animals, and wilderness. Daughter of Zeus and twin sister of Apollo. Her cult was concentrated in Ephesus. The Brauronia festival was held in her honor. Depicted as a woman holding a bow and arrows with a crescent moon over her head.
Asclepius (Asklepios)	Aesculapius	God of medicine and healing. Daughter Hygieia represents sanitary measures and disease prevention. Son Telesforos symbolizes recuperative abilities. A well-known sanctuary was built in his honor in southern Greece. Snakes were sometimes used in healing rites as a way of honoring Asclepius. Depicted as a man holding a rod and as a rooster.
Athena	Minerva	Virgin goddess of strategy, warfare, wisdom, and counseling. Her most famous temple is the Parthenon in Athens. Often paired with Nike, the goddess of victory, and accompanied by an owl. Depicted as armed with various weapons and wearing a breastplate made of goatskin.
Cronus	Saturn	God of farming, harvesttime, and grain, especially corn. Husband of Rhea, father of Zeus, and son of Uranus and Gaia. Leader of the first group of Titans. The Kronia festival was held to honor Cronus and celebrate good crops. Frequently depicted as a man with a sickle.
Demeter	Ceres	Goddess of agriculture, the earth, youth, life and death, marriage, and law. Daughter of Cronos and Rhea, mother of Persephone, sister of Zeus. A seven-day festival was held in her honor at Arcadia. Depicted riding in a chariot, sometimes with Persephone. Associated with aspects of the harvest, including grain, fruit, and flowers.
Dike (Dyke)	Justitia	Goddess of morality and justice. Daughter of Zeus and Themis.
Dionysus	Bacchus	God of wine, civilization, law, and peace. Patron of agriculture and theatrical performances. Son of Zeus and Semele or Zeus and Persephone. Two major festivals in Athens were dedicated to Dionysus: the Dionysia and the Lenaia. The rituals of his cult, the Dionysian Mysteries, were shrouded in secrecy. Depicted carrying a thyrsus (huge staff covered with ivy, with a pinecone on top). Associated with serpents, bulls, figs, ivy, pinecones, pomegranates, centaurs, and satyrs.

* This is only a partial list.

** Olympian gods are in bold type.

Chart 17

Graeco-Roman Deities (continued)

Greek Name	Roman Name	Description/Position
Eros	Cupid	God of love, lust, fertility, and sex. Son of Aphrodite and either Hephaestus or Ares. Usually depicted as a winged baby or very young boy holding a bow and arrows. Sometimes represented as a bull, serpent, or lion, each with a ram's head.
Gaia	Cybele	Goddess who personifies the earth. Present in homes, courtyards, caves, and mothers' wombs. Associated with animals and insects such as pigs, bulls, snakes, and bees.
Hades	Pluto	God of the dead, the underworld, and minerals. Son of Cronus and Rhea. Siblings included Zeus, Poseidon, Demeter, Hestia, and Hera. Rarely depicted in ancient Greek art.
Hephaestus (Hephaistos)	Vulcan	God of metalworkers, blacksmiths, sculptors, artists, and fire. Son of Hera, brother of Ares. Popular in the areas of Greece where craftsmen and various professional trades were concentrated, Athens being one of the main areas. Associated with Mount Etna in Sicily. Depicted as ugly and deformed, often with twisted feet.
Hera	Juno	Goddess of marriage. Wife (and sister) of Zeus; mother of Area and Hephaestus. Some of the shrines erected in her honor are among the earliest in Greek history. Great Daedala festival was held to honor her. Associated with cattle. Often depicted as wearing a crown and veil and holding a pomegranate. Sometimes shown in a wagon being pulled by peacocks.
Hermes	Mercury	God of boundaries, travelers, shepherds, herds of cows, public speaking, poetry, athletics, weights and measures, commerce, and relayed messages from the gods to human beings. Present in any activity that involved "crossing" of any sort: moving objects from one location to another, interpreting texts, and passing from this life to the underworld. Son of Zeus. Inventor of fire, the lyre, racing, and boxing. Depicted earlier as an older, bearded man; later as a young and athletic man.
Hestia	Vesta	Goddess of the household, the family, and domestic affairs. Daughter of Cronos and Rhea. Sister of Zeus, Poseidon, Hades, Demeter, and Hera. No public cults in her name existed. Symbolized the treaties between the Greek colonies and their correlative cities. Sometimes depicted as a woman wearing garb typical of a Greek housewife.
Hypnos	Somnus	God of sleep and dreams. Son of Nyx, the goddess of night. Twin brother of Thanatos. Four of his children were black-winged demons (*oneiroi*) who entered the dreams of emperors. Associated with poppies and other sleep-inducing plants and herbs. Depicted as a naked young man with wings coming out of his head; also as a sleeping man lying on a bed surrounded by black curtains.
Nemesis (Rhamnousi)	Rivalitas	Goddess of justice and vengeance. Enacted retribution on lawbreakers and the proud. Daughter of Oceanus. Associated with Aphrodite. A sanctuary where she was mollified existed near Athens. Depicted holding any number of objects: scales, a measuring rod, reins, or a sword. Depicted riding in a chariot pulled by griffins (creatures with eagle heads and lion bodies).
Nike	Victoria	Goddess of victory, athletic events, military battles, and good fortune. Daughter of Pallas and Styx; attendant of Zeus. Associated with Athena. Popular in Ephesus. Often depicted as a small woman with wings being carried by Athena.

Chart 17

Graeco-Roman Deities (continued)

Greek Name	Roman Name	Description/Position
Ouranos	Uranus	God of the sky and the heavens. First ruler of the universe; father of the Titans (gods who opposed Zeus and the Olympian gods). Son (and husband) of Gaia. Depicted as a man pouring a pot of water.
Pan	Faunus	God of shepherds and their flocks, forests and meadows, and male sexuality. Son of Zeus or Hermes. Depicted as having goat horns, buttocks, and legs, often with an erect phallus.
Persephone (Cora)	Proserpine, Libera	Queen of the underworld and daughter of Demeter. Portrayed with items such as a crown, a scepter, a torch, and stalks of grain.
Poseidon	Neptune	God of the sea, marine life, ships, earthquakes, and horses. Husband of Amphitrite; son of Cronus and Rhea. Popular in Corinth and far southern Italy. Associated with Apollo, a trident (three-pronged spear), and dolphins. Often depicted in a chariot pulled by seahorses.
Prometheos	Prometheus	God of fire and craftsmanship. Inventor of fire and sacrifice; patron of civilization. Brother of Atlas. His shrine was in Athens.
Rhea	Ops	Goddess of female fertility. Wife (and sister) of Cronus. Mother of Demeter, Hades, Hera, Hestia, Poseidon, and Zeus. Daughter of Uranus and Gaia. Associated with Cybele. Popular in Crete. Symbols included swans and the moon. Depicted riding in a chariot pulled by two lions.
Thanatos	Mors	God of death and darkness. Son of Nyx and twin brother of Hypnos. His children were grotesque, nasty, terrible creatures. Depicted as a young man holding a butterfly, torch, or wreath; sometimes shown with wings, with a sword at his belt.
Tyche	Fortuna	Goddess of the affluence and destiny of cities. Daughter of Hermes and Aphrodite. Associated with Nemesis. Popular in areas near the Aegean Sea. Sometimes depicted as holding a fortune wheel, the rudder of a ship, or a cornucopia.
Zeus	Jupiter	Head of the Greek pantheon of gods and god of the sky, thunder, and weather. Husband of Rhea and later Hera (his sister). Son of Cronus. Children included Poseidon, Hades, Demeter, Hestia, Hera, Hephaistos, Ares, Hebe, and Eileithyia. A 40-foot statue of Zeus was built in Olympia. Commonly depicted holding lightning bolts.
	Emperor	Julius Caesar and Augustus Caesar were deified posthumously; Caligula, Nero, and Domitian demanded worship during their lifetimes.

Chart 17

PART 4
WESTERN
RELIGIONS

Historical Relationships of Western Religions

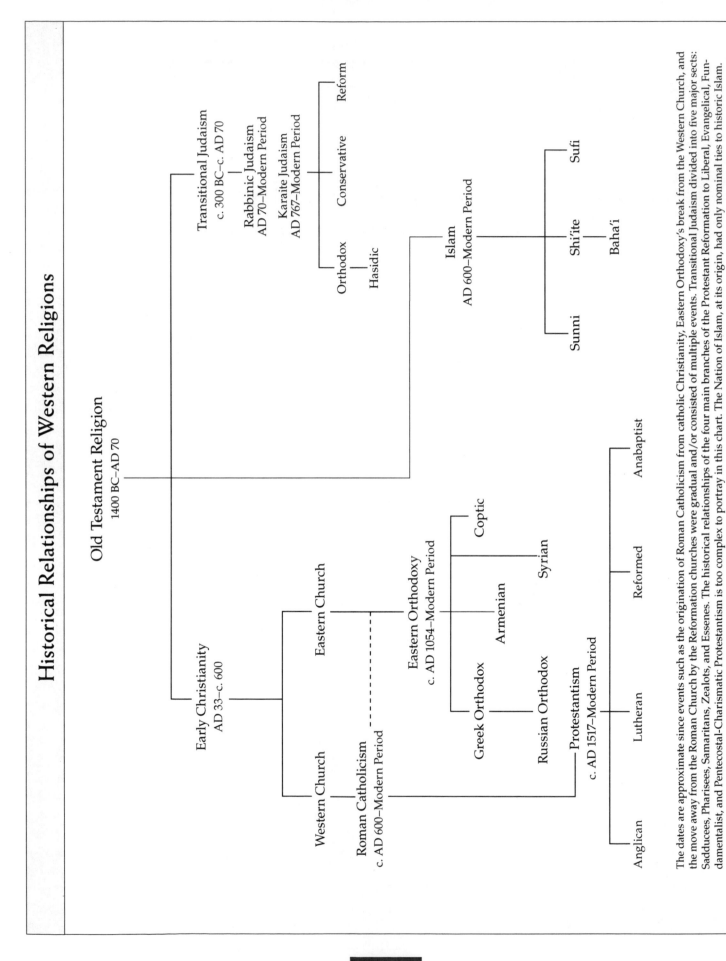

The dates are approximate since events such as the origination of Roman Catholicism from catholic Christianity, Eastern Orthodoxy's break from the Western Church, and the move away from the Roman Church by the Reformation churches were gradual and/or consisted of multiple events. Transitional Judaism divided into five major sects: Sadducees, Pharisees, Samaritans, Zealots, and Essenes. The historical relationships of the four main branches of the Protestant Reformation to Liberal, Evangelical, Fundamentalist, and Pentecostal-Charismatic Protestantism is too complex to portray in this chart. The Nation of Islam, at its origin, had only nominal ties to historic Islam.

Chart 18

Comparison of Western Religions

	Judaism	Christianity	Islam	Baha'i
Birth-date of Founder	c. 2100 BC	c. 5–3 BC	AD 570	AD 1819
Founder	Abraham	Jesus Christ	Muhammad	The Bab (Mirza Ali Muhammad)
Major Branches and Sects	Orthodox Conservative Reform	Roman Catholicism Eastern Orthodoxy Protestantism	Sunni Shi'ite Sufi	Orthodox Baha'is Baha'is Under the Provisions of the Covenant Independent Baha'is
Holy Books	Hebrew Scriptures (Tanach) *Talmud*	Hebrew and Christian Scriptures	Koran (Qur'an)	*The Most Holy Book The Book of Certitude Gleanings from the Writings of Baha'u'llah*
Basic Beliefs	**God:** Yahweh is one in person and nature. **Revelation:** God has revealed himself in the 24 books of the Hebrew Bible. **Salvation:** God has provided a way of salvation through his Law and sacrificial system; various combinations of repentance, prayer, obedience to the Law, maintaining Jewish identity, and improvement of self and society (post-AD 70).	**God:** A Trinity of three persons (Father, Son, and Holy Spirit) subsisting in one nature. **Revelation:** God has revealed himself in the 66 books of the Old and New Testaments. **Salvation:** God has provided salvation in the person and work of the Lord Jesus Christ.	**God:** Allah is one in person and nature. **Revelation:** God has revealed his will in the Koran (Qur'an). **Salvation:** Mankind must obey the revealed will of Allah, yet Allah can bestow or withhold mercy as he sees fit.	**God:** Incomprehensible, but has displayed many Divine Manifestations; sometimes called Primal Will. **Revelation:** God has revealed himself through the writings of the Bab, Baha'u'llah, and 'Abdu'l-Baha. **Salvation:** Can be attained by means of most of the major world religions.

This is a partial list.

Chart 19

Timeline of Judaism

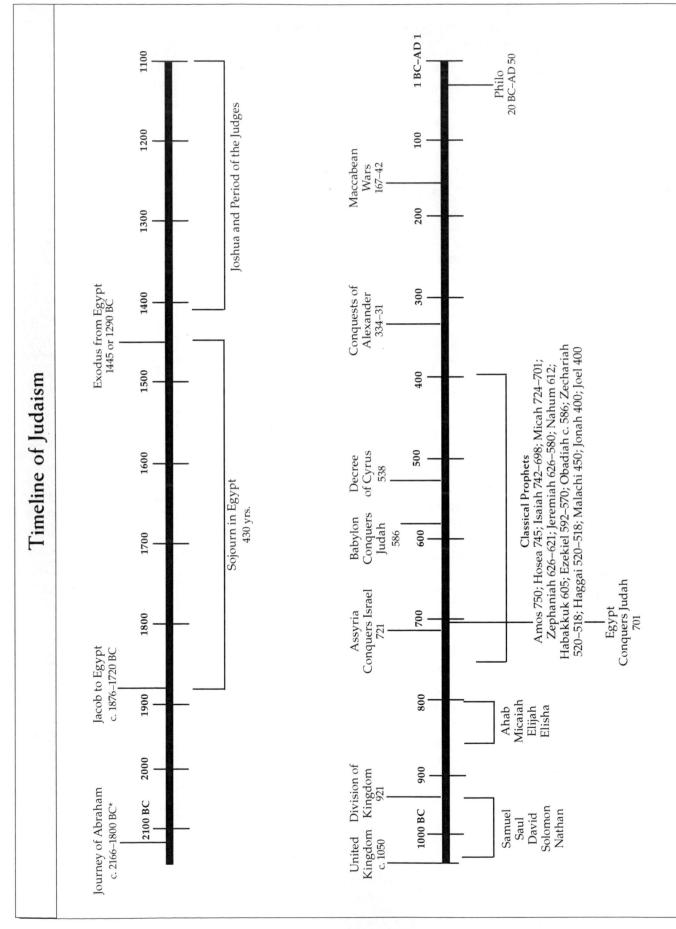

Journey of Abraham
c. 2166–1800 BC*

Jacob to Egypt
c. 1876–1720 BC

Exodus from Egypt
1445 or 1290 BC

Sojourn in Egypt
430 yrs.

Joshua and Period of the Judges

2100 BC 2000 1900 1800 1700 1600 1500 1400 1300 1200 1100

United
Kingdom
c. 1050

Division of
Kingdom
921

Assyria
Conquers Israel
721

Babylon
Conquers
Judah
586

Decree
of Cyrus
538

Conquests of
Alexander
334–31

Maccabean
Wars
167–42

Philo
20 BC–AD 50

1000 BC 900 800 700 600 500 400 300 200 100 1 BC–AD 1

Samuel
Saul
David
Solomon
Nathan

Ahab
Micaiah
Elijah
Elisha

Egypt
Conquers Judah
701

Classical Prophets
Amos 750; Hosea 745; Isaiah 742–698; Micah 724–701;
Zephaniah 626–621; Jeremiah 626–580; Nahum 612;
Habakkuk 605; Ezekiel 592–570; Obadiah c. 586; Zechariah
520–518; Haggai 520–518; Malachi 450; Jonah 400; Joel 400

* The earlier dates in this chart reflect more approximate times according to the clear reading of the Masoretic text. The later dates reflect the views of certain scholars based on external
archaeological evidence or chronologies of countries surrounding Israel. Most early dates are approximate.

Chart 20

Timeline of Judaism (continued)

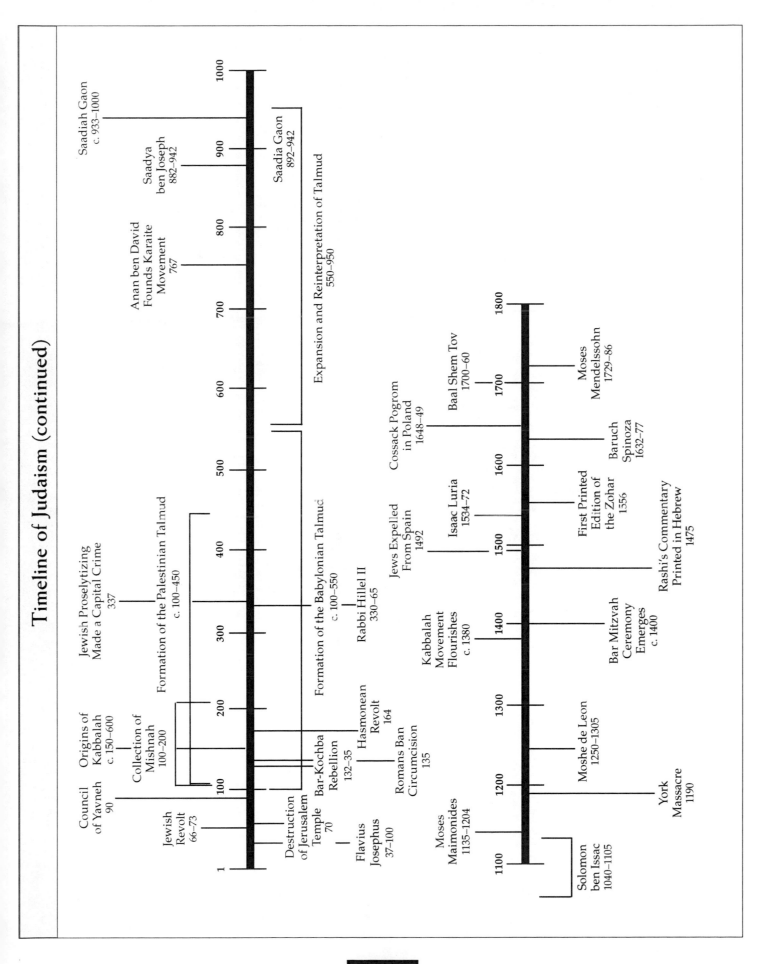

Saadiah Gaon
c. 933–1000

Saadya
ben Joseph
882–942

Anan ben David
Founds Karaite
Movement
767

Saadia Gaon
892–942

Expansion and Reinterpretation of Talmud
550–950

Jewish Proselytizing
Made a Capital Crime
337

Formation of the Palestinian Talmud
c. 100–450

Formation of the Babylonian Talmud
c. 100–550

Rabbi Hillel II
330–65

Council
of Yavneh
90

Origins of
Kabbalah
c. 150–600

Collection of
Mishnah
100–200

Bar-Kochba
Rebellion
132–35

Hasmonean
Revolt
164

Romans Ban
Circumcision
135

Jewish Revolt
66–73

Destruction
of Jerusalem
Temple
70

Flavius
Josephus
37–100

Moses
Maimonides
1135–1204

Solomon
ben Issac
1040–1105

York
Massacre
1190

Moshe de Leon
1250–1305

Kabbalah
Movement
Flourishes
c. 1380

Jews Expelled
From Spain
1492

Isaac Luria
1534–72

Cossack Pogrom
in Poland
1648–49

Baal Shem Tov
1700–60

Moses
Mendelssohn
1729–86

Baruch
Spinoza
1632–77

First Printed
Edition of
the Zohar
1556

Rashi's Commentary
Printed in Hebrew
1475

Bar Mitzvah
Ceremony
Emerges
c. 1400

Chart 20

Timeline of Judaism (continued)

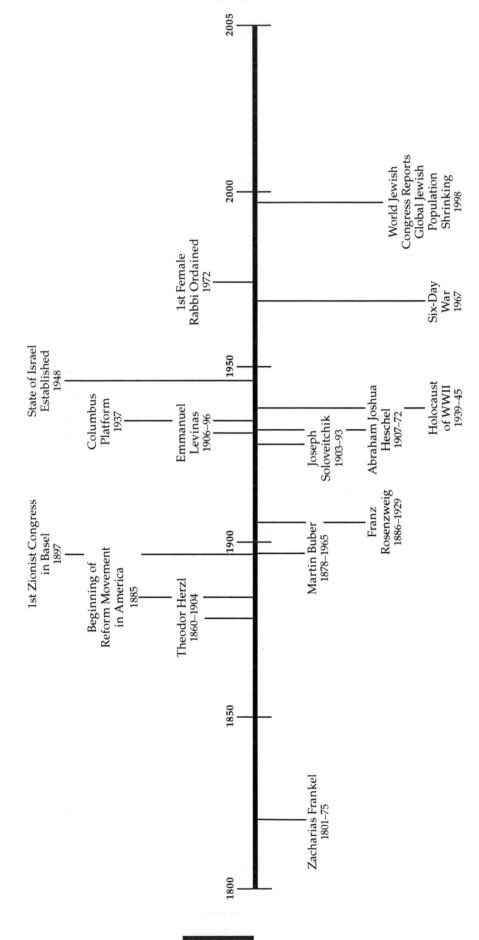

Zacharias Frankel
1801–75

1800

1850

Beginning of
Reform Movement
in America
1885

1st Zionist Congress
in Basel
1897

Theodor Herzl
1860–1904

1900

Martin Buber
1878–1965

Franz
Rosenzweig
1886–1929

Columbus
Platform
1937

State of Israel
Established
1948

Emmanuel
Levinas
1906–96

Joseph
Soloveitchik
1903–93

Abraham Joshua
Heschel
1907–72

Holocaust
of WWII
1939–45

1950

1st Female
Rabbi Ordained
1972

Six-Day
War
1967

2000

World Jewish
Congress Reports
Global Jewish
Population
Shrinking
1998

2005

Chart 20

Judaism

Topic	Facts
Current Data	Historical circumstances in the 20th century—chiefly the Holocaust and establishment of the state of Israel—have transformed Judaism. Its character and traditions worldwide have been reshaped by bitter tragedy and cultural assimilation. The world's largest Jewish community resides in North America. This community includes the three major branches of Judaism—Orthodox, Conservative, and Reform—but also such diverse (and sometimes interrelated) movements as Zionism, Reconstructionism, and Karaite Judaism. Kabbalah (a form of Jewish mysticism) has become somewhat trendy in the United States. Worldwide there are about 14.5 million Jews.
History	At the behest of God, Abraham left his homeland in the area of Ur (ancient Sumer; modern southeastern Iraq) to travel to the land of Canaan (all of the land, and more, that is claimed by the modern state of Israel). God promised this land to Abraham and his descendants through Isaac for an everlasting inheritance (Genesis 12, 15, 17). Abraham and those with him advocated a robust monotheism, in contrast to those among whom they dwelt. This monotheistic religion was passed down through successive generations of Hebrews by Isaac, his son Jacob (Israel), and finally the twelve sons of Jacob. These twelve sons were Reuben, Simeon, Levi, Judah, Zebulun, Issachar, Dan, Gad, Asher, Naphtali, Joseph, and Benjamin. Joseph's brothers, who were jealous of Joseph and the special treatment he received from their father, sold him into slavery, whereupon his new owners took him to Egypt. In Egypt, Joseph gained favor with the pharaoh and became a powerful ruler. Eventually his brothers, because of a famine in Canaan, traveled to Egypt, where they were reunited with Joseph. All twelve brothers and their families and their father then settled in Egypt, where they became a people distinct from the native Egyptians. After a period of peace and prosperity, however, their Egyptian rulers forced them to become slaves of the Egyptian empire. When they cried to God to deliver them, God instructed Moses to confront the Egyptian pharaoh (whom some believe to be Ramses II, in the 13th century, but others believe to be a 15th century pharaoh such as Amenhotep II) and demand that he let the Hebrews go. Initially Pharaoh refused, but after God sent a series of devastating judgments on Egypt, Pharaoh relented and gave Moses permission to lead his people out of Egypt, back to the Promised Land of Canaan. During this exodus from Egypt, God miraculously preserved his people by parting the waters of the Sea of Reeds (which some have identified as the Red Sea), which allowed them to cross over on dry land. At Mount Sinai, God gave Moses the Ten Commandments, and Moses in turn presented these commandments to the people of Israel. It was at this point in Old Testament history that God established a covenant with his people, setting forth promises of blessings for obedience and curses for disobedience. Also, Moses sent twelve spies to look over the Promised Land (Canaan), but ten of the spies reported that any attempt to take the land was too formidable. Since most of the people accepted this report, God judged Israel, causing them to wander for 40 years until the generation of disbelief was dead. After Moses died, Joshua led the new generation into the land promised to Abraham.

Observe the timeline (chart 20) to get a sense of the time periods discussed in this section.

Chart 21

Topic	Facts
History (continued)	Three major periods of Hebrew history followed the entry into the land of Canaan: (1) The Age of Judges. The people were led by judges who were commissioned by God as particular situations developed. (2) The Age of Kings. The first king was Saul, who was followed by David, then by Solomon. David reigned during a time of great military, political, and economic success. After Solomon's reign, the kingdom of Israel split into the Northern Kingdom (Israel) and the Southern Kingdom (Judah). (3) The Age of Prophets. God used messengers (Isaiah, Jeremiah, Ezekiel, and others) in trying to get Israel to give up its sinful ways and repent. The Northern Kingdom (Israel) was conquered by Assyria and its people were dispersed over a wide area. A century and a half later the Southern Kingdom (Judah) fell to Babylonia and the conquerors destroyed Jerusalem, including the temple. The Jews were taken to Babylon. The fall of the Northern and Southern Kingdoms and the Babylonian captivity were perceived as a confirmation of the prophetic predictions of judgment on Israel. Near the end of the 6th century BC, after Babylon was conquered, some of the Jews returned to Jerusalem. They rebuilt the temple and resumed their normal worship of God. Eventually the rest returned. But Judea was not to remain in charge of its own destiny. Military victories again put Judea under foreign control. During this time, a Greek translation of the Hebrew Bible (the Septuagint) was completed in Alexandria, Egypt. A Seleucid king's attempt to force Greek paganism on the Jewish people caused an armed rebellion, led by Judas Maccabeus. While controlled by the Roman Empire, Judaism splintered into three primary sects (Pharisees, Sadducees, and Essenes) and several smaller sects, such as the Zealots. The Pharisees adapted the laws of the Torah to meet the changing needs of the Jewish people by following oral tradition, but with verse-by-verse interpretation of the Scriptures. The Sadducees rejected any doctrine not in the Law (resurrection of the body) and interpreted the Scriptures without the influence of oral tradition or Hebrew customs. The Essenes, whose members wrote the Dead Sea Scrolls, were a reactionary and secretive group concerned primarily with the end times. The Zealots' goal was to get rid of the Romans. But the Roman army destroyed the temple in AD 70, ending Judaism's sacrificial system of atonement (the core of the Mosaic covenant). The Sadducees and the Essenes were destroyed. The Zealots were largely decimated, waiting for their final destruction under Hadrian in the next century. With the temple gone, Judaism changed. The focus turned from the priesthood and blood sacrifices to a belief that the people could have a direct relationship with God. The Pharisees favored participation in local synagogues and Jewish schools of learning. The major blow to Jewish identity as a nation and even survival as a people occurred when, under Emperor Hadrian, Zealots rebelled against the rule of Rome. Hadrian defeated the Jews in AD 135 and made Jerusalem a Roman city. He banned Jews from living there or even being within sight of their holy city. He renamed the Jewish homeland Palestine, after the ancient enemies of the Jews, the Philistines. The Jews became scattered in many areas. In the 8th century the Karaite sect broke away from mainstream Judaism. Members rejected rabbinic tradition and authority and looked only to the Hebrew scriptures for legal

Chart 21

Judaism (continued)

Topic	Facts
History (continued)	decision-making. By the end of the 10th century, many institutions of Jewish learning had been established in Muslim-dominated Spain and North Africa. The Islamic rulers allowed the Jews to be active in shaping the culture. Culminating in the 13th and 14th centuries, the strain of Jewish mysticism called Kabbalah produced a plethora of writings and gained many adherents across Europe. The Enlightenment of the 18th century resulted in many positive changes for Jews in Europe, and by the 19th century the harassment, bigotry, and social marginalization experienced by most European Jews decreased. However, many Jews were confronted for the first time with modern philosophy, science, and historical criticism, which led many leading Jewish intellectuals to engage in a deep and far-reaching re-evaluation of the place of Judaism in the modern world. The majority of Jews developed a new theology that discarded traditional interpretations of the Hebrew Bible and proposed a doctrine of "progressive revelation" wherein divine revelation was taken to be one and the same thing as the combined knowledge of Jews and humanity as a whole. Once the majority of Jews in Europe and the United States accepted this new theology, issues like forming an independent state of Israel, restoring temple sacrifices, and awaiting the Jewish Messiah were dismissed as passé. Modern Judaism looked forward to continued progress in science and technology and further improvement of political, educational, and social conditions.

Alongside this new ideology arose another ideology, that of Zionism. Theodor Herzl (1860–1904) in 1897 organized the Zionist Congress with the intent of establishing a Jewish homeland. Although other areas were considered, eventually Palestine, which was held by the British (1923–48), became the logical place for a Jewish homeland since this was their ancient land. Jews began to buy land and settle there. World War II and the horror of the Nazi Holocaust against European Jewry dealt the plan a crippling blow.

After WWII, in 1947, the newly formed United Nations approved the creation of a Jewish homeland (Israel) by dividing Palestine into Arab and Jewish states. The British occupation of Palestine ended on May 14, 1948. Palestinians and Arab troops from neighboring Egypt, Iraq, Jordan, and Syria quickly attacked Israel, trying by force to drive the Jews out of the area. Israel's military repelled the invading armies and proceeded to occupy additional (previously Arab) territory. In June 1967 the combined military forces of Egypt, Syria, Jordan, Saudi Arabia, Iraq, Kuwait, and Algeria were preparing an invasion to wipe out the fledgling state of Israel, but again the Israeli military won a decisive victory by employing a massive pre-emptive strike. The former line of demarcation now extended into the biblical lands of Judea and Samaria and the land of the Philistines, the Gaza strip. In the Yom Kippur war of 1973, the Arab nations once again attempted to defeat Israel, attacking on the most holy day of the Jews, but the Jews were successful in thwarting off this attack and took control of the Golan Heights above Galilee. Various attempts to find peace for that region have failed. In 2005 Israel, in an effort to end the bloodshed, voluntarily withdrew from settlements in the northern section of the West Bank and in the Gaza Strip, turning the land over to the Palestinians. It's building a security fence along the border of the West Bank. The challenges continue to be great for Israel living in the ancient homeland of the Hebrews in the midst of nearly 300 million Muslims who claim the land as their own. |

Chart 21

Judaism (continued)

Topic	Facts
Summary of Beliefs	Judaism does not focus on official doctrines, emphasizing appropriate actions instead. Judaism allows for a considerable latitude of views on most theological issues. Nevertheless, the Thirteen Principles of Faith enumerated by Moses Maimonides (1135–1204) are thought by many to constitute the minimal theology of Judaism. These principles are: 1. God exists. 2. God is one and there is nothing else like him. 3. God is spiritual in nature; he does not have corporeal aspects (physical form). 4. God is an everlasting God, without beginning or end. 5. God alone is the appropriate object of worship and prayer. 6. The Hebrew prophets spoke truth from God. 7. Moses was the greatest of God's prophets. 8. God gave Moses both the written and oral Torah. 9. There is and will be no other Torah other than the one revealed to Moses. 10. God is aware of every thought and action of human beings. 11. The righteous will receive a reward from God; he will punish the wicked. 12. The promised Messiah will come at the proper time. 13. All human beings who have ever lived will be raised from the dead. Judaism places a premium on relationships, though not just those between human beings. Important relationships in Judaism include those between God and people, between God and the Jews as a group, between Jews and the nation of Israel, and between human beings and God's creation. The Hebrew scriptures narrate the unfolding drama of these various relationships, with a view to God's special covenant relationship with the Jewish people. They also spell out the duties that God has imposed on humans as the pinnacle of his creation and upon his people Israel in particular.

Topic	Summary of View
Creation	The universe was created by God as an act of love and was intended to be a place where his creatures could flourish in their relationship with him. The world reflects and testifies to the wisdom, power, majesty, and goodness of God. God cares for the world he created, ruling over it with justice and compassion.
Scripture and Authority	The Hebrew Bible (the Tanakh), in particular its first five books (Torah), constitute the primary source for Jewish belief and practice. Traditionally, the Torah was viewed as a text whose divine injunctions are perpetually binding on the Jewish people, as well as (to a lesser degree) on Gentiles. The laws contained in the Torah were expanded and given greater clarity before being written down in the *Talmud* and *Mishnah*.

Chart 21

Judaism (continued)

Topic	Summary of View
God	Strict monotheism is declared: God is One; there are no other gods besides him. God is an eternal being, incorporeal, exalted above the heavens and the earth, holy, and supremely wise, loving, and merciful. He cannot (and should not) be represented by any physical object or artifact. He demonstrates his almighty power and authority over all of nature and history by performing signs and wonders for the sake of his covenant people.
Mankind	Human beings are created in the image and likeness of God. Nevertheless, they were given a nature with two aspects, each of which, at times, is in conflict with the other. These two aspects are the *yetzer tov* (conscience), which is aware of God's ethical standards, and the *yetzer ra* (desire to satisfy basic personal needs), which is not concerned with the ethical implications of meeting those needs. The history of Judaism provides abundant witness to God's faithfulness to his covenant and his ongoing presence in the lives of his people.
Sin	It is assumed that, in general, people have the ability to follow the law of God. Grievous sin within Judaism is not anticipated. God disclosed his law to Moses on Mount Sinai. God's revelation of his moral will is the foundation of Jewish belief and practice. The covenant God made with his people at Sinai is permanent and irrevocable. However, the terms and conditions of this covenant have been elaborated by authorized rabbis and can be altered (within limits) over time, as the cultural conditions faced by successive generations of Jews change.
Salvation	What happens to each person when God judges him or her after death is the consequence of how that person lived during life on earth. If the person was generally obedient to the Ten Commandments, that person will be in God's favor. If the person was disobedient, there may be suffering due to just retribution by God. However, even an extremely evil person can come to repentance (*teshuva*; turning) and afterward atone for sins by walking according to the law of God. Three main views about atoning for sin have emerged within Judaism since the Roman army destroyed the Jewish temple in Jerusalem. 1. Atonement can be made by repenting of sins, praying, and doing good works. 2. The corporate sufferings of the Jewish people atone for the sins of every individual Jew. 3. The Jewish people are assured happiness and peace (*shalom*) in the next life just because they are Jews.
Afterlife	According to traditional Judaism, human existence does not end with death of the body. The Hebrew scriptures speak of a shadowy realm called Sheol, but it is never described at length. Death is not considered alien, but a part of God's providential plan. Jews mourn the death of a loved one by means of prescribed mourning rituals for two reasons: to show proper respect for the dead (*kavod ha-met*), and to comfort the living (*nihum avelim*), who feel sorrow because someone they love has died. Jews hold a variety of views concerning life after death: that departed souls go to heaven, that departed souls are reincarnated, or that departed souls will be given a resurrection body when the Messiah comes to earth. Some believe that God torments wicked souls, whereas others believe that God annihilates them. In any case, Judaism focuses mainly on this life rather than on the life to come.

Chart 21

Judaism (continued)

Distinctive Beliefs and Practices

Halakha	Judaism has a system of law regulating civil and criminal justice, family relationships, personal ethics and manners, social institutions, and worship. Included are dietary laws, regulations for Sabbath observance, and instructions on the wearing of phylacteries and fringed shawls (*tallith*) during prayer.
Circumcision	Circumcision is performed on Jewish male infants eight days after they are born. It is performed by a *mohel*, a Jew who has mastered Jewish law concerning circumcision and received extensive training. During the procedure (called Brit Milah), the *mohel* cuts the foreskin from the baby's penis, after which the baby is given a Jewish name. The entire ritual is seen as the perpetuation of the ancient covenant between God and Abraham. It is followed by a meal of celebration called a *seudat mitzvah*.
Bar Mitzvah ***Bat Mitzvah***	When a Jewish child reaches the age of maturity (12 years for girls, 13 years for boys), he or she becomes responsible for keeping all aspects of Jewish tradition, ethics, and ritual law. He or she also gains the privilege of participating in all areas of Jewish community life. On this occasion a boy is said to become Bar Mitzvah ("son of the commandment"); a girl is said to become Bat Mitzvah ("daughter of the commandment").
Star of David	Though it did not become an official symbol of Judaism until the middle of the 20th century, the Star of David (Magen David; sometimes referred to as the shield of David) is now universally recognized as such. Some Jews place great significance on the symbol, explaining that the top triangle points up to God, the bottom triangle points down to the creation, and the interlacing of the triangles creates an unbreakable bond, like the bond of unity among the Jewish people. However, interlaced equilateral triangles, considered a sign of good luck, are a common symbol in many parts of Africa and the Middle East. In the 17th century, the Star of David was used as a symbol on synagogues to identify them as a Jewish house of worship, just as a cross is used on a Christian church.
	In 1897, during the first Zionist Congress, the flag that now is Israel's national flag, with a blue Star of David on a white field between blue and white stripes (like the lines on a Jewish prayer shawl), was adopted as the flag for the World Zionist Movement. Although attempts were made to select a different design for the flag of Israel when the country was established in 1948, opposition faded and the Zionist flag was approved.

Chart 21

Comparison of Beliefs within Judaism

	Scripture and Authority	God	Mankind
Orthodox Judaism	The Hebrew scriptures are divided into three sections: the Law (also called the Torah and Pentateuch), the Prophets (*Nevi'im*), and the Wisdom Writings (*Kethuvim*). The primary focus is on the Books of Moses (Torah), with other Scriptures viewed as subservient to them. It is a revelatory faith as witnessed to by the Scriptures. Both oral and written traditions are revelatory and have a divine origin.	God is One. God is spirit and hence images of him should not be made. He is personal, all-knowing, present everywhere, infinite in power, eternal, and compassionate.	People have inclinations toward both good and evil. People can overcome evil desires and be perfected through their own efforts in following and observing the Law.
Conservative Judaism	The canon of Scripture is the same as that recognized by the Orthodox. The Torah and the other books of Scripture are the Word of God. Scholars in this tradition consider Scripture to be "dynamically" inspired (God inspired the basic idea, but not every single word) rather than verbally inspired (God inspired and intended every word, though each author wrote without any sense of coercion). Revelation is an ongoing process.	The concept of God is non-dogmatic and flexible; there is no consensus of belief concerning the nature of God. Most often God is viewed as being impersonal, unknowable, and indescribable.	People are perfected through enlightenment and are in partnership with God.
Reform Judaism	The Scriptures are considered to be human documents that preserve the history, culture, legends, and hopes of the ancient Jewish people. Scripture is valuable for obtaining moral insights. Revelation is an ongoing process.	This branch of Judaism allows for a broad range of beliefs about who or what God is. It includes the views of mystics, supernaturalists, and humanists.	Human nature is basically good. By means of proper education, moral encouragement, and personal evolution, people can actualize their inner potential.
Hasidic Judaism	Knowledge of God's thoughts can be obtained through mystical communion with him. This direct method of learning the thoughts of God is superior to reading the Jewish Scriptures.	Hasidic Judaism holds to a view of God often termed panentheism, wherein the universe is a part of God, but not the whole of God's being. Nature is thus an aspect of divinity.	Human beings were created to enjoy communion with God at all times. They are able to achieve ecstatic union with God.

Chart 22

Comparison of Beliefs within Judaism (continued)

	Scripture and Authority	God	Mankind
Ancient Judaism	God revealed his will through some of his appointed prophets, priests, and kings. The inspired Scriptures were in the process of being written and compiled by various ancient Hebrew men whom God selected for the task of authoring his Word.	God is viewed primarily in personal-covenantal terms. The Lord of Israel called his covenant people into existence as a nation, continued to interact with them, and providentially superintended their life as a group.	Human beings are wicked and rebellious by nature. Nevertheless, by his covenant presence, upholding power, and restraining grace, God can enable his people to walk in paths of righteousness and receive his covenant blessings.

	Sin	Salvation	Afterlife
Orthodox Judaism	Sin primarily consists of breaking God's commandments.	Repentance, prayer, and obedience to the Law are necessary for securing a proper relationship with God. Focus is not on salvation from the punishment of sin, but on one's relationship with God.	There will be a physical resurrection of all human beings. The righteous (obedient) will exist with God in peace forever in the world to come. The unrighteous will suffer, but disagreement exists over their ultimate destiny.
Conservative Judaism	People sin on an individual level by choosing evil actions. Yet much sin is societal in nature, embedded in unjust social structures. The doctrine of original sin is rejected.	Salvation is obtained by self-improvement and striving for social justice. Maintaining distinctively Jewish identity is important too.	Various views are held, but the emphasis is on improving conditions in this world.
Reform Judaism	Sin primarily has to do with social ills. Original sin on a personal level is denied.	Salvation is obtained through the improvement of oneself and society. The emphasis is almost exclusively on social improvement.	Generally, no concept of personal life after death is taught. It is often said that a person lives on in the accomplishments or the minds of others. Some in this tradition are influenced by Eastern mystical thought, in which departed souls merge into one great impersonal Life Force.

Chart 22

Comparison of Beliefs within Judaism (continued)

	Sin	Salvation	Afterlife
Hasidic Judaism	Evil differs from goodness only by degree. The essence of sin is failing in one's duty to influence God (and be influenced by God) in a good way.	Salvation consists of the experience of spiritual exultation as the soul is elevated toward God during prayer.	Hasidism is unlike other types of Judaism in that it teaches the reincarnation of the soul. Heaven is organized into societies.
Ancient Judaism	Sin stems from the fall of Adam and Eve and has corrupted the whole of human nature. It has many aspects: willful transgression of God's commands, falling short of God's perfect Law, failure to love one's neighbor, and weakness of the flesh, among others.	Salvation is viewed in both societal and personal terms. God provides atonement for the sins of his people through his system of law, priesthood, and sacrifice. However, salvation is ultimately based on his mercy and grace.	The spirits of the deceased go to Sheol, the abode of the dead. The righteous reside in Abraham's bosom, while the wicked are punished.

Other categories of Judaism include Ashkenazic Jews (from France, Germany, and Eastern Europe), Sephardic Jews (from Spain, Portugal, North Africa, and the Middle East), Yemenite Jews, and Ethiopian Jews (also known as Beta Israel and sometimes called Falashas). Sephardic Jews are often subdivided into Sephardim (from Spain and Portugal) and Mizrachim (from Northern Africa and the Middle East). Most of these groups are relatively small and are virtually unrepresented in the United States.

Chart 22

Orthodox Judaism

Topic	Facts
Current Data	Orthodox Judaism can generally be divided into two groups: Modern Orthodox Judaism and Ultra-Orthodox Judaism. Modern Orthodox Judaism is represented by Yeshiva University in New York City. A prominent leader was Rabbi Joseph D. Soloveitchik (1903–92). Examples of Ultra-Orthodox Judaism include the Aguddat Israel movement and the North African group known as Israeli Sepharadic Orthodoxy. Orthodox Jews make up about 6 percent of the North American Jewish population, and 10 percent of Jews in Israel.
History	The term "Orthodox" was not used to refer to conventional Jewish beliefs and practices within Judaism until the influence of modernism and its effects in European society fractured Judaism during the late 18th and 19th centuries. During this time, many rabbinical colleges (*yeshivot*) were built across Europe. Prominent Orthodox Jewish leaders of this era included German Rabbi Samson Raphael Hirsch (1808–88) and Rabbi Yisrael Lipkin Salanter (1810–83) of Lithuania. In the late 19th century, Theodor Herzl (1860–1904) and his political form of Zionism advocated that European Jews relocate to Palestine. There were divergent reactions to this development. Some groups, like Neturei Karta (Guardians of the City), had nothing to do with Herzl because they saw him as having secular aims. Other groups, such as Gush Emunim (Faithful Group), took the lead of Rabbi Abraham Isaac Kook (1865–1935) and began to promulgate a religious form of Zionism. In this view, salvation is tightly linked to retaking the holy land of Israel. Today, there is general agreement among Orthodox Jews concerning such fundamental issues as the authority of the Hebrew scriptures and Jewish law, despite the fact that institutionally, Orthodox Judaism is split into many smaller groups. Orthodox Jews hold opposing views on many issues of secondary importance, including Zionism (Jewish nationalism), the extent of cooperation with non-Orthodox Jews, models of leadership (authoritarian vs. communal), approaches to education, and ethnic styles (as in having a distinctive identity with the nation in which they live, like Russian Jewish identity or American Jewish identity). Other developments that are significant to contemporary Orthodox Judaism include disagreements between traditional faculty members at seminaries and more liberal rabbis in local synagogues, differences of belief regarding pluralism and tolerance, and the demographic shift in congregations from urban to suburban.
Summary of Beliefs	The following are characteristics of Orthodox Judaism: 1. Strict adherence to traditional Jewish law. 2. A range of views concerning modern culture, from cautious acceptance of certain aspects of modernity to outright rejection. 3. The belief that the only legitimate manner of studying Jewish religious texts is that employed by traditional rabbis. Most modern forms of historical scholarship are rejected as being useless at best and often heretical. 4. Uncompromising teaching and acceptance of the basic tenets of the Jewish faith.

Chart 23

Orthodox Judaism (continued)

Topic	Summary of View
Creation	The interpretation of the Genesis creation account varies somewhat within Orthodox Jewish circles. Sometimes the account is understood in a straightforward, literal fashion. God created the universe and all biological life out of nothing in six days, less than 10,000 years ago. Adam and Eve were the first human beings, and they did not evolve from other forms of life. However, for some a "day" in Genesis 1 may be something other than a 24-hour period. Modern scientific discoveries do not contradict, but rather attest to, God's awesome power.
Scripture and Authority	The Hebrew Scriptures are divided into three sections: **The Law** (also called Torah and Pentateuch)—Genesis, Exodus, Leviticus, Numbers, Deuteronomy **The Prophets** (*Nevi'im*)—Joshua, Judges, Samuel, Kings, Isaiah, Jeremiah, Ezekiel, and the 12 Minor Prophets, considered one book (Hosea, Joel, Amos, Obadiah, Jonah, Micah, Nahum, Habakkuk, Zephaniah, Haggai, Zechariah, and Malachi) **The Wisdom Writings** (*Kethuvim*)—Psalms, Proverbs, Job, Song of Songs, Ruth, Lamentations, Ecclesiastes, Esther, Daniel, Ezra–Nehemiah, and Chronicles Though all of the Tanakh (the Hebrew Bible) is seen as being the revelation of God, the main focus is on the Torah, and the remainder is read in light of the Torah. The origin of God's revelation is the history of the Jewish people. Both oral and written traditions are authoritative.
God	The belief in, and worship of, God is so sacred to the Orthodox Jew that God's name is not pronounced. The proper name of God in the Hebrew scriptures, found in the manuscripts, is deliberately written with incorrect vowels, making it unpronounceable. Often scholars, even Jewish ones, will use the name Yahweh, generally recognized as the pronunciation of the four-consonant personal name for God (YHWH), but the Orthodox do not, and in their writing often use G-d as a substitution for God. In Orthodox belief God is everlasting, almighty, glorious, infinitely wise, and supremely benevolent. He rules and judges the nations of the world. He is the only true and living God. Other alleged deities are false, and the idols that represent them are not worthy of worship, for they have no power. God can and does perform miracles. He is faithful to his covenant promises.
Mankind	Human beings are composed of body and spirit and by nature are morally neutral, yet they have propensities toward good and evil. They are capable of overcoming the desire to do evil by observing Jewish law. All persons are descended from Adam, but no one can blame their own wickedness on this association because each person has the ability to make a choice. People are rightly held responsible for their decisions. God chose the Jewish people to be recipients of the Torah, his revelation to mankind.

Chart 23

Orthodox Judaism (continued)

Topic	Summary of View
Sin	The broad definition of sin in Orthodox Judaism means to go astray because of immoral inclinations. Sin is also explained under three types: (1) *pesha*, breaking God's commandments intentionally, (2) *avon*, willingly disobeying the law of God, but as the result of an irresistible impulse, and (3) *cheit*, sinning unintentionally. God revealed his written and oral Law directly to the people of Israel, and this obligates them to obey it.
Salvation	Maintaining a covenant relationship with God occurs through prayer, repentance from sin, and obedience to the Law. Unlike many world religions that center on individual salvation and worship, Orthodox Judaism focuses on redemption of the community.
Afterlife	At the end of human history will occur a physical resurrecton from the dead of all people, with the righteous (those who sought to be obedient to God's Law) living forever with God, and the unrighteous (those who characteristically disobeyed God's Law) suffering the justice of God. There are differences over the final destiny of the unrighteous.

Distinctive Beliefs and Practices	
Messianism	A human Messiah will come to restore the nation of Israel to its biblically prophesied place of prominence, a dominion that will extend over the entire world.
Synagogue	The synagogue serves as the hub of Jewish community life, being primarily a gathering place for prayer and study. Social interaction, while important, is secondary. All prayers are recited in Hebrew, and men and women sit in separate sections of the synagogue. The elders of the congregation face the same direction as the members.
Halakha	Halakha (the body of Jewish Law) provides the underlying structure for Judaism. It is a series of laws (and principles from which new laws can be formed) that God gave to Moses on Mount Sinai. These laws have been accurately preserved over thousands of years. Halakha is the supreme authority for Jews, providing structure and guidance for both individual and community life. The moral goal for an Orthodox Jew is complete dedication to Halakha.

Chart 23

Conservative Judaism

Topic	Facts
Current Data	Conservative Jews (also called Masorti Jews) comprise approximately 35 percent of the Jewish population in North America. They are prominently represented by the Rabbinical Assembly (a worldwide network of Conservative rabbis), the Jewish Theological Seminary of America, in New York City, and the United Synagogue of Conservative Judaism (consisting of more than 800 congregations).
History	Conservative Judaism emerged in Europe and the United States in the 19th century, largely due to social and political changes in which Jews had to make decisions regarding their future in the wake of modernism. Initially designated as Positive-Historical Judaism in Europe, as it settled into the United States it became known as Conservative Judaism. The roots of the movement can be traced to 1854 when Rabbi Zecharias Frankel (1801–75) became the head of the Jewish Theological Seminary in Breslau, Germany. Rabbi Frankel challenged both Orthodox and Reform Judaism because he did not believe they were being faithful to the essence of historic Judaism. He argued that Jewish law was not unchanging, but should develop through a dynamic interaction with contemporary culture. The reaction to his disagreement with Reform Judaism labeled Frankel as not being sufficiently willing to let culture mold the direction of Judaism, whereas Orthodox Judaism considered him far too approving of contemporary culture. During the second half of the 19th century, many Jews emigrated to the United States, especially to New York City, where a Jewish Theological Seminary was founded in 1886. In 1902, the seminary underwent a massive reorganization under the leadership of Solomon Schechter (1847–1915), after which the seminary was recognized as the premier academic institution representing Conservative Judaism. One of the leading figures of this seminary was Abraham Joshua Heschel (1907–72). Since the 1960s there have been a number of significant changes in Conservative Jewish practice. These include a shift from big services at synagogues to smaller prayer groups in homes, a shift from synagogue members' active participation in services to mainly observing during services, more lenient standards of Sabbath observance, institution of retroactive annulments for Jewish marriages, and ordination of female rabbis.
Summary of Beliefs	Conservative Judaism revolves around seven core beliefs: 1. Belief that the modern state of Israel is an essential expression of Judaism. 2. Belief that the Hebrew language is irreplaceable as it functions in worship and scripture study. 3. Strong support of the concept of *Klal Yisrael* (the importance of all Jews). 4. Belief that the Torah is a critical component in the development Judaism. 5. Belief that studying the Torah is a very worthwhile endeavor. 6. Belief that the lives of Jews should be regulated by Jewish law. 7. Belief in God.

Chart 24

Conservative Judaism (continued)

Topic	Summary of View
Creation	Most adherents to Conservative Judaism embrace the view that God is a personal creator with many of the divine attributes that are traditionally ascribed to him. A minority believe him to be a creative force or a symbol of goodness. God is actively involved in the world and cares about his creation, especially human beings. He enjoys being in partnership with the people he created.
Scripture and Authority	God gave the Torah and Talmud to his covenant people, and they are obligated to obey the scriptures to the best of their ability. The Hebrew Bible is a mixture of divine revelation and human interpretation, yet it faithfully expounds the will of God for his people and is historically reliable. Though God's law is authoritative, it has changed over time in accordance with the particular circumstances faced by his people. That is, God's will is expressed not in static codes, but in the gradual and necessary evolution of his law as it interfaces with the realities of human culture. As evidence of this, the Committee on Jewish Law and Standards frequently presents an array of views that satisfies the requirements of both divine law and human society. Rabbis of local synagogues typically defer to the judgment of the CJLS, but they are allowed to dissent under certain conditions.
God	Members of Conservative Judaism are theists, though a wide range of views concerning God's nature and attributes is held and no particular view is required. Minority views include a mystical understanding of God (as found in Kabbalism), panentheism (God is in process, evolving, and is limited), and the belief that God is finite (the classic statement of this position is found in Harold Kushner's *When Bad Things Happen to Good People*).
Mankind	Human beings bear the image of God and thus have great value and dignity. They were created for communion with God and fellowship with one another and should work activvely with God to improve the world. Humans are capable of exemplifying moral virtue and accomplishing great things.
Sin	Human beings are essentially good, though flawed. Individuals sin on both a personal moral level and at a social level, with the social-structural aspect of sin (rather than personal morality) emphasized. Although God plays a significant role in the progress of human history and in the lives of individuals, people can become ethically flawless by education and self-effort. The grace of God is not emphasized as a means to forgive sin.
Salvation	Salvation in Conservative Judaism concerns social progress (rather than individual redemption), such as improving social conditions, ending corruption in government, legal and political progress, making advanced education more widely accessible, scientific advancement, and great cultural achievements. Maintaining Jewish identity is an essential component of being a faithful Jew and is important for the sense of deliverance of the Jewish people that is prominent in Conservative Judaism.

Chart 24

Conservative Judaism (continued)

Topic	Summary of View
Afterlife	Those who espouse Conservative Judaism hold many diverse views of the afterlife, even ones involving reincarnation, but detailed, systematic presentations about this issue are rare. Instead, the emphasis is on dealing with the conditions of this life and world.

Distinctive Beliefs and Practices

Topic	Summary of View
Jewish Identity	One common thread in most Jewish groups is the desire to maintain Jewish identity. Conservative Judaism is no exception. A Jew is any person whose mother is Jewish, regardless of whether the father is a Jew. However, if a person is not born to a Jewish mother but is a sincere convert to Judaism, this person is accepted as a true Jew. Intermarriage with non-Jews is not allowed. The Torah never indicates that matrilineal descent should determine who is a Jew, but it has passages that say that the child of a Jewish mother and a non-Jewish father is considered to be Jewish and passages showing that the child of a non-Jewish woman and a Jewish father is not a Jew. (See Deut. 7:1–5; Lev. 24:10; and Ezra 10:2–3.)

Chart 24

Reform Judaism

Topic	Facts
Current Data	Major organizations include the Union of American Hebrew Congregations, the World Union for Progressive Judaism, and the International Federation of Reform and Progressive Religious Zionists. Approximately 38 percent of North American Jews are affiliated with Reform Judaism.
History	Reform Judaism emerged from the interface between the German Enlightenment of the late 18th century and the teachings of Moses Mendelssohn (1729–86). At first it was merely an attempt to modernize Judaism's practices while maintaining Jewish identity. In the 19th century, under the leadership of Samuel Holdheim (1806–60), David Friedlander (1765–1834), and Israel Jacobson (1768–1828), the Reform movement adopted a different set of goals. These men advocated the assimilation of German Jews into the broader German culture, with its scientific worldview, secular scholarship, and free market capitalism. Guided by Isaac Wise (1819–1900) and David Einhorn (1809–79), the movement largely relocated from Germany to the United States, where it became even more extreme in its attempts at accommodating modern culture. The 1885 Pittsburgh Platform expressed the most radical positions up to that time. It rejected most Jewish rituals, including circumcision, and defined Jews as a purely religious community, without any national or ethnic component. Later, the Columbus Platform of 1937 conveyed a positive attitude toward distinctively Jewish observances of every kind, including Zionism and Jewish national solidarity. Eventually, however, the movement rejected nearly all of the doctrinal claims of historic Judaism. Three major statements of Reform Jewish belief and practice were published during the last quarter of the 20th century: *Reform Judaism: A Centenary Perspective*, adopted in San Francisco in 1976; *Reform Judaism and Zionism: A Centenary Platform*, adopted in Miami in 1997; and *A Statement of Principles for Reform Judaism*, adopted in Pittsburgh in 1999.
Summary of Beliefs	Reform Judaism (also known as Progressive Judaism and, in the United Kingdom, as Liberal Judaism) is characterized by the belief that: 1. The autonomy of individuals has a higher authority than the laws and customs of traditional Judaism. This means that Jews are free to embrace as many or as few Jewish practices as they see fit. 2. Modern culture is a good thing with which Jews should be actively engaged and in which they should be thoroughly immersed. 3. It is acceptable to study the Hebrew Bible and Jewish tradition by using either the methods employed by traditional rabbis or the methods of modern critical scholarship. 4. Jews should decide for themselves whether the doctrines of historic Judaism are plausible in the modern world. Controversial issues in Reform Judaism include the requirement and desirability of using the Hebrew language in prayer, the use of instrumental music in synagogue worship, the nature and extent of Sabbath observance, the status of rituals such as Mosaic dietary laws and circumcision, and the legitimacy of intermarriage.

Chart 25

Reform Judaism (continued)

Topic	Summary of View
Creation	A wide range of views is accepted as valid; there is no official position. However, theistic accounts of the creation and design of the universe are the norm, with the details regarded as relatively unimportant. All of God's creation should be held in high esteem, and humanity has a responsibility to preserve and protect it. Environmental stewardship is thus a moral obligation for everyone.
Scripture and Authority	The canon of Scripture is the same as that affirmed by Orthodox Jews, yet the books of the Hebrew Bible are regarded as merely human documents. Still, they are valuable for deriving ethical insights. These writings preserve the history, culture, legends, and hopes of the ancient Jewish people. Higher criticism, which investigates the origins of the texts of the Hebrew Bible, is a legitimate endeavor. Revelation is an ongoing process, and Jewish tradition is continually adapting to new cultural situations. The autonomy of the individual is the locus, or site, of authority.
God	Official documents of Reform Judaism state that there is one living God who is the source of everything that exists, reigns over the world with love and mercy, and provides moral ideals for all human beings. Nevertheless, a variety of interpretations of God are tolerated, including those of mystics and humanists.
Mankind	Most Reform Jews affirm that human beings are created in the image of God and are children of God. Some think that each person possesses an immortal soul. Human nature is basically good, and all people have free will. As co-laborers with God, humans have a duty to resist evil and fight injustice so as to bring about *tikkun olam* (improvement of the world). To a degree, dissenting views concerning mankind and mankind's relationship to God are tolerated.
Sin	Sin consists primarily of unjust social structures and arrangements; human beings are not innately sinful. The world's problems are not solely the result of evil behavior on the part of humans, but were, to some extent, inherent in the original creation. Sickness and death are a natural part of the created world; they are not the consequence of Adam and Eve's rebellion against God.
Salvation	Salvation is achieved through the betterment of oneself and society; redemption is essentially social improvement. Doctrines of atonement are downplayed; repentance and good works are adequate to remove the guilt of sins. No formal or binding view is espoused.
Afterlife	No one belief concerning life after death is widely held, and no particular view is mandated. It is sometimes said that people "live on" in the accomplishments or minds of others; there is no literal afterlife. Some believe that human souls merge into one great impersonal life force. Others affirm that each soul maintains a distinct personal identity after death. Nearly all maintain that Judaism is a religion that focuses on life in the present world.

Chart 25

Reform Judaism (continued)

Distinctive Beliefs and Practices

Utopian Society	Many Reform Jews embrace the concept of a utopian age of peace and universal goodwill. Mankind is said to be progressing toward a "messianic age."
Worship	Synagogue services have much in common with many Protestant church services, since elements of the latter have been borrowed to make services more appealing. Examples of this include pipe organs, robed choirs, and lecterns. Services are much shorter than those held in Orthodox and Conservative synagogues. Both English and Hebrew are used in services so that members do not feel pressured to learn Hebrew. Men and women are allowed to sit together.
Autonomy of the Individual	Jews must decide for themselves what beliefs and practices they will assent to and live by. No higher authority—whether the Hebrew Bible, Jewish tradition, prominent rabbis, or local synagogues—can judge these personal decisions to be incorrect or unethical.

Chart 25

Hasidic Judaism

Topic	Facts
Current Data	Hasidic Judaism is a thriving minority within Judaism, especially in Israel and the United States. There are approximately 650,000 Hasidic Jews worldwide. Most American Hasidic Jews live in Brooklyn, New York, though there is a sizeable community in Postville, Iowa. Within Hasidism are several sects, including Breslov, Lubavitch (Chabad), Satmar, Ger, and Bobiv. These various groups have had substantial influence in the Naturei Karta anti-Zionist movement.
History	Hasidic Judaism developed during a period of intense misery for most Jews in eastern Europe. By the middle of the 18th century, the Jewish populations of Poland and the Ukraine had endured a century of intermittent poverty, persecution, and pogroms. It was in the midst of these harsh conditions—around 1740—that Israel ben Eliezer (1700–1760), known affectionately as "the Besht," began teaching many of his fellow Jews. He asserted that the essence of Judaism was not to be found in studying the Torah or rigorously adhering to Jewish law, but in an intense, ecstatic, loving relationship with God that includes frequent prayer. Basing his outreach in the Ukrainian town of Miedzyboz, the Besht became quite popular locally, accumulating a sizable following. There he spent 20 years instructing his growing group of pupils before his death in 1760. His most accomplished disciple, Dovber of Mezeritch (1710–72), became the group's leader. Later, two primary branches of Hasidism were formed, one in the Ukraine and one in Lithuania; the latter was led by Rabbi Shneur Zalman (1745–1812). During the Holocaust of World War II, most of the Hasidic Jews in Europe were murdered. The majority of survivors moved to Israel or America and established new communities. Recent years have witnessed a renewed interest in Hasidic Judaism by non-Orthodox Jews. Important Hasidic Jewish authors include Martin Buber (1878–1965) and Arthur Green (1940–).
Summary of Beliefs	The beliefs of Hasidic Judaism are based on two concepts, namely, religious panentheism and the idea of *devekut*. Panentheism is the view that the world is part of God's being, similar to the soul being part of a human's body. *Devekut* (communion between God and mankind) expresses the view that there is interconnectedness between God and humanity—every act and word produces a corresponding reaction in the realm of God. By concentrating one's thoughts on God, one can unite with him and thereby influence him.

Topic	Summary of View
Creation	The world was created by God in seven ordinary days. However, there is no sharp contrast between Creator and creation, inasmuch as God's substance is diffused throughout the world. The world does not exist independently of God and is permeated by his presence. Every material object provides a glimpse of God's reality, though not one is identical to him.

Chart 26

Hasidic Judaism (continued)

Topic	Summary of View
Scripture and Authority	Though the Hebrew Bible is viewed as important and often consulted, personal and group religious experience has greater authority. Still, the Bible contains the literal words of God. Men are encouraged to study and women are expected to learn from the men. Group leaders (*tzaddikim*) often demand unquestioned obedience from members of the group. Local communities typically are small, and the overseeing *tzaddik* keeps a watchful eye on the activities of group members.
God	God is omnipresent in the sense that his "subtle matter" is diffused throughout the world. This divine omnipresence means that God is continually interacting with the world in a proximate, or immediate, way. God is compassionate and desires for humans to commune with him.
Mankind	Human beings were created to have intimate, mystical communion with God. Humans are unique among God's creatures in that they can acquire special knowledge about God and improve their spiritual condition. Humans have the ability to influence the will of God. Everything that a person does results in an accompanying spiritual vibration in God's mind.
Sin	Sin is neglecting the duty to focus one's thoughts on God and consult him in every situation, thereby failing to exert a righteous influence on his will. Persons receive some form of retribution for sinning, though this is not clear. Evil differs from good in degree, not in kind.
Salvation	Righteous people are those who are in continuous communion with God. The *tzaddik* (spiritual mediator) plays a crucial role in atoning for one's sins. Adherents must confess their sins to the *tzaddik* before they can be forgiven. Moreover, the *tzaddik* must release a person from the penalty of sins committed before that person can be healed of any illness.
Afterlife	Heaven is arranged so that souls with similar interests are able to work together in serving God. A different rabbi instructs each one of these groups so that they can increase their ability to do work that is pleasing to God.

Distinctive Beliefs and Practices

Clothing	Hasidic Jews are diligent in taking good care of their clothing. In particular, they do everything they can to avoid soiling or staining them. There are three reasons: (1) their clothes will judge them if those garments are not handled properly, (2) mistreating clothes brings about a rift between God and the *shechinah* (angels), and (3) God deems as rebellious those who neglect to care for their clothing.

Chart 26

Hasidic Judaism (continued)

Topic	Distinctive Beliefs and Practices
Mikveh	In order to cope with the difficulties of life, a Hasidic Jew immerses in a ritual bath called a *mikveh* (this term is also used in Jewish history for the place of the immersing). Doing so (1) solves many of life's problems and results in great blessings, (2) cleanses the bather from all types of sin, and (3) causes negative feelings to be replaced with positive ones.
Tzaddikim	A *tzaddik* (also known as Torah scholar) is a righteous Hasidic Jew who functions as a mediator between God and the faithful. Average Hasidic Jews cannot become holy unless they consult their *tzaddik* in all the affairs of life. There are several reasons: (1) only the *tzaddik* is qualified to give direction to one's spiritual journey, (2) the *tzaddik* alone knows how to make prayers maximally effective, and (3) confessing one's sins to a *tzaddik* is a necessary condition for forgiveness. Adherents can achieve a faultless state of *tikkun* (restoration) if they defer to the *tzaddik* in all things.
Mysticism and Prayer	Prayer is central to the Hasidic life. It lifts up the worshiper's soul to God so that he will bless the worshiper. The prayers of Hasidic Jews often display an indifference to (in some cases a contempt for) the prescriptions for prayer followed by other Jews and often are accompanied by singing and dancing. There are two main components to Hasidic prayer: (1) *devekut* (clinging; constant devotion), which involves being conscious of God's presence at all times; and (2) *hislahavus* (bursting into flame; ecstatic enthusiam), the feeling of euphoria people have when their soul is lifted up to God.

Chart 26

Jewish Scriptures According to Rabbinic Tradition

The Jewish Scriptures normally are arranged in three distinct divisions. Tanakh is the acronym that refers to the three major sections, Torah, Nevi'im, and Kethuvim. The traditional number of books in the Hebrew Bible totals 24.

Torah **(Law or Direction)**	Genesis, Exodus, Leviticus, Numbers, Deuteronomy[1]
Nevi'im **(Prophets)**	Former Prophets: Joshua, Judges, Samuel,[2] Kings Latter Prophets: Isaiah, Jeremiah, Ezekiel, and the Minor Prophets (Hosea, Joel, Amos, Obadiah, Jonah, Micah, Nahum, Habakkuk, Zephaniah, Haggai, Zechariah, Malachi, counted as one book)
Kethuvim **(Writings)**	Psalms, Proverbs, Job Megillot (the Scrolls): Song of Songs, Ruth, Lamentations, Ecclesiastes, Esther Daniel, Ezra-Nehemiah,[3] Chronicles

[1] These are the five books of Moses, also called the Pentateuch.
[2] Samuel, Kings, and Chronicles are not divided in Hebrew Scriptures into "First" and "Second" as is true in Christian editions of the Old Testament.
[3] Ezra and Nehemiah are considered to be one book in the original Hebrew canon.

Chart 27

Jewish Holy Days

Holiday	Time of Year	Observance
Rosh Hashanah (Jewish New Year)	September or October On the 1st and 2nd days of the Hebrew month of Tishri	Joyful atmosphere. Many Jews attend synagogue services. Marks the first part of a ten-day period known as High Holy Days or, less commonly, Days of Awe.
Yom Kippur (Day of Atonement)	September or October, ten days after Rosh Hashanah, on the 10th day of the Hebrew month of Tishri	The most solemn day of the year on the Jewish calendar. Even many nominally religious Jews attend synagogue and recite prayers, asking God to forgive their sins. Many also fast for 24 hours.
Sukkoth (Feast of Tabernacles, Feast of Booths)	September or October, five days after Yom Kippur, begins on the 15th day of the Hebrew month of Tishri	Lasting eight days, it is the annual harvest celebration. Traditionally, a temporary booth (*sukkah*) is constructed in backyards or behind the local synagogue. Fruit is hung from the booth's roof. Customs include waving the traditional *lulav* (branches of various plants) and *ethrog* (citron).
Hanukkah (Feast of the Dedication, incorporates the Festival of Lights)	December, starting on the 25th day of Kislev	A festive holiday commemorating the victory of the Maccabees over the Syrian armies of Antiochus Epiphanes (c. 175 BC) and the rededication of the temple in Jerusalem. Activities include lighting the eight candles of a *menorah* (lampstand) over a period of eight days, spinning the *dreidel* (a top), and eating potato pancakes called *latkes*.
Purim (Feast of Esther, Feast of Lots)	February–March, on the 14th day of Adar	A party-like festival atmosphere often prevails. Purim centers on recounting the deliverance of the Persian Jews from a massacre as described in the book of Esther, which is read aloud. Often participants stage Purim plays, in which the entire story of Esther is enacted in comedic style. Considered by most Jews to be a minor holiday, but is still popular.

Chart 28

Jewish Holy Days (continued)

Holiday	Time of Year	Observance
Passover (Pesach, Feast of Unleavened Bread)	March or April, starting on the 15th day of the Jewish month of Nisan	The most popular of all Jewish holidays, Passover is an occasion for families to gather together, making it something like a Jewish Thanksgiving. The departure of the Israelites from Egypt are recounted by reading through the Haggadah (*seder* lessons and stories). Unleavened bread (*matzah*) is eaten the entire week. The ceremonial meal, called the *seder*, is held on the first two nights.
Shavuot (Feast of Weeks, Feast of Harvest, Pentecost)	May or June, begins on the 6th day of the Jewish month of Sivan	Not widely observed. When observed, it involves themes associated with springtime and harvest and lasts two days. Traditionally, this holiday marked the day when the Law was given at Mount Sinai.

Chart 28

The Jewish Calendar

Lunar Cycles: The Jewish calendar is based on lunar cycles, 12 in all, with an average of 29.5 days in each, totaling 354 days in a year. The Jewish sacred year begins with the new moon of spring, which comes between the Julian calendar months of March and April in 19-year cycles.

Year	Sacred	1	2	3	4	5	6	7
	Civil	7	8	9	10	11	12	1
Month		Nisan/Abib	Iyyar/Ziv	Sivan	Tammuz	Ab	Elul	Tishri/Ethanim
		30 Days	29 Days	30 Days	29 Days	30 Days	29 Days	30 Days
Western Months		April	May	June	July	August	September	October

Year	Sacred	8	9	10	11	12	13
	Civil	2	3	4	5	6	Leap Year
Month		Marchesvan/Bul	Chislev	Tebeth	Shebat	Adar	Ve-Adar
		29 Days	30 Days	29 Days	30 Days	29 Days	29 Days
Western Months		November	December	January	February	March	March/April

Chart 29

The Jewish Calendar (continued)

Festivals						
1 New Moon	1 New Moon	1 New Moon	1 New Moon	1 New Moon	1 New Moon	1 New Year Trumpets
14 Passover	14 2nd Passover	6 Pentecost (Feast of Weeks)	17 Fast / Taking of Jerusalem	9 Fast / Construction of Temple		10 Day of Atonement
15-21 Unleavened Bread						15-21 Tabernacles
16 First Fruits						22 Solemn Assembly

Festivals					
1 New Moon	1 New Moon	1 New Moon	1 New Moon	1 New Moon	1 New Moon
	25 Dedication	10 Fast / Siege of Jerusalem		13 Fast of Ester	13 Fast of Ester
				14-15 Purim	14-15 Purim

Chart 29

The Jewish Covenants

Covenant*	Biblical Record	Occur-rences	Type
Abrahamic	Gen. 12:1–3	7	**Unconditional:** The Abrahamic covenant involved land, progeny (seed, or descendants), and blessing, all of which were part of God's unconditional promise that Abraham's descendants would comprise a great nation that would bless the entire world. At the time this promise was made, Abraham was not a Jew. The boundaries of "the land" are given in Genesis 13 and 15.
The Land	Deut. 30:1–10	12	**Unconditional:** Based on Deuteronomy 30, the Land covenant is God's unconditional amplification of the land promise in the Abrahamic covenant. God declared that the people of Israel, after their disobedience, rejection, and restoration, will possess the land forever. The degree to which they enjoy, or even possess, the land promised to them relates to their obedience. The time of its fulfillment is said to follow Israel's national repentance. It is an everlasting covenant and will eventually bring about the worship and obedience of all the nations. The national aspect of the provision is that the land will be the everlasting possession of Israel (Ezek. 16:60 clarifies this national provision). The provision's universal aspect is that it is meant to benefit all the nations, not just the nation of Israel. People from throughout the world will come to the land to be taught by Israel and to see the glory of the Lord (Isa. 14:1–2).
Davidic (The Seed)	2 Sam. 7:10–16	7	**Unconditional:** The Davidic covenant is the application of the Abrahamic covenant's "seed" promise. David was promised that his kingly lineage would never be broken as the royal line of inheritance in the political kingdom (2 Sam. 7:10–16 and 1 Chron. 17:10–14). Christians see Jesus the Messiah as the culmination of this covenant, whereas many Jews believe that the Messiah promised from the lineage of David has not yet arrived but will in the future. Other Jews believe this promise is only symbolic. There are seven provisions contained within the Davidic covenant: 1. David is promised an eternal dynasty. 2. David is promised victory in defeating all the national enemies of Israel. 3. One of David's sons will be established on the throne after his rule ends; God chose Solomon for this position (*shlomo* = peace).

* Not all of these covenants would be accepted by all branches of modern Judaism, but they are reflective of the historical biblical covenants relating to descendants of Abraham through Isaac and Jacob (Israel).

Chart 30

The Jewish Covenants (continued)

Covenant	Biblical Record	Occur-rences	Type
Davidic (continued)	2 Sam. 7:10–16	7	4. The son of David will build a temple for the Lord; Solomon was chosen to oversee its construction. 5. The throne of David in Solomon's kingdom will be established forever. 6. Solomon will be disciplined for disobedience, but God will not remove his loving-kindness from him. Because of his faithfulness to the covenant, God's loyal love will never be removed from the house of David. 7. The Messiah will come from the line of David (1 Chron. 17:11).
New	Jer. 31:31–40	7	**Unconditional:** The new covenant is God's application of the blessing promised in the Abrahamic covenant wherein Israel will obtain national-spiritual redemption and will be a blessing to all nations. The kingdom of God is the fulfillment of all the covenants. Some Christian theologians believe that the new covenant applies both to the Christian church of today and to national-ethnic Israel. (Compare Jer. 32:40, Isa. 61, Ezek. 16:60, 37:26–28, 43:25–27, and Rom. 7:25–27.) All Israel will be saved when a great number of those Gentiles whom God has elected to salvation are made partakers of the new covenant of grace (Rom. 11:25–30); it has to be this way because this order of events is foretold in Jer. 31. This covenant has eight provisions: 1. Unconditional in nature, involving the houses of both Judah and Israel. 2. Distinct from the Mosaic covenant, ultimately replacing it. 3. Promises regeneration of national Israel. 4. Israel's regeneration will be universal among Jews. 5. Forgiveness of sin grounded in the grace of God. (The Mosaic covenant made apparent the problem of sin, but did not provide for its forgiveness in an ultimate sense.) 6. The indwelling of the Holy Spirit and the circumcision of the heart (Ezek. 36–37; Deut. 30). 7. Israel will receive material blessings (Jer. 32:41; Isa. 61:8; Ezek. 34:25–37). 8. The sanctuary will be rebuilt—a messianic or millennial temple (Ezek. 37:26–28).

Chart 30

The Jewish Covenants (continued)

Covenant	Biblical Record	Occur-rences	Type
Mosaic	Ex. 19:5ff; Deut. 28	Numerous	**Conditional:** The Mosaic covenant was established after the exodus from Egypt by the Israelites. Given at Mount Sinai, it is called Mosaic because Moses received this covenant in the form of the Law (Josh. 8:32; 2 Kings 14:6; Ezra 7:6; Dan. 9:13; see also Luke 24:44; Acts 15:5; 1 Cor. 9:9; Heb. 10:28). This covenant set forth the conditions the nation of Israel must fulfill in order to receive the full blessings of the Abrahamic covenant; it also explained how Israel must go about establishing a relationship between themselves (as subjects) and God (the king of Israel). Often referred to in the New Testament Scriptures as "the Law" or "the law of Moses," many Christian theologians consider this covenant to have ended with the crucifixion of Christ (Rom. 7:6, 10:4; 2 Cor. 3:7–11; Gal. 5:1; Heb. 7:11–12). Some Jews believe this covenant remains in effect today.

Chart 30

Timeline of Christianity

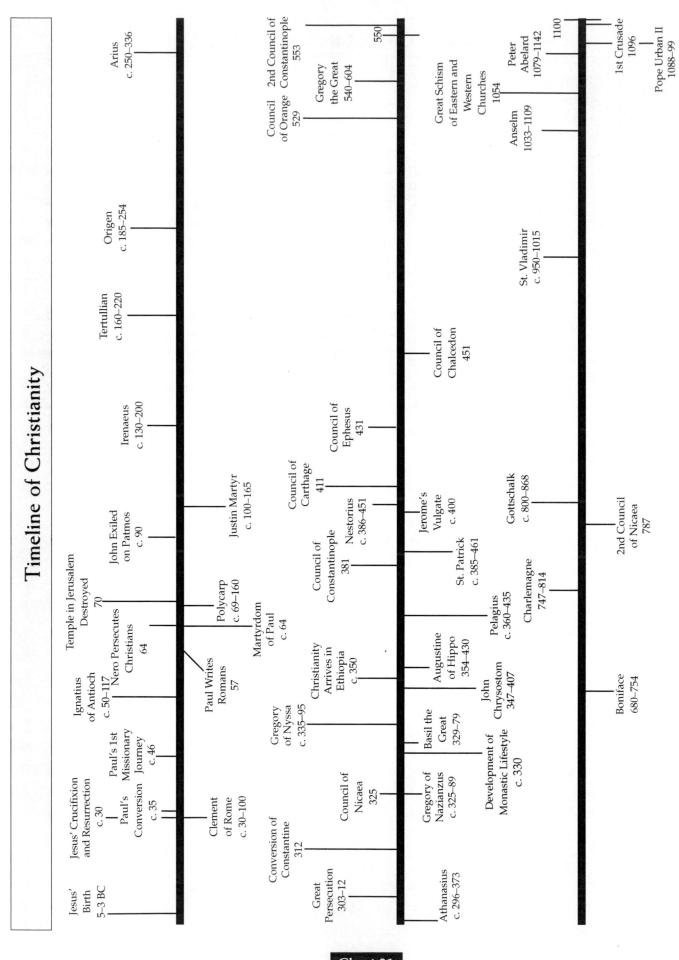

Jesus' Birth
5–3 BC

Jesus' Crucifixion and Resurrection
c. 30

Paul's Conversion
c. 35

Paul's 1st Missionary Journey
c. 46

Clement of Rome
c. 30–100

Paul Writes Romans
57

Martyrdom of Paul
c. 64

Ignatius of Antioch
c. 50–117

Nero Persecutes Christians
64

Temple in Jerusalem Destroyed
70

Polycarp
c. 69–160

John Exiled on Patmos
c. 90

Justin Martyr
c. 100–165

Irenaeus
c. 130–200

Tertullian
c. 160–220

Origen
c. 185–254

Arius
c. 250–336

Great Persecution
303–12

Conversion of Constantine
312

Council of Nicaea
325

Gregory of Nazianzus
c. 325–89

Development of Monastic Lifestyle
c. 330

Gregory of Nyssa
c. 335–95

Christianity Arrives in Ethiopia
c. 350

Basil the Great
329–79

Athanasius
c. 296–373

John Chrysostom
347–407

Augustine of Hippo
354–430

Pelagius
c. 360–435

Council of Constantinople
381

St. Patrick
c. 385–461

Jerome's Vulgate
c. 400

Council of Carthage
411

Nestorius
c. 386–451

Council of Ephesus
431

Council of Chalcedon
451

Council of Orange
529

Gregory the Great
540–604

2nd Council of Constantinople
553

550

Charlemagne
747–814

Boniface
680–754

2nd Council of Nicaea
787

Gottschalk
c. 800–868

St. Vladimir
c. 950–1015

Great Schism of Eastern and Western Churches
1054

Anselm
1033–1109

Peter Abelard
1079–1142

1100

Pope Urban II
1088–99

1st Crusade
1096

Chart 31

Timeline of Christianity (continued)

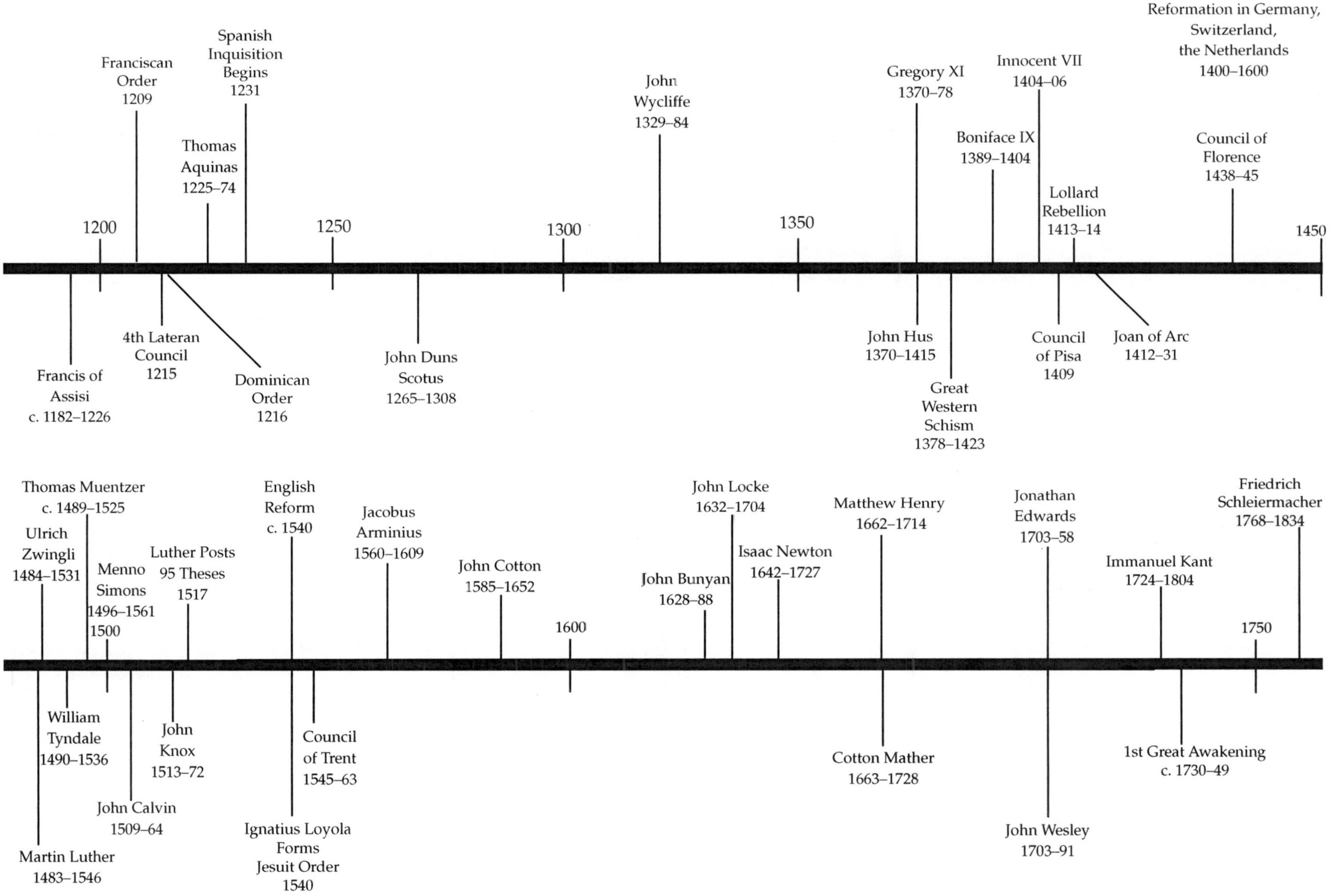

Reformation in Germany, Switzerland, the Netherlands 1400–1600

Council of Florence 1438–45

Joan of Arc 1412–31

Innocent VII 1404–06

Lollard Rebellion 1413–14

Council of Pisa 1409

Boniface IX 1389–1404

Gregory XI 1370–78

John Hus 1370–1415

Great Western Schism 1378–1423

John Wycliffe 1329–84

1450

1350

1300

John Duns Scotus 1265–1308

Spanish Inquisition Begins 1231

Thomas Aquinas 1225–74

Dominican Order 1216

1250

4th Lateran Council 1215

Franciscan Order 1209

Francis of Assisi c. 1182–1226

1200

Friedrich Schleiermacher 1768–1834

1750

Immanuel Kant 1724–1804

1st Great Awakening c. 1730–49

Jonathan Edwards 1703–58

John Wesley 1703–91

Matthew Henry 1662–1714

Cotton Mather 1663–1728

Isaac Newton 1642–1727

John Locke 1632–1704

John Bunyan 1628–88

John Cotton 1585–1652

1600

Jacobus Arminius 1560–1609

Council of Trent 1545–63

English Reform c. 1540

Ignatius Loyola Forms Jesuit Order 1540

Thomas Muentzer c. 1489–1525

Luther Posts 95 Theses 1517

John Knox 1513–72

Ulrich Zwingli 1484–1531

Menno Simons 1496–1561

1500

John Calvin 1509–64

William Tyndale 1490–1536

Martin Luther 1483–1546

Chart 31

Timeline of Christianity (continued)

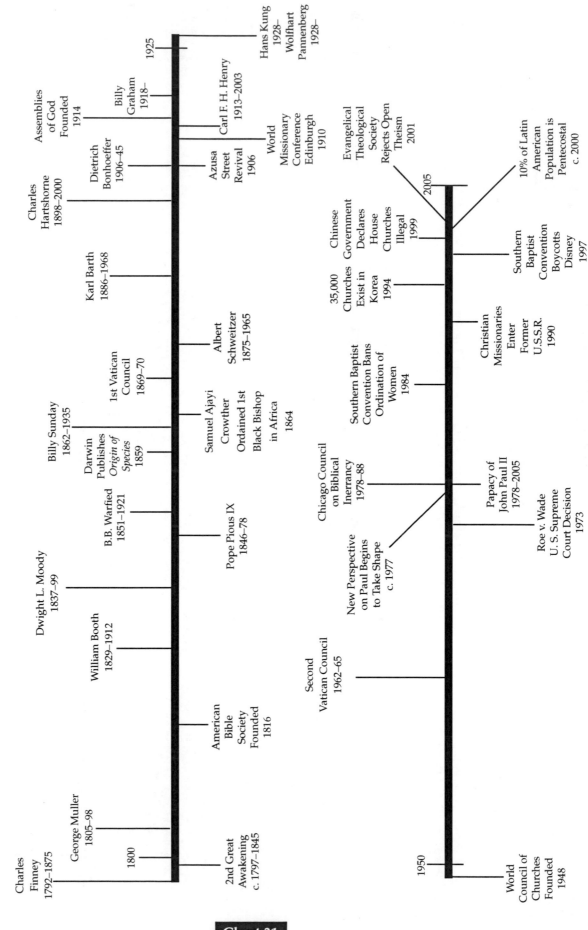

Charles Finney 1792–1875

George Muller 1805–98

1800

2nd Great Awakening c. 1797–1845

Dwight L. Moody 1837–99

William Booth 1829–1912

American Bible Society Founded 1816

Billy Sunday 1862–1935

B.B. Warfied 1851–1921

Darwin Publishes *Origin of Species* 1859

Pope Pious IX 1846–78

1st Vatican Council 1869–70

Samuel Ajayi Crowther Ordained 1st Black Bishop in Africa 1864

Charles Hartshorne 1898–2000

Karl Barth 1886–1968

Albert Schweitzer 1875–1965

Dietrich Bonhoeffer 1906–45

Azusa Street Revival 1906

Assemblies of God Founded 1914

Billy Graham 1918–

Carl F. H. Henry 1913–2003

World Missionary Conference Edinburgh 1910

Hans Kung 1928–

Wolfhart Pannenberg 1928–

1925

Second Vatican Council 1962–65

Chicago Council on Biblical Inerrancy 1978–88

New Perspective on Paul Begins to Take Shape c. 1977

35,000 Churches Exist in Korea 1994

Chinese Government Declares House Churches Illegal 1999

Evangelical Theological Society Rejects Open Theism 2001

10% of Latin American Population is Pentecostal c. 2000

2005

Southern Baptist Convention Boycotts Disney 1997

Christian Missionaries Enter Former U.S.S.R. 1990

Southern Baptist Convention Bans Ordination of Women 1984

Papacy of John Paul II 1978–2005

Roe v. Wade U. S. Supreme Court Decision 1973

1950

World Council of Churches Founded 1948

Chart 31

Christianity

Topic	Facts
Current Data	By some calculations, Christianity is the biggest and fastest-growing religion in the world (Islam, too, claims a large number of adherents and is undergoing rapid growth, though mainly through birthrate). Christians live in nearly every inhabited region of the world, with high concentrations in various parts of Africa, Europe, and the Americas. It is estimated that 50 million to 100 million Christians attend underground churches in mainland China. Several million are found in parts of India, Southeast Asia, and the Philippines. Roman Catholicism is the largest group, though Pentecostalism is growing rapidly, and if its present rate of growth continues, it will eclipse Roman Catholicism as the largest Christian group before the close of the 21st century. Many conservative Protestant groups, especially Baptists, are exhibiting steady growth. Eastern Orthodox populations tend to be regional and ethnic, residing mainly within their respective countries or regions (Armenian, Greek, and Russian Orthodox).
History	The Christian faith was founded by Jesus of Nazareth, a Jewish rabbi, during his ministry in the first third of the 1st century AD in Judea and Galilee. Jesus identified himself as the prophesied Messiah and heralded the kingdom of God. Unlike former prophets and self-proclaimed messiahs, Jesus declared himself to be one with God the Father, able to forgive sins, the creator of the universe, and an authoritative interpreter of God's law. He performed many public miracles. Because of his words and works, certain powerful religious leaders in Judea and Jerusalem became concerned that his popularity might cause a conflict with Roman authorities. After they conspired to have him killed, Jesus was crucified under the Roman procurator Pontius Pilate c. AD 33. The followers of Jesus, though initially emotionally crushed by the death of their Lord and friend, later proclaimed him to have been raised physically from the dead and to have ascended to the throne of God, from which he would return in judgment.

This apostolic faith was carried into the Western world largely through the efforts of another Jewish rabbi, Paul of Tarsus, who wrote at least 13 books of the New Testament and traveled throughout the Mediterranean world during AD 48–64. According to tradition, the other apostles spread the good news (gospel) about Jesus being the Messiah foretold in the Hebrew scriptures. They claimed that Jesus had come to deliver all peoples from their sins through his death on the cross. They preached in various regions of the ancient world, going as far as India and China. Each of these disciples (the Twelve*), except the beloved disciple John, suffered a martyr's death.

After the 1st century, Christians endured ten periods of persecution under various Roman regimes, the last occurring under the emperor Diocletian. He was followed by the first Christian emperor, Constantine, who in AD 313 declared Christianity a legal religion. In AD 394, Emperor Theodosius declared Christianity to be the official religion of the Roman Empire. |

* Matthias was chosen by the apostles to replace Judas (Acts 1:15–26). One tradition says he was stoned to death before his head was cut off at Jerusalem; another that he was crucified in Ethiopia.

Chart 32

Topic	Facts
History (continued)	The early Christian church encountered numerous obstacles that threatened its existence. Government persecutions brought severe trials and the deaths of many Christians, but doctrinal controversies posed the greatest threat to early Christianity, since the very nature of the church and its founder were at stake. Numerous alternative religious movements arose, which challenged the apostolic and early Christian views of the nature of God and Jesus Christ. These were debated and decided at several ecumenical councils, the first held at Nicaea in AD 325 and convened by Constantine. During the medieval period the church saw the rise of the papacy, the spread of monastic communities, developments in the doctrine of salvation in which the role of the sacraments of the church became increasingly important, an increase in political power wielded by the church, the threat of Islam, the Crusades, and the Inquisition. The Christian church underwent a split between its eastern and western branches in AD 1054 (the Great Schism), over both political and doctrinal concerns. Politically the four patriarchal centers of the East were under pressure from the one patriarchal center at Rome, for the pope, from the time of Gregory I in the early 7th century, had ruled over the entire church. These patriarchs of the eastern church played an important part in the split. Doctrinally the split came to a head over "spiration," the relation of the Father and the Son, in what is known as the "filioque clause" (the phrase "and the Son"), which was added to the Nicene Creed in 447 at the Council of Toledo in Spain. The Eastern church maintained that this addition was not legitimate because (according to them) the Holy Spirit proceeds from the Father only, not from both the Father and the Son. The next major challenge to Christian unity was the Protestant Reformation. Many leaders in the church during the 15th and 16th centuries believed that the Roman Catholic Church, the official expression of Christendom in western Europe at the time, had become morally and doctrinally corrupt. Most attempts at reform were met with strong resistance by church authorities and brought persecution on those advocating reform. Martin Luther, an Augustinian monk and theology professor at the University of Wittenberg, in Germany, questioned the practice of offering indulgences to fund the building of Saint Peter's basilica in Rome. On October 31, 1517, he publicly posted his now famous "95 Theses." This act set in motion what has come to be known as the Protestant Reformation. Attempts by church authorities to silence Luther only served to fan the flames of protest regarding the policies and doctrines of the Roman church. Eventually, Protestantism spawned many important leaders and formed various branches (Anglican, Lutheran, Reformed, Anabaptist), each with its own doctrinal distinctives. All Protestant groups, however, stood against the Roman church. In response to the Reformation, the Roman Catholic Church initiated its own Counter-Reformation, which resulted in massive amounts of religious and political upheaval throughout Europe. The doctrinal and ecclesiastical tumult of the 16th century has since produced hundreds of conservative Protestant groups and movements. With a few exceptions, these groups differ on many points of doctrine and practice, but share a common belief in one tri-personal God, salvation being found only in and through the person of Jesus Christ, justification by faith alone, and the Bible as God's unique self-revelation.

Chart 32

Christianity (continued)

Topic	Facts
History (continued)	In the 17th and 18th centuries, the Enlightenment spread throughout Europe and over to America. Its belief in moral and scientific progress, universal standards of reason and scientific method, and the superiority of democratic forms of government, together with its distrust of traditional religious institutions and authority, led to a reinterpretation of historic Christian faith that came to be known as liberal (modernist) theology. Many denominations today can trace their origins to this brand of theology. The 19th and 20th centuries saw a renewed and growing interest in Third World missions. Many foreign mission organizations and Bible distribution societies were organized in Europe and North America during this time, and the spread of the Christian gospel took place at a rapid rate all over the world. The presence of Christian churches in almost every part of the globe today is a testimony to this flurry of mission activity.
Summary of Beliefs	The central elements of Christianity are encapsulated in what is known as *kerygma*, the preaching material of the early church. These basic components are found in the apostle Peter's sermon to the house of Cornelius in Acts 10, the gospel of Mark, and Paul's teaching in 1 Corinthians 15, to name a few places in the Christian Scriptures. These include the incarnation of Christ; his ministry of healing, comforting, and teaching; the death of Jesus on the cross to save from their sins those who believe in him; his physical resurrection from the dead; his ascension back to the Father to be an intercessor for his people; his physical return for his people at the end of the age; and the judgment on those who have rejected him. The death of Jesus on behalf of humanity distinguishes Christianity from other world religions in which a key belief is contributing to one's salvation. Among most Christians, the following refinements are connected to the central elements listed above: 1. There is only one supreme and divine being, but within this divine being or essence are three persons who share equally and indivisibly all of the divine attributes. These three are not separate beings or gods, but they in unity are God without confusion of their persons. God's attributes, as revealed in the Bible, include infinitude, self-existence, omnipotence, omniscience, omnipresence, love, holiness, and many more. 2. The man Jesus is the Messiah, the Son of God. He is fully God and fully man, without mixing the natures of divinity and humanity, nor was the person divided. Thus there are two natures in the one person. None of his eternal attributes were lost or laid aside when the second person of the divine Trinity became a man. Rather, human attributes were added to his person. 3. Jesus was conceived in the young woman Mary while she was still a virgin, and she remained a virgin until after his birth (some Christian groups believe that Mary remained a virgin throughout her life). 4. Jesus of Nazareth lived a sinless life. Through his death and resurrection, those who believe in him are forgiven their sins and reconciled to God. Through faith, believers live by the promise of resurrection from death to

Chart 32

Topic	Facts
	everlasting life through Christ. The Holy Spirit is given to those who have faith in Christ, bringing hope, leading them into true knowledge of God and his purposes, and helping them grow in holiness.
	5. The coming of Jesus as the Messiah was foretold in the Hebrew Scriptures, as were many details of his life. He performed miracles, lived a sinless life, and died on the Roman cross to bear the wrath of God for sinners and to provide redemption and forgiveness for all those who believe personally in his death. Jesus is now at the right hand of the Father in heaven, to represent before the Father those who have put their trust in him as their Savior.
	6. The Holy Spirit is the third person of the Triune God. He comes from God to bring comfort and life to Christians, to dwell within them, and to assist in their spiritual growth. He also brings conviction of sin to the remainder of the world.
	7. Christ will return for the purpose of uniting with him all those who have placed their faith in him and to judge all those who have not. Everyone will be physically resurrected from death and will stand before the judgment seat of God to answer for their lives. The judgment does not evaluate good or bad deeds in regards to salvation (since salvation comes through faith in Christ during one's earthly life), but the level of judgment one receives. Those who believe in Christ will receive eternal life with him, and those who have rejected Christ will be condemned. There is a difference of belief among Christians as to the nature and duration of the condemnation.
	8. The Bible is the revelation of God that he caused to be written by prophets and apostles over a period of approximately 1,500 years. Most Christians believe the Bible is a truthful record of God's work in the world, tells us truth about God, and is sufficient and authoritative for Christian doctrine and practice. Christians differ as to whether the Bible, in the original languages of Hebrew, Aramaic, and Greek, is inspired word for word or in a less exact way, and whether it is without error.
	9. Most in the Christian church recognize two sacraments or ordinances: baptism and the Lord's Supper (also called the Eucharist or Communion).

Topic	Summary of View
Creation	God created the heavens and the earth out of nothing. He fashioned the world into a habitable form and sustains the entire universe in existence. All life owes its existence and preservation to God. The created universe displays the glory, power, and wisdom of God. God has designed the cosmos in such a way that it operates according to physical laws and exhibits regular, predictable patterns of behavior.
Scripture and Authority	God has revealed his identity, plan of salvation, and moral will in the 66 books of the Old and New Testament Scriptures. His creation of the world, mankind's fall into sin, and the redemption provided in Jesus Christ are described therein. The Bible is God's inspired and infallible word and is authoritative for Christian belief and practice.

Chart 32

Christianity (continued)

Topic	Summary of View
God	God is a Trinity: three distinct persons who share one divine nature and set of divine attributes. God is all-powerful, all-knowing, loving, gracious, just, eternal, self-existent, and sovereign. He has revealed himself in a unique and definitive way in the person of Jesus Christ.
Mankind	Mankind is created in the image and likeness of God, capable of having a personal relationship with God and given the task of taking dominion over the earth and all that it contains. Mankind possesses both body and spirit. Mankind has a fallen nature.
Sin	Sin entered the world through the disobedience of the first human beings, Adam and Eve. They were tempted by the Devil to rebel against God's revealed law and to assert their autonomy from God. Disease and death also resulted from the fall of Adam and Eve. All humans born since Adam and Eve stand under the guilt of the original rebellion against God because Adam was the representative head for the human race. This association with Adam spiritually corrupts each person born into the world. People sin against God naturally due to the nature they have inherited from Adam and Eve. Some Christians do not accept the view of inherited sin or judicial sin in Adam.
Salvation	Salvation from sin and death is found in the person and work of the Lord Jesus Christ: his sinless life, atoning death, and physical resurrection from the dead. Faith in Jesus and in his work of redemption are necessary for being justified before God. Protestants have emphasized the Reformation principles of grace alone (*sola gratia*), by faith alone (*sola fide*), and in Christ alone (*Soli Christi*), while Roman Catholics and Eastern Orthodox adherents believe in justification by faith and works together.
Afterlife	All human beings who have ever lived will be physically resurrected and judged by God. After this universal judgment, each person will either live everlastingly with God or be condemned to separation from God, generally viewed as hell.

Distinctive Beliefs and Practices

The Incarnation	Jesus of Nazareth, the historical person, is God incarnate, possessing both a human and a divine nature. His resurrection from the dead served to vindicate his claim to be the promised Messiah and his promise of salvation to those who trust in him.

Chart 32

Comparison of Beliefs within Christianity

	Scripture and Authority	God	Mankind
Liberal Protestantism	The Bible is human in origin, fallible, and a record of religious thought. Some believe that the Bible contains the "word of God," yet this word needs to be demythologized.	God dwells within the world, neither transcendent over nor separate from it. God has not performed supernatural acts. The Trinity is denied; only the Father is God. Jesus was not God incarnate as articulated in the classic creeds.	Mankind is the product of biological evolution. Humans are not sinners in need of divine regeneration, but merely flawed and ignorant, primarily needing better education and social conditions.
Evangelical Protestantism	The Scriptures (66 books of the Protestant Bible) are the final authority and only sufficient guide in matters of Christian faith and practice. Most hold that many present Bible translations are free from error, while some hold that only the original manuscripts were without error.	God exists as a Trinity: Father, Son, and Holy Spirit. Each member of the Trinity is fully God, and each exists as a distinct person with individual responsibilities within the Godhead.	Mankind (male and female) is a special creation of God, made in the divine image, the crowning act of God's creation. Humans were created innocent, but by their free choice sinned against God. The sin of the first man and woman is viewed as having brought sin into the world. Only the grace of God can restore human beings to a right relationship with their Creator.
Fundamentalist Protestantism	The Bible (Old and New Testaments) is divinely inspired, infallible, and inerrant in all matters on which it speaks. It is the supreme standard by which all human conduct, creeds, and beliefs should be tested.	There is one true and living God, the Trinity. Within the Godhead are three persons: Father, Son, and Holy Spirit. These divine persons are coequal in nature and attributes, and they execute distinct yet harmonious offices in God's work of redemption.	Mankind was created in holiness, but by voluntary transgression fell from that state. Consequently, all human beings are sinners by choice, and by nature do not possess the holiness required by the law of God, and are wholly inclined to evil. The human race is under just condemnation from God, without defense or excuse.
Pentecostal-Charismatic Protestantism	The Bible is the inspired, infallible, inerrant word of God. In addition, extra-biblical revelations (such as prophecy and "words of knowledge") in some cases are equal in authority to Scripture.	Most Pentecostal-Charismatic groups affirm the historic teaching of the church concerning the Trinity. However, United Pentecostals and other Oneness Pentecostal groups teach that Jesus is the only God, manifesting himself variously as Father, Son, and Spirit.	Mankind is created in the image of God. Mankind was created innocent, but rebelled against God, thereby polluting human nature and plunging the world into misery and ruin. Humans still possess freedom of will.

Chart 33

Comparison of Beliefs within Christianity (continued)

	Scripture and Authority	God	Mankind
Roman Catholicism	The Bible (66 books + 7 books of the Apocrypha) is revealed Scripture. Scripture and church tradition are equal in authority and are complementary.	One God exists as a "consubstantial Trinity": Father, Son, and Holy Spirit, each of whom is fully God. God is the Creator of all things, whether seen or unseen.	Humans were created in the image of God, holy and perfect, yet humanity abandoned this state through the fall and now is born with the stain of Original Sin.
Eastern Orthodoxy	The Bible (New Testament + Septuagint (Greek) Old Testament = 76 books total) is God's holy revelation. Church tradition, doctrinal statements of the church, and the confessions of the early ecumenical councils have as much authority as Scripture. Revelation has not ceased, but is ongoing in the life of the church.	The Father, Son, and Holy Spirit are one in essence, yet each is distinguishable from the others as a distinct person. Moreover, the Father is the source of the Godhead, the Son is begotten of the Father from all eternity, and the Spirit proceeds from the Father from all eternity.	God created humankind for fellowship with himself, but man rejected that fellowship and thus has alienated himself from God. Human beings possess free will and are capable of genuine goodness because they are made in God's image.

	Sin	Salvation	Afterlife
Liberal Protestantism	The fall of man in Genesis 3, if understood as a historical event, is an absurdity. Humans are not born with a sinful nature. Sin is viewed primarily as a societal rather than a personal issue.	Personal salvation is unnecessary, since sin is a societal problem. Jesus Christ is merely an example of what man should strive to become. The crucifixion, atonement, and resurrection of Christ are mythological or symbolic in significance.	Some reject the idea of an afterlife, while others contend that all people will be saved (universalism). The idea of a literal hell where God exacts retribution on the unrepentant is barbaric and repugnant.
Evangelical Protestantism	Adam and Eve sinned by choice and thereby brought sin into the human race. Through Satan's temptation, man transgressed the command of God and fell from his original innocence. His posterity inherit a nature and an environment strongly inclined toward sin. All persons have broken God's law and deserve his righteous judgment.	Salvation involves the redemption of the whole man and includes regeneration, justification, sanctification, and glorification. This salvation is offered freely to all and is appropriated by accepting Jesus Christ as one's Lord and Savior. By his death on the cross, Jesus has obtained salvation for all who believe in him.	Jesus Christ will judge all human beings at the time of the General Resurrection. Those who rejected him and were lawbreakers will be cast into hell; those who believed in him and were obedient to his law enter into heaven. Some hold to annihilationism rather than the traditional view of everlasting damnation.

Chart 33

Comparison of Beliefs within Christianity (continued)

	Sin	Salvation	Afterlife
Fundamentalist Protestantism	Sin was brought into the human race through Adam and Eve's willful disobedience. When tempted by the Devil, man transgressed God's command and fell from original innocence. His descendants inherit a corrupt nature and an environment contaminated by sin. All are sinners and are under God's just condemnation.	Salvation is wholly of grace, made possible through the priestly mediatorial office of the Son of God, who by his substitutionary death made a full atonement for sins. Sinners are justified freely through faith (alone) in the Redeemer's blood. The eternal redemption purchased by Christ cannot be forfeited.	The end of the present order of things is fast approaching. At the last day, Christ will judge all men. The wicked will be consigned to endless punishment and the righteous will enter into endless joy. This final judgment will seal forever the state of persons in heaven or hell.
Pentecostal-Charismatic Protestantism	Adam and Eve rebelled against God and thereby brought spiritual destruction upon themselves and their descendents. In response to the temptation of Satan, man violated God's commandment and became sinful. Mankind inherits a nature and an environment that is given over to sin. All persons have broken God's law and are the subjects of his righteous anger.	Most Pentecostal-Charismatic groups hold to salvation by grace alone through faith alone. The United Pentecostals, however, believe that salvation can be fully experienced only by being baptized in the name of Jesus, and that salvation is evidenced by "speaking in tongues."	It is commonly (though not always) thought that the time of Christ's return is near. Christ will judge all men at the day of judgment, at which time the wicked will be condemned to endless suffering and the righteous will receive their reward. This final judgment permanently assigns people to either heaven or hell.
Roman Catholicism	Sin entered the world by the transgression of Adam and Eve. Their wounded nature was passed on to their progeny and is called Original Sin. As a result of Original Sin, human nature is weakened in its powers; it is now subject to ignorance, suffering and death, and inclined to sin. Sin falls into two basic categories: mortal (fatal if not forgiven before death) and venial (pardonable).	Salvation is merited through faith, hope, love, and participation in the sacraments of the church. The salvation process begins at baptism and continues primarily through participation in the sacraments (most notably the Eucharist, or Communion). One's salvation can be lost.	Those who die in God's grace and friendship live forever with Christ in heaven and enjoy a full vision of God. Purgatory is the abode of all who die in God's grace and fellowship but are not fully purified. Hell is reserved for those who die in a state of mortal sin and is a state of everlasting ruin.

Chart 33

Comparison of Beliefs within Christianity (continued)

	Sin	Salvation	Afterlife
Eastern Orthodoxy	Spiritually, Adam was a child and his sin is to be understood as "missing the road." Adam's descendants inherit mortality and weakness, but not guilt. Every human child remains innocent until he or she personally sins. Acts of sin result from human finitude and demonic deception, not from antecedent moral corruption.	Salvation is a process of human deification, wherein one can become all that God is, except for identity of nature. Salvation is initially received through the sacrament of baptism. In the sacrament of Holy Chrismation, adherents are sealed by the Holy Spirit and receive gifts of the Spirit.	God gives eternal bliss to the righteous, and the ungodly endure eternal misery. Hell is real, since humans have the freedom to embrace or reject God.

Chart 33

Roman Catholicism

Topic	Facts
Current Data	Official sources indicate that the worldwide membership of the Roman Catholic Church exceeds 1 billion. However, this figure is probably inflated because people who leave the Catholic Church and become members of another church or religion (or who describe themselves as "non-religious") are still included in the Church's membership rolls until their death, unless they are excommunicated. During much of the 20th century Roman Catholics were concentrated in Latin America, Eastern Europe, Italy, Spain, Ireland, Quebec, and parts of the United States. In recent years regions of Africa and Asia have become home to a substantial number of Roman Catholics. A number of closely related groups have branched off from the Roman Catholic Church, most notably the Old Catholics, the Polish National Church of America, the Chinese Patriotic Catholic Association, and the Philippine Independent Church (Aglipayans).
History	The Roman Catholic Church claims its origin in the apostle Peter and the disciples of Jesus, with Peter being the first pope of the Church. The history of the Christian church, from its inception to its formal recognition by Constantine I in the 4th century AD, is viewed as the history of the Roman Church, since Peter and his successors ruled the church from Rome. By the 5th century, five bishops ruled over different jurisdictions—in the ancient cities of Jerusalem, Antioch, Alexandria, Constantinople, and Rome. The bishop in Rome was viewed as having a position of preeminence among the bishops, yet still was seen as equal in power and authority to the others. This changed with the ascendancy of Gregory I, who was recognized in the 6th century as the bishop of the entire Christian Church. By the 10th century, despite Rome's assertion that its authority could be traced back in a line of succession to the apostle Peter, the Holy Roman Emperor and Senate were headquartered in Constantinople. At that time there were tensions between Rome and Constantinople, because the emperors claimed to have authority over the affairs of the Church as well as the right to wield political power. These political tensions were exacerbated by the fact that Rome and Constantinople (the Latin and Greek branches of the Church) did not share the same liturgy for worship. These conflicts—along with a doctrinal controversy concerning the relationship between the persons of the Trinity—came to a head in 1054 in what has come to be known as "The Great Schism." The Church split into two distinct ecclesiastical institutions: the (Western) Roman Catholic Church and the Eastern Orthodox Church. Although proto-Reformers like John Wycliffe (c. 1320–1384), Jon Hus (1369–1415), and William Tyndale (c. 1484–1536) protested against the doctrinal deviations and moral corruption of the late medieval church, it was not until the 16th century that there was another major schism within Christianity. In what has come to be called the Protestant Reformation, leaders like Martin Luther (1483–1546), Ulrich Zwingli (1484–1531), Thomas Muentzer (c. 1489–1525), Menno Simons (1496–1561), and John Calvin (1509–1564) challenged the authority and orthodoxy of the Roman Catholic Church, eventually splitting off into various movements such as the Anglicans, Lutherans, Reformed, and Anabaptists. As a response to these events, the Roman Catholic Church launched an extensive Counter-Reformation. In 1869 Pope Pious IX convened the First Vatican Council to discuss matters pertaining to the

Chart 34

Roman Catholicism (continued)

Topic	Facts
History (continued)	encroachment of secular ideologies on the Church. Pope John XXIII convened the Second Vatican Council in 1962 to deal with the pressing issues of religious pluralism and modernizing the Church. In recent years, Roman Catholic Church authorities in Western countries have begun recruiting priests from Africa to make up for the lack of available priests in their areas. At present, Pope Benedict XVI (1927–) presides over the Roman Catholic Church.
Summary of Beliefs	In addition to the beliefs specific to the Roman Catholic Church, Roman Catholics believe in many basic Christian doctrines in common with other Christians, including the Trinitarian nature of God as described in the Nicene Creed (4th century AD) and the deity and humanity of Christ, as found in the Formula of Chalcedon (5th century AD). The theology of Roman Catholicism ultimately is defined by the pope, who, when he speaks on matters of faith and morals, is considered infallible. Church teaching in the form of official documents written by the pope are called encyclicals. Roman Catholicism teaches that because of Original Sin, mankind is inherently sinful and needs to be saved. Man's fall into sin is described in the story of Adam and Eve in the book of Genesis. Jesus Christ died on the cross as an atonement for Adam's failure and provides Roman Catholics (and, in modern Catholicism, even those outside the formal structure of the Church) with the possibility of meriting eternal life with God in heaven. Salvation may be achieved only through God's grace, though both faith and good works are in some sense necessary. Salvation, in Roman Catholic thinking, includes what Protestants call justification and sanctification. The sacraments are the primary means by which to sustain that grace. The seven sacraments of Roman Catholicism are: baptism, confirmation, holy Eucharist, penance, anointing of the sick, holy orders, and marriage. The Eucharist, which is partaken of during the Roman Mass, is the center of the Church's life. During Mass, Catholics believe that the bread and wine they consume has been changed into the body and blood of Jesus Christ. The Mass is the high point of Roman Catholic worship.

Topic	Summary of View
Creation	The universe was created by God out of nothing and reflects many of his divine attributes. This "natural revelation" of God in his creation provides adequate evidence for his existence and some of his attributes, such that unaided human reasoning is capable of ascertaining these truths. Though insisting that God is the Creator and Sustainer of the world, many modern Roman Catholic theologians teach that this creation does not exclude the possibility that God may have used evolutionary mechanisms in creating life on this planet, up to and including human beings. Although man's fall into sin has brought corruption into the created order, the creation is still fundamentally good.

Chart 34

Topic	Summary of View
Creation (continued)	God's creation is a fitting vehicle for the transmission of his saving grace. In particular, in the Roman Catholic Mass the substance of the body and blood of Jesus Christ is present in and with the physical elements of bread and wine. In this way the very being of God is received by those partaking of the Holy Eucharist (or Holy Communion) and is thus infused into them. There is not as sharp of a contrast between the being of God and the being of man as in classical Protestant Christianity.
Scripture and Authority	There are two equal and ultimate sources of divine revelation: the Scriptures of the Old and New Testaments (including certain Apocryphal writings, which are not recognized as inspired or authoritative by Protestants) and Church tradition. The tradition of the Roman Catholic Church and the teachings of the Bible are complementary. Doctrines and practices not found explicitly in the Bible either exist there in embryonic form or exist alongside Scripture in an unwritten oral tradition. The highest teaching authority of the Roman Catholic Church—the pope and the College of Cardinals—provides the faithful with an infallible and supremely authoritative interpretation of both Scripture and tradition. Whoever holds this infallible teaching position at any given time can maintain continuity with past Church pronouncements while taking the Church's official statements of doctrine in new directions, bringing out previously neglected aspects of tradition.
God	The official view is that presented in the ecumenical creeds (e.g., Apostles', Nicene, Chalcedonian) and, to a lesser degree, in the writings of theologians such as Thomas Aquinas. God is one in substance and yet three distinct persons (Father, Son, and Holy Spirit) share in this one divine essence. The Son is eternally begotten of the Father and the Spirit proceeds from both the Father and the Son. God's attributes include aseity (self-existent), simplicity, goodness, omni-perfection, infinity, immensity, immutability, eternality, invisibility, and ineffability. In contemporary Roman Catholicism, God's love is his supreme defining attribute.
Mankind	Human beings are created in the image of God (the "likeness" of God was lost at the fall), at once physical and spiritual—body and soul are organically united into one person. Mankind was not only created good but was also established in friendship with the Creator and in harmony with other people and the creation around him. The value and dignity of human beings is demonstrated not just in their creation by a wise and loving God and in his making them stewards of his creation but by the Son's incarnation. When the divine Son took on a human nature as Jesus Christ, he demonstrated that God cares about his human creatures and considers their redemption to be worth accomplishing.
Sin	Mankind was created in a state of innocence, having a loving relationship with God and free of any tendency to sin. Unrestricted access to the Tree of Life would have allowed him to continue indefinitely in a state of physical and spiritual life. As a result of the fall, however, human beings now inherit Original Sin and are subject to sickness and death. Disease, pain, and various bodily problems now plague man in his fallen condition. Mankind no longer possesses God's likeness (a

Chart 34

Roman Catholicism (continued)

Topic	Summary of View
Sin (continued)	supernatural gift given to Adam and Eve), but still bears his image. Though Original Sin now stains the soul of every human being from the moment of conception, and all inherit a proclivity toward sin, human beings are still fundamentally good, both morally and in terms of their created being. The fall affected the will (volition) more than a person's intellect. Through his death and resurrection, Jesus Christ achieved victory over sin, sickness, and death. In the resurrection, those who did not die in a state of mortal sin will be given a glorified body, unburdened by fleshly ills and limitations.
Salvation	Though fallen, mankind (with the help of God's grace) is able to cooperate with God in a process of salvation from sin. Faith (conceived primarily as mental assent to the doctrines of Roman Catholicism) and good works both are necessary for meriting eternal life. The grace needed for obtaining salvation comes primarily through the seven sacraments of the Church, especially Holy Communion. Justifying grace is forfeited if one commits a mortal sin, whereas venial sin can be atoned for in purgatory. Those dying in a state of justifying grace go to heaven. Jesus Christ's sacrificial death on the cross provides a way for human beings to be justified before God. Jesus offered himself as a propitiation to (provisionally) satisfy God's wrath against sin, so that God can deal graciously with sinful humans as they work together with him toward final justification and glorification. Historically it was taught that the benefits of this atonement are mediated solely through the Roman Catholic priesthood and Rome's sacraments, and that those not in official communion with the Roman Catholic Church were under God's wrath. More recent Church pronouncements (since Vatican II) indicate that the vast treasury of Christ's merits (accumulated during his life of perfect obedience and his death on the cross) can be applied to "people of good will" who lack explicit faith in Christ and/or have no formal association with the Roman Catholic Church. On this account, such people will receive salvation on the day of judgment, though they will have to endure a period in purgatory before they are allowed into heaven.
Afterlife	Emphasis is on the beatific vision, wherein those who are saved contemplate God in all his glory for eternity. There are four possible final destinations for human beings after death: heaven, hell, purgatory, and limbo. Those who die in a state of grace dwell eternally in heaven, though they may have to spend time in purgatory first. Those who die in a state of mortal sin suffer eternal punishment in hell. Those who die in a state of grace but have unforgiven venial sins must atone for them by suffering in purgatory before being admitted to heaven. Unbaptized infants and unbaptized young children who have not reached the "age of moral accountability" at the time of death reside in limbo, where they experience an everlasting happiness less than that of the blessed in heaven. There are degrees of blessedness in heaven, corresponding to the degree of sanctification achieved in this life.

Chart 34

Roman Catholicism (continued)

Distinctive Beliefs and Practices

Sacraments	Jesus instituted seven sacraments, not two as taught by most Protestant groups. In addition to baptism and the Lord's Supper, Roman Catholicism includes confession (penance), confirmation, marriage, holy orders, and last rites (anointing of the sick) in its list of sacraments.
Mary	The Virgin Mary is the Blessed Mother of God (Council of Ephesus) and Queen of Heaven. As such it is proper to offer prayers and petitions to Mary, who intercedes with God on behalf of faithful Roman Catholics. Though not the official teaching of the Church, some believe Mary is co-mediator and co-redeemer with Christ.
The Papacy	Jesus established the office of pope when he conferred that position and its authority on the apostle Peter. As supreme pontiff of the Holy Roman Catholic Church and the vicar of Christ, the pope is invested with great powers: the right to forgive and retain sin, infallible teaching authority when speaking *ex cathedra* on matters of faith and morals, and authority over all earthly rulers and governments. There is an unbroken line of apostolic succession from Peter to the current pope.
Purgatory	A post-mortem abode where certain souls are purged of any remaining sin before going to heaven. During their time in purgatory, souls are made ready to enter into the presence of God. This process of purification is necessary for two types of people: (1) those who never committed a mortal sin, but whose venial sins still merit a limited period of punishment, and (2) those who committed mortal sins during their life and obtained remission from their eternal penalty in the sacrament of penance, but who still need to suffer the temporary penalty due them. (Those who achieved sainthood before their death by accumulating adequate, or even excess, merit and those who died in a state of spiritual death due to unforgiven mortal sin do not spend any time in purgatory.) A person's stay in purgatory can range from very brief to extremely long, depending on the number and severity of the sins for which they are being punished. Traditional (Tridentine, Vatican I) Roman Catholicism taught that purgatory differed from hell only in duration, not in nature. Post-Vatican II Catholicism emphasizes the cleansing aspect and downplays the retributive aspect.
The Saints	Very religious persons who accumulated an excess of merit in this life are worthy of veneration (*dulia*)—distinct from worship (*latria*)—and have the power to intercede for Roman Catholics who pray to them.
Praying the Rosary	Praying the rosary consists of reciting a series of prayers that follow a predetermined sequence, primarily the prayer "Hail Mary" (a prayer to Mary, Jesus' mother), though sometimes the "Our Father" prayer and others are spoken as well. Persons performing this religious exercise use a string of beads to track their progress; usually these strings have 50 beads arranged in groups of 10. Each sequence of 10 beads is called a decade. Practitioners must utter 20 decades in order to complete the rosary. During the course of saying the rosary, one is supposed to reflect on 20 mysteries of the Catholic faith, which are put in four categories of five each: the joyful mysteries, the luminous mysteries, the sorrowful mysteries, and the glorious mysteries.

Chart 34

Eastern Orthodoxy

Topic	Facts
Current Data	The Eastern Orthodox Church is composed of 14 regional churches whose unity is grounded in a common theology and in their belief in the preeminent (though not unique or highest) authority of the ecumenical patriarch of Constantinople. Included in this family of churches are the eight major ecclesiastical jurisdictions of Constantinople, Alexandria, Antioch, Jerusalem, Moscow (Russia), Bulgaria, Romania, and Serbia as well as the independent churches of Greece, Cyprus, Czechoslovakia, Poland, Albania, and Georgia. Also included are the Orthodox Church of America and the monastery of Saint Catherine in Egypt. Related groups like the Oriental Orthodox churches, the Old Believers, and the Russian Orthodox Church outside Russia are not in communion with Constantinople. Worldwide membership is estimated at 220 million.
History	According to Eastern Orthodox historians, the history of the Eastern Orthodox Church can be traced back to the origin of Christianity itself, with the line of apostolic succession that began with the apostle Peter and has continued until the present day. It is believed that from the apostolic period until the time of Constantine (272–337), the church was unified in its doctrine, liturgy, and government. After the reign of Constantine, a series of gifted theologians worked through a number of important theological issues on behalf of the church. These brilliant thinkers included Gregory Nazianzus (329–389), Basil the Great (330–379), Gregory of Nyssa (c. 335–394), Jerome (340–420), John Chrysostom (347–407), and Augustine of Hippo (354–430). Major ecumenical councils were convened during this period, such as the Council of Nicaea in 325 and the Council of Constantinople in 381.
	There were three major schisms in the Orthodox Church that occurred over the course of the next 700 years. First, in 451, churches now known corporately as Oriental Orthodox separated from the larger body of Christianity as a result of their disagreement with the conclusions (concerning the person and natures of Christ) reached by the majority of delegates at the Council of Chalcedon. Second, during the middle to late 9th century, tensions were heightened between the Eastern and Western branches of the church because of bickering between Patriarch Photius of Constantinople (c. 820–891) and Roman Pope Nicholas I (b. date unknown–d. 867). Third, there was the Great Schism between the Eastern and Western churches in 1054, occasioned by a disagreement over the relationship of the Holy Spirit to the other two persons of the Trinity.
	After Constantinople was sacked and taken over by the Ottoman Turks in 1453, the Islamic government under whose territorial jurisdiction they now fell persecuted the Orthodox Church. The next four centuries witnessed a series of questionable alliances between the Orthodox Church and several European countries, a blurring of the distinction between religious and national identity in many areas where the church dominated the culture. The Russian Orthodox Church as an institution autonomous from Constantinople was founded in 1448. During the 19th century many additional Orthodox churches were established: Greek (1833), Romanian (1859), Bulgarian (1870), and Serbian (1879). Because they existed independently of Constantinople, the amount of power and influence wielded by Constantinople after their formation was greatly reduced. As of 2005, the ecumenical patriarch of the Eastern Orthodox Church was Bartholomew I (Demetrios Archontonis, 1940–).

Chart 35

Eastern Orthodoxy (continued)

Topic	Facts
Summary of Beliefs	In its most common use, the term "Eastern Orthodoxy" refers to those church institutions (and their corresponding traditions) that can be traced back to the Byzantium Empire (c. 395–1453). Just like the Roman Catholic Church, the Eastern Orthodox Church claims (1) to be the One Holy Catholic and Apostolic Church on earth, and (2) to safeguard what is essentially the same set of doctrines and practices that were in place in the primitive church. Eastern Orthodoxy has defined itself in part on the basis of four serious disagreements it has with Roman Catholicism. 1. The Eastern Orthodox Church maintains that the insertion of the filioque clause (the phrase "and the Son") into the Nicene Creed, which was sanctioned at the Council of Toledo in Spain in 447, is in error. According to them, the Holy Spirit proceeds from the Father only, not from both the Father and the Son. 2. The Eastern Orthodox Church contends that the pope of Rome does not have binding authority over all Christians. 3. The Eastern Orthodox Church believes that the Roman doctrine of the immaculate conception of the Virgin Mary is heretical. 4. There are significant differences between Eastern Orthodoxy and Roman Catholicism regarding church liturgy.

Topic	Summary of View
Creation	God was free to create a universe or to refrain from creating one; he was under no external or internal compulsion to decide either way. Because of his great love, however, he brought the universe into being out of nothing; all three persons of the Trinity were involved in this creative act. The divine Logos (intellect) is the ground of existence of all creatures (*logoi*), and bestows each one of them with a divine energy. Through a process known as "Double Movement," God seeks to become united (though not in substance) with his creation, and his creatures seek unity with him. Creation was not in opposition to God prior to the fall, but naturally moved toward him so as to participate more fully in his divine energy and thereby to achieve deification (this should not be understood as becoming God or a god).
Scripture and Authority	There are two main views within Eastern Orthodoxy, the Two Source Approach and the One Source Approach. According to the Two Source Approach, God has given his revelation to the church in two forms: the Holy Bible and Holy Tradition. The early church operated solely on the basis of an oral tradition, which later was used as source material for writing the New Testament. Since neither the New Testament nor the oral tradition of the church exhausts the content of divine revelation, the church has acted as the custodian of the entire Word of God, both written and unwritten. These two sources are entirely consistent, both being valid sources of God's authoritative self-disclosure.

Chart 35

Eastern Orthodoxy (continued)

Topic	Summary of View
Scripture and Authority (continued)	The One Source Approach, on the other hand, alleges that the Two Source approach sets up an unnecessary dichotomy. In this view, the scriptures are simply part of a larger church tradition, and hence the Bible does not ultimately determine the doctrines and practices of the church. Instead, the church, in its God-given role as authorized interpreter of the Bible, infallibly sets forth the teachings of Christianity. This interpretive authority is vested in the episcopate (bishops) of the church, both individually and (primarily) in councils which meet certain criteria.
God	The Father is the fount of the Godhead, with the Son eternally begotten out of the Father and the Spirit proceeding from the Father. The Triune God alone possesses aseity (self-existence); all other beings depend on his free acts of creation and providence for their existence. The three persons of the one God are distinct from each other but indivisible in regards to the essence of deity, with all persons sharing equally the fullness of the attributes of God. All of the attributes of God are infinite, and some of these are shared in a finite manner with human beings. The being of God has three distinguishable aspects: 1. *Ousia*, the inexpressible and unapproachable divine essence. 2. *Hypostases*, the three divine persons whose proper names are Father, Son, and Holy Spirit. 3. *Energeiai*, uncreated energies that God uses to communicate with his creatures. Although positive statements about God provide true (but approximate) descriptions of his attributes, they are incapable of adequately expressing God's most fundamental nature, which is beyond the grasp of the human intellect. God acts in history on behalf of his people.
Mankind	Human beings were created to participate in the divine nature. To make them fit for such participation, they were made to have two different but interrelated aspects: 1. The image of God, which consists of finite rationality and moral freedom. These faculties differentiate human beings from animals. 2. The likeness of God, which consists of the capacity to develop moral virtue and thereby to be deified. These two aspects allow for a point of contact between an infinite, transcendent God and his limited, material human creatures. In terms of their spiritual maturity, Adam and Eve were children. They were given the ability to achieve moral and spiritual perfection by obeying and communing with God, but they were not perfect at the time of their creation. Consequently, Eastern Orthodox theologians view the fall as being substantially less awful than do Christian theologians of most other traditions.

Chart 35

Eastern Orthodoxy (continued)

Topic	Summary of View
Sin	The human proclivity to sin is a consequence of human mortality. Moreover, the conditions of this world, combined with man's estrangement from God, make sin inevitable. While Adam and Eve were still in a state of innocence, all of their physical needs were met by God, so their inclination to sin was far less strong than it is for human beings living after the fall, who suffer from intense and persistent bodily urges. God intended for Adam and Eve to grow in faith and love, eventually becoming perfect. However, at the instigation of the Devil, they willfully disobeyed the clear command of God, which resulted in their losing their perfect fellowship with God and becoming susceptible to disease, decay, and death. From that time forward, rather than acting in accordance with their created nature, they gave themselves over to their senses. This results in three primary sins: 1. Spiritual ignorance stemming from the depraved use of reason. 2. Self-love stemming from perverted desires. 3. Hatred of others stemming from an undisciplined temper. Adam and Eve's rebellion against God was a sin for which they alone must account; the guilt of sin is not inherited by their posterity. The fall did not affect the natural world to the extent maintained by other traditions within Christianity.
Salvation	The sin of Adam resulted in a barrier (his mortality, not a legal sinful impediment) being erected between humanity and God. Since human beings in their present state cannot reestablish friendship with God on their own, the eternal Son of God became incarnate in Jesus Christ, thereby providing the possibility of mystical union with God. (In Eastern Orthodox thinking, Protestant concepts like forensic justification, vicarious atonement, and redemption are either absent or relegated to the distant background; the incarnation itself is seen as the key event enabling humans to achieve salvation.) This mystical union with God is made possible by means of divine energies that flow from God's very being, and by means of the sacraments of the church, which serve as the primary conduit of those energies. Human beings must choose to cooperate with God in the process of salvation; divine grace does not operate unilaterally. Besides the sacraments, good works, prayer, and contemplation of God all aid practitioners in achieving mystical union with God.
Afterlife	At the end of history, Christ will return to the earth in glory to commence the Final Judgment and to renovate the creation, so that it becomes a New Heaven and a New Earth. The righteous (those who have achieved or at least sought mystical union with God) will receive an eternal reward, while the ungodly will have to endure the misery of separation from God. Hell, which is everlasting damnation, is the logical outcome of persistent and willful rejection of God and the salvation he has offered human beings in Christ. Thus hell is not a place to where God sends unrepentant sinners; instead, those who hate God consign themselves to perdition. The torment experienced by the ungodly in hell is not, strictly speaking, a form of divine retribution, but results from their animosity toward the love and goodness of God, which is omnipresent.

Chart 35

Eastern Orthodoxy (continued)

Distinctive Beliefs and Practices

The Church	The Eastern Orthodox Church declares itself to be the one and only true church established by Jesus Christ, founded on Christ and his apostles, and continued by means of unbroken apostolic succession. They staunchly maintain that they alone have preserved the deposit of faith entrusted by Christ to his apostles, which is reflected in their theology and worship practices. Some Eastern Orthodox theologians interpret this exclusive stance more leniently than do others, yet the basic position is the same in each case.
Liturgical Worship	The worship of the Eastern Orthodox Church is permeated with liturgical elements. The interior of Eastern Orthodox churches are aesthetically overwhelming, containing a plethora of eye-grabbing objects like ornate stained glass windows, bright paintings with religious themes, and intricately carved statues. A typical service might include such things as burning incense and large candles, priests wearing elaborate vestments and sporting enormous beards, and worshipers making the sign of the cross and kissing and prostrating themselves before icons.
Icons	Icons are an essential component of Eastern Orthodox theology and worship. They are in abundance in most Orthodox churches, where worshipers embrace them and pray to them, and Orthodox priests perform special rituals with them. The icon is a manifestation of God based on the incarnation of God in human form in Jesus. Thus worshipers receive a vision of the unseen world when they view the physical representation of God the Son in the icon. Orthodox churches celebrate (annually during Lent) the Triumph of Orthodoxy. This event commemorates the acceptance of icons—and the reprimand of the iconoclasts (those opposed to icons)—by the church on March 11, 843. The liturgy of this service includes an anathema (denunciation) on all who disallow the use of icons. Moreover, Orthodox theology, in line with the Second Council of Nicaea held in 787, asserts that the gospel can be communicated as well by icons as it can be by reading the Bible.

Chart 35

Liberal Protestantism

Topic	Facts
Current Data	Since the 1960s, Liberal Protestantism has been in a state of rapid decline, both in terms of church membership numbers and in terms of cultural influence. The 1990s were no exception to this decline. The five major mainline (liberal) Protestant denominations all suffered substantial losses in membership: American Baptist Churches down 5.7 percent, Episcopal Church down 5.3 percent, Presbyterian Church-USA down 11.6 percent, United Church of Christ down 14.8 percent, and United Methodist Church down 6.7 percent. Many liberal denominations are attempting to remake their image so as to recruit more members. Most such groups are witnessing intense infighting over issues such as the ordination of homosexuals, the moral and legal status of abortion, religious pluralism and the exclusivity of Christ, and sexual ethics.
History	German theologian Friedrich Schleiermacher (1768–1834) is generally acknowledged as the person whose thinking gave rise to what later became known as Liberal Protestantism. Following in the footsteps of Schleiermacher, Albrecht Ritschl (1822–1889), another prominent German theologian, desired to forge a form of Christianity that was relevant to modern culture. By the late 19th century, Liberal Protestantism had emerged as a major force within visible Christendom in Western Europe and America. By the early 20th century, the twin doctrines of the fatherhood of God and the brotherhood of man were clearly at the core of Liberal Protestant identity. Continuing to increase both its numbers and its sway in the public sphere, the movement had become a major presence in the United States by the 1920s. During this period of growth and expansion, Liberal Protestantism sought to define itself over and against those expressions of Christian faith that it viewed as traditional or conservative, taking its cues from the surrounding culture. Groups today that are properly designated as Liberal Protestant include the mainline denominations listed above, the Evangelical Lutheran Church in America, and numerous other organizations affiliated with the National Council of Churches and the World Ecumenical Movement. Most of these denominations are shrinking in size, with their strength derived from uniting their church bodies.
Summary of Beliefs	Liberal Protestantism is characterized by several interrelated contentions. 1. God is a wholly loving deity who created such good things as the world, human beings, and human cultures. 2. Reliable knowledge is gained through the means of human reason, the scientific method, and religious experience. 3. Human beings possess great moral, intellectual, and creative capacities, and corporately they have the potential to create a society far better than the one in which they presently live. 4. In order to be relevant to modern men and women, the Bible needs to be "demythologized" (miracles and implausible or objectionable teachings should be seen as myths rather than literal truth). 5. Traditional Christian doctrine and morality is in need of reinterpretation.

Chart 36

Liberal Protestantism (continued)

Topic	Summary of View
Creation	The Genesis creation account is mythological-poetic, not historical or scientific. The writer of the Bible's creation story, along with the writers of other ancient creation myths, was expressing his understanding of God's creative activity from a limited, pre-scientific perspective. Modern scientific developments, such as ancient geologic chronology and earth science, neo-Darwinism, and the Big Bang are readily accepted, and previous religious beliefs are modified or rejected in light of them. An underlying premise is that the scientific method and scientific reasoning are the unquestioned means to achieve human knowledge, and that empiricism (observation and experience) takes precedence over the revelation from God found in Scripture.
Scripture and Authority	The Bible is a human document and was not inspired other than writers of Scripture may have received enlightened religious perspectives that they included in the Bible as they sought to understand God. For God to reveal himself in the way claimed by conservative Christian groups is either impossible because of the limits of human language and culture or is theoretically possible but didn't happen. The Bible informs us about the religious beliefs and practices of ancient peoples, but should not be adopted straightway by Christians today. The locus of authority in the modern world should not be the Bible. Instead, human reason, empirical science, contemporary culture, and personal religious experience form the basis for modern religion. Mankind's intellectual autonomy should not be infringed upon or suppressed by superstitions, outmoded religious beliefs, or religious institutions. The doctrines and ethics of the Bible are outdated and stand in need of reformulation or (in some cases) outright rejection. The Bible is useful or relevant only insofar as it contains inspiring passages or is reinterpreted to meet the needs of modern people and their religious communities. Radical groups look to alternative texts like the Gnostic gospels or even holy books of other world religions as equal to the Bible in value and validity.
God	Views range from generic theism (one God and Creator) to Unitarianism (individual freedom of belief and rejection of Trinitarianism) to deism (God created the world and set it in motion but does not intervene in its working or affairs) to panentheism (God is an evolving being within the finite world, and he is also finite). God's immanence is stressed over his transcendence, his love over his justice, his mercy over his anger, etc. Sometimes traditional divine attributes are redefined. God is supremely benevolent and approves of the values, assumptions, and agendas of the modern world. God is understanding and lenient; he is not a harsh judge. Classic creeds, doctrinal formulations, systematic theologies, etc., are often deemed irrelevant, being seen as exercises in dogmatism.
Mankind	Sometimes affirms the "image of God" in human beings in its classical sense; usually maintains that human beings evolved from lower forms of life by natural processes. Mankind is not morally corrupt, but is basically good. Humans are capable of tremendous improvement if provided with an adequate education, proper socialization and moral training, and a nurturing environment.

Chart 36

Topic	Summary of View
Sin	Whatever evil inclinations men may have are primarily, if not exclusively, due to such things as inadequate education, bad social environments, unjust political structures, and genetic defects. Sin is failing to fulfill the human potential for good. Liberal Protestants firmly reject the doctrine of man's moral pollution and inherent sinfulness, along with the historical existence and fall of Adam and Eve, so no literal Garden of Eden or Devil ever existed—the story of man's fall in the book of Genesis is a mythical-allegorical account. Sickness and death did not come into the world through the sin of Adam, but are simply part of nature.
Salvation	Traditional biblical categories such as justification and atonement are reinterpreted. Atonement is God's demonstration of his love for all humanity, not a blood sacrifice or an outpouring of wrath on an innocent victim. Justification is either automatic (universalism) or is earned by doing good works. Often it is taught that there is no real need of salvation, since there is no serious sin to be saved from in most cases. Jesus is not a Savior from sin in any traditional sense, but was a good man and a great moral teacher, along with other wise sages of the ancient world (Zoroaster, Siddhãrtha Gautama (the Buddha), Confucius, Muhammad, etc.).
Afterlife	Occasionally the afterlife is denied. Often a nebulous view of the immortality of the soul is advocated, rather than belief in the resurrection of the body. God's judgment of individual sin is either repudiated or greatly minimized; such judgment (if it occurs at all) has to do with social-political realities in this life. The existence of hell is emphatically denied. Everyone (or perhaps the vast majority of people) is admitted to heaven, if there is one. Overall, the emphasis is on this world, this life, human culture, human progress, and human achievement as the outworking or manifestation of God's will. Jesus will not return to earth.

Distinctive Beliefs and Practices

Topic	Summary of View
Ecumenism	Great importance is placed on reaching out to other religious groups and joining or merging with larger religious organizations whenever feasible. The ultimate goal is to see humanity united under a global institutionalized religion.
Religious Pluralism	Differences between various religions and sects are downplayed, while beliefs held in common are emphasized. Tolerance of religious beliefs and practices other than one's own is a very important virtue. The great diversity of religious beliefs is a good thing and should be celebrated. Value judgments concerning practitioners of other religions are unacceptable. Claims regarding the exclusivity of Christ are considered bigoted, arrogant, and imperialist.
Universalism	Because the love of God is unbounded, no human being will be consigned to eternal perdition. Any divine judgment of sin that might occur will be temporary. Mankind is a brotherhood united by God's love. The religious and ethical differences between human beings are either minimal or unimportant.

Chart 36

Evangelical Protestantism

Topic	Facts
Current Data	During the 1990s, a number of Christian denominations that can properly be categorized as Evangelical Protestant demonstrated significant—in some cases remarkable—growth. The 41,000-plus local churches that comprise the Southern Baptist Convention increased their membership by 5 percent. The Assemblies of God grew 18.5 percent, the Christian and Missionary Alliance grew 22 percent, the Church of God grew 40 percent, the Presbyterian Church in America grew 42 percent, and the Evangelical Free Church grew an amazing 57 percent.
History	Though broadly speaking there have been "evangelical" groups of various kinds since the days of the apostles, it was not until the time of the Protestant Reformation that the word "evangelical" came into circulation. Martin Luther (1483–1546) dubbed his fledgling movement the *evangelische kirke*, or "evangelical church" (church that preaches the good news of the gospel). Most commonly, though, the term designates Christian groups whose roots go back to the 18th and early 19th centuries, when a series of revivals took place in the United Kingdom and North America. Leading participants in these events included Jonathan Edwards (1703–58), John Wesley (1703–91), and George Whitefield (1714–70), all of whom based their evangelistic methods and the content of their sermons on the Bible alone. Due to the far-reaching and long-lasting influence of these revivals, by 1825, Evangelical Protestantism had firmly established itself in the United States. Later, men like Charles Finney (1792–1875) took Evangelical Protestantism in a different direction, wherein the number of converts was the criterion for the success of a revival, and conversion was based more on emotionalism and social and personal change.
	The middle and later parts of the 19th century witnessed a number of social movements whose inspiration sprang from the distinctive emphases of Evangelical Protestantism. These included charitable organizations, anti-slavery campaigns, the crusade for women's suffrage (in its early days), and the movement to outlaw the sale and consumption of alcohol.
	Evangelicalism's grip on American culture began to wane in the early 20th century, due to such factors as the huge influx of Roman Catholic immigrants and the ambivalence or animosity many people felt toward Fundamentalist Protestantism, whose identity was not yet distinct from that of broader Evangelicalism.
	After World War II, Evangelicalism and Fundamentalism become clearly differentiated movements. Hallmark personalities, institutions, and organizations associated with Evangelical Protestantism (past and present) include evangelists Dwight L. Moody (1837–99), Billy Sunday (1862–1935), and Billy Graham (1918–); Wheaton College in suburban Chicago and Fuller Theological Seminary near Los Angeles; the National Association of Evangelicals; and Youth for Christ.
Summary of Beliefs	For the most part, churches that consider themselves evangelical stress the importance of listening to sermons, personal and group Bible study, and engaging the culture; this distinguishes them from forms of Christianity that believe sacraments and liturgy to be central to the life of the church.
	It is widely agreed that Evangelical Protestantism has at least four characteristics that distinguish it from other Christian groups or movements:

Chart 37

Evangelical Protestantism (continued)

Topic	Facts
Summary of Beliefs (continued	• The belief that being converted (undergoing a definitive spiritual transformation) is essential to being a Christian. Conversion often is referred to as being "born again." It results in the convert having a personal relationship with Jesus Christ. • The belief that the Bible reveals God's will for human beings. It is the sole basis for formulating Christian theology and ethics and the final standard for adjudicating disputes within the church. • The belief that evangelism (sharing the gospel of Christ) is the duty of every Christian, not just pastors or ministers. • The belief that Jesus' death on the cross atoned for the sins of the world and was necessary for the salvation of human beings to be possible.

Topic	Summary of View
Creation	God created the universe out of nothing (*creatio ex nihilo*) by a free act of divine power and rules over it as king. Although there is no universal agreement beyond this basic assertion, the following beliefs are held by many evangelicals: 1. God used the "Big Bang" to create the universe and all that is in it. This happened gradually over the course of billions of years. Others believe that the creation of the universe may have taken only a few thousand years. 2. The days of creation mentioned in Genesis were extremely long periods of time, though many believe that the days were solar days of about 24 hours each. Some who believe the latter also believe that there were long periods of time between each solar day (known as Progressive Creationism). 3. The sun and earth both have existed for billions of years. Others believe that these heavenly bodies are only thousands of years old, and some who would accept a great length of time for the sun, moon, and stars believe that Genesis 1 speaks primarily of the earth, and its formation by God was only several thousand years ago. 4. Animals were created long before Adam and Eve existed. This means that violence in nature and physical death were not due to the rebellion of Adam and Eve, though the fall may have greatly increased the incidence of these things. Some evangelicals, though, believe in a recent creation with the animals and mankind being created in close proximity. 5. The Great Flood in which Noah's family and the pairs of animals were preserved on the ark covered only a limited region of the earth. Since the flood was not worldwide, its geological consequences were negligible. Other evangelicals believe in a worldwide flood that caused many changes in the earth which have had an impact on geological interpretation by scientists. 6. Empirical science and the Bible are both legitimate sources for understanding God's role in the creation of the universe and life on earth.

Chart 37

Evangelical Protestantism (continued)

Topic	Summary of View
Scripture and Authority	The Scriptures (66 books of the Protestant Bible) are the final authority and only sufficient guide in matters of faith and practice. In contrast to Liberal Protestantism that believes the Bible, even the autographs, has error, and Fundamentalist Protestantism that sometimes invests the King James Version of the Bible as being without error, evangelicals hold that only the original manuscripts are inerrant. Some hold to "limited inerrancy" wherein the Bible, when speaking of matters of faith and practice, is free from error, but when addressing subjects such as science and history commits occasional minor errors. On this view, God kept the writers of Scripture free from error when writing about matters of doctrine and Christian living, but allowed them to err on occasion regarding matters not essential to salvation. This view allows for a broader range of interpretive approaches than fundamentalism, yet disavows most of the higher critical approaches common in Liberal Protestantism. Most evangelicals, however, believe that the Bible is a verbally inspired book, and God has preserved it from any error of fact or ethical concept in the original writings.
God	God is a Trinity: three distinct persons—Father, Son, and Holy Spirit—share in one divine nature. The Father exercises sovereign control over creation and history. The Son took on a human nature in the person of Jesus Christ. The Spirit works in and through the church. God's attributes include self-existence, perfect love, omniscience, omnipotence, omnipresence, eternality, and transcendence.
Mankind	Human beings are created in the image and likeness of God, with both physical and spiritual aspects. (Most believe that mankind came into being as a special act of creation, though some maintain that God superintended the process of evolution as his means of creating human beings.) This makes humans unique among God's creatures, and thus it was fitting that they were given the task of exercising dominion over God's creation. Mankind was created morally good and in a loving relationship with the Creator. Mankind is in constant dependence upon God for life, sustenance, and physical and spiritual well-being.
Sin	Adam and Eve sinned against God when they disobeyed his command, seduced by the temptation of Satan. Their fall into sin resulted in a comprehensive moral corruption, which has been passed down to all human beings without exception. This sinful nature manifests itself in sinful decisions, actions, attitudes, and beliefs. Human frailty, disease, and death are among the consequences of sin. There is disagreement as to whether the fall rendered mankind totally incapable of responding to God's grace or whether this incapacity is only partial.
Salvation	The atoning work of Jesus Christ on the cross is necessary for personal salvation. Jesus' death on the cross alone serves as an expiation (act of atonement) for mankind's sin and is substitutionary (takes the place of another) in character. When a sinner trusts in the sufficiency of Christ's atonement for salvation, the perfect righteousness of Christ (his sinless life of perfect obedience) is imputed (credited) to the sinner, and the just penalty for his sin is imputed to Christ. Jesus Christ thus takes

Chart 37

Evangelical Protestantism (continued)

Topic	Summary of View
Salvation (continued)	upon himself the sins of those who trust in him for salvation. Justification (one's right standing before God) is obtained by faith alone and is the result of God's unmerited grace. The resurrection of Jesus Christ from the dead completes, vindicates, and witnesses to the reality of salvation. The Holy Spirit regenerates the heart of all believers, enabling them to live a life of obedience to God's will and to grow in holiness (sanctification). There are divergent views concerning such issues as the basis of God's election of individuals to salvation, the extent of the atonement, precisely how God's grace operates in bringing about salvation, and the possibility of salvation being forfeited.
Afterlife	All human beings who have ever lived will undergo a physical resurrection after death and be judged by God on the basis of how they responded to Christ. Those who trusted in Christ for salvation will escape the just punishment for their sins and enter heaven, while those who did not will suffer the appropriate penalty at the hands of God. Heaven is a place of everlasting peace and fellowship with God. Disagreement exists as to whether hell is temporary or eternal in duration, as well as over the nature of hell. A broad range of views concerning the last times (eschatology) are held, including various positions on the nature and length of the millennium, the nature and timing of the return of Jesus Christ to earth, and the correct interpretive approach to the book of Revelation.

Distinctive Beliefs and Practices

Conversionism	Evangelicals insist that people are not Christians because of their ethnicity, family upbringing, church affiliation, or belief system. Instead, individuals must be changed by the Holy Spirit working through the gospel. Much preaching is designed to press listeners to make a personal decision for Christ, and much practical theology deals with the relationship of conversion to a Christian's spiritual growth.
Activism	Evangelicalism embraces activism, a corollary of the practice of spreading the gospel. This involves expending a great deal of time and energy engaging culture from a Christian perspective and striving to live out the social implications of the gospel. This activism extends to fields as diverse as politics, law, economics, philosophy, medicine, education, the arts, and business.
Biblicism	The Bible is the authoritative source of the gospel and the central defining standard of the Christian life. There is a respect for what the Bible teaches, together with a determination to obey its teachings.
Crucicentrism	Both in their theology and their devotional preoccupations, evangelicals see the atonement of Christ as the heart of the gospel. The cross of Christ is the most important component of Christian preaching and teaching.

Chart 37

Fundamentalist Protestantism

Topic	Facts
Current Data	Typically Fundamentalist Protestant churches are Baptist in doctrine, very conservative, and practice what they call "biblical separation" (from liberal and/or compromised churches). Probably the best-known fundamentalist is pastor Jerry Falwell (1933–). Prominent fundamentalist organizations and institutions include the Independent Fundamental Churches of America (IFCA); General Association of Regular Baptist Churches (GARBC); Bob Jones University in Greenville, South Carolina; Tennessee Temple University in Chattanooga, Tennessee; and Pensacola Christian College in Pensacola, Florida.
History	From the outset, Fundamentalist Protestantism exhibited two related but ultimately divergent strains: Baptist and Presbyterian. In 1883 a Bible conference, attended mainly by Baptists, was held in Niagara Falls, New York, with the stated purpose to set forth the particular doctrines of Christianity that are non-negotiable. It had been convened because of the growing influence of Liberal Protestantism in churches, seminaries, and the larger culture. Around the same time, two leading conservative Presbyterian professors at Princeton Theological Seminary in New Jersey, Archibald Alexander Hodge (1823–86) and Benjamin Breckinridge Warfield (1851–1921), were busy, through their teaching and writing, defending historic Christianity from the onslaught of liberal theology. Both camps believed it was incumbent upon "Bible-believing" Christians to respond in a vigorous way to the inroads of Liberal Protestantism into historic Christianity and American society.

In the years that followed, fundamentalists of all stripes participated in a number of coordinated activities designed to recapture the church and the culture from theological liberals. These included: (1) engaging in political maneuvers designed to take back positions of authority in Protestant organizations, institutions, and missionary societies that were then controlled by theological liberals; (2) supporting a wide range of legislative and judicial efforts to enforce conservative Protestant morality in the United States; and (3) seeking to ban public schools from instructing students concerning Darwinian evolution.

During the first quarter of the 20th century, several pieces of "fundamentalist" literature were published that further defined and shaped the issues: the Bible study notes of Cyrus I. Scofield (1843–1921) in 1909; the first four volumes of *The Fundamentals*, edited by Reuben A. Torrey (1856–1928), also in 1909; and *Christianity and Liberalism* by J. Gresham Machen (1881-1937) in 1923. In 1925, the Scopes "Monkey" Trial took place in Dayton, Tennessee, pitting attorney William Jennings Bryan (1860–1925) against lawyer Clarence Darrow (1857–1938). This trial was to decide whether a Tennessee law forbidding the teaching of evolutionary theory in public schools was constitutional. Though the court ruled to uphold the law, the slant of the media coverage of the trial brought widespread disrepute to fundamentalism, and the movement subsequently withdrew from the American public sphere. |

Chart 38

Fundamentalist Protestantism (continued)

Topics	Facts
History (continued)	Since the late 1970s, fundamentalists have embraced political involvement and the "electronic church" in their fight against threats to their worldview that include secular humanism, Communism, feminism, abortion on demand, homosexual rights, and the judicial ban on prayer in public schools. They have continued to oppose the teaching of biological evolution in public schools and have sought to have scientific creationism taught there as well. Americans who describe themselves as fundamentalists (estimated by some to be 25 percent of the adult U.S. population) have become a political bloc to be reckoned with. During the 1980s they comprised a large portion of the New Christian Right that helped put Ronald Reagan in the White House. The Moral Majority, founded in 1979 by Baptist pastor Jerry Falwell, was the most visible example of this new trend in the 1980s. Currently, the most prominent such group is the Christian Coalition, headed by Roberta Combs (Pat Robertson and Ralph Reed were prominent past leaders). Moderate fundamentalists and conservative evangelicals, such as those in the Southern Baptist Convention, continue to forge new political alliances. Attempting to separate fundamentalists and evangelicals is difficult since they share similar views and concerns regarding social issues, but divide over matters of doctrine and the question of "biblical separation."
Summary of Beliefs	Christian Fundamentalism began in the Fundamentalist-Modernist debates of the early 20th century, the term itself referring to the fundamentals of the Christian faith, such as the inspiration of the Bible, the virgin birth of Christ, and the sacrificial value of the death of Christ on the cross. Those who held to these fundamentals of Christianity, though, divided between what are today called evangelicalism and fundamentalism, with the latter known for its convictions against cultural decadence and apostate churches and persons. Fundamentalism may be summarized by its strong adherence to five basic affirmations: 1. The inerrancy and infallibility of the Bible 2. The virgin birth and deity of Jesus Christ 3. The substitutionary nature of Christ's atonement 4. The literal resurrection of the body of Jesus 5. The future physical return of Christ Among other doctrines staunchly defended are the work of the Holy Spirit in salvation, a historical fall of Adam and Eve, and justification by faith alone. In addition to these basics doctrines, views largely ascribed to by evangelicals, is the issue of separation from worldly lifestyles and from apostasy. Nonetheless, the above five points constitute the doctrinal foundation of the fundamentalist movement.

Chart 38

Fundamentalist Protestantism (continued)

Topic	Summary of View
Creation	God created the cosmos *ex nihilo* (out of nothing) and everything depends on him for its existence and preservation in being. God fashioned every part of the universe, including the earth and every form of life therein, over a period of six 24-hour days. Holding to alternative views of the age of the earth, the length of the days of creation, or the origin of the universe and life are viewed as compromise with apostasy. The earth and its inhabitants are less than 10,000 years old. God did not use evolution as a means of creating life, especially with regard to human beings. Prior to Adam and Eve's fall into sin, there was no physical death. The Great Flood described in the Bible was a global catastrophe that destroyed all life except the passengers on Noah's ark.
Scripture and Authority	Every word of the entire Bible (Old and New Testament Scriptures) is divinely inspired. The Bible is supremely authoritative and without error regarding everything of which it speaks, whether doctrine, morals, history, or science. The accounts of supernatural events given in Scripture are literally true. The true faithful church has been granted the gift of the Holy Spirit, who leads the church into truth and obedience to God's will according to the Scriptures. The Bible is meant to be interpreted in a strictly literal fashion, though figurative language is understood to be present in expressing literal truth; other approaches to biblical interpretation invariably lead to compromise or apostasy. The church is obligated to understand the Scriptures to the best of its ability, to believe what it says, and to obey its commands. Normal practice is to ignore or downplay most interpretations of the Bible that have been set forth during the history of the church, instead leaving biblical interpretation as a matter for each autonomous local church to decide for itself (though most self-described fundamentalist churches agree on most major points of doctrine).
God	Affirms the historic doctrines of the Trinity and Jesus Christ as fully divine and fully human, yet does not look to the classic creeds as the basis for such beliefs. Instead, each local church creates an independent "statement of faith" with its own formulation of the doctrines of God and Christ. The Holy Spirit is God in the fullest sense. The attributes of God include independence, eternality, perfect goodness, unlimited power, perfect knowledge, holiness, graciousness, and wrath against sin.
Mankind	Mankind is created in the image of God and possesses both a body and a soul. Mankind came into being through a direct supernatural act of divine creation and is qualitatively different from all other forms of life. Mankind was created in holiness and in right relationship with God, and was meant to worship and serve him. Mankind was given the stewardship over God's creation. Human beings are totally reliant on God for every facet of their existence.
Sin	Adam and Eve sinned by choice, voluntarily transgressing God's command. This act of rebellion and assertion of personal autonomy was instigated by the Devil. As a result of their disobedience, a universal moral pollution and strong proclivity to sin was passed on to all of Adam and Eve's progeny. This sinful nature shows itself in lawless actions, wicked attitudes, and false doctrine. Pain, sickness, and death have resulted from the fall and are now an inescapable part of a fallen world in which the Devil continues to wreak havoc.

Chart 38

Salvation	God has done all that is necessary to accomplish mankind's salvation. In the blood sacrifice of Jesus Christ on the cross at Calvary, a full atonement for sin has been provided by God. This propitiation acts to avert God's righteous wrath against sin, vicariously satisfying his just demand that sins against him be atoned for before he can bestow mercy upon sinners. This salvation, which is found in Christ alone, can be appropriated only by simple faith. When a sinner believes, God reckons the perfect righteousness of Christ to the sinner; the grace of God alone is sufficient to reconcile a person to God. Jesus' resurrection from the dead completes and attests to the reality of this salvation. The Holy Spirit convicts the hearts of unbelievers and they then must believe to be converted. Persevering in holiness (sanctification) is incumbent upon every believer with the help of the Holy Spirit. God ensures that everyone who believes in him will be spared his wrath on the day of judgment, when all will be judged according to their works. Fundamentalists generally believe in what is called "eternal security."
Afterlife	The return of Jesus Christ to earth is imminent. He will soon return to rapture away his saints before the great tribulation, after which Jesus and his saints will return once more to establish a 1,000-year millennial kingdom. At the end of this millennium, Satan and all who then oppose Jesus and his kingdom will be destroyed in the battle of Armageddon. Next there will be a physical resurrection of all people throughout history and Christ will judge each one. Those who were loyal to Christ and placed their faith in him will enter into a new heaven and a new earth, which will replace the previous universe. All vestiges of sin will be purged from those who are saved (glorification). Those who rejected Christ and continued in sin will be cast into a hell of literal, everlasting fire, where God will enact just retribution for their sins against him.

Distinctive Beliefs and Practices

KJV Only	Some fundamentalists stridently and tenaciously hold to the belief that only the King James version of the Bible is the true Word of God. All other translations are said to be inaccurate, unreliable, and/or the result of liberal or apostate translators. Some even believe that the KJV may be used to correct the "corrupted" Greek manuscripts.
Pretribulation Rapture	Most fundamentalists adhere to what is often termed the Pretribulation Rapture doctrine. This teaching asserts that Jesus will return to earth at any moment to receive his people unto himself. In the rapture, all believers become incorruptible and immortal when their mortal bodies and their spirits are joined. This will be accomplished instantly. After meeting him in the air, believers remain with Jesus until the tribulation on earth is completed.
The Anti-Christ	In the years immediately preceding the return of Christ, a figure called "Antichrist" will increasingly dominate world religious and political affairs, bringing about the existence of a One World Government and a One World Church, both of which will persecute faithful believers.
Biblical Separation	True believers are obligated to separate themselves from compromising and apostate "Christian" churches and organizations, impure social influences, and all forms of immorality. This means refusing to cooperate with Christian groups who do not share the same core doctrines and ethical standards and disassociating from all "worldly" habits and practices.

Chart 38

Pentecostal-Charismatic Protestantism

Topic	Facts
Current Data	Some recent commentators have dubbed Pentecostalism as "World Evangelicalism" because of its tremendous and rapid growth over the last couple decades. Pentecostalism has garnered huge numbers of converts in places like Africa, Central America, and South America. If its current rate of growth continues, Pentecostalism will eclipse Roman Catholicism as the biggest Christian group in many regions of the Third World, especially Latin America. World membership is estimated at 132 million; membership in the United States is estimated at 6.7 million. Pentecostalism includes denominations such as Assemblies of God, United Pentecostal Church International, Church of God of Prophecy, and International Church of the Foursquare Gospel. There are also many closely related Charismatic organizations like the Vineyard International Consortium and the Maranatha movement (though Maranatha International Federation of Churches disbanded in 1990). Two of the most well-known Pentecostals in the United States are televangelist and political activist Pat Robertson (1930–) and faith healer Oral Roberts (1918–).
History	The roots of the movement now known as Pentecostalism can be traced back to 1901 in Topeka, Kansas, according to most Pentecostalism historians, though some others would identify some small Pentecostal types of movements in the latter part of the 19th century. In Topeka, at Bethel Bible School, theology instructor Charles Fox Parham (1873–1929) taught his students that they needed to receive a special outpouring of the Holy Spirit so they could "speak in tongues." Five years later, a massive Pentecostal revival occurred in Los Angeles. Led by preacher William Joseph Seymour (1870–1922), the Asuza Street revival lasted three years and drew people from around the globe. Another major figure in the continuing spread of Pentecostalism was itinerant evangelist and faith healer Aimee Semple McPherson (1890–1944), who founded the Foursquare Gospel church of Los Angeles in 1923. A. J. Tomlinson (1865–1943) was active in Pentecostal church planting and organization during the first several decades of the 20th century, and from his work came what is now a variety of the denominations known as Church of God, or a similar name.
	During these formative years, Pentecostalism was comprised mainly of the poor and uneducated. However, during the 1950s, Pentecostal groups (generally known as Charismatics), such as the Full Gospel Business Men's Fellowship, began to take Pentecostalism into the mainstream of American society. In the 1960s and 1970s, elements of Pentecostalism made their way into a number of mainline Protestant denominations, the Roman Catholic Church, and the Eastern Orthodox Church. In the 1980s, a loose association of neo-Pentecostal (also called Charismatic) and evangelical groups called the Third Wave was formed at Fuller Theological Seminary, largely due to the efforts of professors C. Peter Wagner (1930–) and John Wimber (1934–1997). Pentecostalism continues to grow, adapt, and take on different forms in a variety of cultures around the world.

Chart 39

Pentecostal-Charismatic Protestantism (continued)

Topic	Facts
Summary of Beliefs	Pentecostalism-Charismaticism strongly emphasizes the role of the Holy Spirit in the Christian life. In particular, it emphasizes the gifts of the Spirit, most notably the ability to "speak in tongues" (to talk in unknown or angelic languages). It is also believed that God communicates directly with Christians today using a variety of means. The lordship of Christ is a central concept. Praise is a major aspect of worship and is expressed vocally and physically. Pentecostal churches have a strong end times emphasis, believing that we are living in the last days before the second coming of Christ. Other beliefs include obtaining spiritual power through the Spirit, baptism in the Spirit, victory over sin via the Spirit, and engaging in "spiritual warfare," sometimes understood as literally battling demons who reside in an invisible, spiritual realm.

Topic	Summary of View
Creation	God created the universe out of nothing by an act of awesome power. The Spirit of God played an important role in this creation. God rules and reigns over all of creation, and creation is a living testimony to his love and wisdom. The Spirit of God gives everything life, renewing and sustaining every part of the created world. God created everything in a six-day time period thousands of years ago (though some would differ on this); scientific theories that claim otherwise are viewed with suspicion. Prior to Adam and Eve's fall into sin, the created world was without sin, death, disease, or flaw of any kind.
Scripture and Authority	The Holy Spirit inspired the writers to ensure that the Bible would be God's infallible Word. The Bible (Hebrew and Christian Scriptures) is inerrant and, to most Pentecostals, is the final standard by which all conduct, statements of faith, and church practices are tested. In some cases, however, some subordinate the Bible to the personal-experiential authority of the Holy Spirit and Spirit-inspired, extrabiblical revelation. This perspective would usually come from those Pentecostals who believe that God speaks just as authoritatively through modern prophecy in the contemporary church as he does through Scripture, though arguably the issues spoken of in this manner usually relate to matters of worship or personal life rather than to doctrinal issues. Often for Pentecostals the experiential is given precedence over the intellectual: the Spirit speaking directly to a person or church can trump written Scripture, and the Christian's written source of authority (the Bible) must be understood in light of the living source of authority (the Holy Spirit), who is the source of Christian unity. Doctrinal unity is downplayed and spiritual unity is fostered, though this tends to be the case more in Charismatic churches than in Pentecostal groups.
God	Most affirm the historic doctrine of the Trinity encapsulated in the ecumenical creeds (though the United Pentecostal Church and a few small groups officially espouse modalism, wherein God is said to be one in person and nature, manifesting himself in different forms at various times and places). The incarnate Jesus

Chart 39

Pentecostal-Charismatic Protestantism (continued)

Topic	Summary of View
God (continued)	Christ and his ministry of preaching, teaching, healing, casting out demons, etc., is central. The Holy Spirit is given a place of special prominence and given more attention than is given by many other Christian groups. God is experienced more than he is understood, and he can be understood in a fresh way that supersedes or transcends the dry, formal statements of Scripture. God is loving, merciful, all-powerful, all knowing, all-present, holy, eternal, and sovereign.
Mankind	Mankind is created in God's image and likeness, having a body and a spirit. Unique among God's created beings, man was made from the dust of the ground, after which God breathed the breath of life into him. The Spirit of God gives man his life, movement, and being. Mankind was created in holiness and originally enjoyed a full, loving relationship with God. God intended man to praise, serve, and obey him in all things. Mankind was commissioned as caretaker of God's creation. God gave mankind a free will, which all can use for good or for evil. Moreover, because of free will, people are able to reject the gospel and the call of God to salvation.
Sin	Sin is primarily voluntary transgression. Adam and Eve sinned against God by a free decision, though the Devil tempted them to do so. The fall left Adam, Eve, and all their descendents in a state of spiritual death and with a strong inclination to disregard God's laws. The Fall corrupted the natural world as well: sickness, suffering, hardship, and death are now universal experiences, though they are contrary to God's original intent in creation.
Salvation	The role of the cross of Christ is central: one must be washed in the blood of the Lamb and receive the power of that blood in order to be saved. Christ's sacrificial atonement is necessary for one's sins to be covered and for one to have peace with a holy God. Jesus Christ won a great victory over the Devil and the evil angels (the principalities and powers) through his willing death on the cross and glorious resurrection from the grave. Though three of the four foremost doctrines of the Reformation (faith alone, grace alone, and Christ alone) are affirmed by many groups, some groups give human works a prominent role in their doctrine of salvation. Salvation is primarily something that is experienced, not set forth in legal, judicial, or covenantal terms. Speaking in tongues is an evidence of salvation for some, but the infilling of the Spirit for most Pentecostals. There is emphasis on "full sanctification" in holiness Pentecostal denominations and the role of the Holy Spirit in living a victorious Christian life. Total victory over sin is possible with the aid of the Spirit for holiness Pentecostals. For most, man can choose to live without sin for periods of time.

Chart 39

Facts	Summary of View
Afterlife	The return of Jesus Christ and his judgment of all peoples usually are thought to be imminent, and before a time of tribulation, though a few groups hold to an optimistic, postmillennial view of Christ's second advent. At the end of history there will be a physical resurrection of all human beings, followed by a great judgment in which the evil deeds of all will be exposed and subjected to divine judgment. Those who persevered in following Christ will be saved, and those who continued in rebellion against him will be damned. Heaven is a place of great rejoicing and endless praise of Father, Son, and Spirit; hell is an abode of eternal wretchedness and misery.

	Distinctive Beliefs and Practices
Spirit Baptism	Spirit baptism (also called "The Second Blessing") occurs when the Holy Spirit is poured into a willing believer in a manner that displays the awesome power of the Holy Spirit. When this happens, the believer is said to be "filled with the Spirit." This demonstration of the Spirit's power often is attended by unusual phenomena such as "speaking in tongues" (Pentecostals maintain that this is always the case) and illnesses or injuries being cured. It is said to be different from and unrelated to baptism by immersion in water, and cannot occur until after the person has come to faith in Jesus Christ. Some Pentecostals frequently contend that persons who have experienced baptism in the Spirit are empowered to live lives free of sin or at least to be very holy in their conduct. More modest in their claims, Charismatics typically say that Spirit baptism does much to enhance the believer's walk with the Lord.
"Jesus Only" Baptism	A minority of groups practice water baptism in the name of Jesus only, rejecting the traditional baptismal formula of Father, Son, and Holy Spirit. These groups maintain that God is not Trinity.
Worship	Exuberant and uninhibited worship practices are common: self-prostration, loud clapping, raising of hands, and dancing "in the Spirit" are among them.
Spirit Revelation	God reveals his will through various modes of direct divine communication: "words of wisdom," prophecy, speaking in tongues and interpretation of tongues, visions, dreams, and "inner leadings."
Glossolalia	Glossolalia ("speaking in tongues") is understood somewhat differently by various groups. Some believe that the Holy Spirit allows the speaker to talk in a foreign human language with which he or she is unfamiliar. Others believe that the Holy Spirit enables believers to make utterances in an angelic language that can only be understood by the Spirit himself. Pentecostals often insist that if a person is saved, then he or she will be able to have this experience. Charismatics usually teach that glossolalia is highly beneficial for those who experience it, but that one can be a Christian without ever having that experience. Practitioners point to the book of Acts as evidence that this practice should be occurring in the church today.

Chart 39

Christian Creeds and Councils

Creed or Council	Summary
Apostles' Creed	The content of this creed underwent development over nearly 800 years of church history, yet every doctrine it proclaims is of apostolic origin, with its earliest mention in the 2nd century of the church. The creed summarizes about a dozen of the most basic elements of Christian doctrine. More Christian denominations subscribe to it than to any other creed or confession.
Nicene (Constantinopolitan) Creed	In the early 4th century, disagreements concerning the Trinity and the person of Christ threatened to tear apart the Christian church. In particular, a theologian named Arius (256–336) was teaching that Christ (the Son) was not of the same divine substance as the Father. In response to these doctrinal disputes, Emperor Constantine (272–337) convened an ecumenical council in AD 325 in the city of Nicaea (located in modern-day Turkey). A large majority of the bishops in attendance drafted and gave their assent to a creed that summarized the views of Athanasius (298–373), an Egyptian bishop. The creed condemned the views of Arius as heretical while affirming the two natures (and full deity) of Christ and what has come to be known as the doctrine of the Trinity (there are three, coequal persons who share one divine nature and constitute one God). In AD 381, another church council met in Constantinople (called Nicaea II by many). The bishops in attendance approved a revised and expanded form of the creed, which is now called the Nicene Creed. This creed included a fuller statement on the Holy Spirit, almost entirely lacking from the council's work in AD 325.
Council of Ephesus	This council met in the city of Ephesus (located in modern-day southeastern Turkey) in AD 431. Assembled by Emperor Theodosius II (401–50), this council debated and came to a resolution concerning the two natures of Christ. During the council, it was alleged that Nestorius (c. 386–451), a bishop from Constantinople, had been teaching that Jesus was composed of two distinct persons, one human and one divine. (Nestorius denied this charge.) The council reaffirmed the teaching that Christ is one person with two natures, and asserted that the Virgin Mary could properly be called "the Mother of God" (*theotokos*) since the human Jesus was in fact a person who was also God.
Definition of Chalcedon	This statement was adopted at the Fourth Ecumenical Council at Chalcedon (located in modern-day Turkey) in AD 451. It was a response to several unbiblical views regarding the person of Christ that had resurfaced, including Apollinarianism (Christ had a human body and a divine mind) and Eutychianism (the divine nature of Christ dominated the human nature), both of which were species of Monophysitism (Christ had only one nature). The council's conclusion firmly established the position that Christ is one person who possesses two natures, one human and one divine. It also upheld Jesus' virgin birth and sinless life.

Chart 40

Christian Creeds and Councils (continued)

Creed or Council	Summary
Athanasian Creed	Formulated in the 5th century, the Athanasian Creed provides a brief, clear statement of two core doctrines of historic Christianity: the Trinity and the incarnation. Although named after Athanasius (298–373), bishop of Alexandria (Egypt), it was not written by him. Its language closely resembles that of Ambrose (c. 340–397), bishop of Milan.
Canons of the Council of Orange	During the 5th century, two prominent Christian theologians, Augustine (354–430) and Pelagius (c. 360–435), debated the extent to which fallen human beings are able to procure salvation and the corresponding role of God's grace in salvation. The Council of Orange was a definitive response to this controversy. It addressed (and renounced) the semi-Pelagian contention that fallen human beings, despite possessing a sinful nature, nevertheless have the ability to cooperate with God in salvation.
Statement of Faith of the Third Council of Constantinople	Held in AD 681, this council produced a statement that fleshed out the theological implications of the Definition of Chalcedon. The statement concluded that Christ has two wills, which correspond to his two natures, yet which act in perfect harmony.

Chart 40

Christian Holy Days

Holiday	Time of Year	Observance
Ash Wednesday	Fourth day of Lent	Reminds participants of their mortality and their need to repent of their sins in preparation for the rest of Lent. Somber atmosphere. Primarily observed by Roman Catholics.
Palm Sunday	Sunday before Easter	Recalls Jesus' triumphant entry into Jerusalem in fulfillment of Old Testament prophecy. Marks the beginning of Holy Week (the week before Easter that includes Maundy Thursday and Holy Saturday).
Good Friday	Friday before Easter	Recalls Jesus' suffering and death on the cross. Somber atmosphere. Anticipates Easter Sunday.
Easter	Final Sunday of Lent, falls between March 23 and April 17	Commemorates Jesus' resurrection from the dead and subsequent appearances to his followers. Joyful atmosphere. Originally associated with the spring equinox. Today, often incorporates themes of springtime. (Though not widely observed, some churches also commemorate Jesus' ascension into heaven on Ascension Thursday, 39 days after Easter Sunday.)
Day of Pentecost	Seven weeks after Easter Sunday	Recalls the visitation of the Holy Spirit to the group of Christians described in Acts 2. Originally a Jewish festival day. Not widely observed.
Reformation Day	October 31	Remembrance of Martin Luther posting his 95 theses on the door of the church in Wittenberg, Germany, in 1517. Observed only by some Protestants, usually those in the Lutheran or Reformed traditions.
Christmas	December 25	Celebrates the birth of Jesus Christ. Joyful atmosphere. Marks the end of the Advent season, which begins four Sundays before Christmas. Originally associated with the winter solstice; now often associated with cultural traditions other than the celebration of the birth of Jesus Christ.

Chart 41

Christian Scriptures

Categories	Books	Acceptance
Old Testament		
Law	Genesis, Exodus, Leviticus, Numbers, Deuteronomy	All branches of Christianity
Historical Books	Joshua, Judges, Ruth, 1 and 2 Samuel, 1 and 2 Kings, 1 and 2 Chronicles, Ezra, Nehemiah, Esther	All branches of Christianity
Poetic and Wisdom Literature	Job, Psalms, Proverbs, Ecclesiastes, Song of Songs	All branches of Christianity
Prophets	Isaiah, Jeremiah, Lamentations, Ezekiel, Daniel, Hosea, Joel, Amos, Obadiah, Jonah, Micah, Nahum, Habakkuk, Zephaniah, Haggai, Zechariah, Malachi	All branches of Christianity
Deuterocanonical	Baruch, Judith, Ecclesiasticus (Sirach), Tobit, Wisdom of Solomon, 1 and 2 Maccabees, additions to Esther and Daniel*	Roman Catholicism
Apocryphal	The deuterocanonical books plus 1 and 2 Esdras, 3 and 4 Maccabees, Letter of Jeremiah, Psalms of Solomon**	Eastern Orthodoxy
New Testament		
Gospels	Matthew, Mark, Luke, John	All branches of Christianity
History	Acts	All branches of Christianity
Correspondence (Letters)	Romans, 1 and 2 Corinthians, Galatians, Ephesians, Philippians, Colossians, 1 and 2 Thessalonians, 1 and 2 Timothy, Titus, Philemon, Hebrews, James, 1 and 2 Peter, 1, 2, and 3 John, Jude	All branches of Christianity
Apocalypse	Revelation	All branches of Christianity

Note: Ultradispensationalism (Bullingerism) accepts only the prison epistles of the apostle Paul: Ephesians, Philippians, Colossians, 1 and 2 Timothy, and Titus.

* These include Susanna, Bel and the Dragon, and the Song of the Three Children. Other apocryphal (but non-deuterocanonical) books acknowledged by Roman Catholicism include Azariah, Letter of Jeremiah, Prayer of Manasseh, 1 and 2 Esdras, and Psalm 151.

** For the purposes of this chart, "Eastern Orthodoxy" is defined as those church bodies in communion with the bishop of Constantinople. Other Orthodox groups have somewhat different lists of holy books, and even the Eastern Orthodox list admits some minor variations. This may be because the Eastern Orthodox Church tends to be less concerned than the Roman Catholic Church and traditional Protestant churches with precisely defining the canon of Scripture.

Chart 42

Timeline of Islam

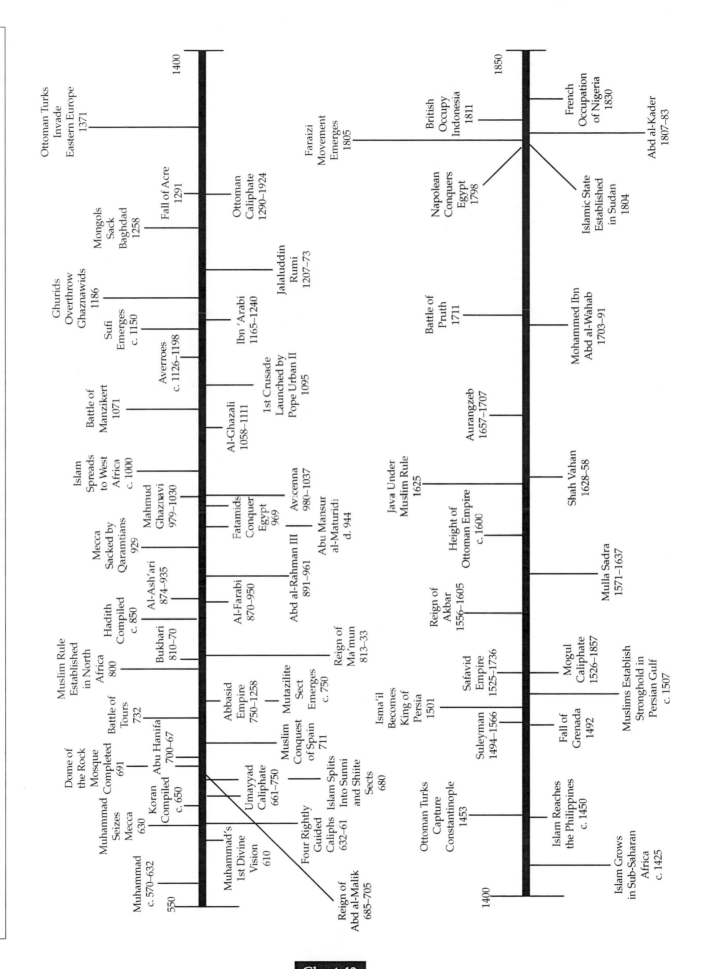

Chart 43

Timeline of Islam (continued)

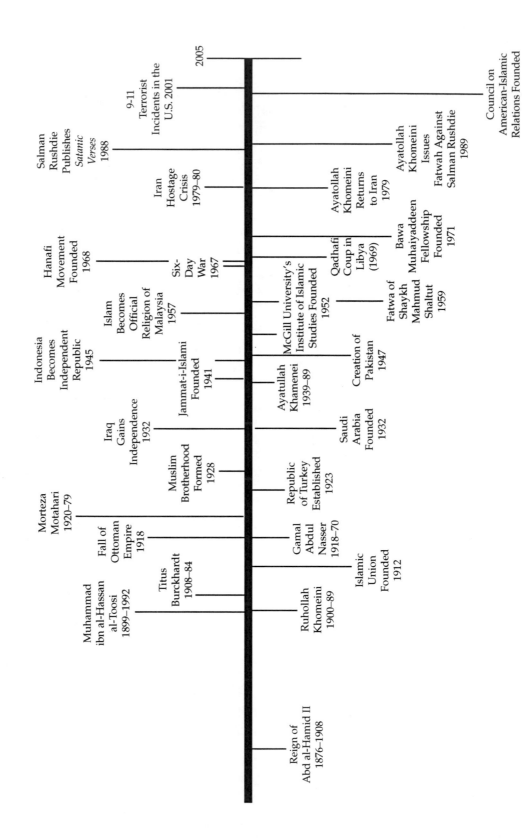

Chart 43

Islam

Topic	Facts
Current Data	Islam is the fastest growing religion in the world, though that rapid growth is largely through birthrate. There are 1.3 billion Muslims worldwide, comprising 23 percent of the world's population. Eighteen percent of Muslims (234 million) reside in various Arab nations, and 20 percent (260 million) live in sub-Saharan Africa. The world's largest Muslim community (over 100 million) is in Indonesia. Nearly 2 million Muslims are in the United States, though some argue that there are several million more. Significant Islamic populations also are in Europe, the former Soviet Union, and South America.
History	Muhammad was born in Arabia in c. AD 570 in what was largely a polytheistic pagan society, though small numbers of believers followed Judaism, Christianity, or Zoroastrianism. Muhammad was married to a wealthy widow named Khadija. Fifteen years after his marriage, when he was 40, he experienced his first prophetic call while meditating in a cave near Mecca. Other revelations followed. At first, Muhammad told only family members and friends about his experiences but finally began speaking publicly. His teachings against idolatry and for socioeconomic equality were at first rejected by most, but over a period of several years he gained a large following from the lower classes of society.
	Muhammad's insistence in a belief in one God came into direct conflict with the paganism of Mecca, centered in the shrine called the Ka'aba, since the sale of idols played an important religious and economic function within the city. Because of this resistance and persecution, Muhammad and his followers in AD 622 moved secretly to the town of Yathrib, which became known as Medina, "the City of the Prophet." After defending Medina against several attacks by tribal groups from Mecca, Muhammad finally conquered Mecca. Arabia became almost entirely Islamic in AD 630.
	After Muhammand's death on June 8, 632, Muhammad's father-in-law Abu Bakr (c. 573–634) became the caliph of the recently created Islamic state and united all of the tribes of Arabia under Islamic rule. He and the next three caliphs, called the Four Rightly Guided Caliphs, were successful in spreading Islam from Persia through northern Africa. Ali ibn Abi Talib (598–661), the third caliph, came from a different tribe than Muhammad and the former two caliphs, which led to a major division within Islam, between Sunnis and Shi'ites, that continues to the present.
	From its inception in the early 7th century, within three generations Islam had gone from obscurity to ruling over the largest empire up to that time, though the attempt to conquer the Byzantine Empire failed. Much of the world that was conquered was Jewish or Christian, and the people were allowed to continue in their faith as long as they were submissive to Islamic religious law and paid a protection tax called *jiszya*. Those who were not Jewish or Christian, however, were made to convert to Islam or be killed.
	In-fighting between various rival Islamic clans, with different emirates seeking independence, brought dissolution to the vast empire. But under the Seljuk Turks, Islam began to expand again. After the defeat of the Byzantines at the Battle of Manzikert (AD 1071), the Roman Catholic Church began crusades to reconquer the

Chart 44

Islam (continued)

Topic	Facts
History (continued)	Holy Land, particularly Jerusalem. Islamic rule of the Middle East suffered setbacks during the Crusades and from the conquests of the Mongols, but finally reached new heights under the Ottomans.
	Though Islamic warriors were not successful in conquering all of Europe, great numbers of Muslims have migrated to historically Christian countries, so that nations such as France and England now have sizable Muslim populations.
	Because of the importance of oil to the world and the fact that the Arabian peninsula has an abundance, Muslims have been able to use this precious commodity to finance the growth of Islam in the West.
Summary of Beliefs	The Arabic word *Islam* means "submission to the will of God." The first and most fundamental pillar of Islam is that there is no God other than Allah (strict monotheism) and that his final, authoritative messenger was Muhammad. The Koran is a holy book that reveals the will of Allah and is his final written message to mankind, teaching the faithful that none is worthy of worship but Allah, and that all people are required to submit unconditionally to his law.

Topic	Summary of View
Creation	Allah created the universe out of nothing. He, then, is before this creation and does not need anything in creation. Allah, however, has made his existence evident within creation. Humans only create secondarily from what Allah has already created.
Scripture and Authority	According to Islamic beliefs, Allah has revealed his message to mankind through written scriptures called the Koran (Qur'an). Over a period of 23 years he revealed to Muhammad this message and had it recorded verbatim in Arabic. Muslims believe that the Koran is the only divinely given scripture in history and that it is preserved without any change whatsoever since the first copy was written. Since it was verbatim in Arabic and not merely thoughts from Allah that human authors penned as they saw fit, it cannot be properly translated into any other language. There are five types of revelation found in the Koran, namely, matters about inanimate objects, about animals lower than man, directions to humans in general, to prophets specifically, and to angels. The manner of divine revelation to humans came in three forms: hasty suggestions (*wahy*), dreams (*ru'ya*), and revelation that is recited (*wahy matluww*). In addition to the Koran, there are three sources of wisdom relied upon by many Muslims, though they contain corruption, the *Tawrat, Zabur,* and *Injil.*
	The word *Koran* (*Qur'an*) (the only infallible source of knowledge of Allah) comes from the Arabic root meaning "to read or recite," expressing the manner it which it is believed to have come to Muhammad. Allah is said to have given the Koran to Muhammad through a monologue. The text of the Koran is not only a word-for-word final communication from Allah but is also engraved on eternally existing tablets. Muhammad received the Koran from the angel Gabriel (Jibreel) during three distinct periods: the Meccan Period (611–615), the Second Meccan Period (616–622), and the Medina Period (623–32).

Chart 44

Islam (continued)

Topic	Summary of View
God	Strict monotheism is a fundamental tenet of Islam. Muslims make a special point, in view of the contact with Christianity, that Allah is by himself and has no son; there is no Trinity. To advocate that Allah has partners or works in conjunction with other gods is the gravest sin. Allah is known by many names, usually listed as numbering 99, but the primary name for God in Islam is Allah, which is the basic generic name for deity. Allah's four primary attributive names are Rabb (Lord), Rahnam (Beneficent), Rahim (Merciful), and Malik (Master).
Mankind	Human beings have dignity, but are not made in the image of God, since the nature of God and the nature of human beings are utterly different. Allah made the first human beings from the dust of the earth and breathed life into them. Humans were created to live in unconditional surrender to the will of Allah.
Sin	The doctrine of Original Sin is denied; human beings do not have sinful natures. People are sinless until they rebel against Allah. People should not behave according to their lower (animal) nature. Instead, they should use their free will to act in total submission to Allah.
Salvation	One must believe the teachings of the Koran and obey Allah's commands and do his will. Islam does not recognize any work by Allah for the benefit of delivering Muslims from their sins. Persons must atone for their own sins by sincere confession and good works. Allah will judge each person by the balance of good or evil that he or she has done (*mizan*). Yet even the most pious Muslim is not guaranteed entrance into paradise; only the martyr can be assured of this. Additionally, Allah is under no compulsion to be merciful.
Afterlife	Like Christianity, Islam believes that there will be a future resurrecton of the body and a time of judgment. There are two possible destinations for humans upon death. Faithful Muslims will receive paradise and all others will go to hell. Paradise is a place of great bliss, often thought to be a beautiful garden. Here all the desires of faithful Muslims are fulfilled, especially those of men, who are rewarded with beautiful young virgins. On the other hand, hell is a place of eternal fiery torment.

Chart 44

Islam (continued)

Distinctive Beliefs and Practices

Theophanies	A theophany is a visible manifestation of God to human beings. There are three theophanies in Islam: The Distant One, The Cold Judge, and The Hater. The Distant One: Islamic religion has no concept of Allah as a benevolent or intimate God. The belief is of Allah as master and humans as servants. Titles for God that seem to convey a sense of mercy relate to an absence of death or peril for the follower of Islam. The Cold Judge: The Muslim comes to Allah with uncertainty as his life is weighed on the scales to determine his final destiny. The Muslim can only hope for mercy from Allah based on good deeds and acts of charity done during one's life. The Hater: There is no need for Muslims to evangelize the non-Muslim world since Allah is said to "hate" the infidel (*kafir*), the non-Muslim. The mission of Islam is conquest, often by means of the sword, with infidels to be defeated, silenced, or expelled.
Jihad	As used by Muslims, the word *jihad* most commonly means "striving" and refers to the attempt to rid oneself of debased behavior or proclivities and to steadfastly persevere in achieving moral excellence. Since Islam does not confine itself to the good of the individual, but extends to the welfare of society and humanity in general, an individual cannot continue improving in isolation from what happens in the community or the world at large. The Koran commands not just Muslims, but all human beings, to do what is good and abstain from what is evil, since all people are meant to obey Allah.
Five Pillars	1. The Confession (*shahadah*): To believe in one's heart that there is no God but Allah and to acknowledge that Muhammad is his Messenger. 2. Prayers (*salah*): Muslims are to pray prescribed prayers during five specific periods of each day. 3. Fasting During Ramadan (*sawm*): This fast, practiced during a month-long period, is accompanied by devotional activities. The daily fast occurs only during daylight hours, so Muslims regularly eat their fill in the evening and early morning. 4. Giving to the Poor (*zakah*): This giving depends on the amount assessed on each Muslim's nonessential property. The money is used to help the needy and to finance construction of mosques, religious schools, and hospitals. 5. Pilgrimage to Mecca (*hajj*): Each Muslim male is expected to make at least one pilgrimage to Mecca, in Saudi Arabia, the birthplace of Muhammad. The journey occurs during the first five days of Dhul-Hijjah, the 12th month of the Islamic calendar. In Mecca the pilgrim visits the famous Ka'aba (in the time before Muhammad, a pagan shrine), which is a rectangular stone building in the center of the courtyard of the Sacred Mosque. The Ka'aba (Sacred House) is draped in black and was purportedly built by Abraham.

Chart 44

Comparison of Beliefs within Islam

	Scripture and Authority	God	Mankind
Sunni	Muhammad is the chosen Prophet and final Messenger of Allah. The Koran is Allah's very word, having come from him in an unmediated way. It contains his unquestionable teaching and decrees.	Allah is One and there is no god beside him; neither is any creature at all like him. He is the eternal Creator, incomprehensible, omnipotent, and sovereign.	Every human being is composed of both body and soul. The ultimate aim of human beings should be to worship and obey Allah, placing oneself in complete submission to his will.
Shi'ite	The Koran is rigidly interpreted and its teachings are strictly adhered to. Twelve heavenly imams (perfect teachers) led the Shi'ites in succession.	Allah is One, utterly unique, eternal, all-powerful, and above every need. He is above any and all descriptions that his creatures might devise and employ in referring to him.	Humans have no choice but to follow religion, which is a path God has provided to reach him. Those who do not follow the way of Islam are headed for damnation because they have neglected the purpose for which they were created.
Sufi	The secret meaning of the Koran takes precedence over its surface meaning. Mystical experience is primary; Muhammad's personal religious experience is also highly significant. The Koran provides instruction for both serious adherents and less committed devotees.	The observable world does not exist in an ultimate sense; its reality is relative to the being of God. Only God exists in the final analysis, since all being is unified at the most fundamental level. God is Perfect Love.	The essence of mankind is Divine Spirit; the body is only a phenomenal manifestation of that Spirit. Looking at things from the perspective of the most fundamental reality (God), human beings do not exist in an ultimate sense.
Nation of Islam	In order for Allah's will to be revealed accurately, it is necessary for the group's leaders to interpret the Islamic scriptures. Both the Bible and the Koran have been corrupted by unbelieving scholars.	God is not a spiritual being. W. Fard Muhammad was Allah in human form and the savior of the black race. Fard's disciple Elijah Muhammad acted as a savior and intermediary between black people and God.	Black people are gods and are of the same race as God himself. Whites are devils who were created by Yakub, an evil black scientist, in a perverse genetic experiment that took place about 6,000 years ago.

Chart 45

Comparison of Beliefs within Islam (continued)

	Sin	Salvation	Afterlife
Sunni	Allah does not require his followers to perform any duty of which they are incapable. Allah has given human beings freedom of choice, and thus he justly holds them morally responsible for their actions.	Prior to the creation of the universe, Allah determined the precise number of those who would go to paradise and those who would be condemned to hell. All of a person's actions, which Allah takes into consideration when he judges that person, are foreknown by Allah.	All human beings who have ever lived will be resurrected and judged on the basis of their deeds by Allah on the day of judgment. After this judgment, each person will spend eternity in either paradise or the fire of torment.
Shi'ite	Human actions are both determined by Allah and free in a morally relevant sense. Allah's grace enables people to refrain from sinning, and some Muslims are able to remain sinless for extended periods of time.	Allah is obligated to supply grace to those who serve him. He always fulfills his promises concerning rewards and punishments for human behavior.	After death, the spirit departs from the body, at which time all must give an account of their actions during life. After a preliminary judgment, each person must wait in a temporary state of happiness or misery until the final judgment, after which each one will be admitted to paradise or consigned to hell.
Sufi	Ultimately, sin does not exist. Nothing except God, who is wholly and perfectly good, exists; therefore sin is illusory. Nevertheless, hurting other human beings is "sinful" and people can commit "evil" deeds.	Salvation in the fullest sense happens in the afterlife, whereas spiritual liberation can be achieved in this life by realizing one's identity with God. Human beings have a duty to love and serve God's creatures as well as God himself.	The supreme attribute of God is love, which is greater than his wrath. One should obey God not out of fear that he will cast the disobedient into hell or because one desires the pleasures of paradise, but out of a longing to be united with God.
Nation of Islam	Blacks are ethically righteous by nature; all other races, especially white people, are inherently sinful. Islam is the religion of black people by nature, whereas whites naturally have Christianity as their religion. The white race was created to be the enemy of Allah.	Salvation comes through seeing that black people are gods and white people are devils. It does not consist in forgiveness of sins or an eternal abode in heaven. Requires conformity to a righteous standard wherein one lives the truth, shuns immorality, practices justice, and worships Allah.	There is no future physical resurrection of the dead. Instead, blacks (and only blacks) can experience a "mental resurrection." The notion of an afterlife is a myth; no one ends up in heaven or hell. Allah's terrible judgment will first be brought down on America, carried out by a giant spaceship that will drop powerful bombs; this judgment will destroy Christianity and all but a few people of the white race. Having destroyed the whites, black people will establish an everlasting Paradise Nation on earth.

Chart 45

Sunni Islam

Topic	Facts
Current Data	The Sunnis (also called Ahlus Sunnah wal-Jamaa'h) make up approximately 80 to 85 percent of the 1.3 billion Muslims worldwide. Most are under 30 years of age, and less than 25 percent are Arabs. Countries with large Sunni populations include Afghanistan, Algeria, Bangladesh, Egypt, India, Indonesia, Libya, Mauritania, Nigeria, Pakistan, Saudi Arabia, Somalia, Sudan, Syria, Tajikistan, Tunisia, Turkey, Yemen, and Zaire (Democratic Republic of Congo). Sects within Sunni Islam include Salafiyyah and Wahabism.
History	Sunnis allege that when Muhammad (570–632) died, he had not yet appointed anyone to succeed him as head of the Islamic community. To resolve this problem, a meeting of prominent Muslims was held; they chose Muhammad's father-in-law Abu Bakr (573–634) to be the first caliph. Sunnis support the election of Bakr; Shi'ites maintain that Muhammad had wanted his cousin Ali ibn Abi Talib (598–661) to take over to keep leadership within his family. In 656 internal strife led to an Islamic civil war (the Fitna) during which Uthman (574–656), the third caliph, was murdered by disgruntled Muslim troops. Talib was appointed as the new caliph, but one of Uthman's relatives, Muawiyah (602–80), would not acknowledge the legitimacy of Talib's authority. A group of insurgents soon assassinated Talib, whereupon Muawiyah took over the caliphate. In the aftermath of the civil war, the previously unified Islamic world broke into three sects: (1) Sunnis, who judge that the first four caliphs after the death of Muhammad upheld the true principles of Islam; (2) Shi'ites, who view Talib as the only rightful caliph; and (3) the Khwarij sect, which is now all but defunct (today the only remnant is the Ibadi subsect in Yemen and Oman).
	During the centuries after this split in Islam, a number of difficult theological issues surfaced. Several schools of theology were formed, each of which viewed itself as having successfully provided the basic framework for dealing with these problems. The three most prominent were the Athariyya, Ash'ariyyah, and Maturidiyyah schools. The Athariyya school was anti-philosophical, limiting the tools of theological inquiry to the text of the Koran and the traditions of Muhammad. The Ash'ariyyah school taught that human reason was subordinate to Allah's revelation, and that human free will was circumscribed by the power and sovereignty of Allah. The Maturidiyyah school asserted that the existence of God can be proven on the basis of unaided reason.
	Two important periods in Islamic history were the Christian Crusades and the Turks' conquest of the Byzantine Empire. Asian people called Turks had migrated westward from their homeland (today's Turkestan). Having encountered Islam as they moved west, they had converted to the religion of Muhammad. These Turkish nomadic tribes moved into the lands of the Persians and the Arabs. In the late 11th century, the defeat of the Christian emperor Romanus Diogenes in Asia Minor turned the cradle of ancient Christendom into a largely Muslim Turkish stronghold. This event gave rise to the first of the Christian crusades twenty-five years later, led by the Franks.

Chart 46

Sunni Islam (continued)

Topic	Facts
History (continued)	This first campaign was successful and Christian soldiers recovered much of what had been conquered, even the city of Jerusalem. For the next century and a half, different crusades continued until finally the Muslims succeeded against the Christian crusaders. In 1453 the Ottoman Turks conquered Constantinople, the jewel of the ancient eastern Christian world. The Ottoman Empire now stretched from Asia Minor down to Egypt, eastward to the lands of the Arabs and Persians, and westward into southern Europe. Not until after World War I, when the Ottomans became linked with Germany, was the Ottoman Empire defeated.
Summary of Beliefs	Sunni Islam is defined by its insistence on an unyielding loyalty to Allah and to the teachings of his final prophet, Muhammad. At the core of Sunni Islam is the desire on the part of adherents to totally submit themselves to Allah, and thereby to obtain his divine favor. Allah is One and has absolute control over the world. As revealed to Muhammad, the Koran is the will of Allah for his followers and for all human beings. Allah sent other prophets before Muhammad, including Abraham, Moses, and Jesus. Each of these prophets served an important function in clarifying and further developing monotheistic religion. However, Muhammad was the greatest and final prophet; any alleged prophets after him are false and to be despised. Allah desires that all human beings join together into a unified religious community (*umma*) that declares with one voice the will of Allah.

Topic	Summary of View
Creation	Allah is the unique omnipotent Creator; the many gods worshiped before Muhammad brought the truth about Allah are false gods. The universe is the work of Allah and was brought into being out of nothing; lesser deities played no role in forming the world because they do not exist. The ways of Allah are just and he deals fairly with all of his creation. Allah created the human race to live a good life on the earth, giving to humans the capacities of hearing, sight, intellect, emotions, and the capacity to enjoy his creation.
Scripture and Authority	Allah chose Muhammad as his servant and messenger, entrusting him with the task of proclaiming and spreading the message of Islam. Allah is very pleased with the work that Muhammad did during his life. Although there were previous prophets who spoke divine truth, it was Muhammad who was commissioned to bring the culmination of Allah's message to the world. All who claim to be prophets after Muhammad are liars and deceivers. The Koran contains words actually spoken by Allah, though the way in which divine speech was transmitted into human writing is a mystery. Any person who hears or reads the Koran and denies that it is of divine origin is an infidel and will be severely punished in hell. Adherents are able to discern Allah's will just by reading the Koran; Shi'ite imams do not have the authority to declare the will of Allah to his followers.

Chart 46

Sunni Islam (continued)

Topic	Summary of View
God	The Oneness of Allah (*Tawheed*) is central to Sunni Islam. There are no gods besides Allah, and he does not work or consult with any of his creatures. Allah is incomprehensible because he is utterly unlike anything he created. Allah has existed from eternity and will never cease to exist. He is in complete control of all things; nothing transpires that he did not decree. He is omnipotent, omniscient, and merciful.
Mankind	Mankind is composed of two basic parts: an organic body and a soul. Humans should be involved in continual worship since the Koran teaches that the purpose of creation is to worship Allah. Worship doesn't mean traditional or ritual worship in which believers perform certain acts prescribed in the *Shariah* (Islamic law). Rather, worship means following Allah's commandments in every situation. The most important aspect of life is truly intending to submit completely to Allah. All people should attempt to please Allah from their hearts and by all possible means, doing everything possible to seek his pleasure and nearness.
Sin	Idolatry is the gravest sin a human can commit. Not one of Allah's commands is unjust, and therefore no one can rightly complain of being burdened by Allah with onerous tasks. Human beings have the God-given ability to make free choices; Allah does not compel them to do either good or evil. At the same time, each person acts in accordance with the will of Allah. Every person is culpable for his actions and will be rewarded or punished accordingly.
Salvation	People are unable to obey Allah unless he shows favor (*tawfiq*) to them. Yet even stellar obedience does not earn or guarantee entrance into Paradise; Allah's sovereign decision whether to show mercy is the determining factor in this regard. Allah has known since before the beginning of time exactly how many human beings would spend eternity in Paradise (*Al-Jannah*) and how many would be consigned to the hell of fire (*Jahannam*). Allah's decree (*Al-Qadr*) ultimately determines the eternal fate of every person, though this fact is difficult to accept. The details of divine predestination cannot be grasped by human minds. Nevertheless, there is considerable debate within Sunni Islam concerning the precise relationship between Allah's decrees and the actions of human beings.
Afterlife (*Al-Akhirah*)	The Angel of Death comes to take possession of a person's soul at the time of death. This angel then travels through the realm of Isthmus, eventually bringing the soul before Munkar and Nakir, angels who interrogate the dead person about their life and the doctrines of Islam. Much later, at the time of the Judgment, every departed soul will be given a resurrection body before Allah pronounces his verdict upon them. This judgment will result in each person either enjoying everlasting paradise or enduring everlasting torment. People who have not yet died can aid the dead by petitioning Allah and giving money to the poor.

Chart 46

Sunni Islam (continued)

Distinctive Beliefs and Practices

Hadith	*Hadith* are holy traditions concerning the history, beliefs, and practices of the first generation of Islamic believers, especially those of Muhammad. These traditions were only passed down orally; Muhammad did not include them when he wrote the Koran. Generations of Islamic scholars have analyzed these traditions and have made judgments as to which ones are most likely to be genuine. Though six groupings of hadith are held in high esteem by Sunnis, two in particular are especially revered: the *Sahih al-Bukhari* and the *Sahih Muslim*.
Nabuwwat (**Prophethood**)	Allah wants all human beings to know his will, so he has sent many prophets to announce his intentions for the world. Starting with Hazrat Adam, the first man he created, Allah has sent prophets all over the world to declare the truths of monotheistic religion. These prophets speak directly from Allah so that his message is not skewed or tampered with. Two words are used in Arabic for the messengers of Allah, prophet (*nabi*) and apostle (*rasul*); a man can be either or both at the same time.
Al-'Ummah (**Nation of Believers**)	*Al-'Ummah* is the organization of Muslims who give their assent to the entirety of Islamic belief and practice as laid down by Muhammad in the Koran. Devout Sunnis never speak irreverently about Allah and disapprove of needless arguments over fine points of Islamic doctrine. In this way they follow the *sunnah* (way or custom) of Muhammad.
Qiyamat (**Doomsday**)	Only Allah knows when Doomsday (*Qiyamat*) will occur. The scope and intensity of Doomsday will be so great that the entire universe will be destroyed as a result. The beginning of this cosmic cataclysm will be signaled by a mighty trumpet blast emitted by Hazrat Israfeel, an angel Allah has appointed to sound this Divine Alarm (Soor). The noise of this blast will be unimaginably loud and piercing, rendering unconscious the earth's inhabitants. Immediately following the blast, a series of massive natural disasters will annihilate the world.
Kiraman Katibin	The Kiraman Katibin (honored writers) are pairs of angels to whom Allah has given the task of recording human behavior. Each pair is assigned to a particular human being; one of the angels records the person's good deeds, and the other angel records the person's evil deeds. These records are then consulted on the Day of Judgment.

Chart 46

Shi'ite Islam

Topic	Facts
Current Data	Shi'ites comprise 15 to 20 percent of the world's Muslims. Most are concentrated in Azerbaijan, Bahrain, Iran, Iraq, and Lebanon. Three major sects have formed due to disagreements concerning the order of the imams (Shi'ite leaders). They are the Twelvers (who believe that the 12th imam, Mahdi, did not die), the Seveners (who believe that the 7th imam, Kazim, did not die), and the Fivers (who do not accept the 5th imam, Baqir, as legitimate).
History	The Shi'ite sect's split from the Sunnis originated with a disagreement regarding leadership in the earliest period of Islam. When Muhammad (570–632) died, after a two-week illness, initially there was some uncertainty as to who should be the next leader of Islam, the caliph. Those who would later be known as Sunnis were convinced that Muhammad failed to appoint a successor before his untimely death. They supported Abu Bakr (573–634), a long-time friend of Muhammad and his father-in-law, who was chosen as the caliph. Those who would later be known as Shi'ites believed that Muhammad had desired for Ali ibn Abi Talib (598–661), his cousin, to be the caliph and viewed the election of Abu Bakr with deep suspicion. After the death of the third caliph, Husayn ibn Ali (626–680), those Muslims who were disgruntled with the line of succession within Islam broke away from the majority Sunnis to form the Shi'ite sect of Islam. After the death of Hasan al-Askari (846–874), the 11th imam, many Shi'ites were mistreated by the Sunnis, who considered them to be an extremist faction, though earlier the Abassid Dynasty (AD 750–945) of that day had begun as a Shi'ite-friendly regime. In AD 945, the Buyids (a Shi'ite tribe from an area in modern-day Iran) established the first Shi'ite government in Baghdad. At about the same time, the Hamdanids, another Shi'ite empire, took political control in a nearby region. The combined influence of these two Shi'ite powers led to the rapid expansion and growth of Shi'ite Islam in many parts of the Middle East. However, in 1055 the Buyids were defeated by the Seljuq Turks, who subscribed to an extremely intolerant form of Sunni Islam and ruthlessly persecuted the Shi'ites. Afterwards, beginning in 1220, the Mongols attacked and overthrew most of the cities in the Islamic world, sending the Sunni power structure into a state of utter chaos. The Shi'ites, however, were affected only minimally, in part because the Buddhist Mongols had considerably less animosity toward Shi'ite Islam than they did toward Sunni Islam. Several decades later a Mongol ruler, Oljeitu (1280–1316), converted to Shi'ite Islam, after which Shi'ism became the state religion in his territory; this lasted briefly since subsequent leaders of the province were Sunnis. The Mongol ruler Timur (1336–1405) led another invasion of the region, yet he also treated the Shi'ites fairly well. As a result, Shi'ism was able to thrive in Iran during the 14th and 15th centuries. In the 1970s, a legal theory called *velayat-i faqih* (rule by jurisprudence) rose to prominence within Shi'ite Islam. The Iranian Revolution of 1979 occurred largely due to the desire on the part of many Muslims to implement these ideas in concrete political ways.
Summary of Beliefs	Shi'ite Muslims hold to the basic pillars of Islam. Differences between them and other Muslims relates to the succession of imams and the matter of openness to culture. The name Shi'ah (partisan; follower) is ascribed to those Muslims who contend that only immediate family members of Muhammad were eligible to succeed the caliphs of early Islam. Shi'ites also have an approach to the study of science and culture that distinguishes them from other Muslims.

Chart 47

Shi'ite Islam (continued)

Topic	Summary of View
Creation	Allah created the universe out of nothing and his providence extends over the whole of creation. The world and its inhabitants will not exist forever, but will come to an end at a future time of Allah's choosing. Allah created thousands of worlds besides the one in which human beings live. Moreover, Allah created seven races of intelligent beings who lived before the creation of Adam and Eve.
Scripture and Authority	All Muslims are able to understand the Koran at a basic level, but only Muhammad and subsequent caliphs and imams have the authority to explain the teachings of the Koran in detail. The Koran contains the fundamental components of Islamic law (*shariah*), but the imams are needed to flesh out its many implications. Each portion of the Koran must be interpreted in light of all other passages, and the Koran as a whole is without discrepancies. Present-day imams have the ability to interpret the Koran and *shariah* with the same level of authority possessed by early leaders. The imams are exceedingly holy and sinless men whose pronouncements are fully authoritative and infallible.
God	Allah is an absolutely perfect and infinite being. Thus he does not possess attributes in the same way as human beings. His many glorious "attributes" exist only as concepts; in reality, his essence is totally unified and unlimited. Allah did not interact with the universe until after it was created because in eternity there was nothing with which he could interact.
Mankind	Human beings are composed of a spirit and a body, each of which is very different from the other. The body is subject to decay and death; the spirit is not. To create the first human being, Allah began by placing a seed in some moist soil. Then, over time, he fashioned the growing seed into Adam. Human beings were created to serve Allah and to comply with his revealed law.
Sin	Allah has decreed all the decisions and actions of human beings, yet humans are still free (*mukhtar*) to do what they desire. This is because Allah executes his will in and through human behavior, and because it is impossible for humans to do anything that is independent (*mustaqill*) of Allah. Allah's grace makes it possible for human beings to go without sinning. A sinless person (*masum*) has the ability to sin, but is so holy that sin is never a temptation.
Salvation	Allah is obligated to provide grace (*tafaddul*) for his human creatures. His corrective oversight of their lives assists their growth in fidelity and ethical purity. It is incumbent upon Allah to recompense people for their virtuous deeds, but he is not duty-bound to punish them for their evil deeds. If Allah decides to punish a sinner, he is being just, and if he decides to forgive a sinner, he is being gracious.

Chart 47

Shi'ite Islam (continued)

Topic	Summary of View
Afterlife	The spirit departs from the body at death and enters a new intermediate stage (*barzakh*) of existence, which transpires before the resurrection of all human beings. During this time, angels question the spirit to find out what the spirit believed and did while embodied on earth. Depending on the findings of these angels, the spirit will undergo either a pleasant existence or a miserable existence until the day of resurrection. At the resurrection each spirit will be united with a new body and will be sentenced either to unending paradise or everlasting ruin. Affirming that there will be a resurrection and judgment is every bit as important as believing in God. Twelver Shi'ites believe that before his death, Muhammad al Mahdi, the twelfth and last imam, was taken away to a realm called Ghaibah by Allah. There he continues to live, and he will return sometime in the future, along with Jesus Christ.

Distinctive Beliefs and Practices	
Adalah	Adalah refers to Allah's justice. Shi'ites contend that Allah's commands are based on the fact that some actions are good in themselves and other actions are intrinsically evil. This is in contrast to Sunnis, who maintain that actions are neither good nor evil when considered in themselves, but become good or evil when Allah either commands them or forbids them.
Jurisprudence (*Fiqh*)	Shi'ite jurisprudence (formal study of law; *fiqh*) involves mastering Arabic and formal logic, reading commentaries on the Koran, and studying Islamic tradition and the lives of the men who transmitted that tradition. Its goal is to deduce further injunctions for the Islamic community so that they are better able to serve Allah and to adapt to the unique cultural circumstances in which they find themselves. It is critical to achieve consensus (*ijma*) on matters of Islamic law.

Chart 47

Sufi Islam

Topic	Facts
Current Data	Sufis are found throughout the world, with significant concentrations in the Balkans, Indonesia, Malaysia, Afghanistan, Pakistan, Kurdistan, Turkmenistan, Western Russia, the Middle East, and Africa. Five of the most prominent orders are Halveti, Naqshbandi, Qadiriyya, Shadhili, and Tijaniyya. Others include Azeemia, Bektashi, Chishti, Halveti, Jerrahi, Murabitun, Mevlevi, Rifa'i, and Tarpa'i. Prominent organizations include the International Sufi Movement, the Sufi Order International, and the Sufi Foundation of America. It is estimated that there are at least 15 million adherents worldwide.
History	Various masters of Sufism (*shaikhs*) founded a great number of Sufi orders between the 7th and the 13th centuries. Because these orders taught several doctrines that departed from the beliefs of Sunni Islam, and partly because of their mystical tendency, most of these orders were persecuted by Muslim authorities in their respective regions. There were many notable masters during this formative period, but one particularly stands out, the philosopher-theologian Al Ghazalli (1058–1111). It was primarily his writings that persuaded many Islamic leaders that Sufism could be justified on the basis of exegesis, or critical interpretation, of the Koran, and that it does not contradict orthodox Islamic theology. By the 13th century political conditions across North Africa, the Middle East, and India had improved to the point where Sufi mosques and universities could be built without harassment from government authorities. For about the next 300 years, Sufism flourished; this period is often said to be Sufism's "Golden Age."
Summary of Beliefs	Unique and central elements of Sufi Islam are the quest for mystical knowledge of God and declaring the absolute unity of God. Divine Love is said to emanate from God to the world. Though Sufis consult the Koran as part of their religious practices, the primary (in some cases nearly exclusive) emphasis is on mystical experience. Sufism is committed to the proposition that Sufi teaching encompasses the core beliefs of all major religions, and that humanity is progressing toward the Sufi understanding of reality. Sufis make an effort to be tolerant of adherents of other religions.

Topic	Summary of View
Creation	God did not create the universe out of nothing because the universe and God are one reality. In other words, God is not independent of, nor can he ultimately be distinguished from, his creation. At the same time, God created human beings and the world in some sense that is difficult to explain. This allows God to see his own beauty in what is called "creation."
Scripture and Authority	The Koran serves as a conduit for experiencing God in an immediate way. It provides teaching for adherents who possess different degrees of spiritual insight. The primary meaning of the Koran is a mystical one, which is not accessible by exegesis, or critical interpretation, alone. Muhammad's mystical experiences also are deemed important guides to spiritual understanding. Adherents learn together under the tutelage of a Sufi master (*shaykh*). Many of these masters prefer teaching by means of parables and metaphors, rather than systematic exposition, or explanations, of topics.

Chart 48

Sufi Islam (continued)

Topic	Summary of View
God	The Islamic doctrine of *Tawhid* (Unity of God) is interpreted to mean that only God is real in an ultimate sense; God, in the final analysis, is the only truly existing thing. This is different from Eastern monism in which the belief is that God is everything and everything is God. Whereas non-Sufi Muslims state Tawhid as *la ilaha illallah* (there is no God but Allah), Sufis declare *la mawjuda illallah* (there is nothing but Allah). Hence the objects of everyday experience only seem to be real, but are not. In this view, called *Wahdatu'l-Wajud* (Unity of Being), God is one in essence and yet that essence somehow manifests itself in creation. Other Sufis have a slightly different understanding, *Wahdatu'l-Shahud* (Unity of Appearance), which asserts that everything other than God is illusory. The mercy of God triumphs over his wrath; his love supersedes all other of his divine qualities.
Mankind	Human beings were created for the sole purpose of serving God. God fashioned the first man out of clay and then breathed into him the Divine Spirit. This spirit is the essence of a person; the body is only a container for it. The body is composed of four elements: earth, air, fire, and water (similar to earlier Greek philosophy), and is equipped with five external senses (sight, hearing, smell, taste, and touch) and five internal faculties (logical thinking, imagination, doubting, memory, and longing). Each human being is a microcosm of the universe. By sincere and sustained devotion to God, human beings can attain a rank higher than that of the angels. The greatest problem in the Sufi theology of God is that if nothing but Allah exists, then the universe, including humans, is only a concept in the Divine Mind.
Sin	At the most fundamental level, sin does not exist. Since sin is a type of evil and nothing exists except a totally good God, it follows that sin is ultimately an illusion. At the same time, inflicting pain on another person (purposefully and without just cause) is the greatest sin possible. If human beings succumb to their demonic propensities, they will do "evil" things. In light of the fact that all things reflect the nature of God, practitioners seek to find beauty in things that appear ugly and to be tolerant even of people who are very "evil."
Salvation	Salvation cannot be obtained until the next life. Spiritual liberation, however, can be attained in this world. This happens when humans recognize their identity with God, the source of all genuine love. At the same time, God should not be the only object of a person's love. People have a duty to care for those who are suffering and to avoid injuring others. To the extent that they fail to do so, they render themselves unworthy of God's help. Serving others in a spirit of love accelerates the process toward liberation.
Afterlife	People should not obey God's commands because they fear the fires of hell or because they anticipate the bliss of paradise. Instead, a person should conform to the will of God out of a deep desire to become closer to God. The doctrines of paradise and hell are simply aids to learning that help people in their quest to unite with God. Because it originated in the world of spirit, the soul does not cease to exist at death. Salvation after death is the total union of a person with God, who is perfect love.

Chart 48

Sufi Islam (continued)

Distinctive Beliefs and Practices

Problem of Evil	God is infinite and omnipotent; therefore all possibilities exist within his creation. One of these possibilities is separation from God, the source of all goodness. The state of being separated from God is evil. Yet evil cannot be a true state of being, since Allah is pure goodness and his reality is all-encompassing. Moreover, evil cannot, in its essential essence, be independent of good, since Allah is the ground of all things. Ultimately, then, there is no evil because only God exists.
Shaykh (Spiritual Mentor)	Each Sufi needs to have a *shaykh* to look to for spiritual guidance. If he does not, then the Devil will lead him into destruction by confusing him and pandering to his ego. A committed devotee trusts his *shaykh* completely and is loved and cared for in return. This is how things were between Muhammad and his disciples.
Dhirk	*Dhirk*, the devotional practice of "remembrance of God," is the central feature of all Sufi orders. It is performed by repeatedly invoking the names and attributes of God. The precise method varies, but its goal is to create spiritual awareness of and love for God in the practitioner. *Dhirk* can be practiced individually or collectively. Some orders perform it silently, others loudly.
Sema	An important practice in Sufism, *sema* literally means "listening." This may involve reciting from the Koran and/or from devotional poetry. Throughout the centuries, Sufi poets have written mystical poems for devotional purposes, some of which have been set to music.
Suluk (Spiritual Journey)	A lengthy and arduous quest for spiritual purification, it consists of three stages. 1. The first consists of a struggle against the *nafs al-ammara* (carnal soul), which is a proclivity to violate God's commands and enjoy doing so. Sufis who subdue this wicked aspect of themselves then are able to begin the next phase of their spiritual journey. 2. In the second adherents heed the *nafs al-lawwama* (reproaching soul), which castigates them for their wickedness and implores them to love and obey God. 3. Stage three is *nafs al-mutma'inna* (station of the contented soul). During this time the practitioner is instructed in the path of unblemished obedience and cultivates higher virtues. Through a regimen of rigorous self-disciple, the person develops the ability to focus solely on God via chanting and mediation, eventually spending as many as 40 days straight doing these activities. At the end, the faithful Sufi has learned perfect contentment.
Fana (Extinction) **Baqa (Subsistence)**	If Allah is gracious to devotees, they are able to reach a mystical state wherein their personal identity is absorbed into the being of Allah, called *fana fi Allah* (extinction of the self in God). This state marks the crossover of the devotee to *baqa billah* (eternal life in union with God). In this final and blessed state the person does not perish, but is granted unending consciousness of God's omnipresence.

Chart 48

Nation of Islam

Topic	Facts
Current Data	At least seven Nation of Islam (NOI) splinter groups have formed since the death of Malcolm X. These include the Lost-Found Nation of Islam, the United Nation of Islam, the Nation of Islam-Canada, the New Nation of Islam, the Messianic Nation of Islam, and the Five Percent Nation of Gods and Earths. Louis Farrakhan has succeeded in making his Nation the best known of these groups, often challenging black Christian churches as a way of gaining converts to his version of Islam. The national membership of Farrakhan's NOI sect is estimated at no more than 20,000.
History	The events that led to the emergence of the group now known as the Nation of Islam can be traced back to 1913, when Timothy Drew (1886–1929) returned to the United States after a trip to Morocco and founded the Moorish Science Temple of America in Newark, New Jersey. He changed his name to Noble Drew Ali. Ali began to teach that blacks could obtain salvation by discovering their roots in Africa, and that Jesus was a black man who had been killed by whites. Over the next 12 years Ali became a controversial figure. In 1925 the temple headquarters was relocated to Chicago, where Ali was murdered in 1929. After the death of Ali, Wallace Dodd Fard (c. 1877–19??) left the Newark temple and formed the Temple of Islam in Detroit. He spent considerable time in poor black neighborhoods, proclaiming he was the reincarnation of Noble Drew Ali. Fard's message was that blacks in the United States are in bondage to their white masters, who use Christianity as a ploy to maintain control over the black population. Fard was soon joined by Elijah Muhammad, born Elijah Poole (1897–1975), who was equally zealous in spreading Fard's message. The Detroit police compelled Fard to leave town in 1934. Elijah Muhammad became the new leader and changed the name to the Nation of Islam. Muhammad spent the next three decades establishing NOI temples in U.S. cities, the most famous of which is Temple #7 in New York City (Harlem).
	During this time, a young man named Malcolm Little (1925–65), while in prison in Norfolk, Mass., became convinced of Elijah Muhammad's teachings. Little corresponded with Muhammad and after his release from prison in 1952 traveled to Chicago to meet Muhammad. Soon thereafter he took Malcolm X as his new Islamic name. Over the next 12 years, Malcolm X's tireless efforts brought a surge of growth to the NOI organization. In 1955, Malcolm X met Louis Eugene Walcott (1933–), who had dropped out of college to pursue a career as a nightclub entertainer. Malcolm X took Walcott to hear Muhammad speak. Walcott converted to the NOI and changed his name to Louis Farrakhan.
	Malcolm X then persuaded Farrakhan to assist him at the Harlem NOI mosque, which Farrakhan did before leaving to oversee the Boston mosque. Over the next several years Malcolm X became increasingly disgruntled with both the teachings and the behavior of Muhammad. Then in December 1963, Malcolm X made incendiary public remarks concerning the assassination of President John F. Kennedy and Muhammad suspended him. Three months later Malcolm X resigned from the NOI. While on a pilgrimage to Mecca, he converted to Sunni Islam. His conversion infuriated the NOI leadership, and soon it was rumored that Malcolm X was a target of assassination. His house was firebombed and eight days later, on February 22, 1965, Malcolm X was assassinated while delivering a speech in Manhattan.

Chart 49

Nation of Islam (continued)

Topic	Facts
History (continued)	As a result of the assassination, the NOI underwent tremendous turmoil. Farrakhan returned to Harlem in an attempt to restore order and unity. Muhammad died 10 years later, in 1975, and the following year his son Warith Deen Muhammed (1933–) assumed the leadership and spearheaded an effort to make drastic changes to the NOI's official doctrines. Farrakhan was angered by these unexpected changes and in 1978 left to start a new NOI committed to preserving the teachings of Fard. In 1995 Farrakhan organized and led a massive rally of African-American men in Washington, D.C., known as the Million Man March. Since 1999 there has been a gradual movement toward Sunni Islamic orthodoxy by Farrakhan and the NOI leadership. In 2000 Farrakhan and W. D. Muhammed declared their unity at the 2nd International Islamic Conference in Chicago. In 2003 Farrakhan instructed NOI members to observe Ramadan at the same time as Sunni Muslims.
Summary of Beliefs	Official beliefs of the Nation of Islam include, but are not limited to: 1. One should use the name Allah when speaking of God. 2. There is no God but Allah. 3. W. Fard Muhammad was Allah in human flesh, the Christian Messiah, and the Muslim Mahdi. 4. The revelation of Allah consists of the Koran and the scriptures of all of God's prophets. 5. Black people need to be mentally resurrected, disassociate themselves from their former status as slaves, and abandon the names they received from their former masters. 6. Blacks should separate from the white race, both culturally and geographically. 7. Programs allegedly aimed at integrating blacks and whites are insincere and duplicitous and are calculated to hinder the division of the United States into a region for blacks and a region for whites. 8. Allah will judge America for its wickedness. 9. True Muslims should refuse to serve in the United States military.

Topic	Summary of View
Creation	According to the Nation of Islam, the creative agents of the universe are all temporal beings who must reproduce themselves to ensure the ongoing survival of the universe and the development of human history. The universe began 78 trillion years ago when a god created himself from a single atom, which in turn had formed itself from nothing. This god created a black man on the earth who also was a god. Twelve trillion years later this newly created god devised a plan for blowing up the earth. He filled the earth with powerful explosives by using a long shaft he had drilled deep into the ground and detonated the explosives, causing the earth to split into two parts, one of which became the moon. However, he had not achieved his goal of

Chart 49

Nation of Islam (continued)

Topic	Summary of View
Creation (continued)	destroying the planet. Since the black creator was not an eternal being, he eventually died, though he produced other gods before his demise. During the 66 trillion years since the death of the universe's first god, the universe has been ruled by a 24-member council of black deities. Allah presides over this council; the remaining members are scientists. These 23 black scientists have determined the history of the world in advance. Approximately every 30,000 years, one of them creates a new civilization.
Scripture and Authority	The Koran and other traditional Islamic scriptures reveal Allah's will, but only as interpreted by the group's leadership. The Bible has been corrupted; the original Scripture revealed to Moses was holy until Jewish and Christian scholars tampered with it, so current copies of the Bible are not the Word of Allah. The Koran also has been tampered with, requiring the assistance of Nation of Islam leaders to understand it.
God	God is not a spirit, he is a man. W. Fard Muhammad was Allah in physical form and he was the return to the world of Christ the Savior—the Muslim Mahdi and the Messiah of the Christians. Fard's disciple Elijah Muhammad serves as a mediator between black people and God. "Allah" can refer to black Muslims as a people. Christians worship an invisible spook in outer space.
Mankind	Blacks are gods and whites are a race of devils. Blacks are of the same race as God. The Black Nation is self-created, while the white race was made by an evil black scientist named Yakub about 6,000 years ago in a genetic experiment on the Mediterranean island of Patmos.
Sin	Blacks are divine and inherently righteous. The other races, in particular whites, are inherently sinful. There is a moral gradient of sinfulness that varies with the darkness of a race's skin. Thus Asians and Native Americans are more sinful than blacks but less sinful than whites. Islam is the natural religion for blacks, and Christianity is the natural religion for whites. Yakub, the evil black scientist, created white people to be enemies of Allah.
Salvation	Achieved by recognizing the true God (blacks) and the true Devil (whites). Christianity is a demonic religion, devised by whites to subjugate the black race. It is a mistake to think that salvation concerns things like being pardoned from sin by God or spending eternity in heaven. Instead, it involves the worship of Allah, living uprightly, and being renamed with a black Muslim name. Though it is extremely difficult to do so, a few white people can escape destruction by becoming Muslims.
Afterlife	In the future there will be a "mental resurrection" of black people, which will liberate them from the system of psychological slavery perpetuated by American whites. The Christian doctrine of a physical resurrection of the dead is a myth. There is no life after death, and thus no heaven or hell. References to heaven in the Koran and the Bible merely speak of favorable conditions in this world. Allah's judgment will be unleashed on America first and will be carried out by a giant spaceship (Mother Plane). Black scientists on board will use powerful bombs to destroy the white race and the Christian religion. Having wiped out white people, gods (blacks) will establish a Paradise Nation on earth and rule over it forever.

Chart 49

Nation of Islam (continued)

Distinctive Beliefs and Practices

Origin of White People and White History	According to Nation of Islam doctrine, one of the significant differences between blacks and whites is that blacks have been in existence for trillions of years and whites came into existence a scant 6,000 years ago.
	The creation of the white race was the diabolical plan of an evil but brilliant scientist named Yakub, who was also a black god. Yakub had been born near Mecca about 600 years earlier, but had been in rebellion against the other gods since his childhood. Eventually he decided to make a race of people who would be the adversaries of blacks and bring them great misery. (Because white people were created for malicious purposes, not for good, whites are a demonic race.)
	Hearing of this, the king of Mecca banished Yakub and his followers to the Mediterranean island of Patmos. There, over time, Yakub created the white race by forbidding marriage between everyone except those with the least dark skin and by killing all newborns whose skin was deemed by him to be too dark. Yukub died 150 years after beginning his eugenics project, but his assistants carried on the work. Over the next 450 years, these scientists were able to gradually alter the skin color of the island's inhabitants, so that brown, then red, then yellow, and finally pure white people emerged.
	All the whites departed Patmos and traveled to Mecca, where they instigated fighting and bickering among the native black population. The king of Mecca deported them to Europe, where they spent 2,000 years in a primitive state. During this time they attempted breeding experiments that would transform them into black people, but they failed, creating gorillas instead. It was at this time that Moses instructed the white people concerning the worship of Allah and the tools and methods of building human civilization.
	Since then, the white race has come to control the political, social, and economic structures of the world. This will end soon, when Allah returns in judgment to destroy whites and return blacks to their natural and rightful place of global dominance.

Chart 49

Islamic Calendar and Holy Days

Holiday	Time of Year	Observance
Lunar Months*	Each month begins with the advent of the new moon. The Western New Year is always on January 1, but the Muslim New Year (Mihama) shifts regularly.	The Islamic month is based on the cycle of the moon. The lunar cycle consists of 12 months, each having either 29 or 30 days, totaling 353 or 354 days for the year. Many Muslims celebrate the New Year on March 21.
Solar Years*	The Islamic calendar begins in the Julian year AD 622, which marks Muhammad's pilgrimage from Mecca to Medina.	Islam has two distinct calendars: lunar and solar. Solar years are approximately 10 days shorter than those on the Julian calendar.
Hajj	Begins on the eighth day of Dhul-Hijjah, the twelfth month of the Islamic year, and lasts for as long as six days.	The fifth pillar of Sunni Islam (and the third "branch of religion" for Shi'ites), this celebration of the requisite pilgrimage to Mecca is a significant rite of passage in the life of a Muslim. The primary purpose of the journey is to worship Allah at the Ka'aba, the Sacred House in Mecca. Pilgrims ceremonially stone the Devil.
Eid-ul-Adha (Big Feast)	The second in a series of major Islamic festivals, it is preceded by the most important day of the Hajj, when all Muslims making the journey gather on the Plain of Arafat.	Celebrates Abraham's willingness to sacrifice everything, including his son Ishmael. Many animals are sacrificed, the meat of which is used to feed the poor.
Eid-ul-Fitr (Little Feast)	The first day of the tenth month (Shawwal) in the Islamic calendar.	Lasting three days, it celebrates the end of Ramadan. Most nonessential work is suspended. Participants dress in their finest clothes and attend a special congregational prayer in their local mosque. There is an obligatory special offering for the poor.
Ramadan	The ninth month (Al-Hijrah) in the Islamic calendar.	The most widely recognized holiday within Islam. Its purpose is to give all Muslims a prescribed period of time to observe the third pillar of Islam, fasting. Participants abstain from food and marital relations during daylight hours. They recite prayers and study the Koran.
The 15th of Sha'baan	The 15th day of the eighth month of the Islamic calendar, it falls between the months of Rajab and Ramadan.	An eschatological holy day in Shi'ite Islam, focusing on the expectation of the coming Messiah. According to Shi'ite tradition the 12th imam, Muhammad Al-Mahdi, never died. Still alive, he remains hidden in an occultic realm, awaiting the final day of judgment.

* Not a holiday.

Chart 50

Timeline of Baha'i

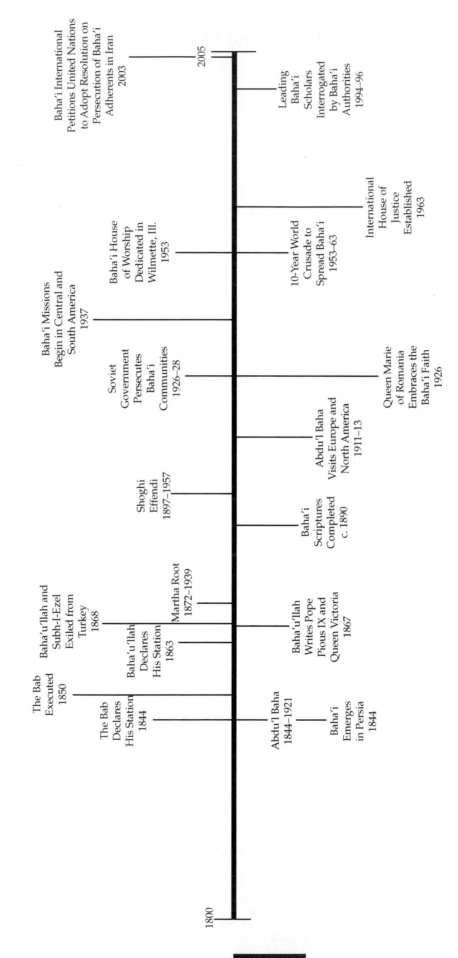

Baha'i International Petitions United Nations to Adopt Resolution on Persecution of Baha'i Adherents in Iran
2003

Leading Baha'i Scholars Interrogated by Baha'i Authorities
1994–96

2005

International House of Justice Established
1963

Baha'i House of Worship Dedicated in Wilmette, Ill.
1953

10-Year World Crusade to Spread Baha'i
1953–63

Baha'i Missions Begin in Central and South America
1937

Soviet Government Persecutes Baha'i Communities
1926–28

Queen Marie of Romania Embraces the Baha'i Faith
1926

Abdu'l Baha Visits Europe and North America
1911–13

Shoghi Effendi
1897–1957

Baha'i Scriptures Completed
c. 1890

Martha Root
1872–1939

Baha'u'llah and Subh-I-Ezel Exiled from Turkey
1868

Baha'u'llah Writes Pope Pious IX and Queen Victoria
1867

Baha'u'llah Declares His Station
1863

The Bab Executed
1850

The Bab Declares His Station
1844

Abdu'l Baha
1844–1921

Baha'i Emerges in Persia
1844

1800

Chart 51

Baha'i

Topic	Facts
Current Data	The Baha'i faith claims about 6 million members worldwide, including about 140,000 in the United States. Unofficial sources drop that to 1 million members worldwide and 28,000 in the United States. Baha'i is widespread globally, with members in at least 235 regions of the world. The international headquarters is located in Haifa, Israel. The main office in the United States is in Wilmette, Illinois.
History	Though the name came later, Baha'i was started in 1844 in Persia (now Iran) by Mirza Ali Muhammad (1819–50) when he proclaimed himself to be the Bab (Gate), a manifestation of God whose mission was to prepare the way for the World Teacher who would unite the human race and bring world peace. The Bab and his teachings became quite popular in Persia, but they also became a concern for the Persian government, which condemned the movement and had the Bab arrested. He was executed in 1850. Thirteen years later one of his followers, Mirza Hysayn Ali, declared that he was the World Teacher prophesied by the Bab. He changed his name to Baha'u'llah (the glory of God) and his followers became known as Baha'is. Baha'u'llah was a prolific author, writing more than 100 books and letters in which he enunciated the Baha'i faith. After Baha'u'llah's death, his son Abbas Effendi took the reins of the organization, naming himself Abdu'l-Baha (the servant of Baha). Though he did not take any divine title as had the Bab and his father, Abdu'l-Baha did claim the sole right of interpreting his father's writings, declaring that his own writings were on the same level of authority as his father's. Until his death in 1921, Abdu'l-Baha wrote and traveled extensively in Europe and North America to advance the Baha'i faith. In accordance with his will, his eldest grandson, Shoghi Effendi, became his successor. Effendi worked to establish Baha'i assemblies that would present the teachings of Baha'u'llah throughout the world. Since Effendi's death in 1957, the Baha'i faith has been led by a group of elected leaders known as the Universal House of Justice.
Summary of Beliefs	Throughout history God has progressively increased the knowledge of truth through various religions, with Baha'i the current stage in the evolution of religion. Previous religious leaders—such as Moses, Jesus, Muhammad, and Buddha—were manifestations of the one God. Baha'u'llah was God's most recent manifestation. Central to the Baha'i faith is the oneness of God, the oneness of religion, and the oneness of mankind.

Topic	Summary of View
Creation	A tension exists within Baha'i in that God is viewed as transcendent and not directly responsible for the creation of the universe, while at the same time the universe, in some way, is said to emanate from his essence. God is viewed as static and unchanging, in no way able to have a personal relationship with his creation. Yet he is able to reveal his attributes to humans in the spatial and temporal realm in which they live.

Chart 52

Baha'i (continued)

Topic	Summary of View
Scripture and Authority	Generally, the scriptures of the Baha'i faith are said to be the writings of the Bab, Baha'u'llah, and Abdul'l-Baha. Historically the authority of the latter two has been questioned even though Baha'u'llah was chosen by the Bab as his successor and as interpreter of his words and Baha'u'llah chose his son Abdul'l-Baha to be the interpreter of his words. Abdul'l-Baha's son Shoghi Effendi considered himself the sole interpreter of his father's words. Baha'u'llah wrote many books and letters, including *The Most Holy Book, The Book of Certitude,* and *Gleanings from the Writings of Baha'u'llah.* A follower of Baha'i is to acquire truth by searching for it without relying on the traditions or prophets of the past. Each person, once adopting this approach, is then capable of discerning the manifestation of God.
God	The God of Baha'i is transcendent, unknowable, and unable to be comprehended, but his attributes are discernible through divine manifestations. These manifestations have come at different periods of human history and progressively reveal more information about the attributes of God. Some of these manifestations were Adam, Moses, Jesus, the Buddha, Muhammad, and the Bab.
Mankind	A fundamental teaching of Baha'i is that the human race is one and, as such, no particular type of human is superior to the rest of humanity. Nationalism, sexism, and racism are prejudices from which everyone should seek to rid themselves. These prejudices work against the goal of a peaceful and just society on this planet. Every individual has an immortal soul that is immune to corruption.
Sin	Human beings, by nature, are neither sinful nor evil. Each person has been given the capacity by God for spiritual growth and progress. Evil, in fact, is seen as only the absence of good. Satan, understood in some religious traditions as an evil angelic being, does not exist, but rather is a personification of a human's lower nature, which can destroy those who fail to gain harmony with their spiritual nature.
Salvation	Salvation, a state of happiness, is realized by those who turn toward God and believe in the manifestation of God that appears in the age in which they live. Salvation does not save anyone from a sinful nature or acts of sin but instead frees humans from bondage to their lower nature. It is this lower nature that threatens the destruction of society. Only through God sending manifestations are people able to reach their true potential. It is through the teachings of these historical manifestations that people evolve to a higher plane of spirituality and unite with God.
Afterlife	When a person dies, the soul separates from the body and travels to the spirit world, which is a part of our universe without time or space. What some persons speak of as the second coming of Christ was actually the time of Baha'u'llah, since he, like the human Jesus, was a divine manifestation. Heaven and hell do not exist as actual places where people go after death, but rather are psychological and spiritual states of being close to God or far away from him. Heaven is realized when spiritual progress is being made; a lack of spiritual progress is hell.

Chart 52

Baha'i (continued)

Distinctive Beliefs and Practices

Ceremonial Minimalism	The Baha'i religion has no clergy, sacraments, or rituals. Adherents regard work as a form of worship.
Unity of Science and Religion	Since science and religion are one, they are in complete agreement. Something cannot be true in science and false in religion or vice versa. But the way in which one discovers truth in these two areas differs. The truths of science are discovered through empirical investigation, whereas the truths of religion are revealed by God through the manifestations he brings to humans. Supposed contradictions between science and religion are the result of human error or being closed minded.
Universal House of Justice	This law-making tribunal, envisioned by Baha'u'llah, was finally founded in 1963. It consists of nine elected judges who have broad authority over the business of the worldwide community of Baha'i. Its primary responsibilities include administering international affairs and preserving the holy places and other property holdings of the Baha'i faith.
Global Commonwealth	Central to the Baha'i faith is the goal of establishing a global commonwealth, viewed as a fraternity of nations working together to resolve disputes and achieve lasting world peace. In this scenario, international leaders would consult with one another regularly so as to bring about political stability on a global scale. Institutions critical to the success of this commonwealth would include an international executive power, a world legislature, and a world court. Top priorities would be compulsory education for every citizen, a universal language, and resolution of economic inequalities.

Chart 52

Timeline of Secular Humanism

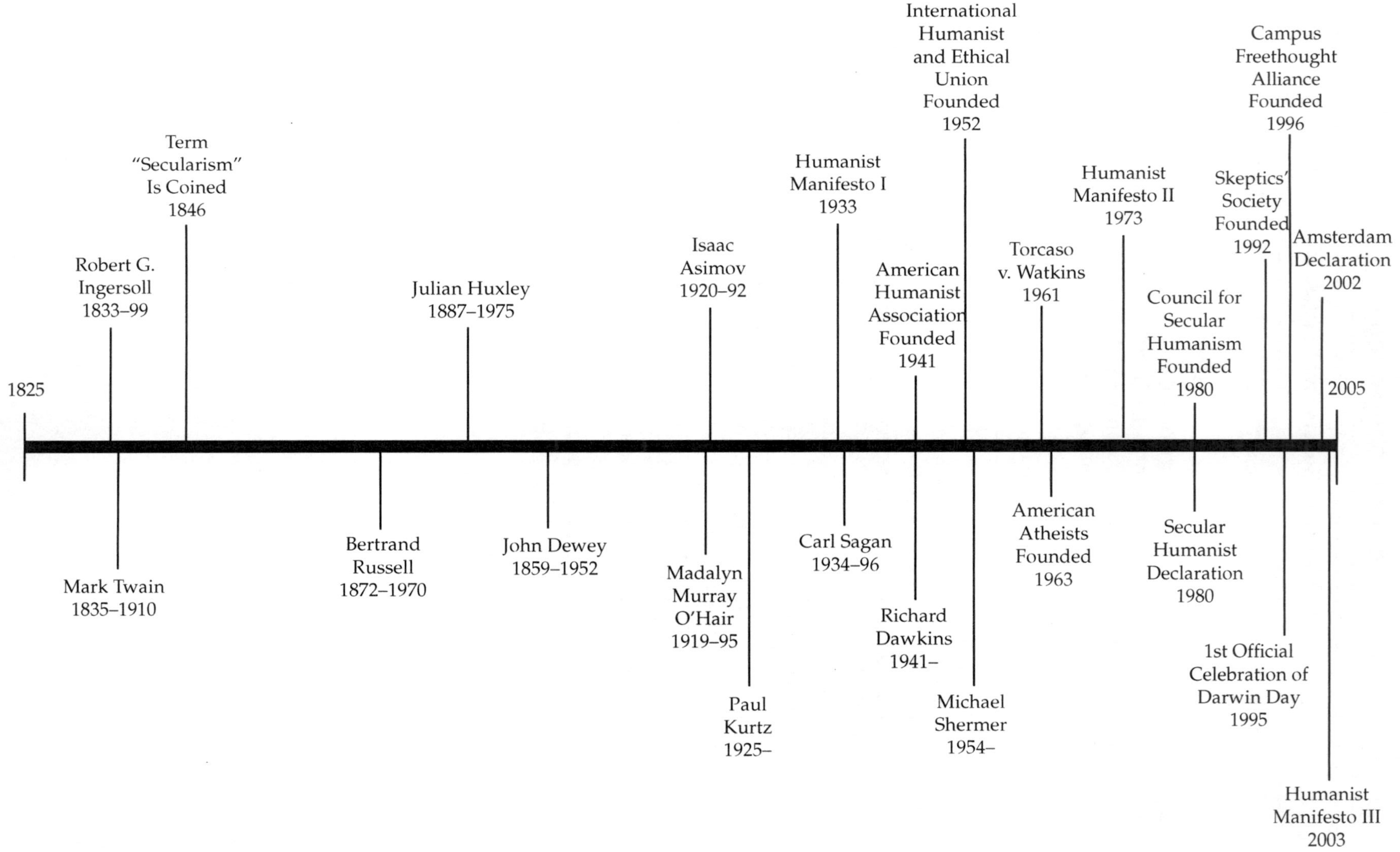

Robert G. Ingersoll
1833–99

Term "Secularism" Is Coined
1846

Julian Huxley
1887–1975

Isaac Asimov
1920–92

Humanist Manifesto I
1933

International Humanist and Ethical Union Founded
1952

Humanist Manifesto II
1973

Campus Freethought Alliance Founded
1996

Skeptics' Society Founded
1992

Amsterdam Declaration
2002

Torcaso v. Watkins
1961

Council for Secular Humanism Founded
1980

American Humanist Association Founded
1941

2005

1825

Mark Twain
1835–1910

Bertrand Russell
1872–1970

John Dewey
1859–1952

Madalyn Murray O'Hair
1919–95

Paul Kurtz
1925–

Carl Sagan
1934–96

Richard Dawkins
1941–

Michael Shermer
1954–

American Atheists Founded
1963

Secular Humanist Declaration
1980

1st Official Celebration of Darwin Day
1995

Humanist Manifesto III
2003

Chart 53

Secular Humanism

Topic	Facts
Current Data	Over the past 35 years, there has been a documented increase in the number of people worldwide who claim no religious affiliation. Major organizations dedicated to the propagation of secular humanist ideas, literature, and agendas exist not only in North America and Europe but in Australia, India, China, and Israel. These include the American Humanist Association, the Council for Secular Humanism, American Atheists, the Skeptics' Society, Campus Freethought Alliance, and the National Secular Society (UK). Some secular humanists celebrate alternative holidays such as Charles Darwin's Birthday, also known as Darwin Day (February 12). Notable secular humanists include Bertrand Russell (1872–1970), Julian Huxley (1887–1975), Isaac Asimov (1920–92), Gene Roddenberry (1921–91), Steve Allen (1921–2000), Kurt Vonnegut (1922–), Paul Kurtz (1925–), Edward O. Wilson (1929–), Carl Sagan (1934–96), Ted Turner (1938–), Richard Dawkins (1941–), and Michael Shermer (1954–).
History	Rejection of a belief in a deity is a recent development in the Western world, having developed out of the Enlightenment's emphasis on man and nature and its de-emphasis on God's special acts in the world, but there were early views similar to this perspective in some ancient Greek philosophy and Eastern religion. The term *secularism* was coined in 1846 by George Jacob Holyoake (1817–1906). The term *secular humanism* is different from the use of the word *humanism* in the Middle Ages. In that context, humanism carried religious aspects. Desiderius Erasmus (1466–1536) was a noted humanist and well-known Christian scholar. The Renaissance opened up a plethora of new ideas, sciences, arts, and exposure to new and different countries and peoples, but it still was within the worldview of, generally, Christian theism. It was with the Enlightenment of the 18th century that bold steps were taken by some to question church authority, the Bible, and even the existence of God. The church persecuted many who opposed its theology, but by the 19th century, the Freethought Movement provided a haven in which people could reject Christianity without incurring public or religious recriminations. Scientists like Charles Darwin and Thomas H. Huxley in England, and skeptics like Mark Twain and Robert G. Ingersoll in America, helped to popularize an early form of modern secular humanism. The first major document stating the core beliefs of secular humanism was the Humanist Manifesto of 1933 (drafted by educator John Dewey), though nowhere in this document was it specifically identified as a religious view. The most public expression of the religious nature of secular humanism is the widely cited phrase "secular humanism" found in the 1961 United States Supreme Court case

Many of its advocates insist that secular humanism should not be categorized as a religion, since it lacks what they take to be essential characteristics of a religion, such as belief in a deity and an accompanying transcendent order. They routinely contend that issues concerning ethics and science are purely philosophical in nature and thus are not part of the domain of religion, which (according to them) deals only with the supernatural. From this point of view, it is more accurate to say that secular humanism is a nonreligious world and life view. While not disputing the sincerity of these claims with respect to most of those who make them, we do not agree with this assessment. In reality, even limiting the discussion to an academic one within the sphere of the work of scholars of religion, the definition of religion is a highly contested one. (See Chart 2: What Is Religion?) Given the diversity of views on this matter and the fact that secular humanism falls within the purview of "religion" on a significant minority of these views, we have deemed it appropriate to include secular humanism in this book on world religions, even though it is not traditionally thought of as such.

Chart 54

Secular Humanism (continued)

Topic	Facts
History (continued)	Torcaso v. Watkins; Justice Hugo Black used the term in a footnote to the text of the judicial decision. In the 1970s the label "secular humanist" came to be embraced by many self-described humanists. Important statements of secular humanism during the last 35 years include the Humanist Manifesto II (1973), A Secular Humanist Declaration (1980), A Declaration of Interdependence (1988), the International Humanist and Ethical Union's Minimum Statement on Humanism (1996), Humanism: Why, What, and What For (1996), the Humanist Manifesto 2000: A Call for a New Planetary Humanism (2000), The Affirmations of Humanism: A Statement of Principles (2001), the Amsterdam Declaration (2002), and the Humanist Manifesto III: Humanism and Its Aspirations (2003).
Summary of Beliefs	Because of the largely unregulated and decentralized nature of the movement, different views are held on a number of issues. Nevertheless, secular humanism is characterized by a commitment to: 1. Free inquiry: The right of individuals to enjoy unrestrained ability to pursue and promote whatever ideas they believe to be worth such efforts, and opposition to any authorities that might attempt to stifle intellectual freedom. 2. Separation of church and state: Religious institutions should not be allowed to use their theological perspectives as a basis for drafting legislation or making judicial decisions to which the larger society is subject, and taxes should not be used to fund activities of religious institutions. 3. The ideal of freedom: Involves vigorous opposition to any and all forms of totalitarianism that would seek to limit freedom of conscience and belief by repressing unorthodox views, as well as support for substantive political liberties for citizens, the practice of democratic decision-making, the rights of minority groups, and the rule of law. 4. Ethics based on critical intelligence: Ethics is seen as an autonomous field of inquiry wherein moral judgments can be made without recourse to revealed religion, and human beings are thought to be capable of cultivating moral wisdom and living virtuous lives independent of their belief in or reliance on God or gods. 5. Moral education: Moral education of children is essential to maintaining an open democratic society, and it is the task of a public education system to develop and nurture good moral character in children. 6. Religious skepticism: A tenacious skepticism concerning supernatural claims and traditional views of God/divinity prevails. This skepticism stems in part from the conviction that the physical universe can be properly understood only by means of scientific inquiry. 7. Reason: The only rational modes of inquiry are ones that rely solely on logic, evidence, and empirical testing; genuine knowledge and objective truth cannot be obtained in any other manner.

Chart 54

Secular Humanism (continued)

Topic	Facts
Summary of Beliefs (continued)	8. Science and technology: The scientific method is believed to be the most reliable way of understanding the world, and the natural, social, and behavioral sciences are the most effective means of procuring knowledge about the world. 9. Evolution: Efforts to require that creationist (or intelligent design) theories of human origins be taught to public school students and attempts to include criticisms of Darwinian evolution in biology textbooks are deplored. 10. Education: Secular public education is seen as the key to building humane, free, and democratic societies since it is thought to effectively transmit knowledge, train young people for their future jobs and for their roles as citizens in a democracy, and to develop the capacity for critical intelligence.

Topic	Summary of View
Creation	The material universe is either eternally existent or the Big Bang brought it into existence without a supernatural cause. Metaphysical naturalism is held as an all-encompassing ontology: there are no supernatural entities of any kind, the laws of physics suffice to describe all events, and all phenomena can be explained without invoking the agency of anything beyond the natural world (at least in principle).
Scripture and Authority	All alleged holy books/sacred texts are rejected as guides to human behavior or as revealing special truths. Religion in general is held to be the result of ignorance and superstition, and religious authorities are denigrated as being irrational, oppressive fraudulent, and/or severely misguided. "Reason" is touted as the highest and final authority in adjudicating all contested matters. Dogma, creeds, ideologies, and traditions are eschewed, though certain basic principles and beliefs are central and nonnegotiable, and a number of writings that serve to define the movement are held in high esteem by most adherents.
God	Some secular humanists contend that God does not exist (atheists); others withhold judgment on this issue (agnostics); a small minority are deists who see God's existence as irrelevant to the practical affairs of human life. There is a tendency among secular humanists to "deify" reason and human potential, wherein they boast that they do not rely on God, gods, or other supernatural forces to solve their problems or provide guidance for their personal conduct. Most have a strong conviction that proper use of reason, an open marketplace of ideas, goodwill, and tolerance comprise the necessary tools and conditions for making progress in creating a better world; God is not needed to help man achieve such goals.
Mankind	Human beings are the result of evolutionary processes that are devoid of intentionality; they were not created or designed by God. Human beings have value and dignity and are fully capable of solving their problems. Fulfillment of human potential and the display of human creativity are seen as significant and worthwhile endeavors. Cultural pluralism is a good thing and should be encouraged.

Chart 54

Secular Humanism (continued)

Topic	Summary of View
Sin	Strictly speaking there is no such thing as sin; nevertheless there is an insistence that certain fundamental moral precepts be obeyed. There is no transcendent ground for ethics, and moral virtue can be achieved without supernatural assistance. Some secular humanists are moral relativists, though most would say that ethics is in some sense objective, or at least has a practical value, inasmuch as there are normal standards of human behavior. The former state that ethics and its prescriptions for action are merely a cultural construct; the latter argue that human beings discover viable moral arrangements via corporate assessments of their ability to enhance human well-being. Most desire to secure social justice, eradicate discrimination and intolerance, and encourage "common moral decencies" such as altruism, integrity, honesty, truthfulness, and personal responsibility. Most secular humanists tend to be progressive or liberal in their perspectives on social issues such as abortion, homosexuality, and health care.
Salvation	None in the usual sense. However, harnessing human potential, the proper application of reason, science and technology, tolerance, cooperation, and compassion are means to attaining human happiness, economic prosperity, and political freedom. The 1980 Secular Humanist Declaration says: "We deplore efforts … to look outside nature for salvation."
Afterlife	There is no life after death; humans cease to exist after their bodies no longer function in such a way as to provide the biological conditions necessary for living. Therefore the focus is entirely on improving conditions in this world for the betterment of human life. Overall, belief in bodily resurrection or immortality of the soul has a negative effect on achieving the human good in this life.

Distinctive Beliefs and Practices

Topic	Summary of View
Anti-Supernaturalism (Metaphysical Naturalism)	All that exists is contained within the realm of nature. Corollaries include a steadfast skepticism regarding anything supernatural, paranormal, or mystical; the firm conviction that all phenomena have a naturalistic explanation; and a robust confidence in the ability of reason and empirical science to provide an adequate understanding of reality.
Skeptical Epistemology	The intellectual prescription that dogmas, ideologies, and traditions of all kinds ought to be critically analyzed by individuals and not simply accepted "on faith." This involves a commitment to employ careful reasoning, factual evidence, scientific methods of inquiry, personal experience, and the lessons of history in seeking solutions to problems and answers to questions.
Humanist Universalism	The quest for social justice is paramount. Global justice cannot be achieved unless "divisive parochial loyalties" based on religion, creed, race, ethnicity, nationality, class, gender, and/or sexual orientation are transcended, and diverse groups of people strive to work together for the common good of humanity. Adherents are resolute in their promotion of pluralism.

Chart 54

PART 5
EASTERN
RELIGIONS

Historical Relationships of Eastern Religions

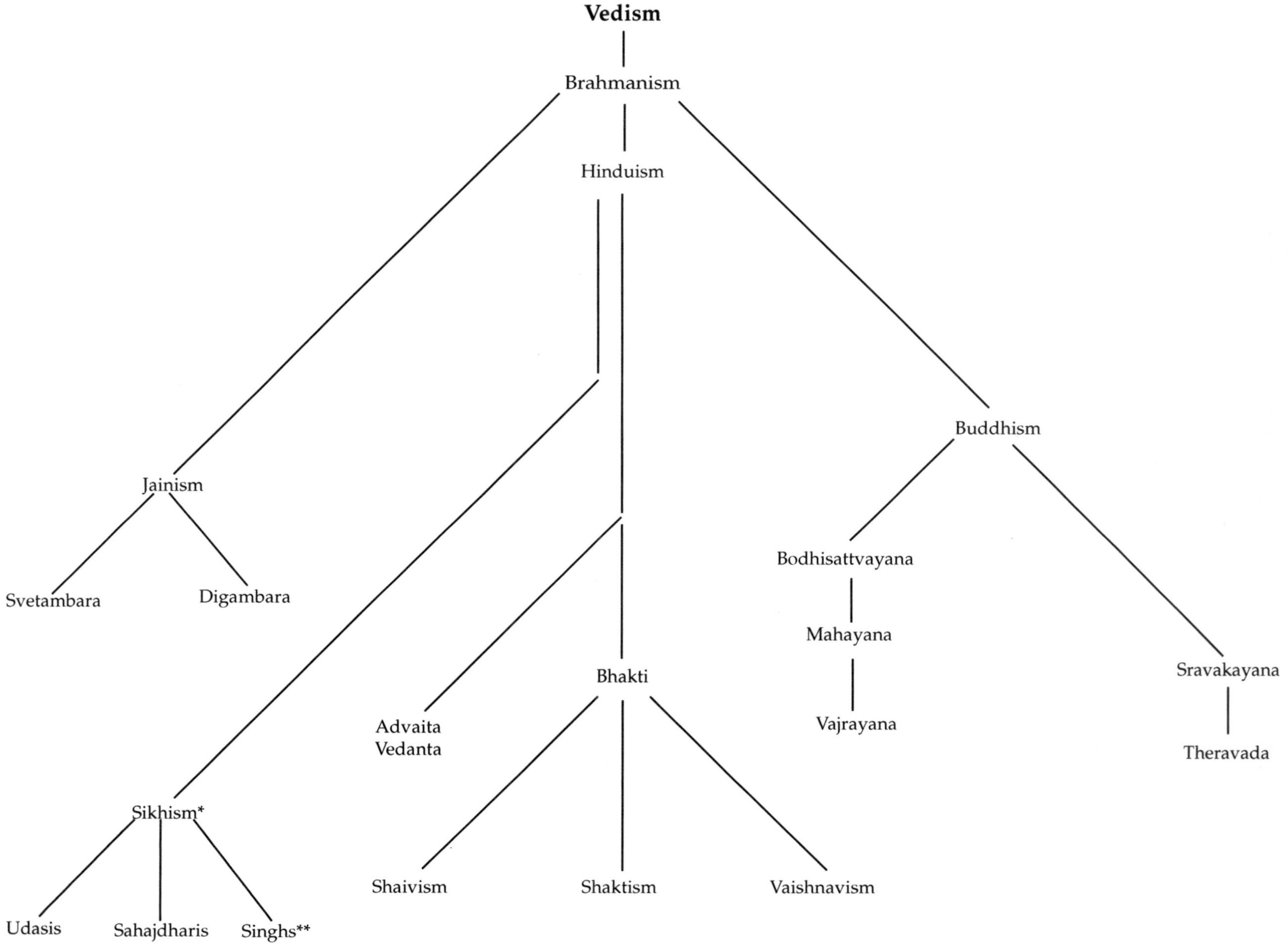

Vedism — Brahmanism

Brahmanism — Buddhism

Buddhism — Sravakayana — Theravada

Buddhism — Bodhisattvayana — Mahayana — Vajrayana

Brahmanism — Hinduism

Hinduism — Jainism — Digambara

Jainism — Svetambara

Hinduism — Advaita Vedanta

Hinduism — Bhakti

Bhakti — Vaishnavism

Bhakti — Shaktism

Bhakti — Shaivism

Hinduism — Sikhism*

Sikhism* — Singhs**

Sikhism* — Sahajdharis

Sikhism* — Udasis

* Sikhism was also influenced by Islam.

** The Singhs divide into three sects: Nihang, Nirmalae, and Kukae.

Chart 55

Historical Relationships of Eastern Religions (continued)

Shinto

- Jinja
- Koshitsu
- Minzoku
- Shuha

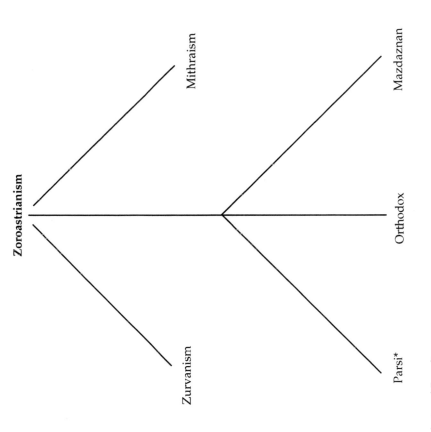

Zoroastrianism

- Zurvanism
- Mithraism
- Parsi*
- Orthodox
- Mazdaznan

* The Parsis divide into three sects: Shahenshai, Kadmi, and Fassali.

Chart 55

Historical Relationships of Eastern Religions (continued)

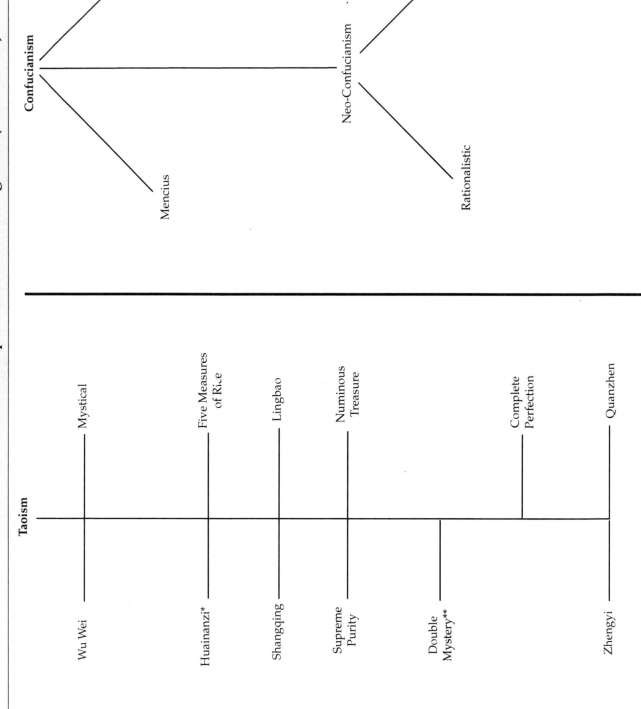

* This school was influenced by Confucianism.
** This school was influenced by Hinduism.

Chart 55

Comparison of Eastern Religions

	Hinduism	Buddhism	Taoism
Birthdate of Founder	c. 1800 BC (early formation)	c. 560 BC	c. 604 BC
Founder	None or unknown	Gautama Buddha	Lao-tzu
Major Branches and Sects	Brahmanism Advaita Vedanta Bhakti	Mahayana Theravada Vajrayana	Zhengyi Quanzhen
Holy Books*	*Vedas* *Upanishads* *Bhagavad Gita*	Pali Canon (*Tripitaka*)	*Tao-te-ching* *I-ching*
Basic Beliefs*	**God**: View varies from one sect to another: theism, monism, and polytheism all have adherents. Major deities include Brahman, Shiva, Vishnu, Shakti, and Krishna. **Revelation**: The two major categories of sacred texts are *Shruti* (what is heard) and *Smriti* (what deserves to be remembered). **Salvation**: Consists of escaping the endless cycle of death and rebirth, and attaining union with Brahman.	**God**: Functionally atheistic, since it is thought that belief in God is not helpful for living properly. However, many practitioners venerate various Buddhas and *bodhisattvas*.** **Revelation**: The Pali Canon is divided into three sections: the *Vinaya Pitaka* (code of ethics), the *Sutta Pitaka* (accounts of the Buddha's life and teachings), and the *Abhidhamma Pitaka* (systematic presentation of doctrine). **Salvation**: Liberation from attachment, desire, and ignorance can be attained by following the Eightfold Path.	**God**: The Tao is a ubiquitous force that keeps the cosmos in a state of harmony and balance. **Revelation**: The wisdom of the Tao is found in many scriptures authored by Taoist sages. **Salvation**: The Way or Path is to become "one with the Tao" by not striving against it.

* Not necessarily a complete list.

** It should be noted that although Buddhas and *bodhisattvas* function as gods in Buddhism, they are not identified as gods by many practicing Buddhists.

Chart 56

Comparison of Eastern Religions (continued)

	Jainism	Zoroastrianism	Shinto
Birthdate of Founder	599 BC	c. 1300 BC (early formation)	c. 600 BC (early formation)
Founder	Mahavira	Zarathushtra	None or unknown
Major Branches and Sects	Svetambara Digambara	Parsi Orthodox Mazdaznan	Jinja Koshitsu Minzoku Shuha
Holy Books	*Angas* *Upangas* *Pakinnakas*	*Avesta*	*Ko-ji-ki* *Nihon-shoki*
Basic Beliefs	**God**: Many gods (*Tirthankaras*) are affirmed; Mahavira is preeminent among them. **Revelation**: The *Angas* is the primary collection of sacred writings. **Salvation**: Freeing oneself from impurity of thought, word, and deed, thus achieving liberation from death and rebirth.	**God**: The supreme being is Ahura Mazda. Lesser deities (*Amesha Spentas*) communicate his will to human beings. **Revelation**: The *Avesta* reveals the will of Ahura Mazda. **Salvation**: Devotees follow a threefold path consisting of good thoughts, works, and deeds, obtaining salvation by doing more good than evil.	**God**: The *kami* are spirits that include forces of nature, clan ancestors, and the souls of deceased national leaders. **Revelation**: The *Ko-ji-ki* and *Nihon-shoki* are the earliest and most important sacred writings. **Salvation**: The *kami* will grant protection and good fortune to those who undergo ritual purification and worship them in accordance with proper shrine protocol.

Chart 56

Comparison of Eastern Religions (continued)

	Confucianism	Sikhism
Date of Founding	551 BC	AD 1469
Founder	Confucius	Nanak Dev
Major Branches and Sects	Rationalistic Idealistic	Udasis Sahajdharis Singhs
Holy Books	*Analects* *Book of Mencius* *Hsiao Ching*	*Guru Granth Sahib*
Basic Beliefs	**God**: Confucius believed in T'ien (heaven), a personal, supernatural being. Later Confucian thinkers came to regard God as an abstract principle. **Revelation**: The *Analects* are the most significant sacred writings. **Salvation**: Maintaining ethical purity and cultivating harmonious relationships with those in one's family, government, and society.	**God**: True Name has two natures: one personal and immanent, the other incomprehensible and transcendent. **Revelation**: God's will is disclosed in the *Granth Sahib*. **Salvation**: Freedom from the cycle of reincarnation by abandoning self-centeredness and embracing God-centeredness.

Chart 56

Timeline of Hinduism

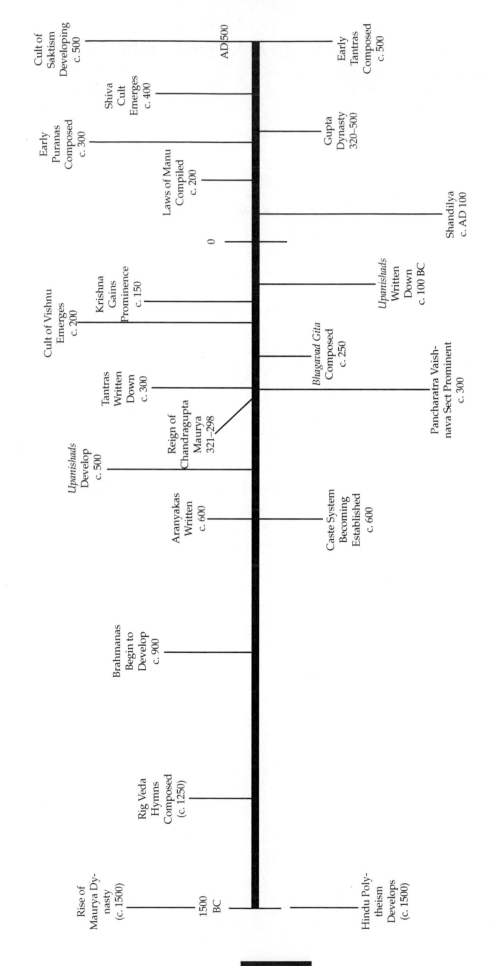

Chart 57

Timeline of Hinduism (continued)

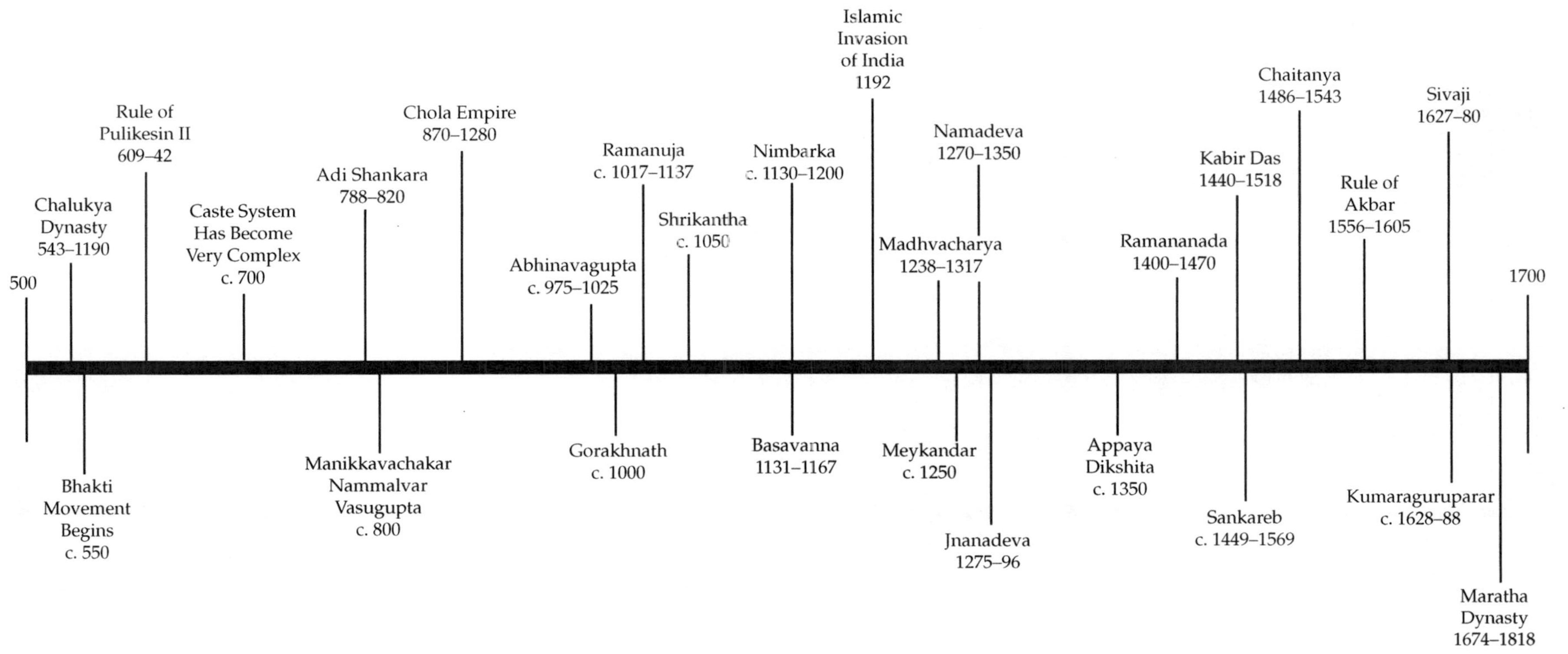

Chalukya Dynasty 543–1190

Rule of Pulikesin II 609–42

Caste System Has Become Very Complex c. 700

Adi Shankara 788–820

Chola Empire 870–1280

Abhinavagupta c. 975–1025

Ramanuja c. 1017–1137

Shrikantha c. 1050

Nimbarka c. 1130–1200

Islamic Invasion of India 1192

Namadeva 1270–1350

Madhvacharya 1238–1317

Ramanananda 1400–1470

Kabir Das 1440–1518

Chaitanya 1486–1543

Rule of Akbar 1556–1605

Sivaji 1627–80

Bhakti Movement Begins c. 550

Manikkavachakar Nammalvar Vasugupta c. 800

Gorakhnath c. 1000

Basavanna 1131–1167

Meykandar c. 1250

Jnanadeva 1275–96

Appaya Dikshita c. 1350

Sankareb c. 1449–1569

Kumaraguruparar c. 1628–88

Maratha Dynasty 1674–1818

500

1700

Chart 57

Timeline of Hinduism (continued)

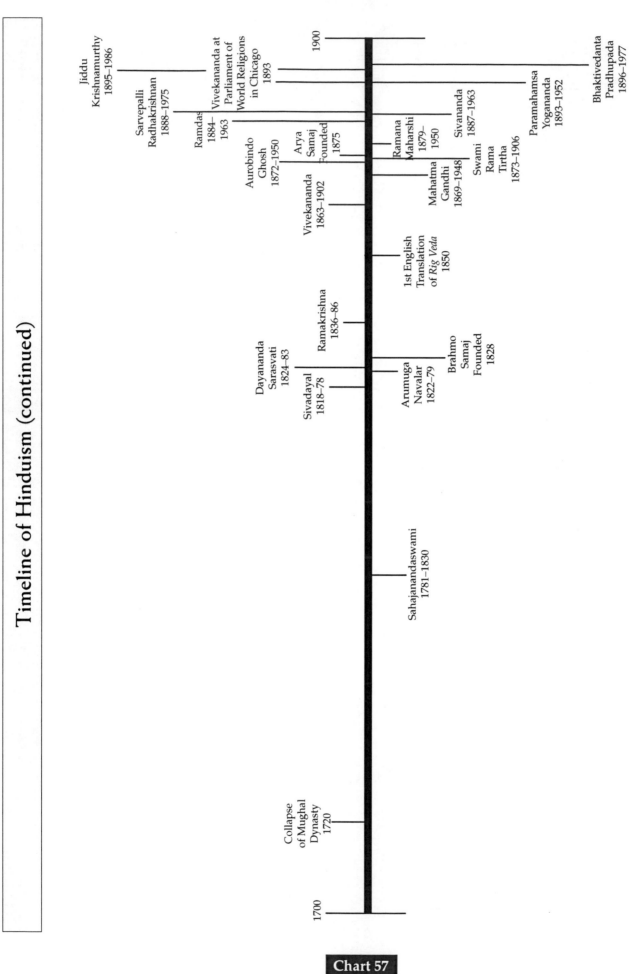

Jiddu Krishnamurthy 1895–1986

Vivekananda at Parliament of World Religions in Chicago 1893

Sarvepalli Radhakrishnan 1888–1975

Ramdas 1884–1963

Bhaktivedanta Pradhupada 1896–1977

Paramahamsa Yogananda 1893–1952

Aurobindo Ghosh 1872–1950

Arya Samaj Founded 1875

Ramana Maharshi 1879–1950

Sivananda 1887–1963

Mahatma Gandhi 1869–1948

Swami Rama Tirtha 1873–1906

Vivekananda 1863–1902

1st English Translation of *Rig Veda* 1850

Ramakrishna 1836–86

Dayananda Sarasvati 1824–83

Brahmo Samaj Founded 1828

Sivadayal 1818–78

Arumuga Navalar 1822–79

Sahajanandaswami 1781–1830

Collapse of Mughal Dynasty 1720

1900

1700

Chart 57

Timeline of Hinduism (continued)

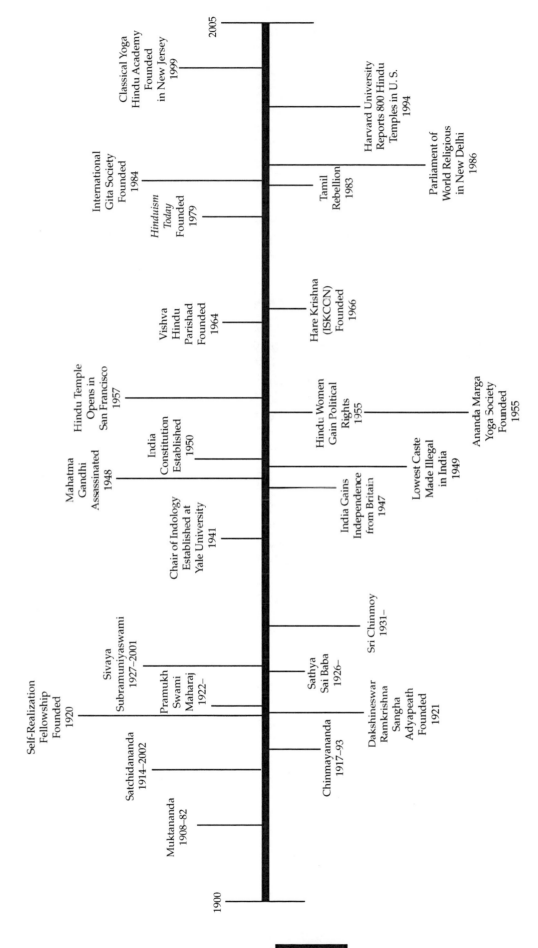

Muktananda
1908–82

Satchidananda
1914–2002

Self-Realization
Fellowship
Founded
1920

Sivaya
Subramuniyaswami
1927–2001

Pramukh
Swami
Maharaj
1922–

Chinmayananda
1917–93

Sathya
Sai Baba
1926–

Dakshineswar
Ramkrishna
Sangha
Adyapeath
Founded
1921

Sri Chinmoy
1931–

Chair of Indology
Established at
Yale University
1941

Mahatma
Gandhi
Assassinated
1948

India
Constitution
Established
1950

Hindu Temple
Opens in
San Francisco
1957

India Gains
Independence
from Britain
1947

Lowest Caste
Made Illegal
in India
1949

Hindu Women
Gain Political
Rights
1955

Ananda Marga
Yoga Society
Founded
1955

Vishva
Hindu
Parishad
Founded
1964

Hare Krishna
(ISKCON)
Founded
1966

International
Gita Society
Founded
1984

Hinduism
Today
Founded
1979

Tamil
Rebellion
1983

Harvard University
Reports 800 Hindu
Temples in U. S.
1994

Parliament of
World Religious
in New Delhi
1986

Classical Yoga
Hindu Academy
Founded
in New Jersey
1999

1900

2005

Chart 57

Hinduism

Topic	Facts
Current Data	Hinduism is the third largest religion in the world; only Christianity and Islam have more adherents. Thirteen percent of the world's population is Hindu, totaling about 762 million. Hindus are concentrated in India, Nepal, and parts of Sri Lanka. There are between 750,000 and 1.1 million Hindus in the United States and approximately 160,000 in Canada.
	During the past few years, a Hindu nationalist political party has controlled the government of India. The combination of religion, federal government, and nationalism has led to less separation between church and state in India than in previous decades. This, in turn, has decreased the level of religious tolerance in that country, with disputes and even violence between Hindus and Muslims. In some areas, Christian missionaries and churches are not welcome.
History	Scholars have theorized that Hinduism began in the Indus Valley (present-day Pakistan and western India) as a melding of two forms of religious practice: Vedism and the traditional beliefs of the Indus Valley civilization. One theory is that Indo-European tribes (Aryans) from eastern Europe invaded northern India about 1800 BC, destroying the Indus culture. These tribes brought with them their religious beliefs (Vedism), which became mixed with the beliefs of the Indus Valley people. However, an increasing number of scholars now dispute the invasion theory, basing their conclusions on archeological findings and other studies. They think Vedism had been practiced by that Indus Valley civilization and was not brought in by invaders. The destruction of the Indus culture, they say, which contributed to the development of Hinduism, was due to natural disasters and internal social problems.
	The story of Hinduism may be divided into four epochs. (1) The Pre-Vedic Period (c. 3000–1500 BC). During this time the inhabitants of the Indus Valley may have practiced animism, with cult centers where a great goddess and a divine bull were worshiped. (2) The Vedic Period (c. 1500–700 BC). This period witnessed the rise of Hindu polytheism and the Hindu caste system. The hymns of the *Rig Veda* developed during this time. (3) The Upanishadic Period (starting c. 700 BC). During this period Hinduism experienced many changes. Vedic views of the gods began to fade and the focus turned from the present world to concern about the next life, the cycle of death and rebirth, enlightenment, asceticism, and how a guru and his disciples related. (4) The Post-Upanishadic Period (c. 200 BC–AD 200). During this period came the writing of the Bhagavad Gita, the reemergence of the Vedic scriptures, and increasing devotion to the gods Brahma, Krishna, and Shiva.
	Between the 4th and 8th centuries AD, the religion continued to grow, largely due to the influence of the *Puranas*, Hindu scriptures explaining many of the doctrines of Hinduism. Also during this period, acrimony began to develop between Hinduism and Islam. Islamic invaders in the 11th century limited the practice of Hinduism for nearly 500 years. Better times came for Hindus, however, under the reign of Muslim sultan Jalaluddin Akbar (1542–1605). Due to the spread of Sikhism during this time, the possibility that Hindu and Islamic beliefs could be joined to produce a religion promoting peace and harmony emerged, but a revival of Islam in the

Chart 58

Hinduism (continued)

Topic	Facts
History (continued)	18th century, and the subsequent colonization of India by Great Britain in the 19th century, frustrated the efforts of those who were working for this syncretism. Beginning in the 1880s and continuing well into the 20th century, Hinduism began to spread into Europe and the United States. This outreach included groups such as Theosophy, the Divine Light Mission, Self-Realization Fellowship, Ananda Marga, and Hare *Krishna*.
Summary of Beliefs	Hinduism teaches the following: 1. There is only one Ultimate Reality. This is true despite the fact that the world of appearances contains many discrete objects. 2. Essentially all human beings are the same, since each person is identified with the one Ultimate Reality. (This belief stands in an uneasy tension with the social inequalities inherent in India's caste system.) 3. The Law of Karma ensures that everyone receives just recompense for their behavior. This law is built into the very fabric of the universe and cannot be thwarted. 4. People should refrain from harming any creature except in cases where inflicting violence is necessary for some greater good. Causing as little pain and suffering to others as possible is the highest moral virtue. 5. When the people of the world fall into ignorance and immorality, Brahman manifests himself as an avatar (incarnation in the form of a deity) to help humanity regain its former knowledge and righteousness.

Topic	Summary of View
Creation	The cosmos is an eternal emanation of Brahman, whose essence is without form or attribute, ubiquitous, pure consciousness, and bliss (*sat-chit-ananda*). The male aspect of the creation (Sri Bhagavte) is immutable and unending. The female aspect of the creation (Sri Bhagavati) acts through its creative power (*shakti*) to fashion the world into a suitable form. The entire cosmos is permeated by Paramatma, a divine energy. In some types of devotional Hinduism (Bhakti), Brahma is the personal creator of the world.
Scripture and Authority	The Hindu scriptures developed over a period of 2000 years. Their classification and organization are a contentious issue, since there are equally valid ways of grouping the texts and there is no clear consensus among practicing Hindus or scholars of Hinduism. It is common, however, to divde these texts into two main groups, the Shruti and Smriti. Shruti (what is heard) is the record of God's truth heard in the cosmos. It is thought to consist of four Vedas (collectively the Brahmanas): 1. the *Rig Veda* (knowledge of praise), a collection of more than 1,000 hymns; 2. the *Atharva-Veda* (priestly knowledge), dedicated to topics of medicine, warfare, and different rituals;

Chart 58

Hinduism (continued)

Topic	Summary of View
Scripture and Authority (continued)	3. the *Sama-Veda* (knowledge of chants), containing hymns and various chants to be recited; and 4. the *Yajur-Veda* (knowledge of sacrifice), describing a number of liturgies and rituals. These *Vedas*, in turn, are often divided into subdivisions. Those texts not part of Shruti comprise the Smriti (what deserves to be remembered). The Smriti is divided into six major sections: 1. the *Dharma Shasta* (Knowledge of the Laws); 2. the *Mahakayyas* (Epics); 3. the *Puranas* (Ancient Writings); 4. the *Sutras* (Proverbs); 5. the *Agamas* (consisting of devotional texts of various Hindu sects); and 6. the *Dyasanas* (Philosophies). The *Puranas* are arguably the most widely consulted sacred writings in Hinduism. An important subtext is the *Mahabharata* (Epic of the Bharta Dynasty), a collection of dialogues and parables within a larger narrative. It includes the *Bhagavad Gita* (Song of the Lord)—one of the most popular and influential writings within Hinduism—and the *Ramayana*, an epic interspersed with discussions of religious devotion and philosophy.
God*	Early Hinduism taught that there was one absolute reality having two natures: Atman, the Universal Spirit, and Brahman, the power of God. This one reality (Atman-Brahman) is the source and ground of the entire cosmos and is omnipresent. Human beings observe Atman-Brahman in the objective world of phenomena and in the subjective world of personal experience. Later Hinduism, though, believed that God has three aspects: (1) Brahma, the omniscient, unfathomable, self-existent (*swayambhu*) ground of the world; (2) Vishnu, the sustainer and preserver of the world in its present form; periodically, Vishnu embodies some of his divine attributes by means of avatars (personal manifestations of the divine essence); and (3) Shiva, who is capable of both uniting and destroying the cosmos. Other gods (avatars) include Krishna, Rama, Ganesh, Durga, Saraswati, Kartikeya, Lakshmi, Gauri, and Hanuman. Even in later Hinduism, though, God is often viewed as being Absolute in the final analysis; he is then referred to as Parabrahma.

* Hinduism has been characterized variously as pantheistic (monistic), polytheistic, henotheistic, and monotheistic. Though this is due in part to the differing emphases of different schools of Hindu thought, much of the seeming inconsistency in characterizing Hinduism can be attributed to the fact that traditional Western categories of deity don't apply in a straightforward manner to the most common Hindu concepts of God.

Chart 58

Hinduism (continued)

Topic	Summary of View
Mankind	Every human being possesses an imperishable soul (*atman*) that continues to exist throughout the entire cycle of death and rebirth. However, this "individual" *atman* is actually an aspect of Atman-Brahman, sharing all of Atman-Brahman's qualities, including infinity and eternality. For at least 1,500 years, Hinduism has sanctioned a rigid caste system comprised of five distinct castes: (1) Brahmins (priests and scholars); (2) *kshatriyas* (rulers and military personnel); (3) *vaisyas* (people involved in business and commerce); (4) *sudras* (farmers and domestic servants); and (5) *dalit* (untouchables). A person's caste is determined by the community (*jat*) into which that person is born, though today an increasing number of Hindus support either caste mobility or eradication of caste distinctions.
Sin	Sin consists of two primary elements: (1) *avidya* (ignorance concerning reality) and (2) *maya* (the illusion that persons are real). The persistent quandary in which human beings find themselves involves misapprehending the nature of the self and the cosmos. By recognizing that everything is one undifferentiated reality, including oneself, a person escapes from the otherwise endless cycle of reincarnation (*samsara*). Evil actions, especially violent ones, result in a person accumulating bad karma, which inhibits the person's ability to break free from ignorance and illusion.
Salvation	People who realize their identity with Brahman obtain release (*moksha*) from their ignorance and are no longer subject to the karmic laws that cause one's soul to be reincarnated. Instead, they have attained enlightenment and provisional union with Brahman that will become final at death. Spiritual paths that can assist a person in this quest include *bhakti marga* (the path of devotion) and *jnana marga* (the path of knowledge). In all cases, a person must act consistently with *dharma* (the ways of Hindu spirituality).
Afterlife	After death, a person's soul migrates to another body, a process called the Transmigration of the Soul. A person's next life may be spent in a human body or in the body of an animal or insect. Until a person attains spiritual liberation, there is a continuous cycle of birth, life, death, and rebirth, which may last numerous (even millions) of lifetimes.

Distinctive Beliefs and Practices

Mark on Forehead	A female Hindu who wears a colored dot on her forehead (known variously as a *tilaka*, *bottu*, *bindiya*, and *kumkum*) does so to make it known to all that she is a pious Hindu. The dot symbolizes the "third eye," which is supposed to be focused on the divine essence within. In previous times most unmarried women wore black marks, while most married women wore red ones. More recently in India, Hindu women frequently wear dots that match the color of their sari (a garment consisting of a long strip of cloth that can be wrapped around the body in various ways).

Chart 58

Hinduism (continued)

Topic	Summary of View
Three Debts During Life	For Hindus, there are three Debts during life: 1. Debt to God, repaid by committing one's life in service to God by helping others, showing respect to teachers and elders, telling the truth, being non-violent to all creatures, and refraining from consumption of meat; 2. Debt to saints and gurus, repaid by venerating gurus and saints, by passing on Hindu doctrine and culture, and by caring for the needy; and 3. Debt to ancestors, repaid by living in accordance with Hindu ethics.
Ten Great Observances	The Ten Great Observances of Hinduism are: 1. *indriya nigraha* (subduing the senses and sexual urges), 2. *asteya* (refraining from theft and/or being selfish), 3. *akrodha* (not being controlled by anger), 4. *kshama* (forgiving others), 5. *saucham* (purity and truthfulness), 6. *dama* (self-restraint and contentment), 7. *dhruti* (steadfastness), 8. *satya* (truth and social justice), 9. *dhee* (proper understanding of the Hindu scriptures), and 10. *vidya* (knowledge of the divine).
Four Stages of Hindu Life	Traditional Hinduism acknowledges four stages in life: 1. Brahmacharya Ashrama: Beginning (as a young boy) and completing (as a young man) the process of formal education, during which the boy learns the things he will need to know in order to succeed in life as an adult. 2. Grhastha Ashrama: Getting married, paying the Three Debts, and taking pleasure in life within the bounds of Hindu standards of behavior. 3. Vanaprastha Ashrama: Entered into once his children have grown up, it involves a gradual withdrawal from society so that the middle-aged man can spend most of his time in study and meditation. 4. Sannyasa Ashrama: The older Hindu man completely withdraws from social relationships and focuses entirely upon contemplating spiritual things.

Chart 58

Hinduism (continued)

Topic	Summary of View
Four Ends of Hindu Life	The Four Ends of Hindu Life are: 1. *dharma*: acting righteously in every sphere of life in accordance with Hindu teachings; 2. *artha* (wealth): earning enough money to support the basic needs of a family and establish a household, with excess being shared with others in need; 3. *kama*: satisfying legitimate human desires by enjoying things like music, good food, fine clothing, and loving relationships in a restrained and measured manner; and 4. *moksha*: attaining liberation from the cycle of death and rebirth.
Yoga	Yoga is a set of methods employed by many Hindus in their quest to attain liberation from an endless series of reincarnations. Its main goal is to bring about a radical change in consciousness by means of exercising strict control of the mind and body. All sects of Hinduism practice some form of yoga. Prerequisites of successful yoga include the realization that all legitimate religions lead to the same goal, and a striving for purity and contentment. The practice of yoga involves assuming prescribed postures, controlling the rate of breathing, blocking out the senses, intense concentration, meditating on a single object, and going into *samadhi*, an altered mental state wherein the mind is totally at peace.

Chart 58

Comparison of Beliefs within Hinduism

	Scripture and Authority	God	Mankind
Brahmanism (Vedism) "The Way of Works"	Scriptures include the *Vedas*, early *Upanishads*, *Brahmanas*, *Agamas*, and *Puranas*. Generally, no single sacred text or small group of texts is considered to be more authoritative than any others. The Brahmins possess the authority to explain the meaning of the sacred scriptures.	A Trinitarian view is common wherein God has three primary manifestations: Brahma (Creator), Vishnu (Preserver), and Shiva (Destroyer). Other divine manifestations are also possible, and in some cases great numbers of lesser deities fall under the umbrella of Brahma-Vishnu-Shiva.	Human beings have an immortal soul (*atman*) that continues to exist through the course of successive deaths, transmigrations of the soul, and rebirths. On some accounts, this *atman* is ultimately the same as Atman, the Universal Spirit, which is identical to Brahman. In these cases, the true self is eternal, infinite, and has the same essence as Ultimate Reality. Nevertheless, making a distinction between the self and Brahman can aid in attaining liberation.
Advaita Vedanta "The Way of Knowledge"	Main scriptures are the *Upanishads*. The *Brahma-Sutras* and the *Bhagavad Gita* are also consulted. The *Vedas* have always existed and bear testimony to their own eternality; their authoritative character is seen in the fact that they are free from any fault (*dosa*) or limitation. Moreover, the *Vedas* provide knowledge about things that cannot be known by any other empirical means.	God (Brahman) is simultaneously both the instrumental and the material cause of the universe; nothing exists independently of Brahman. Yet Brahman cannot be identified with the universe because Brahman is beyond all change, whereas the perceived universe continually changes. To truly understand Brahman is to know Brahman to be devoid of parts, diversity, or attributes of any kind.	In reality, the true nature of the human self (*jiva*) is the Atman, which is unchanging and identical with Brahman. The "individual" is thus not truly a person, since all is Brahman. Making any sort of distinction between the self and Brahman jeopardizes one's attempt to attain liberation.
Bhakti* "The Way of Devotion"	Scriptures include the *Bhagavad Gita*, *Vedas*, *Upanishads*, and the writings of prominent gurus and saints. There is more emphasis on devotion and less on the study of Hindu scriptures than in other forms of Hinduism.	Any one of the gods or goddesses might be worshiped at any given time for a specific purpose. Many of the deities have histories associated with particular geographic regions of India.	Views often are similar to those of other Hindu traditions, though there is a greater tendency to disregard caste distinctions.

* Bhakti devotees can be divided into three main classes based on the primary god they worship: (1) Vaishnavites, who worship the Lord as Vishnu, Krishna, and/or Rama; (2) Shaivites, who venerate the Lord as Shiva; and (3) Shaktites, who adore the Mother aspect of the Lord as Devi, Durga, Kali, Parvati, or Uma. Additionally, there are the Sauras, who worship the Sun-God; Ganapatyas who worship the elephant god Ganesh as supreme; Kumaras who worship Skanda as the godhead; and those who are devotees of Hunuman, the monkey god.

Chart 59

Comparison of Beliefs within Hinduism (continued)

	Sin	Salvation	Afterlife
Brahmanism "The Way of Works"	Often the emphasis is on particular evil acts and the Law of Karma. In some cases the fundamental human predicament is taken to be the problem of *avidya* (ignorance of the truth) and *maya* (attributing reality to personhood; the illusion of individuality). On this view, all people begin life misunderstanding the nature of the self and of ultimate reality.	Attained when the soul realizes its identity with all that is; when this occurs, the soul becomes One with Brahman. *Raja yoga* meditation techniques can aid in this quest. Brahmans (priests) speak mystical words that aid in liberation.	In early Brahmanism, the dead are absorbed into the natural world, living in another form on this earth. In later Hinduism, the belief was that after death one's soul is transferred into another body; this body could be human, animal, or even an insect. One undergoes an unending cycle of reincarnations until liberation is achieved.
Advaita Vedanta "The Way of Knowledge"	People suffer from bondage in this life because they are caught in an endless cycle of death and rebirth. Bondage arises from ignorance (*avidya*) of mankind's true nature.	Consists in being released from bondage and thus breaking the cycle of reincarnation and attaining liberation (*moksha*). Liberation comes when a person knows his true nature. One who fully grasps this by a personal experience of Atman-Brahman, is liberated even before death. Such a person is a *jivanmukta*.	One either undergoes rebirth (if one failed to break free from the false perception of oneself as a truly existing and abiding self) or else enjoys liberation from the cycle of reincarnation (if one was enlightened regarding the reality of one's nature).
Bhakti "The Way of Devotion"	Views often are similar to those of other Hindu traditions, though more emphasis is put on particular acts of evil-doing. People are overly conscious of the body and do not focus adequately on the mind.	Aim is union with God. Intense love for God and surrender to him, reliance on his grace rather than on rituals, learning, or ascetic practices and the continuous repetition of his name are the means to liberation. Inner feelings are stressed and institutional forms of religion are downplayed. Nevertheless, popular means of expressing love for God include *puja* (ritual devotion) and *bhajans* (devotional songs).	Frequently viewed not as the dissolution of the devotee into Brahman, but as an eternal resting place for the individual personality in the arms of a loving, personal deity.

Chart 59

Brahmanism

Topic	Facts
Current Data	The influence of Brahmanism in India has lessened substantially since the British colonization of India. As of 1998 about 12 percent of Hindus in the upper Ganges plains were Brahmans. However, the number of Brahmans drops dramatically in other regions of India. For example, in Assam, Orissa, and Tamil Nadu, Brahmans comprise less than 3 percent of the Hindu population.
History	Brahmanism developed its worship and philosophy from the Vedas beginning around 1100 BC. Over many centuries, Indian society developed a rigid caste system, which took solid form around 600 BC. Brahmanism came to view the Brahmin caste as a group of hereditary clergy. During the first stages of its history, an evolution took place from early Brahmanism (Vedism) to later forms, both popular and priestly. The founder of Buddhism, Siddhãrtha Gautama (c. 563–483 BC), contended that the Vedas were not revelatory scripture, denied the efficacy of Brahmanical ceremonies, and rejected the Brahmanical priests' claim that they were the repositories and divinely appointed teachers of sacred knowledge. Gautama also vigorously opposed the caste system of his day, which favored the Brahmins (clergy). This led to the rapid decline of the authority of orthodox Brahmanical dogma and a corresponding development of sects within Hinduism. Around AD 200, Brahmanism began to be seriously challenged by other schools of Hindu thought, some of which later took form as different types of classical Hinduism, like Advaita Vedanta. In the 20th century, B. R. Ambedkar (1891–1956) revived Buddhism in India and campaigned against Brahmin supremacy and the existence of the "untouchable" caste.
Summary of Beliefs	Brahmanism is a very early form of Hinduism, or proto-Hinduism. The fundamental aspects of Brahmanism developed from a series of priestly commentaries on the original four Vedas, commonly known as the *Brahmanas*. Brahmanas is a Sanskrit word meaning "explanations of Brahman," or "sacred word." Each of the four Vedas acquired corresponding Brahmanas: the Aitareya and Kausitaki (Sankhayana) for the *Rig Veda*; the Kathaka, Taittiriya, and Satapatha for the *Yajur Veda*; the Pancavimsa (Tandyamaha) and its appendix, the Sanvimas and Jaiminiya (Talavakara), for the *Sama Veda*; and the Gopatha for the *Atharva Veda*. These extensive discourses served as guides for the priests (Brahmins) as they performed rituals and sacrifices and as explanations of the nature of Brahman and the basic beliefs of Brahmanism as a religion. Within this general framework, there exists a range of views on a number of particular doctrines. Moreover, in many respects Brahmanism is difficult to characterize because what is referred to as Brahmanism underwent extensive historical development and, in some stages, begins to overlap with subsequent schools of thought.

Chart 60

Brahmanism (continued)

Topic	Summary of View
Creation	The universe as a whole embodies a divine structure. Brahman is the metaphysical ground of the world. There is no uniform belief concerning the creation of the universe. Broadly speaking, two main views are held: a theistic view in which Brahman creates (by fashioning preexisting substance, not *ex nihilo,* out of nothing) a world of real particulars and a "pantheistic" view in which a cosmos (composed of different aspects of the same underlying substance) emanates from the being of Brahman. A number of mythological accounts circulated among adherents of early Brahmanism (Vedism).
Scripture and Authority	The primary holy texts are the *Rig Veda,* the early *Upanishads,* and the *Brahmanas.* Others include the *Agamas* and the *Puranas.* Occupying the highest Hindu caste, Vedic priest-shamans (Brahmins) are the keepers of sacred hymns, and cosmic power is thought to reside in their inspired utterances. Brahmins are said to have come from the mouth of the Purusha (Cosmic Man).
God	There is no single, coherent view. Brahmanic thought has taken on pantheistic, polytheistic, henotheistic, and monotheistic forms, though it is not always clear precisely how to differentiate between these "competing" conceptions. An ancient classification of the gods had 33 deities, 11 in each of the three realms of nature. Later the notion of a threefold divine government, consisting of Agni, Indra or Vayu, and Sirya, emerged. Yet even in cases where there is a plurality of gods, each individual deity is addressed as being supreme. On some accounts Brahman created the lesser gods; on others these deities are but manifestations of one God. Many adherents see Brahman as transcending finite individuality, omnipresent, having non-dual self-awareness, beyond human thought, and the essence of all things. Most common is a Trinitarian view in which God takes on three main manifestations: Brahma (Creator), Vishnu (Preserver), and Shiva (Destroyer).
Mankind	On some accounts, human beings are creatures who can attain a place among the gods. On others, the self (Atman) and Brahman are ontologically distinct, but can be united in a way that diminishes this metaphysical difference. The Atman exists throughout the course of successive deaths, transmigrations of the soul, and rebirths. Sometimes Atman is said to be ultimately the same as Brahman. Even in these cases, however, making distinctions between the self and Brahman is thought to help in attaining liberation.
Sin	One emphasis is on particular evil acts. Here every good action guarantees a future recompense, and every evil action destines its perpetrator to reap correlative misery (Law of Karma). Another emphasis is ignorance (*avidya*) of the nature of Brahman and *maya* (falsely attributing independent reality to the self).

Chart 60

Brahmanism (continued)

Topic	Summary of View
Salvation	In early Brahmanism (Vedism), this was pursued by means of an extensive and complex system of prayers, sacrifices, ceremonies, sacramental rites, and recitation of the *Vedas*. In this system, the transcendent cosmic order and the whole of the spoken and acted proceedings of the rituals were seen as concentrated and internalized in the person of the priest, such that the sacred words he spoke had real potency. Escape from rebirths and their attendant misery was achieved by storing up the merits of good deeds; morally pure persons obtain an eternal life of conscious bliss in heaven. Later in the historical development of Brahmanism, the attainment of final emancipation (*moksha*) was dependent on having perfect knowledge of the divine essence. This knowledge could be obtained only by ceasing to focus the mind on external objects and meditating intensely on the divinity, and involved a number of austere practices (*tapas*). Liberation is attained when the soul realizes its identity with Brahman and is thereby united with him.
Afterlife	In early Brahmanism (Vedism), the dead are assimilated with the natural world and live in some other form on this earth. The concepts of reincarnation and attaining heaven became popular at a later stage in the development of Hinduism. Here lasting bliss in heaven was held out to those who were righteous, while various post mortem fates were reserved for the wicked. These varied according to the nature and degree of moral guilt, ranging from long periods of torture in a graded series of hells to a series of rebirths in successive forms of plants, animals, and human beings. This process continues until liberation is attained. Later in the historical development of Brahmanism, the few who succeed in gaining complete mastery over their senses and procuring an accurate knowledge of the divine nature are absorbed into the Universal Soul immediately upon the dissolution of the body.

Distinctive Beliefs and Practices

Samskaras (Sacramental Rites)	There are 16 of these rites, which are described in a group of texts called *Grihyasutras*: (1) *Garbhadhan* (Sacrament of Impregnation), (2) *Punsavanam* (occurs during the second or third month of pregnancy), (3) *Simantonnayana* (takes place between the fifth and eighth month of pregnancy), (4) *Jatakarma* (performed during childbirth), (5) *Namakarana* (naming the child), (6) *Niskramana* (when the three- or four-month-old infant is brought out of house), (7) *Annaprashana* (the first feeding of cereal when the child is six months old), (8) *Chudakarma* (the first time the child gets a haircut, usually at one to three years of age), (9) *Karnavedha* (piercing the child's ears in the third to fifth year), (10) *Upanayana* (Investiture of the Sacred Thread, when young boys are assigned to a spiritual teacher, usually at age eight), (11) *Samavartana* (when studies are completed), (12) *Vivaha Samskara* (marriage ceremony), (13) *Grihasthashrama* (sacraments relating to householders), (14) *Vanprasthashrama* (renouncing the life of a householder), (15) *Sanyasashrama* (becoming a monk), and (16) *Antyeshti* (funeral rites).

Chart 60

Brahmanism (continued)	
Distinctive Beliefs and Practices	
Vegetarianism	Traditionally, as a matter of cultural identity, most Brahmins (priests) were known for practicing vegetarianism. Today the practice is based on geographical region and orthodoxy more than on caste. For instance, many Brahmins from West Bengal eat fish. Brahmins who act as priests are strict vegetarians. Milk and most dairy products are allowed, however, so this does not constitute veganism.
Devotion to the Fathers (*Pitris*)	The happiness of dead people depends in part on their living relatives performing prescribed acts of devotion. These include offerings of *soma* (an intoxicating juice), rice, and water and feast offerings (*sraddhas*). In return for these acts of love and respect for one's ancestors, the grateful *pitris* (ancestors) protect the living from harm and promote their welfare.

Chart 60

Advaita Vedanta

Topic	Facts
Current Data	It is impossible to estimate the number of adherents worldwide with a degree of accuracy sufficient to merit its inclusion in this chart. Prominent organizations include the Vedanta Society of Southern California and Maharishi Mahesh Yogi's Transcendental Meditation program.
History	The first Hindu thinker to systematize the principles of Advaita Vedanta was Adi Shankara (788–820). Basing his views in part on previous Upanishadic teachers, including Gaudapada, his own instructor, Shankara expounded the doctrine of Advaita (ultimate reality as monistic). This teaching entailed the position that the phenomenal world has only a relative, and ultimately unreal, existence. Subsequent Vedantins debated whether the reality of Brahman was *saguna* (with attributes) or *nirguna* (without attributes). Partly as a result of these philosophical conversations, a proliferation of serious devotion to Vishnu and Shiva emerged in India. Advaita Vedanta philosophy also had a remarkable impact on Tantric Hinduism and supported the Yogic teaching that Brahman and Atman are One. The emergence of Advaita Vedanta also led to debates regarding Vishishtadvaita (qualified non-dualism) versus Dvaita (dualism). In the 19th century, Ramakrishna (1836–86) did much to spread the message of Advaita Vedanta. In the 20th century, some followers of Advaita contended that Einsteinian physics served to establish the Advaitic unity of the universe.
Summary of Beliefs	Human beings suffer from bondage to the illusions of life in this world (*maya*) and thus are caught in an endless cycle of births and deaths (*samsara*). The Advaitan quest is to escape from this bondage by breaking the cycle of rebirths and attaining liberation (*moksha*). Overcoming ignorance (*avidya*) of human nature ends this bondage. The key to—and the essence of—liberation is knowledge (*jnana*) of one's true nature. This true nature is mankind's innermost essence, the *Atman*, which is the same as Brahman.

Topic	Summary of View
Creation	There are three main ways of understanding creation: *Ajati Vada* (creation is not an absolute, real event), *Srshti-drshti Vada* (what has been created is perceived), and *Drshti-srshti Vada* (perception is simultaneous with creation). On all three views, Brahman is simultaneously the instrumental and material cause of the universe, and the universe participates in reality only insofar as it is dependent on Brahman. In general it can be said that what people refer to as "the universe" is merely a mental construct that they superimpose on the underlying reality of Brahman. Moreover, all accounts of causality ultimately are deficient, since they presuppose an ontological distinction between cause and effect.
Scripture and Authority	The primary scriptures are the *Upanishads*, though the *Brahma-Sutras* and the *Bhagavad-Gita* also are considered important. The *Vedas* are eternally existent, their authority stems from their perfection, and they provide knowledge about things that cannot be otherwise known.

Chart 61

Advaita Vedanta (continued)

Topic	Summary of View
God	God (Brahman) possesses no attributes (*nirguna*) or diverse aspects whatsoever, nor does he act; he is the eternal, changeless cause of the universe. Though the world of appearances, the world that can be seen, is ultimately unreal, Brahman is not to be identified with the universe, because whereas the universe undergoes continuous change, Brahman transcends all change. The reality of Brahman cannot be captured by human language.
Mankind	The true nature of the human self (*jiva*) is eternal and unchanging, being identical with Brahman. Thus "individuals" are not really persons; the deceptive superimposition of the concept of a self onto Brahman causes the illusory belief in personhood.
Sin	Human beings cannot directly perceive Brahman due to a pervasive and systemic illusion (*maya*) concerning the true reality of things. They also suffer from ignorance (*avidya*) of the actual nature of human beings. As a result, people are in bondage, trapped in an endless cycle of death and rebirth (*samsara*).
Salvation	Consists of being released from bondage, thereby breaking the cycle of rebirths and attaining liberation (*moksha*). Making any sort of distinction between the self and Brahman jeopardizes one's attempt to attain liberation. Liberation occurs when individuals come to have knowledge (*jnana*) of their true nature by means of both intellectual acknowledgment and the experience of their metaphysical unity with Brahman. Once the illusion of selfhood is recognized, the individuals see the unreality of their own existence, inasmuch as all is Brahman. A liberated person is known as a *jivanmukta*.
Afterlife	After death, those who failed to disabuse themselves of the belief that they are a really existing and abiding self undergo rebirth. Those who became enlightened as to the reality of their true nature gain liberation from the cycle of reincarnation.

Distinctive Beliefs and Practices	
Worship	Vishnu, Shiva, and Shakti are worshiped not as independent gods or as manifestations of a single theistic God, but as forms of Saguna Brahman.
Metaphysical Monism	All of reality is ultimately of one and the same substance, in this case Brahman.

Chart 61

Bhakti

Topic	Facts
Current Data	It is estimated that there are more than 750 million devotees worldwide. The most well-known Bhakti movement in the United States is the International Society for Krishna Consciousness (ISKCON), also known as the Hare Krishnas.
History	Though not widespread before the 13th century, various forms of Bhakti have probably been a part of Hinduism since its earliest stages. There are traces of it in some of the *Upanishads*. The *Mahabharata* epic, written sometime before AD 200, contains ideas found in later Bhakti movements. The first documented Bhakti movement was founded in the 6th century AD by Karaikkal-Ammaiyar, who wrote poems in Tamil describing her love for Shiva. In the 13th century, Basaveshwara (1131–67) founded the Vira-Shaiva school of Hinduism. He repudiated the caste system, denied the supremacy of the Brahmins, condemned ritual sacrifice, and insisted on worshiping Shiva alone. Shri Madhvacharya (1238–1317) was one of the fathers of the Vaishnava Bhakti movement. He propounded a dualistic view of reality (Dvaita Vedanta) in which there is a fundamental ontological difference between the ultimate Godhead and the individual soul. Around 1300, the Saiva-Siddhanta school was founded in southern India. It maintained that Shiva is God and that his love is revealed in the creation, preservation, and destruction of the universe and in the liberation of souls. A sizable Bhakti movement swept through northern India during the period 1400–1650. This period witnessed a spate of devotional literature in the ethnic languages of various Indian provinces, including many poems praising Vishnu and the now-legendary songs of Ramprasad Sen that proclaim love for Devi. It also saw the emergence of Ramananda's teachings, which maintained that Rama is the supreme Lord, and that salvation could be attained only through devotion to him, including the repetition of his name. Other major figures in the proliferation of Bhakti during this time included Vallabhacharya (1479–1531), who taught that only by God's grace can one obtain release from bondage and attain the highest heaven of Krishna; Chaitanya Mahaprabhu (1485–1533), whose Achintya Bheda-Bheda (incomprehensible dualistic monism) philosophy attempted to combine elements of monism and dualism into a single system; and Srimanta Sankardeva (1449–1569), who introduced special prayer halls called *naamghors*. Since being established, Bhakti Hinduism has remained the dominant factor in Indian religious life.
Summary of Beliefs	Bhakti movements are popular Hindu religious movements in which the main spiritual practice is the fostering of loving devotion to God. They are theistic and usually devoted to the worship of Shiva, Vishnu, or Shakti. The appeal of Bhakti lies in the fact that devotees do not have to bear the burdens of ritual and/or caste, nor do they have to work through the complexities of Hindu philosophy; instead, they can simply express their overwhelming love for God. The Bhakti tradition stresses authentic inner feelings as opposed to institutional forms of religion and typically disregards caste distinctions. Although Bhakti has some general characteristics, its particular manifestations can vary considerably, often reflecting local and regional idiosyncrasies. Even many of the deities worshiped are regional, many of them having had their names and forms changed over time.

Chart 62

Bhakti (continued)

Topic	Summary of View
Creation	In every case there is a theistic account in which God orders the universe, though some stories tend toward a monistic view of reality while others tend toward a dualistic understanding of the world and God. Details vary depending on the particular deity worshiped and the corresponding creation myth to which devotees subscribe.
Scripture and Authority	There is less emphasis on the classical Hindu scriptures and more focus on singing hymns, chanting, performing dramas, dancing, and reciting the heroic deeds or erotic sports of various gods. Unlike Brahmanism, wherein authority is vested in a priestly class, individuals decide what deity to worship and how to worship him or her. The most popular devotional book is the *Bhagavad-Gita*. Other holy texts include the *Vedas*, *Upanishads*, *Vedangas*, *Darshanas*, *Dharma Shastras*, *Puranas*, *Mahabharata*, *Ramayana*, *Agamas*, and the writings of the *jagadgurus* (great gurus, the best in the world), *acharyas* (prominent gurus who teach by example), and saints.
God	Typically, God is viewed as an extremely wise, powerful, and loving divine person, totally distinct from his worhipers. In some cases, however, God and his worshipers are thought to consist of the same substance and thus to be identical (in the final analysis). Nearly all views affirm that the divine reality is infinitely superior to human beings, and that finite souls and material objects are a subordinate reality. The three most common deities worshiped are Shiva, Vishnu, and Shakti. Still, any god or goddess might be worshiped at any time for a specific purpose. Many of the gods have histories associated with specific areas of India. Usually Brahma is considered to be the supreme god, but is not seen as a personal god, and is not often worshiped.
Mankind	(See Hinduism: Mankind for the basic view.) A strong religious egalitarianism (equality of all humans) is espoused, along with an emphasis on the maintenance of communities of good people (*satsang*). Metaphysically speaking, views are typical of those found in other Hindu traditions, though socially there is a much greater tendency to downplay caste distinctions.
Sin	Any kind of evil-doing, as defined by the ethical standards of traditional Hinduism. Most significantly, failing to demonstrate devotion to a worthy deity.
Salvation	Consists of an intense and passionate love between devotee and deity wherein the devotee surrenders to the deity. Sometimes this involves a particular kind of yoga in which the devotee contemplates God. There is a firm reliance on the grace of the deity rather than on rituals, learning, or austerities. God acts through the devotee in such a way that the person's sins fall away of their own accord, without effort on the part of the devotee. The continuous repetition of the deity's name is the primary means for coming into the deity's constant presence. The devotee's goal is total union with God.
Afterlife	Liberation (*moksha*) from material embodiment in the present imperfect world and the attainment of a state of abiding communion with God. In most cases this is understood merely as being in the loving presence of God; sometimes it is thought to consist of a spiritual or even quasi-physical union with God in which the individual ego is dissolved.

Chart 62

Bhakti (continued)

	Distinctive Beliefs and Practices
Five Attitudes Toward God	The devotee may adopt different attitudes, or modes, in relation to the deity. These include: 1.　*Shanta Bhava*, the peace and stillness felt in the presence of God; 2.　*Dasya Bhava*, the attitude of a servant toward master; 3.　*Sakhya Bhava*, the attitude of a friend toward a superior friend; 4.　*Vatsalya Bhava*, the attitude of a child toward a parent; and 5.　*Madhura Bhava*, the attitude of a lover toward the beloved.
Four Degrees of Communion with God	The devotee's communion with the deity admits of varying degrees. They are: 1.　*salokya* (being in the same heaven as God, with a continuous vision of him), 2.　*samipya* (residing close to God), 3.　*sarupya* (having the same form as God, which is the privilege of his intimate attendants), and 4.　*sayujya* (complete union with God through entering his body).
Puja	Ritual devotion, frequently using the aid of a *murti* (statue) in conjunction with the singing or chanting of meditational prayer in the form of mantras. Devotional songs called *bhajans*, *kirtan* (praise), and *arti* (a modified form of Vedic fire ritual) are sometimes sung in conjunction with performance of *puja*. This syncretistic system of devotion is meant to aid the devotee's quest to unite with God.

Chart 62

Self-Realization Fellowship

Topic	Facts
Current Data	The Self-Realization Fellowship has over 450 meditation centers worldwide, but the number of members is unknown, since the group does not keep membership records. The headquarters is located in Los Angeles, California. An annual conference is attended by thousands of practitioners from around the globe.
History	Paramahansa Yogananda (1893–1952) was known in his youth as Mukunda Lal Ghosh. He was born in Gorakhpur, India. During his childhood Mukunda was keenly interested in Hindu spirituality. When he was 17, Mukunda began to follow the teachings of Sri Yukteswar Giri (1855–1936) and became a disciple. In 1915 he graduated from Calcutta University and became a monk in India's Swami Order, receiving the title Paramahansa Yogananda. In 1917 he opened a school for boys in which instruction in Hinduism and traditional education were integrated. His prime achievement was the founding, in 1920, of Yogananda Self-Realization Fellowship as a means of propagating his understanding of meditation and yoga; five years later the organization's international headquarters was operating smoothly in Los Angeles, California. He spent the next 10 years giving lectures in the United States, Europe, and India. Around 1935 Yogananda began writing a series of lessons for study at home. After his death in 1952, Rajasi Janakananda (1892–1955) became the leader of SRF; he in turn was succeeded by Sri Daya Mata (1914–). By the 1990s SRF had become fairly well-known in the United States.
Summary of Beliefs	Self-Realization Fellowship does not have a body of doctrine similar to many world religions. Human beings need to be freed from their bondage to bodily diseases, wrong thinking, and spiritual ignorance. If God is acknowledged as the foundation of unity of the world's peoples, a global spiritual brotherhood that selflessly serves humanity can be formed. Self-Realization Fellowship advocates certain principles which they believe will further world harmony and progress. 1. Scientific methods for achieving direct and personal experience with God are known and should be taught to all people of the world. 2. The one pathway to which all religions ultimately lead is found through daily scientific and devotional mediation on God. 3. Christianity, as taught by Jesus Christ, is not different from yoga as Bhagavan Krishna explained it. 4. Self-Realization Fellowship temples have been established to lead all people to the purpose of their lives, to move from their limited consciousness to God Consciousness. 5. The mind is superior to the body and the soul is superior to the mind, so meditating daily is the surest path to accomplish health, peace, and unity.

Chart 63

Self-Realization Fellowship (continued)

Topic	Summary of View
Creation	The world of appearances, which is a pervasive illusion, is the result of God's *lila* (divine play). Although God is infinite and all-knowing, he desired creatures with whom he could share his divine bliss, so he divided himself into many finite souls and gave them a universe in which to live. In so doing, he changed himself from a purely spiritual being into a being having spiritual and natural aspects.
Scripture and Authority	Monks who are personally trained by Paramahansa Yogananda oversee the organization's activities. They teach classes, lead retreats, and provide spiritual guidance to students. There is no one sacred text recognized as superior to all others, but several popular religious books are significant, including the New Testament, the *Bhagavad Gita*, and Yogananda's autobiography.
God	Ultimately, nothing is real except God, the Absolute. All seemingly independent things are actually part of God, who is both impersonal and personal. The impersonal aspect is primary, but the personal dimension is also important, inasmuch as God has become personal and visible to human beings through the medium of the cosmos.
Mankind	Humanity is an illusion. The apparent existence of persons as enduring, separate selves is the result of God causing human beings, in his act of creating them, to be ignorant of their true nature. In reality human beings are part of the one Divine Substance, which is their true identity.
Sin	The fundamental human problem is ignorance of the fact that God and the world are ultimately one undifferentiated substance. Thinking of reality in dualistic (the world and God are different) rather than monistic (the world and God are the same) categories is the cause of all apparent suffering and evil. Ultimately, evil, suffering, and death are illusory.
Salvation	People achieve salvation when they overcome their ignorance of who they are and grasp their true divine identity. Self-realization is attaining Christ Consciousness (Divine Awareness). Special techniques of concentration and meditation, patterned after the yoga of Patanjali (c. AD 200), allow for this direct experience of God.
Afterlife	Affirms the standard Hindu view of karma and reincarnation, in which the deeds a person performs in this life determine the type of body into which the soul is deposited at the time of rebirth. The final goal is to attain Christ Consciousness, when the cycle of death and rebirth ceases.

Chart 63

Self-Realization Fellowship (continued)

Distinctive Beliefs and Practices

Kriya Yoga	One is able to calm inner turmoil through the Kriya Yoga method, based on Patanjali's Eightfold Path: 1. Moral conduct (*yama*) 2. Religious observances (*niyama*) 3. Right posture (*asana*) 4. Control of energy (*pranayama*) 5. Withdrawal of the senses (*pratyahara*) 6. Concentration (*dharana*) 7. Meditation (*dhyana*) 8. Superconscious experience (*samdhi*) When people follow this path, they are able to focus their energy around the six spinal centers of the body, bringing feelings of tranquility as the energy moves around the spine. Those who are most successful in the method will become oblivious to the world around them and unite with the forces of energy pervading them.

Appendix: Transcendental Meditation

Basic Beliefs and Practices	Similar in many ways to Self-Realization Fellowship, Transcendental Meditation (TM) is a program that presents itself as a religiously neutral set of meditation techniques, though many would argue that in fact it presupposes a number of distinctive Hindu beliefs. Maharishi Mahesh Yogi (1917–) founded TM by combining insights from the Hindu Vedas into a system known as the Science of Consciousness, TM being the main component. The Maharishi instructed his students to perform this technique for 15 to 20 minutes each morning and evening while sitting in a comfortable position with their eyes closed. The technique aims to calm practitioners and bring them into a state of restful alertness. According to practitioners, as the body relaxes deeply, the mind transcends all mental activity and experiences Transcendental Consciousness, the most fundamental mode of awareness. The claim is made that entering into Transcendental Consciousness develops the practitioner's creativity, releases stress, decreases fatigue, and activates latent powers of organization. This, in turn, increases the practitioner's effectiveness and general success. The Maharishi has established several institutions of learning, which teach what is dubbed "Vedic Science and Technology" as a way of improving social conditions and governments worldwide. The most prominent of these is Maharishi University in Fairfield, Iowa. There is considerable debate on whether the Maharishi Mahesh Yogi is dead or alive. He has been away from public view for many years.

Chart 63

Ananda Marga Yoga Society

Topic	Facts
Current Data	Ananda Marga adherents are concentrated largely in India and the Philippines, though members are scattered worldwide. The organization claims nearly 1 million members and has centers in more than 160 countries. Ananda Marga coordinates disaster relief efforts through the AMURT (Ananda Marga Universal Relief Team) and its sister organization, AMURTEL (Ananda Marga Universal Relief Team Ladies).
History	Ananda Marga (also known as Ananda Marga Yoga Society) was founded in 1955 in Bihar, India, by Prabhat Rainjain Sarkar (1921–90). The mission of Ananda Marga was to help individuals achieve complete self-realization. Sarkar also emphasized charitable service. Sarkar's movement soon spread into other regions of India. In 1962 Sarkar inducted the first monk into Ananda Marga, and four years later the organization included nuns. He started the Education, Relief, and Welfare Section (ERAWS) of Ananda in 1963. During the rest of the 1960s, Ananda greatly expanded the range of social welfare programs it offered, and by 1970 it had become a global presence.
Summary of Beliefs	Central to Ananda Marga is the importance of working toward social unity and human progress of all kinds. High on the agenda are bringing an end to religious bigotry and helping the impoverished and the marginalized. A major tenet of Ananda Marga is what is called "economic democracy." This involves guarding against human rights violations and working to strengthen local economies. Other issues important to the organization are eliminating government corruption, establishing an international constitution, promoting sustainable farming practices, funding railroads, advocating the use of science and technology in accordance with Ananda principles, and defending the rights of women. An interesting aspect of Ananda's teaching is that people are not only to love people and animals, but also plants.

Topic	Summary of View
Creation	Nirguna Brahma, an infinite consciousness that is the foundational unity of the universe and controls everything in the universe, transformed itself into the universe with the assistance of *prakrti* (the other aspect of Brahma). *Prakrti* (the aspect of Brahma which is consciousness, in contrast to Brahma, the operational aspect of deity) created a world containing distinct things by employing three methods, known as *gunas*, to modify Nirguna Brahma. *Sattva guna* brought forth human consciousness, *rajah guna* allows for the experience of acting in the present, and *tamah guna* makes memories possible; another *guna* also created physical objects.
Scripture and Authority	No sacred text has final authority in matters of doctrine and practice. However, several works by P. R. Sarkar are used as outlines of Ananda Marga philosophy and guide devotees in their daily lives. Sarkar's first book (written under the name Shrii Shrii Anandamurti) was *Ananda Marga: Elementary Philosophy*; it provides a sketch of Ananda Marga beliefs. Other similar books set forth important teachings of the society.

Chart 64

Ananda Marga Yoga Society (continued)

Topic	Summary of View
God	Nirguna Brahma has two aspects, consciousness (*purusa*) and energy (*prakrti*). Despite this, Nirguna Brahma is one being in the sense that these aspects cannot exist independently of one another. *Purusa* sees all that happens in the universe and makes possible every event therein. *Prakrti* is the basic substance of which the universe is composed.
Mankind	The fundamental nature of the human being is pure consciousness, since the immaterial mind is the true reality. Yet that pure consciousness has been modified by *prakrti* so that it has three functioning aspects: *mahat* (I am), *aham* (I do), and *citta* (I have done). The human mind consists of six layers: (1) *kamamaya kosa* (conscious mind), (2) *manomaya kosa* (subconscious mind), (3) *atimanasa kosa* (the desire for spiritual realization originates here), (4) *vijinamaya kosa* (a faculty that allows for esoteric knowledge to be gained, including *viveka* [true discrimination] and *vaeragya* [non-attachment]), (5) *hiranmaya kosa* (the golden layer), and (6) *annamaya a kosa* (physical body).
Sin	The fundamental human problem consists of three interrelated flaws: failing to regulate one's mind and actions, non-perfection of the mind, and lack of a spiritual connection with Nirguna Brahma. The emphasis is on overcoming destructive behaviors and addictions that impede spiritual progress rather than on following rules. Negative actions are inflicting unnecessary harm on other creatures, lying, stealing, and hoarding wealth. People should love animals and plants along with human beings. The immutable Law of Action and Reaction ensures that everyone will reap the consequences of their actions.
Salvation	To have a spiritual connection with Nirguna Brahma requires the operation of a variety of disciplines. This connection cannot be realized without breaking free of addictive behaviors and practicing yoga and meditation, the final goal being the experience of Eternal Bliss. *Acharyas* (gurus) instruct new practitioners on how to engage in these spiritual activities. The Path to Salvation (Bha'Gavad Dharma) includes: (1) Upavasa (fasting the 11th day after a new moon); (2) Sa'Dhana' (conscious effort to attain enlightenment); (3) Is'ta (the goal of connecting with Nirguna Brahma); (4) A'darsha (an uncompromising path toward enlightenment); (5) strict adherence to prescribed rules of conduct so as to maintain mental equilibrium; and (6) Dharmacakra (weekly collective meditation sessions).
Afterlife	A person merges with Nirguna Brahman after death only if all *samskaras* (units of negative karma) have been eliminated. In every other case the deceased will be reborn in a different body. The post-mortem disembodied mind has a particular wavelength, depending on the type of *samskaras* that remained in it at the moment its accompanying body died. If there is a physical body with a wavelength suited to a particular disembodied mind anywhere in the universe, that mind will be reborn in the suitable new body. The interim between death and rebirth can range from a few minutes to millions of years. Heaven and hell relate to the results of good and bad actions of the past. A doctrine of endless suffering or punishment is a superstition.

Chart 64

Distinctive Beliefs and Practices

Neo-Humanism	Neo-humanism is the view that the nature of the human mind dictates that it have the freedom to progress toward Supreme Consciousness. When persons make spiritual progress, they come to love and be devoted to the Supreme Consciousness and to love all living things.
Jaeva Dharma	*Jaeva Dharma* ("maintenance of existence") consists of a number of practices to assist persons in their spiritual growth, though it is understood that few persons will be able to do all of these things: 1. A person should pour water over the genitals after urinating, both to increase health and to minimize sexual stimulation. 2. Males should be circumcised in order to maintain health and cleanliness. 3. One should not shave hair under the arms, on the legs, or in the pubic area, and these areas should be cleaned daily with soap and oiled with coconut. 4. Males should wear a *laungota* to protect the genitals and prevent excessive sexual stimulation. Women should dress in a similar fashion as it pertains to the female body. 5. People should take ceremonial baths (half-baths) before meditation, meals, and sleep to relax the body; a full bath should be taken at least once each day. 6. Additional baths should be taken at four specified times each day, including morning, evening, and midnight. 7. Eat meals and drink water at prescribed intervals throughout the day, consuming a maximum of four meals per day.
Nr Yajna	*Nr Yajna* means "service to humanity." There are four different ways to perform this duty: engage in physical labor, provide financial support, demonstrate strength and courage, and use one's intellectual powers. *Paincaseva* (special works of service) are to be performed daily. They can be accomplished by performing such tasks as selling vegetarian food inexpensively and distributing free clothing, medical supplies, educational materials, etc.
Pa'shas	Eight social *pa'shas* (bondages) result from contact with the world: fear, shame, doubt, hatred, hypocrisy, self-centeredness, pride of lineage, and cultural arrogance. Additionally, there are six internal bondages that plague humans: pride, envy, anger, greed, physical desire, and attachment. Practitioners follow *yama* and *niyama* (moral guidelines) to curb the former bondages, and perform *sadhanas* (spiritual exercises) to restrain the latter ones.
Kiirtan	A spiritual dance sometimes done before engaging in meditation. It prepares the body for movements associated with yoga and helps calm the mind.

Chart 64

Hare Krishna

Topic	Facts
Current Data	Due to their once-frequent public presence in such venues as airports and outdoor plazas, many Americans recognize Hare Krishnas. Their worldwide organization, ISKCON (International Society for Krishna Consciousness), has established many centers across North America, including locations in Atlanta, Boston, Chicago, Dallas, Miami, New York, St. Louis, San Francisco, and Toronto, to name just a few. They publish a magazine called *Back to Godhead*.
History	The Hare Krishna religion can be traced back to a 16th century guru by the name of Caitanya Mahaprabu, whom devotees believe to be an incarnation of Krishna, but the International Society for Krishna Consciousness (ISKCON) did not actually begin in a formal sense until the 1960s under Bhaktivedanta Prabhupada (1896–1977). Prabhupada lived most of life in his homeland of India until 1959, when he decided to embark on a mystical path (*sannyasa*). At that time he started translating the *Srimad-Bhagavatam*, a Hindu scripture dealing with the life of Krishna, into English. By 1965 he was able to travel to the United States, where he lived briefly in New York City. In New York's Tompkins Square Park, Prabhupada performed his first outdoor chanting session outside the borders of India. One year later he established the International Society for Krishna Consciousness. During the early years of its existence, funds for its operation were raised exclusively through selling incense and the writings of Prabhupada. In 1967 Prabhupada moved to the Haight-Ashbury district of San Francisco, where his fortunes changed. He began to attract a number of followers, in part because certain celebrities joined ISKCON, most notably rock musician George Harrison of the Beatles (whose song "My Sweet Lord" introduced Hare Krishna chanting to the general music public), part of the rock band The Grateful Dead, and poet Allen Ginsberg. In 1968, Prabhupada founded a farm community called New Vrindaban in West Virginia. In 1970 a twelve-member governing board was set up to oversee ISKCON's affairs, and in 1972 Prabhupada established the Bhaktivedanta Book Trust. ISKCON incurred difficulties in June 1992, when the United States Supreme Court made a landmark ruling in the case of ISKCON v. Walter Lee. In its decision, the court upheld a ban on solicitation in certain public venues, including some airports. This ruling resulted in severe financial difficulties for ISKCON, because the organization had raised the bulk of its support through outdoor fund-raising efforts.
Summary of Beliefs	Srila Prahupada has listed the following tenets as the primary convictions of the Krishna Consciousness Movement (Hare Krishna Society), which is a form of Bhakti: 1. The scriptures of all major world religions contain truth, but the *Bhagavad Gita*, in particular, is a record of God's very words. 2. Krishna (God) is eternal, all-powerful, all-knowing, all-present, and all-attractive, and sustains the universe. 3. Human beings should not be understood as identical to their physical bodies, but rather as a "spirit souls," which are a part of God. 4. All humans are related. 5. Every action done by a person should be performed as a sacrifice to Krishna.

Chart 65

Topic	Facts
Summary of Beliefs (continued)	6. Any food, before it is eaten, should be offered to Krishna. 7. Humans can achieve a continual state of bliss in this life. 8. By chanting the holy name of the Lord Krishna, one is best able to assure spiritual maturity. The Hare Krishna mantra is said as follows: "Hare Krishna, Hare Krishna, Krishna Krishna, Hare Hare Hare Rama, Hare Rama, Rama Rama, Hare Hare."

Topic	Summary of View
Creation	Krishna created everything that exists. This act of creation continues, however, because Krishna dwells within his creation and his Supersoul pervades all things.
Scripture and Authority	The Scriptures of ISKCON include all the Vedic literature of classical Hinduism, the *Bhagavad Gita* (especially Prabhupada's authorized English translation) being preeminent. Stories in these scriptures are interpreted as literal historical events. The Bible, too, is scripture and is in agreement with the *Vedas*; however, the *Vedas* contain specific information about God that is lacking in the Bible. Devotees of Krishna need to be under the authority of a spiritual master (*pujari*) who is in a line of succession from the guru Caitanya (or who is part of one of three other lines of succession whose adherents worship Krishna as the Supreme God). Prabhupada is worthy of the same honor people would give God, because he is God's authorized representative on earth.
God	Krishna is the Supreme Personality of the Godhead, eternal, all-powerful, all-knowing, present everywhere, and all-attractive. There are three aspects to the Godhead: (1) the transcendent Krishna, (2) the Krishna who is immanent in his creation, and (3) Brahman, the impersonal spirit, who possesses only 78 percent of Krishna's attributes. Whereas mainstream Hinduism believes Krishna to be the eighth incarnation of Vishnu, ISKCON regards Krishna as the supreme Lord over all deities, Vishnu included. The gods worshiped in other religions, including classical Hinduism, are merely differing manifestations of Krishna. Jesus Christ was one of the demi-god manifestations of Krishna and worshiped Krishna; he only intended to serve as a spiritual guide to 1st-century Palestinians. Prabhupada is the mediator between Krishna and humanity and deserves worship. Only Prabhupada is to be referred to as His Divine Grace, for he is the greatest example of Krishna consciousness.
Mankind	The core of every human being is an eternal soul (*atma*) that is a part of Krishna. The body and the mind act to conceal the true nature of persons, and thus humans do not know their real identity. This ignorance causes people to attempt to secure permanent happiness in a world that is fleeting. Such ill-fated efforts produce bad karma that results in reincarnation.

Chart 65

Hare Krishna (continued)

Topic	Summary of View
Sin	The most fundamental problem people have is that they lust for temporal pleasures instead of loving and serving the Lord Krishna. Humans commit sin when they are disobedient to the different rules and regulations given by Prabhupada, including the worship of Prabhupada, singing devotional songs (*kirtanas*), placing authorized depictions of Hare Krishna on temple walls, and celebrating the festivals of Hare Krishna. The Four Rules are prohibitions against (1) consuming harmful substances, (2) killing animals, (3) gambling, and (4) sex for any purpose other than conceiving children within marriage.
Salvation	Human beings are reincarnated due to accumulated bad karma, and it is possible that a person could be reincarnated more than 8 million times. Liberation from the cycle of death and rebirth is achieved through practicing the spiritual disciplines of ISKCON, one of the most important of which is *sankirtana* (congregational singing of God's names). Nine Processes of Devotional Service also aid in attaining Krishna Consciousness: (1) hearing about Krishna, (2) chanting the names of Krishna, (3) remembering Krishna by reading approved ISKCON literature and associating with other Hare Krishnas, (4) serving Krishna in the ISKCON temple, (5) worshiping Krishna by preparing special foods for him, decorating him appropriately, and bringing others to see him, (6) praying to Krishna, (7) encouraging others to chant, (8) developing an intimate relationship with Krishna, and (9) relinquishing everything one owns to Krishna, including one's body. If a devotee is painstaking enough in his or her efforts, Krishna will atone for this karma, yet the person receives Krishna's mercy only if Prabhupada approves. Union with Brahma and devotion to Vishnu or Shiva are not proper spiritual goals.
Afterlife	A person's eternal soul survives the death of the body and lives on. The karma people have accumulated at the time of death determines the kind of body into which they will be reincarnated. Moreover, karma is the consequence of what a person has done in all previous lives, not just the most recent one. Some people are reborn as human beings—often into a higher or lower caste—while others are downgraded to lower species of life, such as animals or insects. Hell is a temporary post-mortem destination for people who have sinned greatly while on earth, which ends when they have suffered adequately for their bad karma.

Distinctive Beliefs and Practices

Order of Monks	Monks shave most of their heads, leaving only a long tuft of hair called a *sikha*; they also wear a special mark on their foreheads called a *tilaka*, which symbolizes Krishna. They wear saffron-colored robes (*dhotis*) to indicate that they are celibate; monks who are married wear white *dhotis*. Females who live at a temple wear traditional Indian saris. Their hair is not shaved off. All monks get up very early in the morning and spend much of the day chanting and praying.

Chart 65

Hare Krishna (continued)

Distinctive Beliefs and Practices

Ritual Food Preparation	Eating food that has been prepared for and offered to Krishna is a form of communion with him. When such specially prepared food is eaten, Krishna purifies the body of the devotee with his divine energy.
Chanting	Chanting the Hare Krishna mantra (Hare Krishna, Hare Krishna, Krishna Krishna, Hare Hare Hare Rama, Hare Rama, Rama Rama, Hare Hare) is perhaps the most frequently-performed activity of ISKCON devotees. A string of 108 prayer beads is used by devotees to help them keep track of how many times they utter the chant. ISKCON members are to chant 16 rounds of these beads daily (1,728 chants total), which can take as long as two hours.
Sankirtan	*Sankirtan* includes both public chanting and distributing ISKCON literature. Passing out literature is done by most members as often as possible, since they believe that it can bring liberation both for those handing out the literature and for those who accept it.

Chart 65

Timeline of Buddhism

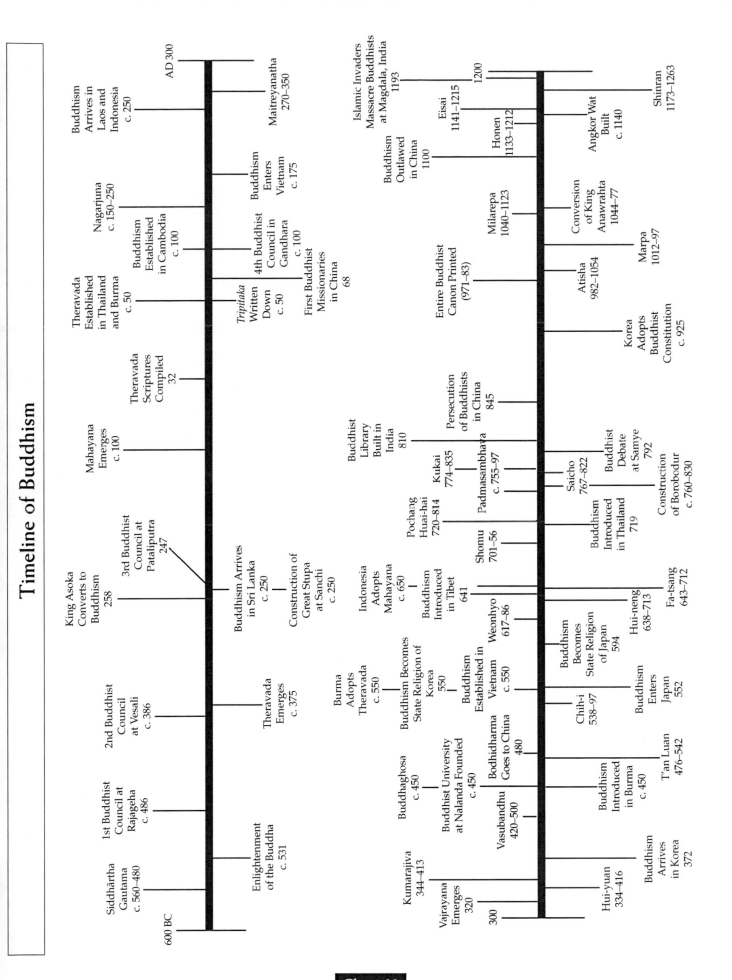

Chart 66

Timeline of Buddhism (continued)

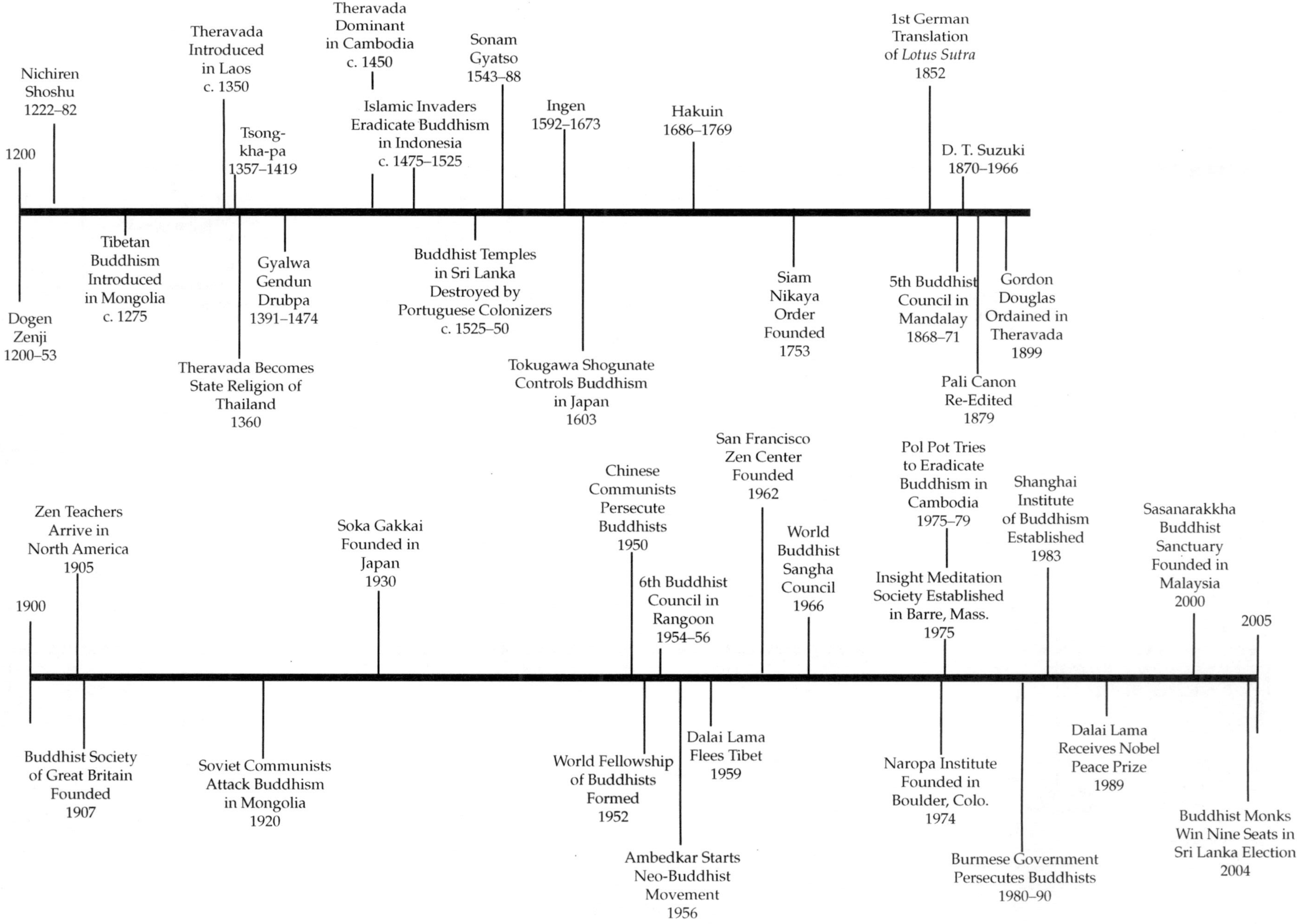

1200

Nichiren Shoshu
1222–82

Dogen Zenji
1200–53

Tibetan Buddhism Introduced in Mongolia
c. 1275

Theravada Introduced in Laos
c. 1350

Tsong-kha-pa
1357–1419

Theravada Becomes State Religion of Thailand
1360

Gyalwa Gendun Drubpa
1391–1474

Theravada Dominant in Cambodia
c. 1450

Islamic Invaders Eradicate Buddhism in Indonesia
c. 1475–1525

Buddhist Temples in Sri Lanka Destroyed by Portuguese Colonizers
c. 1525–50

Sonam Gyatso
1543–88

Ingen
1592–1673

Tokugawa Shogunate Controls Buddhism in Japan
1603

Hakuin
1686–1769

Siam Nikaya Order Founded
1753

1st German Translation of *Lotus Sutra*
1852

D. T. Suzuki
1870–1966

Gordon Douglas Ordained in Theravada
1899

5th Buddhist Council in Mandalay
1868–71

Pali Canon Re-Edited
1879

1900

Zen Teachers Arrive in North America
1905

Buddhist Society of Great Britain Founded
1907

Soviet Communists Attack Buddhism in Mongolia
1920

Soka Gakkai Founded in Japan
1930

Chinese Communists Persecute Buddhists
1950

World Fellowship of Buddhists Formed
1952

6th Buddhist Council in Rangoon
1954–56

Ambedkar Starts Neo-Buddhist Movement
1956

Dalai Lama Flees Tibet
1959

San Francisco Zen Center Founded
1962

World Buddhist Sangha Council
1966

Naropa Institute Founded in Boulder, Colo.
1974

Pol Pot Tries to Eradicate Buddhism in Cambodia
1975–79

Insight Meditation Society Established in Barre, Mass.
1975

Burmese Government Persecutes Buddhists
1980–90

Shanghai Institute of Buddhism Established
1983

Dalai Lama Receives Nobel Peace Prize
1989

2000

Sasanarakkha Buddhist Sanctuary Founded in Malaysia
2000

Buddhist Monks Win Nine Seats in Sri Lanka Election
2004

2005

Chart 66

Buddhism

Topic	Facts
Current Data	The number of Buddhists in the world is estimated at roughly 350 million to 400 million. Countries whose populations are 60 percent or more Buddhist include Bhutan, Cambodia, Laos, Myanmar, Sri Lanka, Thailand, and Tibet. Prominent organizations include Buddha's Light International Association, the World Fellowship of Buddhists, and the Buddhist Association of the United States.
History	Scholars are uncertain as to the origin of Buddhism since historical information is incomplete. According to tradition, Siddhārtha Gautama (563–483 BC) was born in northeast India. Siddhārtha's father was a king, so Siddhārtha lived in luxury and was destined, it was said, to be a great king himself. One day, at age 29, when he was walking in his father's kingdom, he observed what is called the Four Passing Sights: a crippled old man, a sick man, a decaying corpse, and a wandering holy man. This sight caused him to reflect on the fact that everyone is destined to become old, get sick, and die innumerable times. Based on this reflection and his thoughts about the holy man he had observed, Siddhārtha decided to abandon his worldly life—which included his wife, child, and position in the kingdom—to become a wandering holy man, seeking to solve the puzzle of old age, sickness, and death. In India at the time, it was thought that one could end the cycle of birth, death, and rebirth by enduring pain and suffering. After much struggle, Siddhartha found this solution unacceptable. Finally he decided to meditate while sitting under a tree, now called the Bodhi tree (*bodhi*, meaning enlightenment). Freed from distraction during his meditation, he finally achieved spiritual enlightenment and became a Buddha.
	Buddhism spread throughout eastern Asia during its first several centuries. By the middle of the 6th century AD it had made significant inroads in China, Sri Lanka, Korea, Japan, and much of southeast Asia. However, a revival of Hinduism in the 4th century and invasions of the Huns (6th century AD) and Muslims (11th century AD) led to the near-extinction of Buddhism in India by the 13th century.
	The Buddhist philosopher Nagarjuna (c. AD 150–250), arguably the most significant Buddhist teacher in India besides Gautama Buddha, founded the Madhyamaka school in the late 2nd century. In the 4th century, Vasubandhu and Asanga (both born c. AD 300) put forth the teachings of the Yogacara school. An important literary phase of Buddhism began with the writings of the Theravadan Buddhist scholar Buddhaghosa (5th century AD). The 6th century is noted for the formation of several important schools of Buddhism in China, including T'ien-t'ai, Hua-yen, Ch'an, and Pure Land. Subsequent competition with Confucianism and Taoism slowed the growth of Buddhism in China, and a severe persecution in the 9th century reduced its numbers there. In the 7th century Buddhism entered Tibet, where it flourished. After World War II new Buddhist sects in Japan, such as Soka Gakkai and the Risshokoseikai, attracted many followers.

Chart 67

Buddhism (continued)

Topic	Facts
Summary of Beliefs	Buddhism revolves around three foci called the Triple Gem, namely, the Buddha (teacher), the teachings (*dharma*), and the monastic order (*sangha*). Common to all schools of Buddhism are the doctrine of reincarnation, the Four Noble Truths, the Four Seals, and the Eightfold Path.
	Reincarnation is the term used for the cycle of birth, life, death, and rebirth which persons must experience as they travel toward enlightenment. The type of body one receives upon rebirth depends on the good or evil actions a person performed in a former incarnation (or perhaps in all previous incarnations) and the karma accrued through such actions.
	The Four Noble Truths were embodied in the journey of Gautama Buddha as he traveled toward enlightenment. They are *duhkha* (life is full of suffering), *samudaya* (suffering has a cause), *nirodha* (suffering can cease), and *marga* (the path to the cessation of suffering).
	The Four Seals are basic teachings of Buddhism: All things in the world of appearances are impermanent, there is no true "self," existence is characterized by suffering, and nirvana is the release from suffering.
	The Eightfold Path explains how to move toward enlightenment through eight steps: right understanding, right thought, right speech, right action, right livelihood, right effort, right mind, and right concentration.
	In addition to these doctrines are two doctrines that relate to reincarnation and the movement toward enlightenment, the law of Karma and the transmigration of the soul.

Topic	Summary of View
Creation	Buddhism does not refer to the creation of the universe. Instead it refers to everything in the universe as "reality," with all phenomena of the world originating interdependently. Reality is characterized by impermanence, insofar as everything eventually perishes. Reality is understood in terms of processes and relations rather than entities or substances. Human experience is analyzed in five aggregates (*skandhas*). Form (*rupa*) denotes material existence. The other four refer to psychological processes: sensations (*vedana*), perceptions (*samjna*), mental constructs (*samskara*), and consciousness (*vijnana*). The causal conditions for such human experience are found in a 12-membered chain of dependent origination (*pratityasamutpada*). The links in this chain are ignorance, predisposition, consciousness, name-form, the senses, contact, craving, grasping, becoming, birth, old age, and death.

Chart 67

Buddhism (continued)

Scripture and Authority	The primary Buddhist scripture is the *Tripitaka* (Pali Canon). The *Tripitaka* is divided into three groups: 1. *Vinaya Pitaka*, texts concerning rules of conduct that regulate the community of monks; 2. *Sutta Pitaka*, discourses said to have been spoken by Gautama Buddha or his close disciples; and 3. *Abhidhamma Pitaka*, texts in which the basic teachings of the Sutta Pitaka are organized to assist in the study of the nature of mind and matter. There are different perspectives on the authority of the Buddhist scriptures within Buddhism. One view asserts that no text is capable of conveying rationally warranted beliefs, and thus the Buddhist scriptures possess no real authority. Another claims that Gautama Buddha provided reliable knowledge through his lectures, but no Buddhist texts are authoritative. A third view maintains that the entire Pali Canon is authoritative.
God*	God is not a personal being to be worshiped, though in Pure Land Buddhism the person of Amitabha Buddha is worshiped. There are two schools of thought regarding the concept of Buddha-nature. One is that the Buddha (refers to Gautama Buddha) occupies all space and time and may even suspend the laws of nature; the other is that the Buddha can exist only where his body is located and is himself bound by natural law. The former considers the Buddha an omnipresent and eternal being who guides humans into truth, while the latter says the Buddha was only a mortal who possessed knowledge of how to achieve peace and happiness.
Mankind	The Buddhist idea of a human being is radically different from Western concepts of humanness and even from many Eastern views. Rather than an individual possessing an eternal soul or even an enduring substance that grounds personal identity, in Buddhism the person is a bundle of properties that are in constant flux. This aggregate of properties survives the death of the body and is transferred into a new body during reincarnation.
Sin	In Buddhism, sin is not viewed primarily in ethical terms, but as ignorance of the true nature of reality. Since all existence is one undifferentiated unity, evil and good are ultimately the same. Nonetheless, individuals are responsible to have a proper sense of virtue and decency, and acting in a vicious manner will inhibit one's movement toward liberation. Rather than the absolute sense of right and wrong, good and evil found in some religions, Buddhist ethics seeks to avoid moral extremes which cause struggles and to avoid viewing the world as a reality that is independent from oneself. The Five Precepts refer to the manner of life that adherents are to follow, including commandments not to kill, steal, lie, or be unchaste, and to avoid alcohol and drugs.

* It should be noted that although Buddhas and *bodhisattvas* function as gods in Buddhism, they are not identified as gods by many practicing Buddhists.

Chart 67

Buddhism (continued)

Topic	Summary of View
Salvation	Humans are presumed to be within a recurring cycle of birth, death, and rebirth known as *samsara*. The body in which one is reincarnated is dictated by the karma from one's previous life. Karma is the sum of a person's actions in a previous life (or lives). Good karma assists one in receiving a body conducive to attaining enlightenment and liberation from the cycle of reincarnation, while bad karma can result in a person being reincarnated into a lower form of existence.
	Sects within Buddhism vary on how best to achieve liberation, with Theravada considering rigorous asceticism the best path to liberation, while in Mahayana, a person who has been liberated renounces it in order to help others. The predicament in which humans find themselves is described by the doctrine of the Four Noble Truths. The first is that suffering (*dukkha*) is universal. The second is that this suffering (*samudaya*) is caused by the desire for possessions and the selfish enjoyment of things in life. The third is that suffering will cease (*nirodha*) when one's desires for worldly existence and things of the world have been done away with. The fourth is that the way to eradicate these desires (*magga*) is through the Eightfold Path, which serves to deprive people of all that otherwise would keep them within the cycle of reincarnation. The steps on the Eightfold Path always occur in the same order, though they are not always related as cause and effect:
	1. Right views, belief in the Four Noble Truths and rejection of false views concerning one's person and destiny.
	2. Right resolve, ridding oneself of improper thoughts.
	3. Right speech, speaking clearly and truthfully.
	4. Right conduct, performing proper actions.
	5. Right livelihood, living simply.
	6. Right effort, working to achieve detachment from the world.
	7. Right awareness, understanding the nature of oneself and reality.
	8. Right concentration, putting aside all distractions and focusing one's thoughts totally on enlightenment.
Afterlife	The goal to which every Buddhist aspires is total liberation from illusion, detachment from desire, and cessation of suffering, a state called nirvana. To achieve this, one must follow the Eightfold Path that leads to the endless bliss of nothingness wherein the illusion of enduring personhood is decisively defeated and all desires and suffering are extinguished. When this transpires, the person is liberated from the endless cycle of birth, death and rebirth. Failing to reach nirvana means that the person must either begin the cycle of rebirth again or, in the case of wicked persons, suffer for a time in one of the hundreds of hells taught in Buddhism. To which hell one may be consigned depends on the nature and extent of one's wickedness. However, even those in hell eventually are released and once again can work toward nirvana.

Chart 67

Buddhism (continued)

	Distinctive Beliefs and Practices
Buddha	Contrary to popular understandings of Buddhism, Buddha is not a god and is not a person ("Buddha" is a title, not a name, and means "teacher"). In fact, all schools of Buddhism understand that there are many Buddhas (awakened ones), for a Buddha is anyone—regardless of age, sex, race, or caste—who has come to understand the true nature of reality and been transformed, or enlightened, by this recognition. The principles that lead a person to be a Buddha are principles of thinking that exist outside of temporal and spatial existence, known as Buddhadharma. "The Buddha" refers to Siddhartha Gautama, the founder of Buddhism.
The Four Boundless States	Adherents are helped to achieve nirvana by the four boundless states (*brahmaviharas*). These states of love, compassion, joy, and having an even temper assist practitioners in recognizing that the self is not a separate entity from the one reality of existence.
Buddhist Shrines	The purpose of a Buddhist shrine is to house images or representations of the Buddha's body, speech, and mind. These images assist devotees in reflecting on the final goal of Buddhist practices. When a devotee develops spiritual traits, all of life—human and animal—is thereby helped. Respectful veneration of the Buddha requires setting aside a separate room for this purpose, but if space is limited, any clean room may be used, provided the altar is higher than the devotee's head when facing the altar.
Three Marks of Conditioned Existence	All phenomena (*dharmas*) are marked by three fundamental attributes. 1. *Anatman* (no-self; without an unchanging, permanent essence). The Hindu concept of the soul is that of an immutable, enduring essence wherein reincarnation involves the soul "putting on" a new body. The Buddha challenged this notion, maintaining that the soul cannot be found in the body; nor is it the body or part of the body, or the mind or part of the mind. According to him, if the soul were permanent and unchanging in nature, then any change whatsoever in it would be impossible. 2. *Anitya* (all things and experiences are inconstant, unsteady, and impermanent). In one sense, all things are made up of parts and are dependent on just the right causes and conditions for their existence, thus they are subject to inevitable decay and dissolution. 3. *Duhkha* (because people fail to grasp the first two conditions, they suffer needlessly). People desire lasting satisfaction, but seek it in the flux of impermanent phenomena. Falsely perceiving a self (locus of personhood), people act to gratify that self by pursuing and seeking to prolong pleasure, yet such pleasure is fleeting.

Chart 67

Comparison of Beliefs within Buddhism

Group	Scripture and Authority	God	Mankind
Mahayana (Northern Buddhism)	Canon is comprised of the *Tripitaka* of disciplines, discourses (sutras), and dharma analysis. Almost all the Theravada *Tripitaka* and many additional sutras are included. These writings are normally translated from Sanskrit into local languages, though some languages (e.g., Tibetan, Chinese, and Japanese) are considered untranslatable.	Popular Buddhas include Sakyamuni, Amitabha, and Bhaisajyaguru. Popular *bodhisattvas* include Maitreya, Avalokitesvara, Mansjuri, Ksitigarbha, and Samanthabadra.	Every person possesses a Buddha-nature as their true nature.
Theravada (Southern Buddhism)	The Pali Canon is divided into "three baskets" (*Tripitaka*): the five books of the *Vinaya Pitaka*, the five collections of the *Sutta Pitaka*, and the seven books of the *Abhidhamma Pitaka*. The *Tripitaka* is written only in Pali, though *dharma* teaching can be supplemented by writings in local languages.	Only the historical Gautama Buddha (Sakyamuni) and past Buddhas are accepted as legitimate. Contemporary Buddhas are rejected. Only Maitreya is accepted as a true *bodhisattva*.	Persons are identical with *Nirmana-kaya* or *Dharma-kaya*, the Truth or Reality Body of the Buddha. This state is empty, timeless, permanent, devoid of characteristics, and free from duality.
Vajrayana (Tantrayana or Tibetan Buddhism)	Canon consists of two parts: the *Kangjur* and the *Tanjur*. Because the *Tanjur* contains writings by teachers other than the Buddha, it is deemed only semi-canonical. The Dalai Lama is the most esteemed interpreter of the tradition.	Venerated beings include the five Dhyani Buddhas, many *bodhisattvas* including Manjusri and Avalokitesvara, and 16 *arhats* who are reincarnated lamas. The hundreds of thousands of other "deities" are not regarded as gods but as *sambogakaya* (enjoyment bodies) of the Buddha.	All humans possess a Buddha-nature as their true nature; its essence is emptiness.

Chart 68

Comparison of Beliefs within Buddhism (continued)

Group	Sin	Salvation	Afterlife
Mahayana	Sin, sickness, and the self are ultimately unreal. Ignorance of this fact keeps people in bondage. Death results in either liberation or reentry into the cycle of death and rebirth (*samsara*).	Strong emphasis on rituals, such as feeding *petas* (hungry ghosts). Some schools use mantras in their daily liturgy. Liberation from *samsara* (the cycle of death and rebirth) is the ultimate goal. Nevertheless, it is important to help other sentient beings attain liberation.	Souls experience an in-between stage after death and prior to rebirth (*bardo*) during which they can spend time in various heavens and hells. Nirvana, a state of indescribable bliss, is the highest destiny of the soul.
Theravada	Ignorance of the illusory nature of the self keeps people trapped in the cycle of death and rebirth.	The performance of rituals is not central, though chanting certain sacred texts is thought to be helpful in attaining liberation. No distinction is made between the nirvana attained by an *arhat* and that of a Pratyeka Buddha. Devotees rely solely on themselves to get rid of their defilements (self-liberation).	The soul does not reside anywhere between death and rebirth. Until nirvana is attained, rebirth immediately follows death. Nirvana is the "blowing out" of all cravings, a state of nothingness.
Vajrayana	Sin is ignorance of one's true nature as identical with the Primordial Buddha. The cultivation of virtue is stressed more than the eradication of defilements.	Tantric practices are a helpful way to bring about enlightenment. Humans attain enlightenment when they understand that nothing exists except the Primordial Buddha. Liberation can be attained in this life.	After death, one can receive merit from more righteous persons; this allows the deceased to be reborn in a better body than would otherwise have been the case. There are three stages of *bardo* (rebirth) that last a total of 49 days. At the conclusion of *bardo*, the soul either enters nirvana or returns to earth to be reborn.

Chart 68

Mahayana Buddhism

Topic	Facts
Current Data	There are 187 million adherents worldwide, most of whom are concentrated in northern India, Japan, China, Korea, and Vietnam. The most popular sect of Mahayana is Pure Land. Other leading sects include Madhyamika, Yogacara, and Tien-tai. Prominent organizations in the United States include Soka Gakkai-USA, the Amitabha Buddhist Society, and Dharma Drum Mountain, a sect of Zen.
History	Buddhism had been in existence in India for more than 400 years when, at the beginning of the first century BC, Mahayana began to emerge as a distinct Buddhist tradition. At first it developed slowly and incrementally and was not viewed as a competitor to Theravada Buddhism (also known as Nikaya or Hinayana).
	Differences in doctrine and practice, however, began to be observed, which culminated in the Fourth Buddhist Council at Gandhara (c. AD 100). The Mahayana school then officially split from Nikaya. Over the next 500 years, Buddhist missionaries took Mahayana to many parts of Asia, including Tibet, Mongolia, China, Korea, Japan, Burma, Thailand, Laos, Cambodia, and Vietnam. The first Indian Buddhist missionaries arrived in China in AD 67 and were well-received by Emperor Ming (reigned AD 28–75). By the next year a major Buddhist temple had been built near the capital city of Luoyang. By the end of the 2nd century, a highly developed form of Mahayana had taken root in China, in large part due to the efforts of Buddhist scholars from India who translated Sanskrit texts into Chinese. By 372 it had spread to Korea, and in 538 (possibly 552), through a delegation of Korean ambassadors, to Japan, and in 594 Buddhism was officially endorsed by the Japanese government.
	During the 11th century the influence of Mahayana waned in southeast Asia; Theravada Buddhist missionaries from Sri Lanka convinced the rulers of that region that their form of Buddhism was superior to Mahayana. Islamic raiders from Turkey invaded India in 1193, and within a decade Mahayana Buddhism had been virtually eliminated from that country. What few remnants survived were further marginalized by a revival of Advaita Vedanta Hinduism in India in the 14th century. In 1392 the Confucian rulers of Korea began to persecute adherents of Mahayana in Korea.
	During the last half of the 20th century, various schools of Mahayana Buddhism spread to Europe and North America, where they have continued to grow until the present day.
Summary of Beliefs	Mahayana (Greater Vehicle) Buddhism is not monolithic. The term "Mahayana" refers to an ensemble of Buddhist traditions that includes Madhyamika, Yogacara, Avatamsaka, Vinaya, T'ien T'ai, Pure Land, Zen, and Tantric. The Buddhas (enlightened ones), as taught by Mahayana, exist *lokottara* (beyond this world) and thus have only a tangential relationship to the affairs of the present life. In contrast to Theravada Buddhism, whose adherents seek to attain their own enlightenment as quickly as possible, practitioners of Mahayana strive to emulate the *bodhisattvas*, compassionate persons who have postponed their enlightenment in order to assist those still suffering in this world. Though their spiritual gratification is delayed, *bodhisattvas* eventually attain the very highest level of enlightenment (*bodhi*).

Chart 69

Mahayana Buddhism (continued)

Topic	Summary of View
Creation	Eternally existent, the cosmos undergoes a never-ending and recurring succession of epochs in which it is created, annihilated, and reborn. Each one of these epochs (*kalpas*) begins with there being only darkness and water. At a later stage land takes shape and emerges from the water, and all who had died, but had not yet been reincarnated when the previous *kalpa* ended, appear on the land. After billions of years the cosmos is obliterated once more and the cycle begins anew.
Scripture and Authority	The *Tripitaka* comprises the basic canon. It is divided into three sections, which deal with rules of conduct among ordained Buddhist monks and nuns, conversations attributed to the historical Buddha and his disciples, and the analysis of Buddhist doctrine. The third section sometimes is further arranged into 12 categories of doctrine. However, unlike Theravada, Mahayana schools often accept additional sacred texts as being normative for Buddhist doctrine and practice; these supplementary scriptures vary from one school to another.
God	There is no God in the sense of classical theism, but many Buddhas (fully enlightened beings) and *bodhisattvas* (powerful beings striving toward enlightenment) are venerated. Popular Buddhas include Sakyamuni Buddha (the historical Buddha), Amitabha Buddha, and Bhaisajyaguru (also known as the Medicine Buddha). Among the most well-known *bodhisattvas* are Maitreya, Avalokitesvara, Mansjuri, Ksitigarbha, and Samanthabadra.
Mankind	Every person's true nature is a Buddha-nature, but most people are ignorant of this fact. The degree to which it is legitimate to make distinctions between persons and the Buddha-nature varies among adherents.
Sin	The fundamental human problem is ignorance of the fact that nothing exists except a ubiquitous Buddha-nature. Evil, suffering, and disease are ultimately unreal. Nevertheless, certain codes of conduct are expected of adherents. Death brings about one of two consequences: liberation or reentry into the cycle of reincarnation.
Salvation	Liberation from *samsara* (the cycle of death and rebirth) is the ultimate goal. There is a strong emphasis on rituals, such as feeding *petas* (hungry ghosts); some schools employ chants and magical incantations. Adherents are encouraged to help others in the quest for liberation. After death, practitioners can avoid rebirth into this world under certain conditions, remaining for a time in a much better world where, in ideal circumstances, they are able to strive to become a Buddha. Depending on the sect, entry into the realms of paradise is attained by faith, visualization techniques, or invoking the Buddha's name.
Afterlife	Souls experience a period after death and before rebirth (*bardo*) during which they may spend time in various heavens and hells. The highest destiny of the soul is nirvana, a state of ecstasy that is beyond description.

Chart 69

Mahayana Buddhism (continued)

Distinctive Beliefs and Practices

Karuna (Compassion)	*Karuna* is a corollary of the wisdom that accompanies the quest for enlightenment. Noble *bodhisattvas* vow to delay their entrance into nirvana until all sentient beings have attained liberation. They aid the less fortunate by transferring excess spiritual merit from themselves to those who need it. Although all schools of Buddhism sanction compassionate actions, seeking to benefit others who are still in ignorance is a distinguishing aspect of Mahayana.
Bodhicitta	Cultivating a mind of great compassion (*bodhicitta*) is central to Mahayana practice. Related to this is the importance of obtaining wisdom (*prajna*), so that one's compassion will be demonstrated in a proper manner. Possessing a *bodhicitta* is a crucial step on the path toward Buddhahood. Once Buddhahood is attained (which includes omniscience), the person will be free from suffering and thus capable of working continuously, without becoming fatigued, for the benefit of others who are not yet liberated.
Paramitas	*Paramitas* are key virtues, six of which are embodied by *bodhisattvas*: transcendent wisdom, patience, generosity, moral perfection, unflagging effort, and concentration in meditation.
Universalism	Mahayanas maintain that every individual is endowed with Buddha-nature, in contrast to Theravada Buddhists, who contend that only a few can attain nirvana.

Appendix: Pure Land Buddhism

History	Pure Land Buddhism (a sect of Mahayana) began to form in China during the latter part of the Jin Dynasty (265–429), primarily through the efforts of Hui-yuan (334–416). One of the most ancient and enduring sects of Chinese Buddhism, its teachings stem from Hui-yuan's interpretation of the *Sukhavati Vyuha* sutras.
	In AD 402, at a monastery he had established in the Chinese province of Jiangxi, Hui-yuan and about 30 other Mahayana adherents made a vow that they and all other sentient creatures would eventually be reborn in a celestial realm called the Pure Land. They believed that the most effective method of attaining this rebirth was meditation. However, Hui-yuan's successor Tan-luan (476–542) maintained that reciting the name of Amitabha Buddha (Buddha of Limitless Light) was the key to being reborn in this paradise.
	Next in the line of succession from Hui-yuan, Shan-tao (613–81) was responsible for the founding of Pure Land as a formal school of Mahayana in China. His teachings were attractive to the vast majority of Chinese Buddhists who were not disciplined enough to pursue the rigors of traditional Mahayana meditation and study, and so the school gained a sizable following within a few decades after its introduction. During this same period, Pure Land teachings were exported to Korea by the Buddhist scholar Weon-hyo (617–86). In the 12th century, the intrepid monk Honen Shonin (1133–1212) brought Pure Land Buddhism to Japan. More recently, Yin-kuang (1861–1940) was a significant advocate of Pure Land teaching.

Chart 69

Mahayana Buddhism (continued)

Appendix: Pure Land Buddhism

Summary of Beliefs	The main tenet of Pure Land Buddhism is that in the end, all beings that are capable of attaining liberation will be reborn in the Pure Land (Sukhavati) of Amitabha Buddha. However, this does not just happen automatically. Instead, one can be guaranteed a place in Amitabha's paradise only by means of steadfast devotion to him (often through the medium of images) and frequent recitation of his name. If a devotee is diligent, this can be attained in one lifetime.
	Amitabha grants liberation from the world of suffering and the cycle of death and rebirth on the basis of his grace (*tariki*), not because of the efforts (*jiriki*) of his devotees. At the same time, adherents employ a number of practices aimed at facilitating their journey toward liberation and subsequent bliss. These include ritual worship, chanting the name of Amitabha, and the veneration of images of Amitabha. The most important ingredient in this process, though, is faith—all who trust in Amitabha and aspire to have fellowship with him in the Pure Land will be reborn there. Moreover, after one has come to reside in the Pure Land, it is impossible to relapse and thereby forfeit one's dwelling place with Amitahba. One controversial teaching within Pure Land Buddhism is the contention that even wicked persons can gain entrance into the Pure Land merely by earnestly repeating the mantra "Namo Amitabha Buddha."

Chart 69

Theravada Buddhism

Topic	Facts
Current Data	Theravada Buddhism is the dominant school of Buddhism in most of Southeast Asia, including Sri Lanka, Myanmar (formerly Burma), Thailand, Laos, Cambodia, and parts of Malaysia, with a total of 127 million adherents worldwide. Prominent organizations in the United States include the Buddhist Study Center of New York, Washington Buddhist Vihara, Wat Carolina Buddhajakra Vanaram, the Bhavana Society, Vipassana Meditation, and Mahasati Meditation.
History	Theravada Buddhism began in the early 4th century BC at a time when Buddhism was relatively unified. This changed in the middle of the 3rd century BC when, in order to combat what was perceived to be Buddhist heresies, the Third Buddhist Council, held at Pataliputra, adopted the texts of the Pali Canon and endorsed teachings called Nikaya (later referred to as Theravada). Differences in doctrinal views erupted among the council participants and led to a schism between Theravada Buddhism and what later became known as Mahayana Buddhism. Later Theravada Buddhism also split into the Sarvastivadin and Vibhajjavadin sects.
	In contrast to the missionary zeal of Mahayana Buddhism, Theravada grew slowly in Asia and was nearly destroyed in India and Sri Lanka in the 11th century AD by invading Muslim raiders. From the 11th to the 15th centuries Theravadan missionaries established their religion in Burma, Thailand, Laos, Cambodia, Vietnam, Malaysia, and Indonesia, causing considerable impact on these cultures. Several monarchs in these nations based their empires on Theravada Buddhism. That influence was curbed in the 14th century in many of these countries by Islam. In the late 19th century and the 20th century Theravada Buddhism began to filter into Europe and the United States, where it took root and continues to have steady growth.
Summary of Beliefs	Theravada (Teaching of the Elders) Buddhism is the only remaining school of the approximately 20 Buddhist schools that existed during the first several centuries of Buddhism's history. The tradition out of which it formed was known as Sravakayana. Distinctive traits of Theravada include the affirmation of the historicity of the Buddha, a view of human nature as fundamentally spiritual, and a strong emphasis on the critical role of meditation in attaining enlightenment. According to Theravada, the Buddha directed his disciples to do three things that are essential to attaining liberation: refrain from doing any evil, pursue whatever is good, and cleanse the mind. These three aims can be accomplished by means of three corresponding disciplines: cultivate righteous conduct, meditate properly, and seek spiritual insight. Attaining the state of nirvana, wherein one escapes the cycle of death and rebirth and achieves perfect holiness, is the final goal of Theravada.

Topic	Summary of View
Creation	The cosmos is impersonal and has always existed. It passes through countless eons in an everlasting cycle of formation and destruction. The world, as it appears, is characterized by transience, impermanence, and inability to provide satisfaction. All things that are made of parts have both material (*rupa*) and immaterial components. The immaterial components possess four primary qualities: consciousness (*vijnana*), perception (*samjna*), sensation (*vedana*), and mental images (*sankara*).

Chart 70

Theravada Buddhism (continued)

Topic	Summary of View
Scripture and Authority	The Pali Canon, referred to by adherents as the *Tripitaka* (Three Baskets), is a collection of sacred texts upon which the teachings of Theravada Buddhism are primarily based, though some lesser texts are also used. The *Tripitaka* is customarily separated into three sections: 1. The *Vinaya Pitaka*, which describes the behavior fitting for those who have taken vows of ordination as monks and nuns and joined a monastic community (*sangha*). 2. The *Sutta Pitaka*, which contains discourses given by the Buddha that set forth the core of Theravada beliefs. 3. The *Abhidhamma Pitaka*, in which the teachings of the *Sutta Pitaka* are given systematic treatment.
God	The Buddhist "God" is not a personal deity, but is impersonal (and eternal). Only the historical Siddhãrtha Gautama (Sakyamuni Buddha) and other past Buddhas are deemed legitimate; there are no true Buddhas today. Maitreya alone is accepted as a genuine *bodhisattva*.
Mankind	Persons are the same as the Truth (Reality) Body of the Buddha (*nirmana-kaya* or *dharma-kaya*), and the Body is equated with the state of Buddhahood itself (pure mind and emptiness), which is timeless, permanent, lacking any characteristics, and free of duality.
Sin	Sin is ignorance of one's true nature, though committing certain wicked acts will result in the spiritual defilement of the person who perpetrated them. Human beings do not need divine assistance to overcome the effects of sin, and thus they ought to be self-reliant in this area.
Salvation	Rituals do not have a prominent place in Theravada Buddhism, though chanting *parittas* (texts which, when recited, bring favorable conditions) is important. The highest goal of the devotee is to attain nirvana by becoming an *arhat* (a person who grasps the true nature of existence and as a result will not be reborn) or a Pratyeka Buddha (an enlightened one who learned the nature of reality without the aid of others). Nirvana can be reached by diligently adhering to a rigorous program of meditation and study. However, it is usually thought that only ordained monks, who have demonstrated the seriousness of their commitment by renouncing worldly possessions and desires, have a realistic chance of attaining nirvana.
Afterlife	People approaching death often spend time meditating on the realities of human misery, the impermanence of phenomena, and nothingness. Until nirvana is attained, death is followed immediately by rebirth. Between death and rebirth, the soul does not reside anywhere. Nirvana itself is neither the continued existence of the soul nor its annihilation.

Chart 70

Theravada Buddhism (continued)

Distinctive Beliefs and Practices

Sravaka	A Theravadan monk who takes a highly ascetic approach to attaining nirvana, one involving suppression of desire, separation from the world, and periods of solitude.
Meditation Techniques	Practitioners engage in *anapana* (mindfulness of breathing; used to remove defilements), *metta* (unconditional loving-kindness; used to develop love and compassion toward others), *jhana* (a type of meditation involving four or eight successive stages), and *vipassana* (insight meditation; used to prepare the mind for enlightenment).
Four Levels of Spiritual Attainment	Theravada recognizes four kinds of disciples, corresponding to four stages of progress toward enlightenment. 1. A Stream-Enterer is one who no longer is plagued by doubt, believes in self-existence, or trusts in Buddhist rituals. Such a person will not be reborn as an animal, hungry ghost, or demonic entity and will have to endure a maximum of seven further rebirths before attaining nirvana. 2. A Once-Returner has accomplished the Stream-Enterer stage and has curtailed the extent of being affected by illusion, lust, and hatred; such a person will undergo only one more rebirth before attaining nirvana. 3. A Non-Returner is one who has completely overcome the handicaps of human existence in the world. Such a person will be reborn in a realm of paradise, and after dwelling there for a time, will attain nirvana. 4. An Arhat is one who has attained enlightenment and is rid, once and for all, of bad karma and thus is forever free from ignorance and worldly attachments and cravings.
Temporary Ordination	In Theravada Buddhism it is common for young men to be ordained as monks for a temporary period. For example, in Thailand and Myanmar, young men often are ordained only for the three-month-long Rain Retreat.
Pratyeka Buddha	A person who is a Pratyeka Buddha needs no assistance to gain insight into the true nature of existence and attain enlightenment. A Pratyeka Buddha arises only during times when Buddhist teachings are being neglected or have been lost. Such persons contemplate the doctrine that reality is one though the phenomenal "parts" of this reality appear to have individual existence. There is difference of opinion among schools of Theravada as to whether Pratyeka Buddhas are omniscient.

Chart 70

Vajrayana Buddhism

Topic	Facts
Current Data	There are approximately 10 million adherents worldwide, primarily concentrated in Tibet, Nepal, Bhutan, and Mongolia. Many organizations and institutes devoted to the promulgation of Vajrayana have been established in North America, including the Nyingma Institute in Berkeley, California, and the Tibetan Buddhist Learning Center in New Jersey. The Dalai Lama (Tenzin Gyatso) is the most recognizable representative of Vajrayana Buddhism in the West. The two major sub-schools are Shingon in Japan and Tibetan Buddhism. Major Tibetan lineages include Kagyu, Nyingma, Sakya, and Gelugpa.
History	Historians of Buddhism hold one of two competing views regarding the origin of Vajrayana. One group argues that Vajrayana began in the Udyana region of northern India (located in modern-day Pakistan). The other group contends that southern India was its birthplace. The earliest extant texts of Vajrayana date to the early 5th century AD. The refining and transmission of Vajrayana occurred in the 5th century due to the founding of Nalanda University, which had a major influence on Vajrayana until the 12th century.
	Several key missionaries also contributed to the spread of Vajrayana beyond India. In the middle of the 7th century, Buddhist scholars from northern India brought Vajrayana to the Chinese city of Chang'an, the capital of the Tang Dynasty (618–907). In 747 King Trisong Detsen (reigned 742–797) of Tibet summoned Padmasambhava (c. 730–805), a Buddhist scholar from Afghanistan, to come to Tibet and present to him the teachings of Vajrayana. (During much of its history, Tibetan Buddhism developed independently of Mahayana and Theravada due to the geographical isolation of Tibet.) In 804, the Japanese Emperor Kammu (reigned 781–806) sent the Buddhist monk Kukai (774–835) to China to learn about Vajrayana Buddhism, and upon his return he established a sect of Vajrayana which he called Shingon. By the late 8th century, Vajrayana missionaries had journeyed as far as the island of Java in Indonesia, but Islamic conquests into India in the late 10th and 11th centuries stopped its growth, so that by the 13th century hardly a trace of Vajrayana Buddhism was to be found there. Though Vajrayana was largely gone from India, it had been preserved in Tibet. Another boon to the spread of Vajrayana during these difficult times was the visit to the Mongolian capital by three eminent Tibetan masters: Drakpa Gyaltsen (1147–1216), Sakya Pandita (1182-1251), and Chogyal Phakpa (1235–80). Prince Godan converted to Vajrayana, and when Mongol Emperor (and Vajrayana adherent) Kublai Khan (1215–94) took control of China, Tantric practices were established there again. The prominence of Vajrayana in China was short-lived, however, so when the Yuan Dynasty (1271–1368) ended, Pure Land Buddhism, Taoism, and Confucianism replaced Vajrayana as the dominant religion. In the 17th century political ties were once again established between Mongolia and Tibet, which allowed for Tibetan religious leaders to advise Mongol rulers. In the 20th century, when the Chinese Communist military took over Tibet, Vajrayana Buddhists fled, with many of them establishing Tibetan communities in northern India.

Chart 71

Vajrayana Buddhism (continued)

Topic	Facts
Summary of Beliefs	The name Vajrayana (Thunderbolt Vehicle or Diamond Vehicle) is meant to elicit thoughts of both the sudden flash of enlightenment (*bodhi*) toward which practitioners strive and the indestructible nature of enlightenment itself. The most distinguishing feature of Vajrayana Buddhism is its claim to provide practitioners with a process for attaining enlightenment that is much faster than those prescribed by other Buddhist schools, who usually maintain that one must go through a great number of reincarnations before reaching nirvana. Though different in many respects from its parent tradition, Vajrayana (sometimes called Tantrayana) is actually a species of Mahayana Buddhism, albeit modified to the point where it can rightly be considered as a distinct school. Adherents of Vajrayana view their tradition as the pinnacle of the historical progression of Indian Buddhism. From their perspective, early Buddhist practitioners did not know the fullness of Buddhist teaching. Thus Hinayana Buddhism (including Theravada) was less developed than Mahayana, which in turn needed further amplification and correction in the form of Vajrayana. Each successive Tibetan lama (guru) functions as the spiritual leader of most of the Vajrayana tradition.

Topic	Summary of View
Creation	There is no initial act of creation as understood in the West, but rather, all phenomena originate in (and proceed from) the Primordial Buddha (the ultimate source of reality). Unlike the Hindu Brahma, which exists independently of individual persons, the Primordial Buddha does not exist apart from the consciousness of each person.
Scripture and Authority	The scripture of Vajrayana consists of two parts: the *Kangjur* (Translation of the Word [of the Buddha]) and the *Tanjur* (Translation of the Teachings [of the Buddha]). Because the *Tanjur* includes the writings of teachers besides the Buddha, it bears less authority than does the *Kangjur*. The Dalai Lama is the authoritative interpreter of the Vajrayana tradition.
God	A transcendent personal deity does not exist. All reality is one, and distinctions within this reality are merely phenomena of the mind, not the true nature of things; only those who have been enlightened have this comprehension. The Primordial Buddha (Buddha Samantabhadra) is contained within the Reality Body (*Dharmakaya*) of each person who has attained Buddhahood; here the phenomena that appear in the world of non-Buddha minds dissolve into nothingness. Many enlightened beings with divine qualities are venerated, the foremost of which are the five Dhyani Buddhas: Vairochana, Akshobhya, Ratnasambhava, Amitabha, and Amogasiddhi. Popular *bodhisattvas* (powerful beings striving for enlightenment) include Vajragarbha, Manjusri, Maitreya, and Sagaramati. Sixteen *arhats*—reincarnated lamas who are destined to become *bodhisattvas*—are worshiped as well. Additionally, there are innumerable quasi-deities who do not have the status of gods, but are respected as being *sambogakaya* (enjoyment bodies) of the Buddha.

Chart 71

Vajrayana Buddhism (continued)

Topic	Summary of View
Mankind	Vajrayana Buddhism is similar to the Mahayana view. However, internal to each person is the realm of emptiness (*Dharmakaya*), which is the true nature of the human mind. The spiritual core of a person can rightly be called Luminous Source and Inherent Clear Light.
Sin	The essence of sin is ignorance of one's true nature as identical with the Primordial Buddha. Adherents are charged with working to achieve the virtues germane to their particular role in advancing the Vajrayana tradition. It is imperative that devotees not break any of their vows regarding the path to liberation, and that they be willing to put forth the intense effort required of those whose minds are in the process of awakening to the reality of their existence as pure emptiness. Practitioners focus on cultivating virtues rather than eradicating spiritual defilements, yet the recognition that one suffers from such defilements indicates wisdom.
Salvation	A wide range of tantric practices (offerings, chants, visualization techniques, etc.) are employed as aids in the quest for enlightenment; transmitting the Vajrayana tradition through approved channels and by means of proper protocol also serves to bring a person closer to spiritual liberation. Nirvana is attained when a person sees that all is the Primordial Buddha. The soul of a person who remains ignorant of this fact will be consigned to wander in other realms after death. It is possible for a committed devotee to remain in a continuous state of spiritual lucidity and indescribable bliss in this life.
Afterlife	Similar to the Mahayana view, except that instead of only one, there are three stages of *bardo* (the intermediate state) that last a total of 49 days. During its stay in *bardo*, the soul returns to its original source: the Primordial Buddha. When the soul's time in *bardo* has been completed, it either enters nirvana or returns to the world of appearances, where it is reincarnated in a new and different body.

Distinctive Beliefs and Practices

Topic	Summary of View
Tantra	A number of special techniques and learning aids, known as tantras, are used to accelerate the process of reaching nirvana. Many of them involve the extensive use of symbols and visualization. Though differing greatly in their details, each technique is designed to help the devotee recognize his identity with the Primordial Buddha in the present moment, rather than thinking of enlightenment as something that is far off.
Esoteric Transmission and Initiation	The methods that are used to speed up the process of reaching nirvana are shrouded in secrecy, passed down directly from lamas to disciples during private ceremonies. This teaching is not made public because the methods are ineffective outside the Vajrayana community. In fact, they are potentially dangerous; if not performed in a proper manner, those utilizing them may cause great harm to themselves.

Chart 71

Vajrayana Buddhism (continued)

Distinctive Beliefs and Practices

Vairocana Buddha	A Buddha who is the embodiment of the Reality Body of the Buddha (*dharma-kaya*) and thus is the universal expression of Siddhārtha Gautama, the historical Buddha.
Trikaya	The Trikaya (Three Bodies) Doctrine is a way of explaining the nature of a Buddha, and, by extension, the nature of all existence. In essence, it affirms that a Buddha has three bodies, each of a different kind. 1. A created body (*nirmana-kaya*), which displays itself in the phenomenal world of space and time. 2. A body of mutual enjoyment (*sambhoga-kaya*), which is the epitome of, but not precisely the same as, the state of enlightenment. 3. A reality (or truth) body (*dharma-kaya*), which manifests enlightenment itself.
Yidam	A *Yidam* is an enlightened being upon whom practitioners concentrate during times of spiritual reflection, seeking to become one with the Yidam. It is hoped that by identifying with a particular Yidam, practitioners will be enabled to see that they are one with the Primordial Buddha. Popular Yidams include Cakrasamvara, Guhyasamaja, Hayagriva, Hevajra, Kalacakra, Kurukulle, Samputa, Vajrakilaya, Vajrayogini, and Yamantaka.
Dorje **(Vajra)**	A ritual object that functions as a symbol of true existence (*sunyata*) and its properties of potency and creativity.
Ghanta	A ritual bell used in Vajrayana rituals that symbolizes wisdom.
Damaru	A small drum shaken by Vajrayana monks during certain rituals.
Mandala Diagram	An intricate, colorful map of the cosmos that pictures various paths to enlightenment and represents the transitory nature of existence. Monks who build mandalas prepare for the task by drawing very precise geometric measurements that aid in their construction of the chart. The Kalachakra Mandala is a famous example; its complex structure depicts 722 Vajrayana deities.
Tantric Sex	Ritual sexual practices involving an experienced female teacher and a young male monk. These practices aim to prepare monks to become *bodhisattvas* via meditating on the act of sexual union. According to this approach, the bliss of sexual union is analogous to the bliss of nirvana.

Chart 71

Zen Buddhism

Topic	Facts
Current Data	Reliable statistics regarding the number of adherents are difficult to discover since most schools of Zen do not keep membership records and there are many practitioners of Zen who are not affiliated with any organization. There are roughly 11 million adherents in Korea (where it is called Seon), 8.5 million adherents in Japan, and 200,000 adherents in the United States. There has been a resurgence of Zen in China (where it is known as Chan). Rinzai, Soto, and Obaku are the three most popular sects in Japan.
History	Bodhidharma (440–528), an Indian Buddhist monk, founded Zen in China. Some reports say that in the early 6th century he traveled to southern China, where he presented Buddhist doctrine and practice to Emperor Liang Wudi (502–549). Soon after that he went to the eastern Chinese province of Luoyang, where it is alleged that he meditated next to a cliff for nine years. After this he gathered some disciples, one of whom, Hui-k'o (c. 487–593), became his successor, who, along with those who succeeded him, carried on the Bodhidharma form of Buddhism in China (known as Chan) for many years. One of the successors, Hui-neng (638–713) taught a doctrine of "Sudden Awakening," in contrast to the doctrine of "Gradual Awakening" expounded by Shen-hui (684–758). Later important figures in Chan Buddhism were Ma-tsu (709–788) and Lin-chi (c. 810–866).
	Hearkening back to the 6th century, Korean monks studying in China learned of Bodhidharma's account of Buddhism, which by then had been significantly influenced by Taoism and Confucianism. These monks took Chan Buddhism to Japan during the 7th century, where it came to be called Zen. However, Zen Buddhism did not become widespread in Japan until the late 12th or early 13th century, when a number of Japanese aristocrats embraced it. By this time, Zen had been somewhat modified by its interaction with Shinto.
	In 1191, Myoan Eisai (1141–1215) founded the Rinzai school of Zen. One of Eisai's disciples, Dogen Zenji (1200–1253), later founded the Soto school, which taught *zazen* (sitting meditation). Coming from China, the Obaku school was introduced in Japan in 1654 by Yinyuan Longqi (1592–1673). Recently, several prominent teachers of Zen in Japan have criticized it because of its excessively formal and ritualistic nature and because the vast majority of Zen practitioners never attain enlightenment. In the West, Zen has received a popular status with many not understanding the underlying precepts of Zen.
Summary of Beliefs	Zen means "to meditate" or "to concentrate." Even more so than is the case with other schools of Buddhism, Zen eschews a systematic approach to doctrine and disavows the use of formal logic. Although it proceeds on the basis of certain assumptions, Zen focuses on methods that aid practitioners in their quest for enlightenment. These methods include the observation of Zen precepts (*sila*), the development of the power to focus the mind (*samadhi*), and the practice of wisdom (*prajna*). There are five major types of Zen. 1. Non-Buddhist Zen, in which adherents of other religions use Zen meditation techniques for practical purposes other than seeking enlightenment. 2. Mundane Zen, which is embodied in such forms as haiku (a form of Japanese poetry).

Chart 72

Zen Buddhism (continued)

Topic	Facts
Summary of Beliefs (continued)	3. Theravada Zen, which Buddhist monks follow as a path to great spiritual ac complishments. 4. Mahayana Zen, which *boddhisattvas* practice as a means of attaining enlightenment for themselves and others. 5. Zen of the Highest Vehicle, which stresses the nature and qualities of enlightenment.

Topic	Summary of View
Creation	Ultimately, reality consists of nothing but pure, indivisible Buddha-nature; the world of appearances is illusory. Every kind of existing thing has as its true nature a Buddha-nature. Thus seemingly individual objects exist only as illusory phenomena; they do not exist as real entities. Even the properties of good and evil do not exist in an ultimate sense, since the all-pervading Buddha-nature is beyond such apparent dualities.
Scripture and Authority	In the end, authority is vested in each "individual." Neither Buddhist scriptures nor Buddhist traditions possess binding authority, though in many cases they can serve as practical aids in the quest for enlightenment. In particular, the *Avatamsaka-sutra* (Flower Ornament Scripture) is deemed helpful in this regard. The key to attaining enlightenment is found in the mind of each person, since enlightenment comes directly from within.
God	In common with other forms of Buddhism, Zen believes that there is no personal deity. All reality is one without distinctions; the existence of a divine being with distinguishable attributes is an impossibility.
Mankind	There are no such things as persons; each "self" is actually one in being with undifferentiated Buddha-nature. The primordial state of mind, to which each person should try to return, is utterly clear and pure of ignorance and delusions. The truths of Zen originate in the mind of a person, not in any "outside" source.
Sin	Zen advocates Ten Moral Precepts (*Kai*). 1. Do not kill. 2. Do not steal anyone's property. 3. Do not misuse sex. 4. Do not tell lies. 5. Do not imbibe alcohol or harmful drugs. 6. Do not gossip about others. 7. Do not speak well of yourself while criticizing others. 8. Conduct yourself in such a manner that observers will see in you the Original Perfection. 9. Do not become angry.

Chart 72

Zen Buddhism (continued)

Topic	Summary of View
Sin (continued)	10. Do not malign any of the Three Treasures: the Buddha of history (Siddhārtha Gautama), his precepts (*dharma*), and the fellowship of his disciples (*sangha*). Most people fail to see that they are Buddha-nature because of their insatiable appetites, proneness to rage, and spiritual ignorance. To talk as though one has achieved enlightenment, when in fact one has not, is indicative of a terrible spiritual illness.
Salvation	When people describe things in the world of appearances, they presuppose that the things of which they speak are discrete, abiding objects that can be assigned to classes and divided into constituent parts. Because they use language in this way, a false construct of permanent, particular things is imposed on the undifferentiated Buddha-nature of which reality truly consists. Therefore, in order to grasp the true nature of reality, a person must reach a point where it is possible to transcend this ordinary way of thinking about and perceiving the world. Since most human's minds are muddled and lack focus, this goal is facilitated by consistently engaging in *zazen* (sitting meditation). Yet paradoxically, no amount of striving can bring about enlightenment; it simply happens when it happens. The essence of enlightenment is "seeing into one's own nature" (*kensho*). This occurs with one's realization that the person and all other "things" are in fact nothing other than the one, all-encompassing Buddha-nature. This realization (*satori*) results in liberation from the cycle of death and rebirth.
Afterlife	Most adherents to Zen believe in an afterlife in which the mind is separated from the body. Those who hold to this view believe that the mind after death desires an embodied existence and so searches for a body in which to reincarnate, one that is compatible with that mind's karma. This view teaches that minds are reborn into one of six realms: those of gods, demigods, humans, animals, hungry ghosts, and various hells. The former three are relatively pleasant and free of suffering, whereas the latter three are unpleasant and filled with suffering. Even though persons are happier in the realms of the gods and demigods than in the realm of human beings, the latter is the one most conducive to attaining nirvana (liberation). This is because those reborn into one of the former realms are so distracted by their intense happiness that they often neglect to pursue enlightenment.
Distinctive Beliefs and Practices	
Rejection of Formal Logic	Employing formal logic confirms people in their false interpretation of reality because it involves making distinctions and analyzing arguments. It is this very proclivity to divide the world into parts and categories that inhibits the attainment of liberation. In light of this, students of Zen are encouraged to move beyond logic by means of *gong-ans*, absurd or silly questions asked of Zen students by their masters. These questions function as a means of helping students break through their erroneous perceptions to the truth that only Buddha-nature exists.

Chart 72

Zen Buddhism (continued)

Distinctive Beliefs and Practices

Koan	Zen masters use stories of everyday events or sayings of other Zen masters or the Buddha to circumvent the habitual patterns of discursive thought and rational scrutiny that are common to human beings in their unenlightened state. Most *koans* deal with normal, everyday events. Yet the silliness or absurdity of these *koans* is designed to shock the hearer and thereby elicit the intuitive aspect of the mind. Once the ordinary thought processes of the student have been disengaged and the student's intuition has been activated by means of these *koans*, the student is in a better position to break through into an awareness of reality as nothing but Buddha-nature. More than 1,700 *koans* are known to be used in Zen training.
Full Lotus Posture	A posture for meditation in which the right foot is placed with the sole up on the left thigh and vice versa, with both knees touching the ground. The palms of both hands are facing up, with the fingers and thumbs making an oval that lies on the lap just under the navel. The backbone is straight, the nose is in line with the navel, and both ears are in line with their respective shoulders.
Three Aims of Zazen	*Zazen*, a type of meditation done while seated in one of several prescribed positions, is used to relax the mind for the purpose creating the conditions necessary for having a sudden insight into the true nature of reality. *Zazen* has three primary, inextricably interconnected aims: 1. Improving the ability to engage in sustained concentration (*joriki*). 2. Bringing about *satori*-awakening (*kensho-godo*). 3. Making it possible for practitioners to manifest the Supreme Way in daily activities (*mujudo no taigen*).
Chan Khong **(Emptiness)**	Chan Khong means "nothingness" or "emptiness" and refers to the Zen metaphysics in which all phenomena are, in the final analysis, "empty" or unreal. This is because all things originated interdependently in such a way that existence is an indissoluble unity. Thus persons cannot successfully define things as they are in themselves, nor can they properly conceive of a thing's structure. All allegedly distinct entities in the world are merely the illusory result of faulty perception and knowledge.

Chart 72

Nichiren Shoshu Buddhism

Topic	Facts
Current Data	Nichiren Shoshu is experiencing extremely rapid growth in Europe and the United States, especially in Hawaii. Not including Japan, there were approximately 600,000 lay members in 40 countries in 1998; Japan alone had about 10 million members at that time. There are more than 700 Nichiren temples in Japan, 8 (total) in the United States, Spain, and Brazil, and 4 (total) offices in France and Taiwan. The main Nichiren Shoshu temple is located in Yamanashi, Japan, near Mount Minobu.
History	The founder of Nichiren Shoshu, Nichiren Daishonin (1222–1282), established his peculiar brand of Buddhism during the Kamakura Dynasty (1185–1333) in Japan. As a Buddhist priest who had studied Tendai, a form of Mahayana that had come to Japan from China in the 9th century, Nichiren was able to forge a new form of Tendai Buddhism that was responsive to the needs of the Japanese people in his day. The core of his teaching was that people from all walks of life need only devote themselves to the *Lotus Sutra* (a Buddhist devotional text) in order to experience happiness and enlightenment.

	Then on April 28, 1253, Nichiren had a vision in which he obtained knowledge of a particular chant (*Nam-myoho-renge-kyo*) that would become foundational to the subsequent development of his sect. Having received this special knowledge, Nichiren announced that his sect of Buddhism alone was the true way to enlightenment. This declaration brought considerable persecution upon Nichiren and his followers. In particular, the audacity he demonstrated in attempting to proselytize the rulers of Japan, and thereby to challenge the official Japanese Buddhism of the day (Shingon), incited the wrath of the Japanese government. In 1271 Nichiren was almost killed, and after this he was exiled to the Japanese island of Sado, where he spent 11 years. Despite this, Nichiren continued to spread his message and teach his students until his death.
	After he died, Nichiren's students were very active in spreading his teachings, so much so that by the 15th century Nichiren Shoshu was well-established in Japan. During the Tokugawa Dynasty (1600–1868), in part because of the desire of the Japanese government to create a unified society and stop the spread of Christianity, local Nichiren Shoshu temples were integrated into a nationwide system of townships.
	In 1940 the Religious Organization Law was passed in Japan, which mandated that all Buddhist sects associate themselves with state-sponsored Shinto. Members of the Nichiren sect refused to comply with this new law, and in July 1943 Japanese law enforcement officials arrested several leading members of Soka Gakkai, the lay branch of Nichiren Shoshu. After the defeat of Japan in World War II and the subsequent dismantling of the old regime with its restrictions on religious liberty, dozens of new religious groups formed.
	In 1960 Daisaku Ikeda (1928–), the president of Soka Gakkai, visited the United States to establish Nichiren Buddhism. At that time there were less than 500 adherents in the U.S., but due to the efforts of Ikeda and others in the movement, by the mid-1970s there were more than 200,000 registered members in the United States. In 1991 Soka Gakkai and Nichiren Shoshu split. Soka Gakkai has continued to grow and is beginning to have a measurable impact on North American culture.

Chart 73

Nichiren Shoshu Buddhism (continued)

Topic	Facts
Summary of Beliefs	Nichiren Shoshu, which expounds the True Law and Teachings of Nichiren Daishonin, has three fundamental elements: faith, practice, and study. All adherents are expected to be diligent in attending to these matters. (1) Faith, which is foundational to the practice of Nichiren Shoshu, consists of placing unconditional trust in the doctrines taught by Nichiren Daishonin and in the power of the Gohonzon (supreme object of worship). (2) Practices must be done in complete sincerity and include daily *gongyo* (recitation of sutras) to the Gohonzon, chanting the *daimoku* (mantra) of *Nam-myoho-renge-kyo* as a means of attaining purity, praying for global happiness and enlightenment, and sharing the teachings of Nichiren with others. (3) Nichiren Daishonin's teachings should be studied regularly. Doing these three things will achieve many good results: the happiness of the practitioner and the practitioner's family, practitioners' wishes being granted, many people being freed from suffering (mankind attaining Buddhahood), and the furthering of prosperity and social justice.

Topic	Summary of View
Creation	No creator God exists, and thus there was no act of creation wherein the universe was brought into being. Instead, the universe has always existed. The synchronized changes that take place in the universe are caused by a single rhythmic, fundamental law (*Nam-myoho-renge-kyo*), which sustains and animates human life. This single law has several aspects and effects. These include *myoho*, the law that guides the outworking of *Nam-myoho-renge-kyo*; *renge*, the karma of simultaneous cause and effect; and *kyo*, the vibrations of the universe. Enlightened people understand the nature of the universe apart from knowledge obtained by the scientific method.
Scripture and Authority	The *Lotus Sutra* is the holy book that is given the most attention; Nichiren Daishonin's distinctive doctrines and practices are rooted in a careful analysis of this text. Other important writings of Nichiren include *Kaimoku Sho* (The Opening of the Eyes), *Honzon Sho* (On the Supreme Object of Worship), *Kanjin-no Senji Sho* (The Selection of the Time), *Ho-on Sho* (Requital for the Buddha's Favor), and *Rissho Ankoko Ron* (On Securing the Peace of the Land through True Buddhism). Nichiren Daishonin was authorized to establish True Buddhism because it had been prophesied that he would replace Shakyamuni, the One True Original Buddha. Nichiren transmitted his teachings to his chosen disciple Nikko Shonin (1246–1333), who in turn passed them on to the High Priest of the next generation. This process has continued to the present day, when Nikken Abe (1922–) became the guardian of the teachings of Nichiren.

Chart 73

Nichiren Shoshu Buddhism (continued)

Topic	Summary of View
God	God is an eternal, ubiquitous, impersonal essence that undergoes alternating periods of activity and being dormant. The Gohonzon is the visible form of this God, yet somehow is personal and worthy of worship. Other properties of the Gohonzon include eternality, omnipotence, omniscience, and being the source of all reality. The Gohonzon has the power to impart wisdom, grant prayer requests, bring about purification and healing, pardon sin, and punish evil. Although many gods exist, their ability to act is constrained by *Nam-myoho-renge-kyo*, the highest law of the universe. Since the gods can employ their protective powers only within strict limits, they cannot mete out retribution or deliver people from bondage. In fact, practitioners can compel the gods to carry out their wishes by invoking them with the chant *Nam-myoho-renge-kyo*.
Mankind	Human beings are neither good nor evil by nature. There are ten fundamental states in which human beings can be; these states of being are described in the Theory of Ten Worlds (*Jikkai*). These worlds do not objectively exist, but are subjective experiences of individuals. 1. Hell, in which the person experiences excruciating suffering. 2. Hunger, defined as greed and the lust for power, fame, and wealth. 3. Animality, acting according to instinct rather than being guided by morality and reason. 4. Anger, which is animosity resulting from being competitive and egotistic. 5. Tranquility, or acting in a serene and detached manner. 6. Rapture, experienced as intense happiness due to being satisfied with life. 7. Learning, which consists of accumulating knowledge. 8. Absorption, wherein a person feels great joy upon engaging in creative activities. 9. Aspiration for Enlightenment, which involves working to improve the lives of others. 10. Enlightenment of Buddhahood, when a person awakes from spiritual slumber, grasps the true nature of things, and experiences deep and lasting happiness. There are three main goals of human life: experiencing beauty, procuring basic necessities, and sharing beauty and necessities with others. Nichiren Shoshu emphasizes ritual equality. Any person, regardless of age, race, or gender, can attain enlightenment.
Sin	All human beings live in a state of constant suffering. This is true despite the fact that many people truly think they are happy, taking comfort in the things of this world. People will continue to endure the pains and tribulations of this life, such as uncertainty, disappointment, illness, bodily infirmity, and death, unless they embrace the One True Way of Nichiren Shoshu.

Chart 73

Nichiren Shoshu Buddhism (continued)

Topic	Summary of View
Salvation	Absolute faith in the Gohonzon, and dedicating one's life to it, is the key to solving one's problems and obtaining such blessings as good health, material prosperity, and Buddhahood. At the same time, no one can be totally happy until the entire world has attained enlightenment. This goal of bringing about global peace and happiness is called *Kosen-rufu* and will be accomplished only by the practice and dissemination of Nichiren Shoshu Buddhism. Every member is given the task of faithful adherence and proselytizing, known as *Shakubuku*. There are three proofs (*sansho*) that are useful in carrying out this task: utilizing the scriptures of Nichiren Shoshu, logical demonstrations, and explaining the practical benefits of the religion. The most important means to attaining enlightenment for oneself and others is reciting *Nam-myoho-renge-kyo* while worshiping the Gohonzon. This activity awakens the Buddha within each person.
Afterlife	Focus is on this life and transforming this world. The ultimate goal is to create a worldwide civilization of peace, based on the teachings of Nichiren Daishonin. Heaven and hell are not places that exist outside of human beings. Rather, they are inner states that are experienced here and now.

Distinctive Beliefs and Practices	
Gongyo	Gongyo (ritual worship) is to be performed each day and has three primary elements. 1. Reciting portions of the *Lotus Sutra* while kneeling in front of the Gohonzon. 2. Chanting *Nam-myoho-renge-kyo* with the aid of special prayer beads known as *juzu*. 3. Saying prayers of gratitude to Nichiren and the Gohonzon, praying to the dead, and praying that one's virtuous desires would be granted.
Ichinen Sanzen	Meaning "Three Thousand Realms in a Single Moment of Life," this experience occurs when one attains Buddhahood. According to Nichiren Shoshu teaching, Buddhahood is not a static state of being, but involves grasping all ten realms of experience simultaneously.

Chart 73

Timeline of Taoism

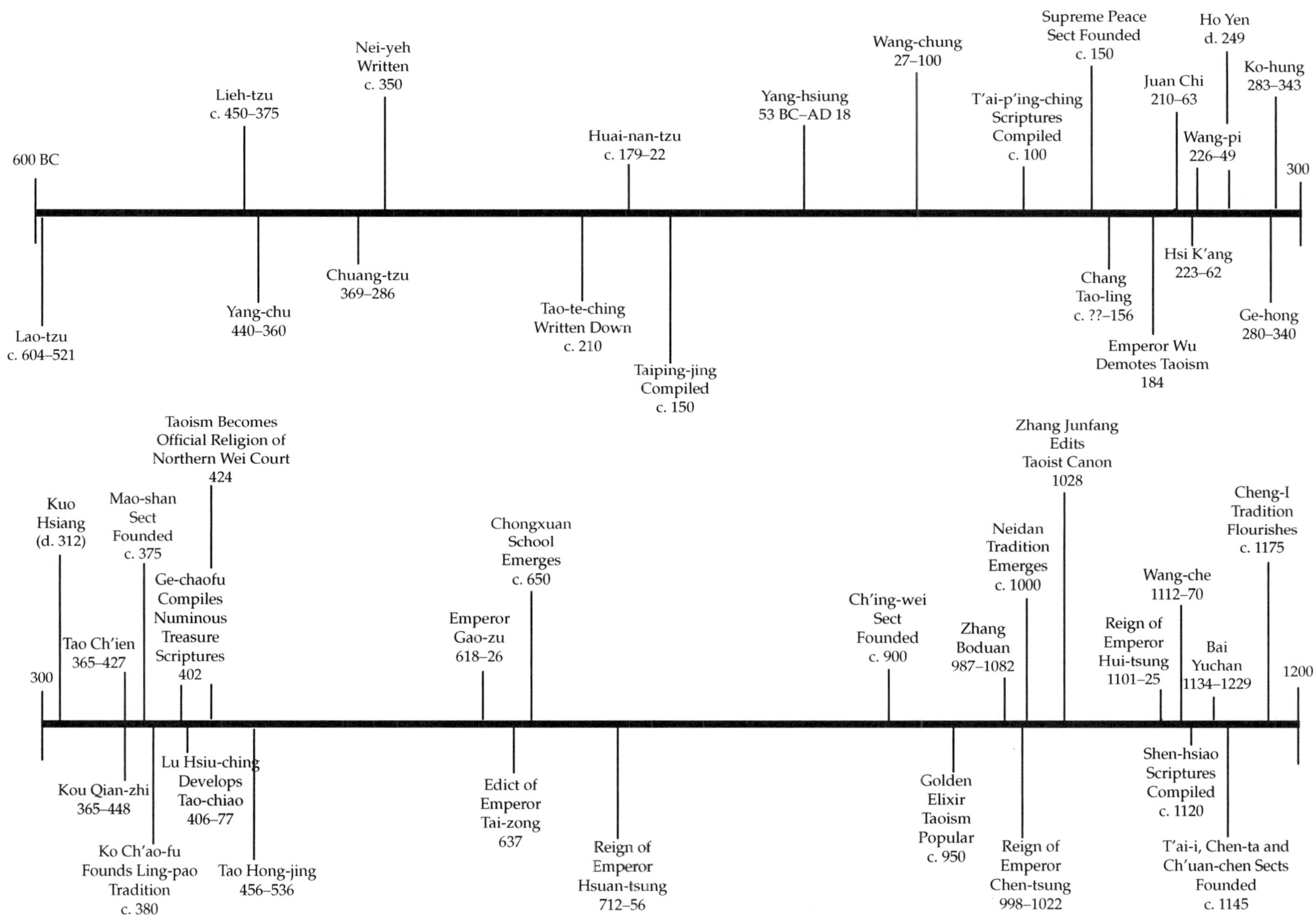

Lao-tzu
c. 604–521

600 BC

Lieh-tzu
c. 450–375

Yang-chu
440–360

Nei-yeh
Written
c. 350

Chuang-tzu
369–286

Huai-nan-tzu
c. 179–22

Tao-te-ching
Written Down
c. 210

Taiping-jing
Compiled
c. 150

Yang-hsiung
53 BC–AD 18

Wang-chung
27–100

T'ai-p'ing-ching
Scriptures
Compiled
c. 100

Supreme Peace
Sect Founded
c. 150

Chang
Tao-ling
c. ??–156

Emperor Wu
Demotes Taoism
184

Ho Yen
d. 249

Ko-hung
283–343

Juan Chi
210–63

Wang-pi
226–49

Hsi K'ang
223–62

Ge-hong
280–340

300

Kuo
Hsiang
(d. 312)

Tao Ch'ien
365–427

Mao-shan
Sect
Founded
c. 375

Ge-chaofu
Compiles
Numinous
Treasure
Scriptures
402

Taoism Becomes
Official Religion of
Northern Wei Court
424

Kou Qian-zhi
365–448

Ko Ch'ao-fu
Founds Ling-pao
Tradition
c. 380

Lu Hsiu-ching
Develops
Tao-chiao
406–77

Tao Hong-jing
456–536

Chongxuan
School
Emerges
c. 650

Emperor
Gao-zu
618–26

Edict of
Emperor
Tai-zong
637

Reign of
Emperor
Hsuan-tsung
712–56

300

Ch'ing-wei
Sect
Founded
c. 900

Golden
Elixir
Taoism
Popular
c. 950

Reign of
Emperor
Chen-tsung
998–1022

Zhang
Boduan
987–1082

Neidan
Tradition
Emerges
c. 1000

Zhang Junfang
Edits
Taoist Canon
1028

Cheng-I
Tradition
Flourishes
c. 1175

Wang-che
1112–70

Reign of
Emperor
Hui-tsung
1101–25

Bai
Yuchan
1134–1229

Shen-hsiao
Scriptures
Compiled
c. 1120

T'ai-i, Chen-ta and
Ch'uan-chen Sects
Founded
1145

1200

Chart 74

Timeline of Taoism (continued)

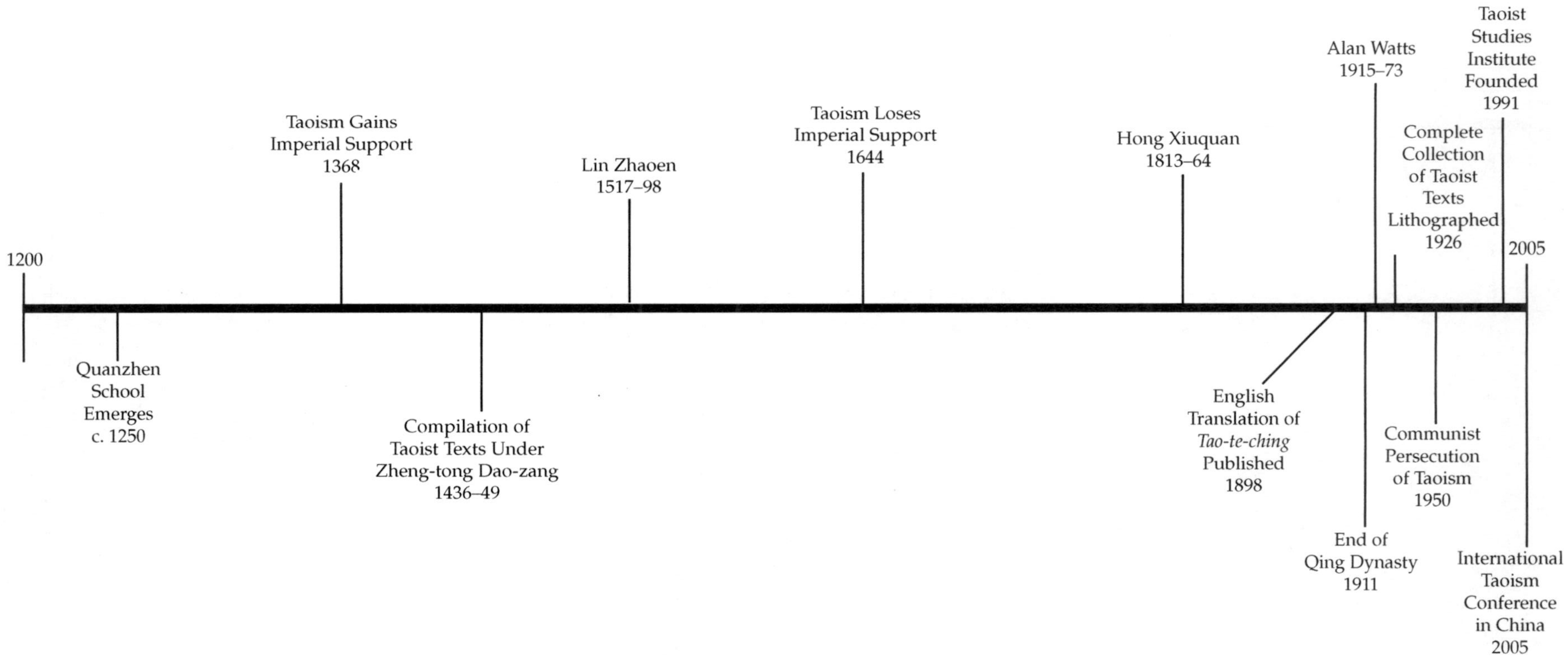

Quanzhen School Emerges c. 1250

Taoism Gains Imperial Support 1368

Compilation of Taoist Texts Under Zheng-tong Dao-zang 1436–49

Lin Zhaoen 1517–98

Taoism Loses Imperial Support 1644

Hong Xiuquan 1813–64

English Translation of *Tao-te-ching* Published 1898

End of Qing Dynasty 1911

Communist Persecution of Taoism 1950

International Taoism Conference in China 2005

Alan Watts 1915–73

Complete Collection of Taoist Texts Lithographed 1926

Taoist Studies Institute Founded 1991

1200

2005

Chart 74

Taoism

Topic	Facts
Current Data	The estimated number of people worldwide who identify themselves as practitioners of Taoism (pronounced DOW-izm) is 55 million; 31 million live outside mainland China. About 30,000 live in North America. Precise figures are difficult to obtain partly because Taoism has been banned in China since 1949. Apart from China, the greatest concentrations of Taoists are in Taiwan and Singapore. Prominent organizations in the United States include the Foundation of Tao, the Integral Way Society, and the Center of Traditional Taoist Studies in Boston.
History	Scholars of the history of Taosim are divided in their views of Lao-tzu (604–521 BC), traditionally said to be the founder of Taoism. One camp is convinced that Lao-tzu was a contemporary of Confucius; others believe the accounts of his life are merely legends, that he was not a historical person. The traditional view asserts that Lao-tzu was in search of a way, or path, that if put into practice would curtail the myriad conflicts that were disrupting Chinese society in his day. He committed his thoughts on these matters to writing, and the result was the *Tao-te-ching*.

The subsequent history of Taoism in China can be divided into eight periods.

1. Warring States Period (453–222 BC): Two competing understandings of Taoism emerged during this time. The first maintained that political stability in China could be achieved only through *wuwei* (non-action). The second held to the ideal of the Taoist mystic who casts aside traditional social norms.

2. Han Dynasty (206 BC–AD 220): The Huainanzi and Huang-lao schools blended principles from Confucianism and Taoism. Toward the end of this period a number of unusual sects emerged, the most notable of which was the Way of the Five Measures of Rice.

3. Chinese "Middle Ages" (AD 220–581): Ge Hong Baopuzi (280–340) advocated alchemy, including the production of pills that conferred immortality. Around AD 370 Yang Xi allegedly received the Supreme Purity (Shangqing) revelation. In 402 the Numinous Treasure (Lingbao) school was founded; it assimilated a number of ideas from Indian Buddhism.

4. Tang Dynasty (618–907): For the most part the Tang emperors supported Taoism, but many practitioners mixed Taoist ideas with teachings from Buddhism and/or Confucianism; the Double Mystery school (Chongxuan) was a prime example of this syncretism.

5. Song and Yuan Dynasties (960–1368): Many emperors were favorably disposed toward Taoism, in particular the Divine Empyrean (Shenxiao) school. The Filial Piety (Jingming Zhongxiao) school incorporated Confucian ethics into Taoism, while the Complete Perfection (Quanzhen) school sought new advances in alchemy.

6. Ming Dynasty (1368–1644): Taoism received tremendous backing from the rulers of China during this period.

7. Qing Dynasty (1644–1911): Taoism lost the support of the Chinese emperors and started to decline.

Chart 75

Taoism (continued)

Topic	Facts
History (continued)	8. 20th Century to the Present: Imperial support of Taoism ended in 1911, but it was not until after the Communist takeover of China in 1949 that severe restrictions were placed on religious freedom, which forced Taoist activity to limit itself to the private sphere. The social upheaval that occurred during Chinese Cultural Revolution (1966–76) nearly wiped out the last vestiges of Taoism in China. Since 1982 a degree of religious tolerance has been afforded adherents of Taoism (and of other religions) in China, but it has not been substantial.
Summary of Beliefs	Unlike many other religions, Taoism has few organized forms and does not boast a systematic presentation of its doctrine. Instead it is a way of living in the world in harmony with the Tao, a ubiquitous force that permeates the cosmos, regulating and upholding the natural order of things. It is critical that the Tao be in proper balance; when it is, the cosmos is characterized by tranquility. A circular Yin-Yang drawing is often used to depict the optimal balance of opposites in the cosmos that the Tao seeks to maintain. Because the Tao is everywhere, it is necessary to be attuned to it at all times in order to live rightly and obtain enlightenment.

Topic	Summary of View
Creation	A personal, transcendent creator God does not exist. Yin, the dark side of things, formed the earth; yang, the light side of things, formed the heavens. The fundamental reality is the Tao (Way or Path), which can be experienced more readily than it can be defined. The Tao is a mystical power that surrounds and flows through everything in the cosmos. It nurtures all forms of life, empowers the workings of nature, and restores cosmic balance. The Tao harmonizes pairs of opposites in the world like light and darkness, love and hate, male and female.
Scripture and Authority	Traditionally attributed to Lao-tzu, the *Tao-te-ching* (Book of the Way) is the most important sacred text. It instructs its readers concerning the natural order of the cosmos, the way of peace and harmony, and the path that rulers should take in governing their people. Further wisdom concerning the Tao and related subjects is found in the *Chuang-tzu* (Master Zhuang), the *I-ching* (Book of Changes), and the *Lieh-tzu* (Scripture of the Perfect Emptiness).
God	Various views are held. Taoist philosophers view the Tao as an active, creative force that envelops and permeates every living being. Taoist priests believe in numerous gods, yet think they are but expressions of the one Tao. The majority of practitioners believe the world is full of spirits and that heaven and hell contain a vast number of gods, many of whom are very unruly.
Mankind	Human beings are divine by nature, since they are filled with and participate in the Tao. The yin has given each person *ch'i* (air or breath) that sustains them. Certain parts of the human body correspond to the elements of which the sky is composed. Developing moral virtue is the most important duty that a human being can fulfill.

Chart 75

Taoism (continued)

Topic	Summary of View
Sin	The fundamental human problem is that people do not act in harmony with the Tao. Instead of flowing with it, they strive against it and act in ways that are not natural. This striving upsets the natural equilibrium between the opposing forces of yin and yang. If the Tao is thwarted on a large enough scale, turmoil and confusion can beset an entire society, possibly throwing even nature itself into disarray. The primary virtues (known as the Three Jewels) are humility, compassion, and moderation.
Salvation	The way to achieve inner harmony and balance is through non-doing (*wu-wei*). This does not mean being passive or idle, but involves a continuous process of adapting to change and being responsive to the natural flow of events in the world rather than trying to make things happen differently. By gaining a deep awareness of the Tao, a person can follow its path with minimal effort.
Afterlife	For those with a philosophical orientation, the sole focus is on being in harmony with the Tao in this life. These practitioners either deny there is an afterlife or are agnostic (undecided) in this regard. Adherents of more "religious" and popular forms of Taoism believe the soul of a person can go to heaven or hell.

Distinctive Beliefs and Practices

Tai Chi	Tai chi is a distinctively Taoist art of carefully performed bodily movements. Historically, Chinese medicine taught that bodily ailments resulted when a person's *ch'i* (life force; *qi* in Chinese) was imbalanced or blocked. In addition to promoting good health, the practice of tai chi is thought to restore balance to this spiritual energy.
Chen-jen	A *chen-jen* (realized man) is a Taoist master who has become so attuned to the Tao that he has become deified and thereby obtained immortality. These men were often thought to possess magical powers.
Emptiness	Emptiness is a moral ideal for which each Taoist adherent should aim. It requires displaying impartiality and not harboring hostility toward others.
P'u	*P'u* is the state of perceiving the world with an untainted mind, like a block of wood that has not been made into a carving. It also means seeking to be plain and unpretentious when pursuing wisdom, since overly complicated thinking can prevent a person from being in tune with the Tao.
T'ai-hsi (Embryonic Breathing)	The precise manner in which practitioners went about performing this breathing exercise varied from one sect of Taoism to the next. Those who engaged in it sought to become immortal by emulating the breathing patterns of a child in the womb.
Feng Shui	Ancient Chinese study of the natural environment undertaken to determine the most favorable and least desirable locations for a person to be in any given environment. These determinations are based on the year in which the individual was born, the particular features of the immediate environment, and the movements of the planets and stars.

Chart 75

Taoism (continued)

Appendix: Religious Taoism

History, Basic Beliefs, and Practices	Alongside Taoism as a philosophical worldview, other more popular and religious forms of Taoism developed. In general, the focus of this religious-popular Taoism was living a long life that was disturbed by as few adverse conditions as possible. To aid in achieving this end, a complex system of symbols, priests, ceremonies, and temples was formed, along with a pantheon of gods whose deities stood for various attributes of the Tao. These deities included Yuan-shih T'ien-tsun (the First Principal), who was the eternal, changeless, infinite source of all truth; Yu-huang (also known as the Jade Emperor), who meted out justice; the San-ch'ing (Three Pure Ones) who represented Lao-tzu; and the San-kuan (Three Officials), who kept a record of each person's good and evil deeds. At certain times in the history of Taoism, occult practices like alchemy, divination, sorcery, and astrology were quite popular. This led to the emergence of Taoist rites dealing with things like exorcisms, fortune telling, ghosts, and paranormal healing. Many practitioners sought to master magical arts such as controlling internal bodily functions, turning non-precious metals into gold, necromancy, levitation, and numerology. Many forms of religious Taoism also were influenced by their interaction with Chinese Buddhism.

Chart 75

Timeline of Jainism

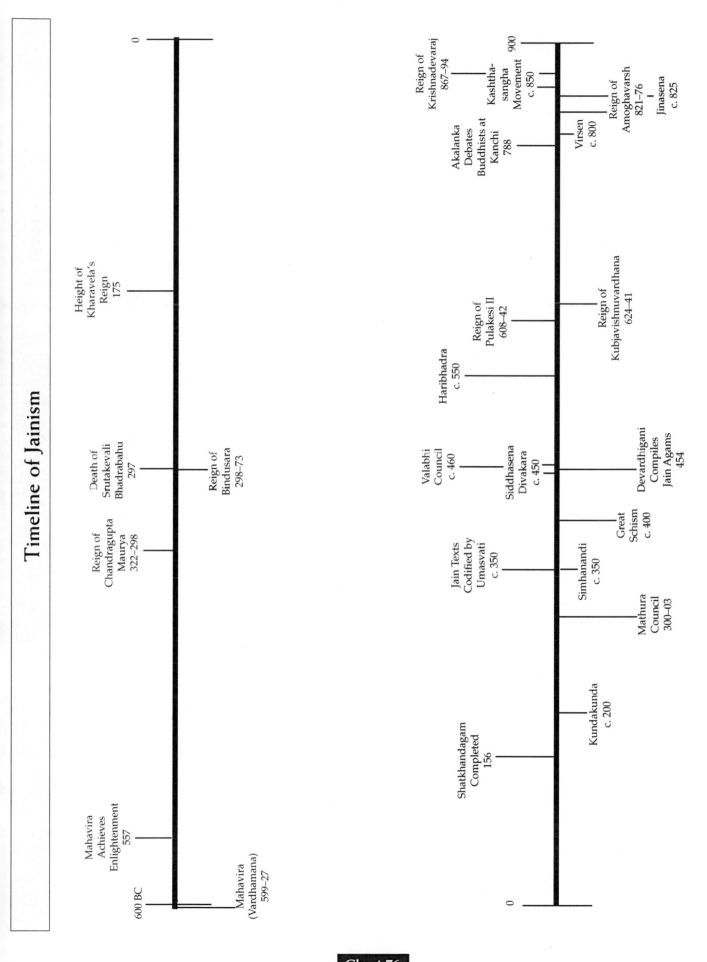

Mahavira Achieves Enlightenment
557

600 BC

Mahavira (Vardhamana)
599–27

Reign of Chandragupta Maurya
322–298

Death of Srutakevali Bhadrabahu
297

Reign of Bindusara
298–73

Height of Kharavela's Reign
175

0

Shatkhandagam Completed
156

Kundakunda
c. 200

Jain Texts Codified by Umasvati
c. 350

Simhanandi
c. 350

Mathura Council
300–03

Great Schism
c. 400

Valabhi Council
c. 460

Siddhasena Divakara
c. 450

Devardhigani Compiles Jain Agams
454

Haribhadra
c. 550

Reign of Pulakesi II
608–42

Reign of Kubjavishnuvardhana
624–41

Akalanka Debates Buddhists at Kanchi
788

Virsen
c. 800

Reign of Krishnadevaraj
867–94

Kashtha-sangha Movement
c. 850

Reign of Amoghavarsh
821–76

Jinasena
c. 825

900

Chart 76

Timeline of Jainism (continued)

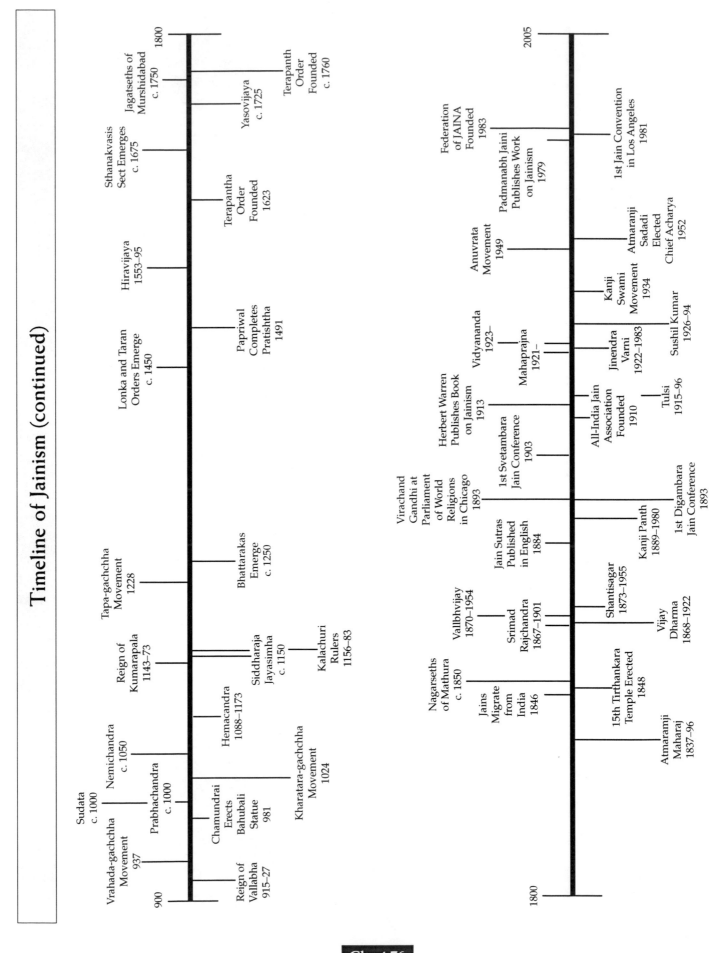

Chart 76

Jainism

Topic	Facts
Current Data	Estimates of the number of Jains worldwide vary greatly, ranging from 3 million to 8 million. The vast majority of Jains live in central and southern India. The two primary sects are Svetambara and Digambara. Sub-sects of the former include Murtipujak, Sthanakwasi, and Terapanthi. Sub-sects of the latter include Bagherwal, Lad, Khandelwal, and Saitwal. Prominent organizations include the Federation of Jain Associations in North America, Young Jains of America, Jain Meditation International Center in New York City, and Anekant Education Foundation.
History	Traditional Jainism alleges that its history began 8.4 million years ago with a *jina* (overcomer, conqueror) who was a giant. However, historical research places the origin of Jainism somewhere in the early to middle 6th century BC. It was during this time that Vardhamana (599–527 BC)—also known as Mahavira—formed the first Jain community. Mahavira was a prince who had been raised in an Indian royal family. However, when he was about 30 years old, Mahavira left his household and its comforts and embarked on 12 years of rigorous asceticism. During this time he became recognized as an outstanding teacher and developed a number of religious ideas that differed significantly from traditional Hinduism. At the end of this period, believing that he had attained perfect enlightenment (*keval-jnana*), Mahavira began traveling around India, proclaiming his message to all who would listen. (He continued to do this for 30 years.) After amassing a sizable number of followers, Mahavira organized them into an ordained order of monks and nuns. Finally, when he was 72 years old, Mahavira ended his life by starving himself to death (*salekhana*).
	Though at first Jainism was largely unified, by the late 1st century AD a schism had arisen between the Svetambara (white-clad), a moderate order of Jainists, and the Digambara (sky-clad; unclothed), who abandoned all material possessions, even clothes. During the Gupta Dynasty (320–550) many of the emperors supported Jainism, which experienced an era of stability and growth. Beginning in the 7th century, the Svetambaras splintered into more than 80 sects. In the 13th century Muslim invaders advanced far enough south that segments of Jainism suffered considerable persecution, including subjugation and the destruction of many Jain temples. Farther south in India, however, the rulers of the Hindu Vijayanagar Empire (1336–1660) offered protection to Jains who had been displaced by the Islamic invasions. Here Jains were allowed to be active participants in shaping the culture. During the 20th century, a number of Jains migrated to East Africa, the United Kingdom, and the United States. Many of these immigrants have played integral roles in the construction of Jain temples on non-Indian soil and have formed regional associations that promote Jain religion and culture.
Summary of Beliefs	The core of Jainism is the belief that all sentient beings are in spiritual bondage, unaware of their true being (godhood) and its inherent perfection. Because of this ignorance, people are trapped in their bodies and are unable to experience the state of freedom and bliss that comes from enlightenment. The path to attaining liberation requires a radical reorientation of priorities, since it involves abandoning all superstitions, rigorous spiritual discipline, and daily contemplation of the highest

Chart 77

Topic	Facts
Summary of Beliefs (continued)	reality. In order to make progress toward liberation, three realities (called the three jewels, *ratna-traya*) must be present in cooperation, namely, having a proper conception of reality (right perception), thinking correctly (right knowledge), and performing proper actions (right conduct). Jainism is characterized by exacting ethical demands, gentle treatment of all living things, a contentment with one's lot in light of one's eventual liberation, and tolerance of other religions.

Topic	Summary of View
Creation	The universe is eternally self-existent and operates according to laws that are woven into its very fabric. It consists of seven cosmic layers. 1. Supreme Abode: the highest layer, the dwelling place of liberated souls (*siddha*) 2. Upper World: 30 celestial abodes in which heavenly beings reside 3. Middle World: the earth and the visible universe 4. Nether World: seven hells, each with a distinct kind and degree of suffering 5. Nigoda: the abode of the very lowest forms of life 6. Universe Space: clouds that envelop the Upper World 7. Space Beyond: an immeasurable realm without properties The Middle World is filled with two fundamental kinds of entities: living beings (*jiva*) and nonliving objects (*ajiva*). Nonliving objects fall into five categories: space (*akasa*), time (*kaal*), matter (*pudgala*), medium of motion (*dharmastikay*), and medium of rest (*adharmastikay*). Together these two major classes of things comprise the Six Universal Substances. Each one of these substances (*dravyas*) has always existed and cannot be destroyed, though they are constantly being modified in appearance. That is, despite these countless outward changes, the fundamental, underlying substance of each thing, along with its basic qualities (*gunas*), remains unaltered in a condition of permanence (*dhrauvya*). In sum, then, every entity in the universe has three fundamental aspects: origination (*utpada*), destruction (*vyaya*), and permanence (*dhrauvya*). The substance and attributes of a thing are permanent (*nitya*); its various forms are transient (*anitya*).
Scripture and Authority	There are 45 sacred texts in all, divided into six major groupings: *Angas, Upangas, Pakinnakas, Chedas, Mulasutras,* and *Sutras*. The teachings found in these books initially were transmitted by means of oral tradition but were finally written down in the early 4th century BC. Though it does not possess the same authority as the canonical Jain scriptures, the *Kalpa Sutra*, which contains the biographies of all 24 Tirthankaras, is held in high esteem. There are five primary roles that a person can play in a Jain community, those of leader (*acharya*), monk (*sadhu*), nun (*sadhvi*), layman (*shravak*), and laywoman (*shravika*).

Chart 77

Jainism (continued)

Topic	Summary of View
God	Jainism is polytheistic, affirming the existence of a countless number of gods, the number of which continues to increase as more living beings attain liberation. Nevertheless, Mahavira is usually deemed the preeminent deity. He is a savior who has perfect knowledge and unlimited power and is the last in a series of 24 Tirthankaras (perfect souls) who have lived in the Middle World. Each of these Tirthankaras was born as an ordinary human but went on to attain perfect enlightenment. A Tirthankara is a type of Arihanta, which is one of the two main classes of gods who have overcome all four kinds of destructive karma (*ghati*) and continue to teach Jain doctrine and practice after attaining enlightenment. (The other type of Arihanta is the Kevali.) The other main class of gods is the Siddhas (Perfect Souls), who have destroyed all eight kinds of karma. Each Siddha is a free soul (*mukta*) that will never be reborn.
Mankind	Each human soul (*samsari*) is embodied, covered with karma particles, and caught in the cycle of death and rebirth. Human beings are composed of eight types of matter (*vargana*): <ol><li>*audaric*, of which the physical body is composed;</li><li>*tejas*, which allows for bodily heating and digestion;</li><li>*karman*, of which the karmic body is composed;</li><li>*aharac*, which fashions an additional tiny body with its own soul;</li><li>*vaikriya*, which fashions a body that can grow or shrink;</li><li>breathing, which allows for breathing;</li><li>mind, which allows for thinking; and</li><li>speech, which allows for language.</li></ol> Only a very small number of people possess an *aharac* body, which can be used to travel other realms. Similarly, very few people have a *vaikriya* body, which can become extremely large or extremely small. Human life is of great value, yet all living beings are equal and ought to be treated with love and respect.
Sin	Actions that result in the accumulation of negative karma are sin. Adherents commit themselves to abide by prescribed ethical standards by means of vows, which are taken very seriously. In particular, obeying five rules of conduct (*samitis*) and three prohibitions (*guptis*) are essential to spiritual progress. The five samitis are: <ol><li>*iriya samiti* (regulation of walking),</li><li>*bhasa samiti* (regulation of talking),</li><li>*esnna samiti* (regulation of begging),</li><li>*adana nikshepana samiti* (regulation of taking and keeping), and</li><li>*utsarga samiti* (regulation of disposing of waste).</li></ol> The three guptis are: <ol><li>*mana gupti* (regulation of the mind),</li><li>*vachana gupti* (regulation of speech), and</li><li>*kaya gupti* (regulation of using the body).</li></ol> Ascetics also take vows regarding things like *ahimsa* (non-violence toward all sentient beings) and *agarigrapha* (complete detachment from the world).

Chart 77

Jainism (continued)

Topic	Summary of View
Salvation	Attaining liberation (*moksha*) from endless reincarnations involves three key elements: 1. right perception (*samyak darsana*), which makes a person aware of the true nature of reality, 2. right knowledge (*samyak jnana*), which compels a person to take the proper steps in pursuing enlightenment, and 3. right conduct (*samyak charitrya*), which rids a person of negative karma. Moreover, these three disciplines must be done concurrently or else they will be of no benefit to the practitioner. During the process of purifying the soul, a devotee will destroy all eight types of karma in the following order: *mohaniya* (illusion), *jnana-varaniya* (knowledge), *darasna-varaniya* (vision), *antaraya* (natural qualities), *nama* (body), *ayu* (life span), *gotra* (social status), and *vedniya* (bodily pleasures and pains). Every soul (*jiva*) is capable of attaining godhood, which is pure consciousness and supreme bliss.
Afterlife	A person cannot attain liberation without an *audaric* body, so if the person has not been purified of all bad karma at the time of death, the *tejas* and karmic bodies accompany the soul and fashion a new *audaric* body for the person to inhabit. If all of a person's bad karma (*nirjara*) has been eliminated before death, the soul is liberated from the confines of this world, never again to be trapped in a physical body.

Distinctive Beliefs and Practices

Topic	Summary of View
Vegetarianism	Because all living beings are of great value and have the potential to become gods, and also because most are capable of experiencing pain, killing animals as a source of food is prohibited. Eating the flesh of animals is also forbidden. Thus Jains follow a strict vegetarian diet.
Kalchakra	Jainism teaches that time has no beginning or end. Rather it is divided into cycles called *kalchakras*. Each cycle has two equally long sub-cycles, a progressive-ascending one (*utsarpini*) and a regressive-descending one (*avasarpini*). During *utsarpini* conditions in the world get progressively better; during *avasarpini* they get progressively worse. Both of these sub-cycles are further divided into six time periods of unequal lengths called *aras*. By Jain reckoning, the universe is presently in the fifth *ara* of an *avasarpini* phase. This series of cycles is everlasting.
Panch Parameshthi	Known collectively as *Panch Parameshthi*, there are five kinds of benevolent beings who guide Jains in their conduct: (1) supreme human beings (*arihantas*), (2) perfect souls (*siddhas*), (3) master teachers (*acharyas*), (4) scholarly monks (*upadhyayas*), and (5) ascetics (*sadhus*).
Anekantvada	A Jain philosophical theory of non-absolutism. It maintains that because human knowledge is limited in substantial ways, human beings should be open to the possibility that they are mistaken in their beliefs, especially religious beliefs.

Chart 77

Jainism (continued)

Distinctive Beliefs and Practices

Namaskar **Mantra**	The daily prayer said by all practicing Jains is called the Namaskar Mantra. It is composed of nine parts: 1. *namo arihantanam* (bowing to the Arihantas), 2. *namo siddhanam* (bowing to the Siddhas), 3. *namo ayariyanam* (bowing to acharyas), 4. *namo uvajjayanam* (bowing to upadhyayas, or learned teachers), 5. *namo loe savva sahunam* (bowing to all holy men), 6. *eso panch namukkaro* (performing five obeisances), 7. *savva pavap panasano* (eradicating all defilements), 8. *mangalancha savvesin* (the first form of happiness), and 9. *padhamam havai mangalam* (auspicious praise). Jains do not say this prayer in order to receive material blessings, nor do they petition specific divine beings. Rather, it is said as one of many means to the attainment of liberation from suffering.

Chart 77

Timeline of Zoroastrianism

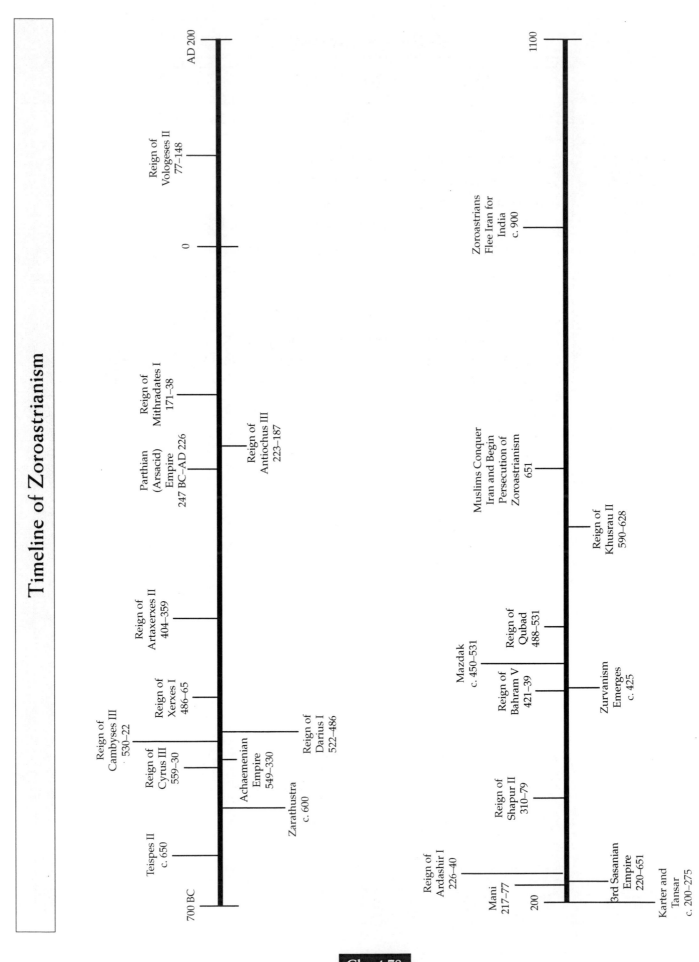

Chart 78

Timeline of Zoroastrianism (continued)

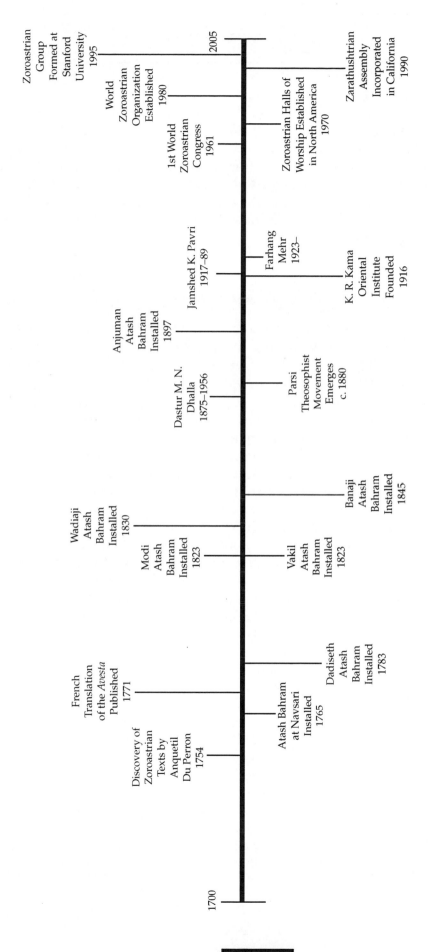

Chart 78

Zoroastrianism

Topic	Facts
Current Data	The worldwide population of Zoroastrians is estimated at 2.5 million. Communities of adherents are located in India, Iran, Pakistan, Afghanistan, and the United States. Zoroastrians are called Parsis (Persians) in India, where their social influence greatly exceeds their numbers. Sects include Zurvanism, Mithraism, Orthodox, and Mazdaznan. Prominent organizations include the World Council of Zoroastrian Federations, the Federation of Zoroastrian Associations of North America, the Council of Iranian Mobeds of North America, and the Stanford University Zoroastrian Group.
History	Zoroastrianism was founded by Zarathushtra (c. 1300 BC) in Persia (modern-day Iran). According to legend, his birth had been prophesied many years before he was born. Zarathushtra did not adhere to the religious status quo, preaching monotheism in the midst of a thoroughly polytheistic culture. After initial opposition, Zarathushtra persuaded the king of Persia to establish Zoroastrianism as the official religion of the empire. In part because Zoroastrianism portrayed itself as a religion for all peoples, it spread rather quickly.
	Beginning in the 6th century BC, a series of Zoroastrian empires rose and fell. The first two were the Achaemenid Empire (549–330 BC) and the Arsacid Empire (220 BC–AD 227). The Avestan Empire (800 BC–AD 200) also prospered during this period. Another was the Sassanid Empire (AD 220–651), during which the sacred texts of Zoroastrianism were compiled and Zoroastrian eschatology underwent significant changes. In 651 Islamic armies besieged Persia, leading to a mass exodus of Zoroastrians to India over the next 300 years. After coming into contact with Hinduism, mystical Zoroastrian sects formed. Over the course of the next 1,000 years, Zoroastrianism suffered a number of setbacks that caused its number of adherents to dwindle, including persecution from other religious groups, successful Christian missionary activity within its ranks, colonialism, and the influence of secular education. In the 20th century small numbers of Zoroastrians moved from Iran and India to Europe and the United States.
Summary of Beliefs	Zoroastrian beliefs can be summarized as follows: Ahura Mazda is the One, Good, Eternal God. A cosmic battle rages continually between Good and Evil. Human beings possess a free will and should choose to love and obey Ahura Mazda. Maintaining inner and outer purity by performing prescribed rites brings about harmony between this world and the realm of spirit. With the help of his servants, Ahura Mazda will decisively triumph over evil and restore the world to its original condition of goodness. There will be a resurrection of the dead and a final judgment. After this judgment, good souls will be rewarded in heaven and evil souls will be punished in hell.

Many Zoroastrian beliefs have evolved during the course of its history. Some are vague and thus are open to a range of interpretations; some are difficult to reconstruct historically with accuracy. Because of these considerations, the descriptions of Zoroastrian doctrines offered in this section might not be accepted by all scholars of religion who are considered authorities in Zoroastrianism.

Chart 79

Zoroastrianism (continued)

Topic	Summary of View
Creation	Ahura Mazda created the universe, and he has already determined its final destiny. Although there are several competing creation accounts, a standard one is as follows: In Infinite Time there was a realm of light and a realm of darkness. Ahura Mazda lived in the former realm and Angra Mainyu lived in the latter realm. After 3,000 years, Angra Mainyu left his dwelling and attacked Ahura Mazda. Wanting to avoid an eternal battle, Ahura Mazda spoke the Ahuna Vairya (the most holy prayer in Zoroastrianism), which caused the horrified Angra Mainyu to return to the realm of darkness for another 3,000 years. While Angra Mainyu was dormant, Ahura Mazda created all things. First he created the Six Beneficent Immortals (Amesha Spenta), whose task it is to govern the material creation, and a host of preexistent souls (*fravashis*). Then he made the material world, including the earth, sky, water, the Primeval Ox, and the first man, Gayomart. Next, Ahura Mazda told the souls that they could either remain as mere souls forever or become embodied and help him in the fight against Angra Mainyu; they decided on the latter option. Meanwhile, Angra Mainyu created six demonic creatures to oppose Ahura Mazda and his good creation. When the 3,000 years had passed, Angra Mainyu entered Ahura Mazda's creation and slew the Ox and Gayomart. The corpse of the ox was used to fashion animals and plants, while Gayomart's dead body was used to fashion metals and human beings. Seven parts of the creation are considered especially worthy of preservation: fire, earth, sky, water, humans, cattle, and plants.
Scripture and Authority	The central holy book of Zoroastrianism is the *Avesta*. The portion of it that was written earlier, the *Gathas*, contains sacred hymns concerning such topics as worship, cosmic order, moral freedom, personal righteousness, and social justice. Centuries later the remaining parts of the *Avesta* were written; they deal primarily with law, liturgy, and the elaboration of doctrines found in the *Gathas*. Zoroastrians are sharply divided between those who contend that the *Gathas* alone are authoritative, and those who maintain that later sacred writings in the *Avesta* have equal authority. Modern copies of the *Avesta* are arranged into five sections: *Yasna*, *Yashts*, *Visperad*, *Vendidad*, and *Khordeh Avesta*. Other significant texts include *Bundahishn*, *Shayest Na-shayest*, *Dadestan-i Denig*, *Menog-i Khrad*, and *Shkand-gumanig Vizar*.
God	There are two views: 1. strict monotheism, wherein only Ahura Mazda is God and Angra Mainyu is relegated to the status of a powerful but finite being, and 2. monotheism within a cosmic dualism, which can be construed as a kind of henotheism. In this view, Ahura Mazda is the supreme deity in a moral sense (and thus is the only God worthy of worship), yet Angra Mainyu is his equal in an ontological sense, despite his wicked and violent nature. According to both views, Ahura Mazda is everlasting, exceedingly wise and powerful, transcendent and immanent, immaterial, and perfectly loving. Ahura Mazda communicates with human beings via *amesha spentas* (bounteous immortals). In some cases these immortals are viewed merely as concepts; in others they are thought to be real persons.

Chart 79

Zoroastrianism (continued)

Topic	Summary of View
Mankind	Human beings were created by Ahura Mazda as free agents with the power to choose between good and evil. They are part of Ahura Mazda's good kingdom by birthright, but they can choose to rebel against him. Human beings are endowed with mind, conscience, insight, wisdom, and desire, the combination of which is designed to guide them into truth (*asha*). Moreover, each person possesses both an incarnate soul and a (previously) preexistent soul (*fravashi*) that will be resurrected at the final judgment. There are three types of *fravashis*: living, dead, and not yet born. The two most important tasks of human beings are protecting the sacred fire (*empyrean*) and fighting against the demonic forces.
Sin	Sin is choosing to violate the law of *asha*, which is rooted in the nature of Ahura Mazda. Ahura Mazda holds people accountable for their actions because they have genuine moral freedom. According to some interpretations, the battle between good and evil is not a cosmic clash between rival gods, but an ethical dualism within the human heart.
Salvation	The salvation of each individual depends solely upon the choices the person makes. People should strive to have good thoughts (*humata*), words (*hukhta*), and deeds (*huvarshta*). One view maintains that those whose good actions outweigh their evil actions will be rewarded with eternal life in heaven after death, while those who committed more evil than good in this life are punished in hell, though hell is limited in duration. Another view holds that heaven and hell are terms that refer to the consequences of sin in this life. Although good and evil coexist in the present world and are locked in a fierce struggle, if enough people are steadfast in doing good works, the world will gradually become conformed to the perfect righteousness of Ahura Mazda.
Afterlife	After death, the soul (*urvan*) stays near its corpse for three days. (The performance of death rituals during this time restrains the demonic forces.) Then the soul walks across the Chinvat Bridge until it reaches a sword. If the soul is righteous, the sword turns so that its broad side faces the soul. If the soul is wicked, the sword remains with its sharp edge facing the soul so that the soul cannot get past it. Wicked souls are then slashed by the sword and fall off the bridge into hell, a four-storied realm of intense misery, each level of which is more miserable than the last. If the soul has committed an equal amount of good and evil deeds, it goes to Hammistagan, a neutral realm where it must wait until the resurrection. Righteous souls are permitted to cross the bridge into heaven, which also has four levels (of increasing joy). In a future millennium, all human beings who have ever lived will be resurrected. During this period, a savior named Saoshyant, whose lineage traces back to Zarathusthra, will be born of a virgin. At the end of the millennium, a massive battle will take place between the forces of good and the forces of evil. The latter will prevail in this cosmic combat, and then the final judgment will commence. During this judgment, the divine fire of Ahura Mazda will try all people. Good people will have their moral impurities burned away, whereas evil people will be utterly consumed, suffering annihilation. Next, Angra Mainyu will be cast into everlasting darkness and torment. The entire earth will be purified at this time, so that the resurrected righteous can live forever on the new earth with Ahura Mazda. Finite Time will then merge with Infinite Time.

Chart 79

Zoroastrianism (continued)

Distinctive Beliefs and Practices

Conversion	In most cases Zoroastrian communities will not accept converts, limiting members to those who are born into Zoroastrian families. Some Zoroastrian groups, however, dispute this and allow (or even encourage) converts to join them.
Nou Rouz (New Day)	*Nou Rouz* (New Day) is an important Zoroastrian festival that centers around the arrangement of seven special items on a table. Traditionally this festival occurred only once every several hundred years, but today it is observed annually.
Gahambars	*Gahambars* are special activities performed by Zoroastrians in open fields that point to the integral relationship between human beings and nature and express gratitude to animals and plants. Zarathushtra taught that human beings should respect and coexist peacefully with the natural world, learn about its practical uses, and apply this knowledge in a responsible way, one that does not result in damage to the environment.
Haoma	*Haoma* refers to both a sacred plant and a ritual drink made from that plant by pounding it. Drinking *haoma* is an important feature of many Zoroastrian rituals. Zoroastrian myth asserts that heavenly birds bring twigs of the *haoma* plant from a shining white tree in paradise to the earth. Haoma is also the name of a deity who grants human beings health, fertility, and marriages.
Navjote	An affirmation ceremony that serves to confirm a candidate's belief in and commitment to Zoroastrianism; most candidates are 15 years old or younger. Candidates wear a *sudre* under their outer clothing; this thin white garment represents purity. Once they have worn the *sudre*, adherents usually do not remove it unless they are preparing to take a bath. Candidates also wear a *kushti*, a cord made of 72 threads of wool, each of which represents a chapter from the *Yasna*; it too is worn nearly all the time. The *kushti* is wrapped around the body three times to remind the devotee of the obligation to think good thoughts, speak good words, and perform good deeds.
Sacred Fire	Zoroastrian myth states that the Great Fires have been burning since before the world was created. In one account, the first fire was transported from heaven to earth on the back of the mythical ox Srishok. This was done so that the fire could serve as protection for human beings against the cores of darkness and evil. Ahura Mazda himself is symbolized by fire. Zoroastrians perform elaborate purification ceremonies in which sacred fires are tended to 1,128 times over the course of a year. Most of these sacred fires have been burning for centuries in Zoroastrian temples in Iran and India.
Jashan	A memorial and thanksgiving ceremony, Jashan is performed with the intent of inducing residents of the world of spirit to meet with devotees in the material world. Ahura Mazda, the Amesha Spentas, the *yazates* (angels), and the unborn *fravishes* are invited to take part in the festivities. Afterward celebrants partake together of a ritual meal.

Chart 79

Zoroastrianism (continued)

Distinctive Beliefs and Practices

Boi Machi	This ritual is performed five times daily in conjunction with tending the sacred fires. The priest recites prescribed prayers before placing six pieces of sandalwood in a special urn (*afargan*). He then puts the urn and six measures of frankincense on the fire, and soon the fire emits a pleasant fragrance. Next, holding a ceremonial ladle, the priest walks around the fire and says a series of eight prayers. After this the priest strikes a ceremonial bell to summon the presence of Ahura Mazda. Afterward the priest gives worshipers ashes from the sacred fire.
Amesha Spentas	The *amesha spentas* (holy immortals) are the six beings through whom Ahura Mazdu created the material world. One view holds that they are independently existing divine beings. Another contends that they are divine emanations or aspects of Ahura Mazda. The names of these six beings are (1) Asha (the spirit of the Highest Law), (2) Khshatra (the spirit of Holy Dominion), (3) Vohu Mano (the spirit of the Good Mind), (4) Haurvatat (the spirit of Perfection and Well-Being), (5) Spenta Armaiti (the spirit of Benevolent Devotion), and (6) Ameretat (the spirit of Immortality).

Chart 79

Timeline of Shinto

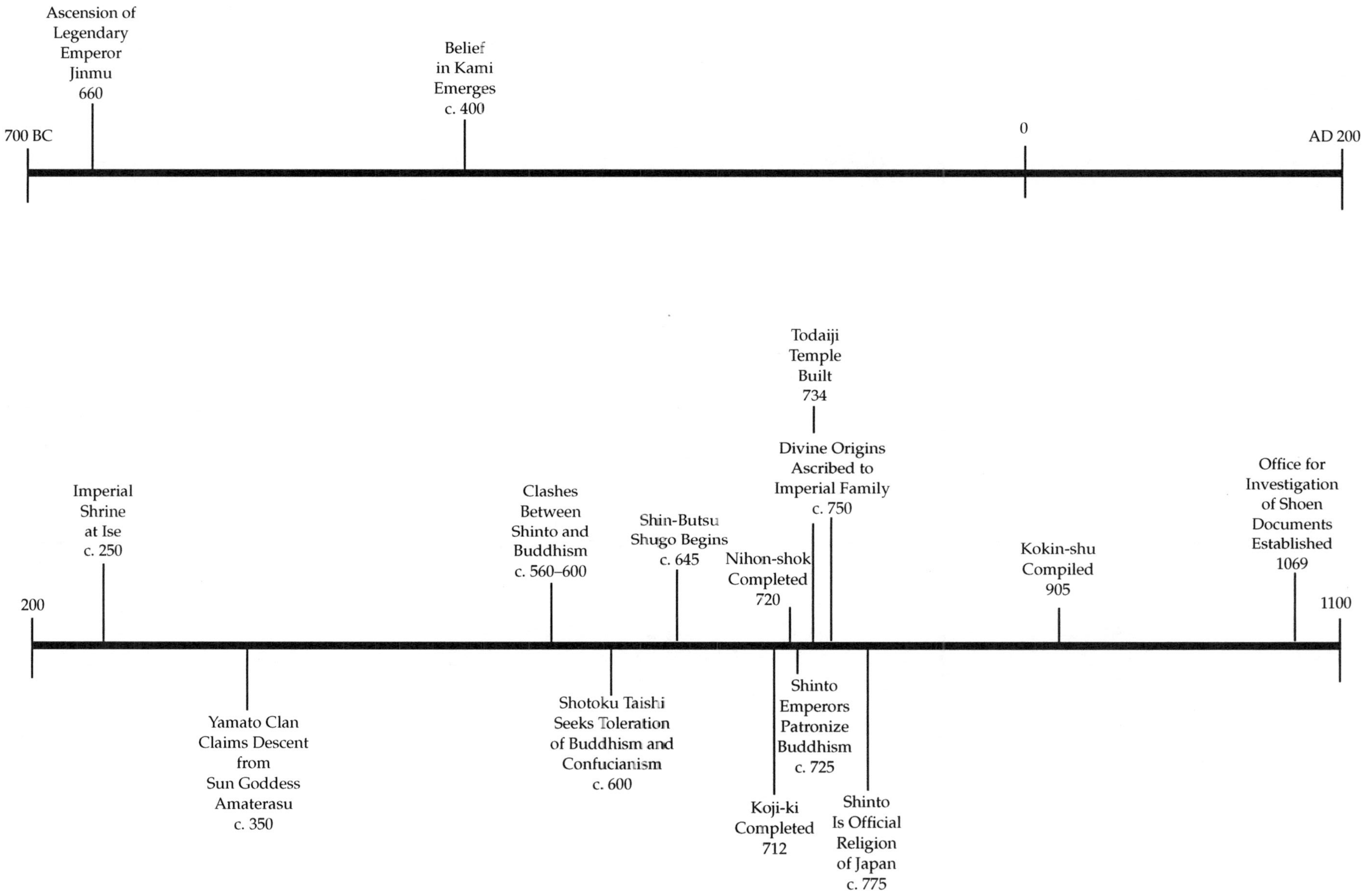

Ascension of
Legendary
Emperor
Jinmu
660

Belief
in Kami
Emerges
c. 400

700 BC

0

AD 200

Imperial
Shrine
at Ise
c. 250

Yamato Clan
Claims Descent
from
Sun Goddess
Amaterasu
c. 350

Clashes
Between
Shinto and
Buddhism
c. 560–600

Shotoku Taishi
Seeks Toleration
of Buddhism and
Confucianism
c. 600

Shin-Butsu
Shugo Begins
c. 645

Nihon-shoki
Completed
720

Todaiji
Temple
Built
734

Divine Origins
Ascribed to
Imperial Family
c. 750

Koji-ki
Completed
712

Shinto
Emperors
Patronize
Buddhism
c. 725

Shinto
Is Official
Religion
of Japan
c. 775

Kokin-shu
Compiled
905

Office for
Investigation
of Shoen
Documents
Established
1069

200

1100

Chart 80

Timeline of Shinto (continued)

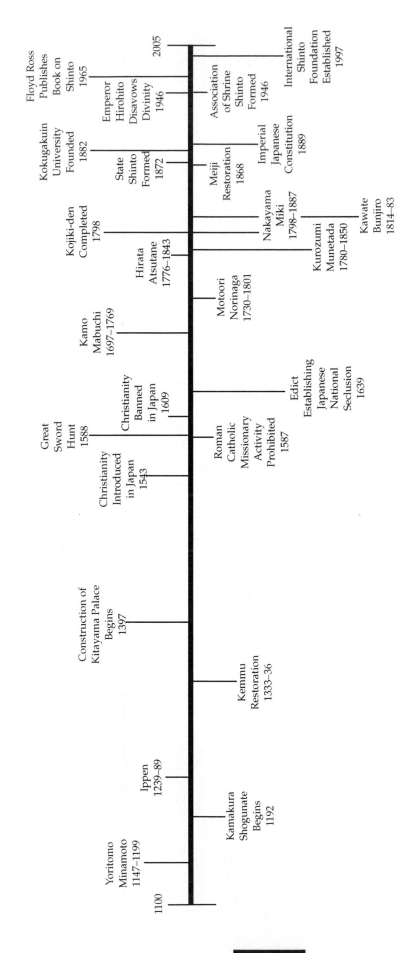

Chart 80

Shinto

Topic	Facts*
Current Data	Many estimates of the number of adherents are thought to be unreliable, in part because estimates vary by such substantial margins and because there is no widely agreed-upon set of criteria for determining whether a person is properly designated as a practitioner of Shinto. Sources employing strict criteria estimate as few as 3 million, while other sources claim that approximately 40 percent of Japanese adults are at least nominally affiliated with Shinto (putting the number at about 50 million). Some estimates count all Japanese citizens who identify themselves as Buddhists yet incorporate aspects of Shinto into their religion, in which case as many as 117 million people can be considered adherents of Shinto. More than 99 percent of all adherents live in Japan. Fewer than 1,000 live in the United States. There are more than 80,000 shrines in Japan. The largest sect is Shinshu Kyo. Prominent organizations include the International Shinto Foundation and the Tsubaki Grand Shrine of America.
History	The origins of Shinto are shrouded in mystery and thus only the most general (and tentative) things can be said about its early development. None of the teachings of Shinto were written down until the 5th century AD, and no single individual seems to have founded the religion. Many historians of Japan believe that the practices which led to the formation of Shinto as an organized religion go back as far as the 6th or 7th century BC. (According to Shinto legend, Emperor Jimmu founded the nation of Japan in 660 BC.) These practices may have included nature worship, shamanism, divination, hero worship, and fertility cults. In the late 6th century AD, the various beliefs and devotional activities that had become common in Japan were called the "Way of the Kami."
	During the Nara Dynasty (710–94) three pivotal events occurred: the Japanese imperial family declared itself to be divine; Shinto, along with Buddhism, was recognized as an official religion of the Japanese state; and the *Kojiki* (Records of Ancient Matters), a central Shinto holy book, was completed. Much of the next 500 years, however, was marked by internal warfare that went deeply against the principles of Shinto.
	In 1543 Jesuit missionaries arrived in Japan, setting in motion a series of events that threatened the dominance of Shinto. This in turn led to an attempt by the Japanese government to restore Shinto to its previous position of cultural ascendancy. The Meiji Restoration of 1868 resulted in the restructuring and centralization of Shinto in Japan. Although many Shinto ceremonies were significantly altered, the basic worldview remained unchanged.
	In 1882 all Shinto shrines were divided into two categories, those administered by the Japanese government (state shrines) and those allowed to oversee their own affairs (sectarian shrines). In the decades that followed, the myths and legends of ancient Japan were revived as a means of bringing greater honor to the emperor of Japan. After World War II, however, this practice came to an abrupt halt. Since then, Shinto has remained popular in Japan, but it now sees itself primarily as a way of preserving Japanese cultural traditions.

* The name "Shinto" can be misleading, for it is a combination of two Chinese words that mean "the way of the gods" (*shen*: spiritual power, divinity; and *tao*: the way or the path) and was first used at the beginning of the Early Modern Period. The Japanese word for the religion is *kannagara* (the way of the *kami* [spirits]).

Chart 81

Shinto (continued)

Topic	Facts
Summary of Beliefs	The term "Shinto" covers a broad range of beliefs, practices, and attitudes that were deeply embodied in traditional Japanese culture. Although Shinto does not concern itself with the systemization of doctrines, a supreme being, or sin and salvation in ways common to many other religions, it is nonetheless religious in the sense that it places its approach to the world in the context of an intimate relationship with a spiritual reality that lies partly beyond (though also partly within) this world. Shinto is greatly concerned with such social and relational issues as order, serenity, purity, and right sensibility. There are Four Affirmations in Shinto: 1. The central role of tradition and the family. Traditions are guarded and handed down within families. 2. A love of the natural world. Nature and the realm of spirit are closely interwoven and thus a preoccupation with the latter entails a respect for the former. 3. A commitment to personal hygiene. Shinto practitioners frequently wash their hands, bathe, and rinse out their mouths. 4. Celebrating *matsuri*, festivals in honor of the *kami* (spirits).

Topic	Summary of View
Creation	One account states that in countless ages past, long before the creation of the world, there was nothing but an infinite and formless chaos. From this chaos emerged the Plain of High Heaven and its attendant trio of gods: Ame-no-Minaka-Nushi-no-Mikoto, Takami-Musubi-no-Mikoto, and Kammi-Musubi-no-Mikoto. After many more eons had passed, the earth materialized from this chaos. The earth then gave birth to the deities Umashi-Ashi-Kahibi-Hikoji-no-Mikoto, Tokotachi-no-Mikoto, and a number of others. It was then suggested that Izanagi-no-mikoto and Izanami-no-mikoto fashion the earth into a suitable dwelling place for the gods. Using his spear to stir the chaos waters, Izanagi formed the Japanese islands of Onokoro, Awaji, Shikoku, Oki, Kyushu, Tsushima, Hokkaido, and Honshu, naming them as a group as Oyashi-ma-kuni (Country of the Eight Great Islands). Next Izanagi and Izanami formed dozens of additional islands in the vicinity of the primary eight. Later they begat many other gods, including the sun goddess Amaterasu Omikami.
Scripture and Authority	For the most part, the teachings of Shinto are not codified in a sacred book or collection of holy writings. Instead, Shinto is handed down from one generation to the next through spoken narratives and local participation in an ensemble of prescribed rites. Nevertheless, four texts are widely revered as being crucial to a proper understanding of Shinto in its broader historical context: (1) *Ko-ji-ki* (Record of Ancient Matters), (2) *Nihon-shoki* (Continuing Chronicles of Japan), (3) *Rokkokushi* (Six National Histories), and (4) *Jinno Shotoki* (a study of Japanese history and politics).

Chart 81

Shinto (continued)

Topic	Summary of View
God	*Kami* are the "gods" of Shinto and can roughly be thought of as spirits. However, there are many different kinds of *kami*: those related to natural objects and living things, guardians of particular areas and clans, family ancestors, souls of dead national leaders, and abstract creative forces, to name but a few. In fact, there are *kami* associated with nearly everything in the world, from mountains to waterfalls to rice paddies. Because the *kami* have such an intimate relationship with all aspects of nature, many animals and plants are given deference. Other types of *kami* include those involved in fertility (*musuhi*); "straightening" *kami* who solve personal, family, and even national problems; and "bending" *kami* who bring calamity. The most popular and highly esteemed *kami* is the sun goddess Amaterasu Omikami. Shinto legend has it that the Japanese emperors, beginning with Emperor Jimmu in 660 BC, can trace their genealogy back to the sun goddess. Until the end of World War II, the emperors of Japan were thought to be living *kami* (*ikigam*). Emperor Hirohito (1901–89) ended this tradition when he relinquished his claims to deity in 1946.
Mankind	Human nature is inherently good. People do evil when their otherwise pure nature has become contaminated through contact with evil or foreign influences. Every human being is a child of the *kami*, and thus human life is sacred. Up until the end of World War II, the people of Japan believed themselves to be divine and therefore to have a privileged place in the world.
Sin	Shinto does not have a well-developed system of personal ethics, in part because right action is defined in terms of its consequences for the family, clan, or nation. To this end, it is the will of the *kami* that people develop sincerity of heart (*makoto*). Some practitioners take a Confucian approach to ethics; others follow what is called The Code of the Noble. The three basic virtues involved in this moral code are (1) courage, which includes an antipathy toward cowardice and stealing; (2) loyalty, which involves devotion to one's rulers and clan; and (3) physical and ritual cleanliness. Other common moral precepts include: do not thwart the will of the gods, do not neglect your duties to your ancestors, do not break the laws of the government, and do not be lazy at work. Major sins include infant murder, incest, poisoning someone, and cursing. Things like natural disasters and ferocious animals are viewed in a similar manner to willful sin, because all such harmful events (*kunitsu-tsumi*) threaten social harmony and stability. Death, corruption, and grief entered the world after the divine Mother Izanami perished.
Salvation	The shrine is the focal point of religious rites and ceremonies. When devotees enter a shrine, they pass through a gateway (*tori*) that the *kami* use to go back and forth between worlds. Inside each shrine is a sacred object in which the *kami* of that shrine resides. Each shrine's *kami* listens to and answers the sincere prayers of the faithful and accepts worship from them in exchange for providing health and safety. Shrine *kami* also expect devotees to make offerings, perform ritual cleansings, recite prayers, and perform special dances. Traditionally, before entering the shrine, devotees washed their bodies (this washing was called *misogi*) in a sacred river near the shrine. Most Shinto homes feature an altar called the *Kami-dana* (Shelf of the gods). Many adherents wear *mamori* (charms thought to provide healing and protection from harm).

Chart 81

Shinto (continued)

Topic	Summary of View
Afterlife	When someone dies, the members of the family arrange for a cremation ceremony to be held. After the ceremony, relatives use chopsticks to remove the bones of the deceased from the ashes. The urn in which the body was burned is left out for 35 days and then buried. If cremation is not chosen, the corpse is buried wearing a kimono, the right part of which is placed over the left (ordinarily a kimono is worn with the left side over the right). This switch symbolizes the fact that the abode of the dead is a reflection of the present world. After death, every person becomes a *kami* and maintains a vital link with those who are still living. Good people go on to be *kami* who benefit their families, communities, and nation; evil individuals become malicious and destructive *kami*. No one faces divine judgment, but persons who have committed grave sins cannot enter the next world until the proper rituals have been performed on their behalf by those still living. Some traditions mention the High Plain of Heaven and the Dark Land as dwelling places of the dead, though little is known about them.

Distinctive Beliefs and Practices

Topic	Summary of View
Types of Shinto	1. Koshitsu (Shinto of the Imperial House): This is the official Shinto of Japan. The emperor of Japan performs specified ceremonies which symbolize the nation and its people. 2. Jinja (Shrine Shinto): Currently the largest type of Shinto, many of its practices can be traced back to ancient times. Nearly all Japanese shrines are part of a larger association that provides cohesion to the movement. 3. Kyoha (Sectarian Shinto): Consists of thirteen distinct sects, all of which were established during the last 200 years by different founders, and each of which has its own distinctive beliefs and practices. 4. Minsoku (Folk Shinto): This takes the form of local and regional variations of Shinto, many of which are distinctively rural. Sometimes the residents of a locality select a particular individual to worship the local *kami* on behalf of the entire community.
Origami	Origami (paper of the spirits) is the Japanese art of paper-folding. It originated during the Edo Period (1603–1867). Only a few basic folds are used, but the different combinations of folds produce an array of aesthetically pleasing objects. Used for a variety of purposes and occasions, origami shapes are frequently found in or near Shinto shrines. Some practitioners do not cut the paper, in deference to the spirit of the tree from which the paper came.

Chart 81

Timeline of Confucianism

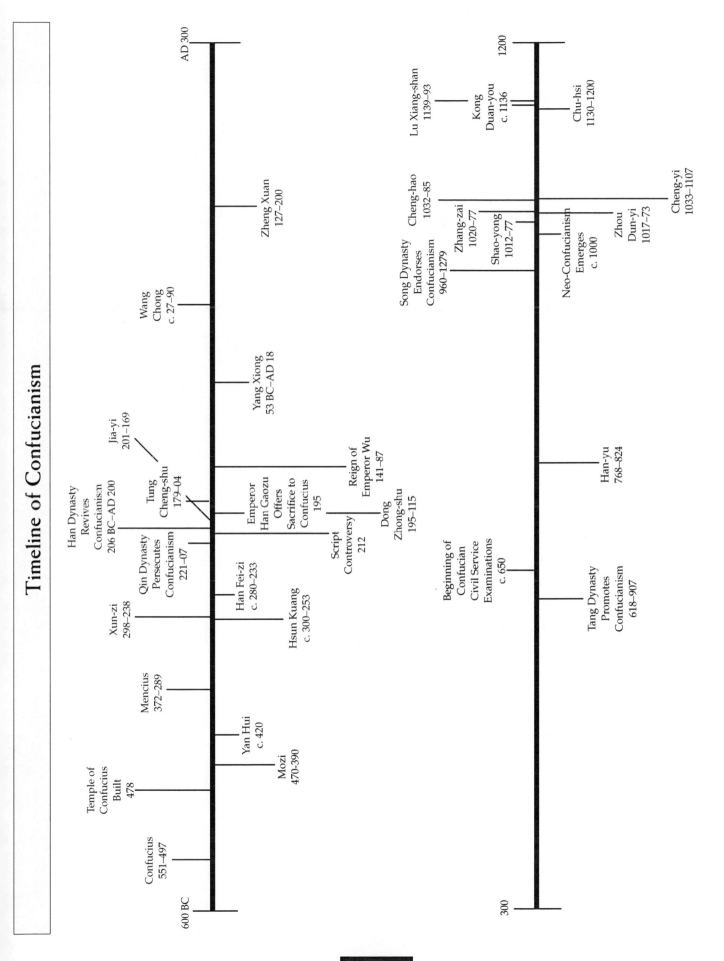

Confucius 551–497

Temple of Confucius Built 478

Mozi 470-390

Yan Hui c. 420

Mencius 372–289

Xun-zi 298–238

Han Fei-zi c. 280–233

Hsun Kuang c. 300–253

Qin Dynasty Persecutes Confucianism 221–07

Han Dynasty Revives Confucianism 206 BC–AD 200

Tung Cheng-shu 179–04

Jia-yi 201–169

Emperor Han Gaozu Offers Sacrifice to Confucius 195

Reign of Emperor Wu 141–87

Dong Zhong-shu 195–115

Script Controversy 212

Yang Xiong 53 BC–AD 18

Wang Chong c. 27–90

Zheng Xuan 127–200

Song Dynasty Endorses Confucianism 960–1279

Cheng-hao 1032–85

Zhang-zai 1020–77

Shao-yong 1012–77

Neo-Confucianism Emerges c. 1000

Zhou Dun-yi 1017–73

Cheng-yi 1033–1107

Lu Xiang-shan 1139–93

Kong Duan-you c. 1136

Chu-hsi 1130–1200

Han-yu 768–824

Beginning of Confucian Civil Service Examinations c. 650

Tang Dynasty Promotes Confucianism 618–907

600 BC

AD 300

300

1200

Chart 82

Timeline of Confucianism (continued)

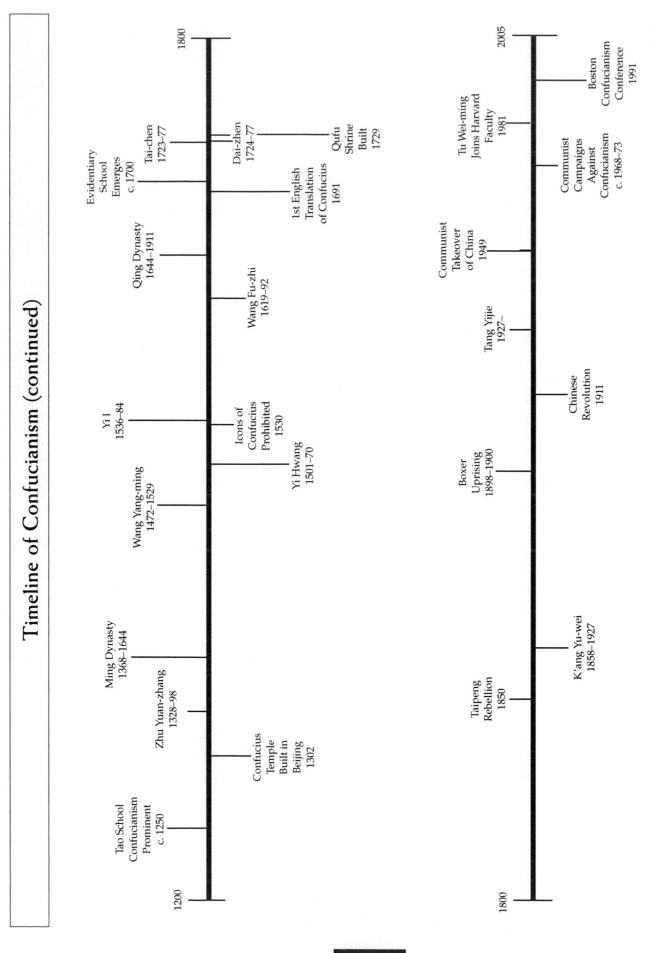

Chart 82

Confucianism

Topic	Facts
Current Data	The number of Confucians worldwide is very difficult to determine. Estimates range from 6 million to 350 million. This huge discrepancy is the result of different criteria for determining whether a person should be considered an adherent of Confucianism. Lower estimates include only those who strongly adhere to the entire Confucian worldview. Higher estimates include those who have been significantly influenced by cultures that have been shaped by Confucianism. Nearly all Confucians live in China and other parts of East Asia; only about 25,000 live in North America. There are five main schools of Confucianism: Neo-Confucianism, Singapore Confucianism, Japanese Confucianism, Korean Confucianism, and Han Confucianism. The most prominent organization in the United States is the Boston Confucians, based at Harvard University.
History	Confucius (551–479 BC) was born Kong Qui in the Chinese territory of Lu (present-day Shandong province). During the first few decades of his adult life he taught using the traditional Chinese curriculum, but began to form ideas of his own. During his 50s and 60s Confucius may have worked in regional government, but this is unclear. He did begin teaching a small group of followers his novel philosophy during this time. When Confucius died his ideas had not gained a wide audience, but some of his disciples wrote them down; these texts are now known as the *Analects*. In the 4th and 3rd centuries BC, Mencius (372–289 BC) and Hsun-tzu (310–237) were staunch advocates of Confucian teachings. During the Han Dynasty (206 BC–AD 220), Tung Vhung-shu (179–104 BC) supported the incorporation of Confucian teaching into the state-sponsored education curriculum. This period also witnessed the canonization of Confucius's writings and the establishment of a cult of Confucius. After the fall of the Han Dynasty, however, Buddhism and Taoism played a greater role in shaping Chinese culture than did Confucianism; this state of affairs lasted for several centuries. Confucianism made a comeback during the Tang Dynasty (618–907), when it was endorsed by the Tang emperors. Temples in honor of Confucius proliferated during this time. Neo-Confucianism developed during the Song Dynasty (960–1279) largely due to the efforts of Zhu-xi (1130–1200). The Qing Dynasty (1644–1911) witnessed a proposal by Chinese scholars to return to the type of Confucianism practiced during the Han Dynasty. In 1906 K'ang Yu-wei (1858–1927) tried (but failed) to establish Confucianism as the official religion of China. The Chinese Revolution of 1911 put an end to Confucian religious practices that had been in place for centuries. After the Communist takeover of China in 1949, Confucianism was greatly suppressed by the government. During the late 1960s and early 1970s there was a government-sponsored crackdown on Confucian practices, though this ended in 1977. Led by Tu Wei-ming (1940–), the organization known as the Boston Confucians was formed in Boston during the 1990s.
Summary of Beliefs	Though certainly containing many religious elements, the core of Confucianism is a concern for maintaining social harmony and stability that works itself out in a complex system of ethics that penetrates into every sphere of life. The primary purpose of Confucianism is to establish and preserve the basic social structure, values, and rites of traditional Chinese culture. Three fundamental ideas are central to Confucianism.

Chart 83

Confucianism (continued)

Topic	Facts
Summary of Beliefs (continued)	1. The rectification of names. Confucius firmly maintained that people should behave in a manner fitting to their social position, thereby conforming to the Universal Law that governs relationships in the world. Acting inconsistently with one's position causes dissension and strife at every level of society. 2. The relationship between "human-heartedness" and righteousness. Confucius taught that every social position carries with it certain prescribed responsibilities (righteousness). He insisted that love for others (human-heartedness) ought to motivate the meeting of these obligations. 3. Knowing *ming*. Confucius taught that acting virtuously always provided some significant benefit to the person who so acted, and thus that people should not base their moral decisions on the possible consequences of actions. Knowing *ming* amounts to the determination to behave virtuously regardless of possible outcomes.

Topic	Summary of View
Creation	The question of whether the universe had a beginning in time or was created by an omnipotent deity is not addressed. The fundamental units of social order—marriage, family, and government—are reflections of the structure of the universe. In particular, the office of king is deeply embedded in the cosmic order of things.
Scripture and Authority	Confucianism has no revealed scripture but does have a number of writings that are highly esteemed. These include the *Analects of Confucius* (*Lun-yu*), *Book of Mencius* (*Meng-tzu*), *Hsiao Ching*, *Doctrine of the Mean* (*Chung-yung*), *Great Learning* (*Ta-hsueh*), *Book of Odes* (*Shih-ching*), and *Book of History* (*Shu-ching*). These works are part of a larger collection of 13 honored classic texts.
God	Confucius believed in a personal deity named T'ien (Heaven), though his teaching focused far more on personal and social ethics than on the nature of God or the duties human beings have with respect to God. This caused later Confucian intellectuals to view T'ien as a mere concept or philosophical principle, and hence belief in a personal divine being dropped out of Confucian thinking. Much of popular Confucianism concerns itself with the activities of spirits (*shen*) and ghosts (*guei*), who can affect social relationships. During much of Chinese history the emperors viewed the *shen* and *guei* as Chinese citizens, subject to many of the same sanctions as human citizens.
Mankind	Human beings are social creatures and maintaining proper relationships between them is the most important human activity. Only in relation to others can one establish virtuous character. The universal law known as the Rectification of Names is the standard to which human behavior ought to conform. The way in which social relationships are organized and conducted either promotes human flourishing or causes great damage to individuals and society. Relationships that are integral to the proper functioning of families and society include those between wife and husband, son and father, younger brother and older brother, subjects and rulers, and friendships of

Chart 83

Confucianism (continued)

Topic	Summary of View
Mankind (continued)	various kinds. In all these relationships, the submissive party should not criticize the dominant part except in extreme situations. Showing honor and respect to one's parents—known as filial piety (*xiao*)—is extremely important. Ancestors are worthy of reverence and, in many cases, of worship. Human beings are morally neutral, but the practice of virtue makes them good. The example of rulers has a significant effect on swaying their subjects toward good or evil.
Sin	The Mandate of Heaven sets forth the moral obligations that are incumbent upon each person. To ignore or willfully violate this mandate is sin. The emperor is a mediator between heaven and earth, appointed by Heaven (T'ien) to govern his subjects in such a manner that they can prosper. If he abdicates this duty by refusing to rule in accordance with virtue (*te*) or by failing to embody humaneness (*ren*) in his dealings with his subjects, then he has sinned. The most important ethical principle is that of social propriety (*li*), which has implications for the nature and structure of human government, provides critical norms for social etiquette, and prescribes specified rituals. *Li* is embodied when fathers are loving and kind (*jen*), when sons love and honor their parents (*hsiao*), when wives obey their husbands, when older brothers are gentle in their dealings with younger siblings, when younger people show respect for their elders and treat them humanely, and when subjects are loyal to their rulers (*zhong*). To upset social order by rejecting *li* is a grave sin. Other virtues include honesty and trustworthiness (*xin*) and practicing peace (*wen*).
Salvation	Unlike many religions that have a doctrine of rewards and punishments in the next life, in Confucianism salvation is understood as a society characterized by harmonious relationships and benevolent government rule. This kind of social order can be brought about if the individuals in a society are committed to moral improvement over the course of their entire lives. Participating in proper rituals and appeasing the spirits of one's ancestors help to prevent conflict and disorder in society.
Afterlife	Some Confucians believe that T'ien (Heaven) holds all people accountable for their behavior. Confucius rarely spoke to his disciples about death and the afterlife. He also said very little about the veneration of ancestors, but did advise treating them as though they were still observing the affairs of this world. The spirit of a deceased ancestor may behave spitefully if living relatives do not perform fitting rites of ancestor veneration. Popular Confucianism teaches that after death, a person's two souls go to separate destinations: the upper soul (*hun*) becomes a spirit (*shen*) and rises to the heavenly realms, while the lower soul (*p'o*) becomes a ghost (*guei*) and is buried with the corpse.

Distinctive Beliefs and Practices

Topic	Summary of View
Foretelling	*Yi-jing* diagrams are used to prognosticate future events and, on the basis of that information, to choose appropriate courses of action. Each diagram is composed of 64 hexagrams, each of which represents an epoch in the cyclical history of the universe; 49 sticks are cast as a means of selecting which hexagram to use as the basis for the prediction. Many Confucians believe that the universe is always progressing through one of these 64 stages. Chinese concepts of time and personhood have been influenced by this kind of diagram.

Chart 83

Confucianism (continued)

Distinctive Beliefs and Practices

Life Passages	Traditional Confucianism involves the celebration and regulation of four major life passages.

Traditional Confucianism involves the celebration and regulation of four major life passages.

1. Birth. The pregnant woman is protected by the spirit of her unborn baby (*t'ai-shen*). After the child has been delivered, there is a ritual disposing of the placenta.

2. Reaching maturity. The young adult eats a specially prepared chicken dish along with family and friends.

3. Marriage. Confucian marriages involve six progressive stages.

   a. Proposal. The marriage proposal is turned down if an inauspicious event transpires during a three-day period after the proposal is made.

   b. Engagement. The bride sends wedding invitations to invited guests, along with moon-shaped cookies.

   c. Dowry. The father of the bride presents a dowry to the groom's parents, they send a bride price to the parents of the bride, and the groom gives his bride gifts whose value is the same as the dowry.

   d. Procession. The groom goes to the home of his future in-laws, at which time his bride accompanies him to his own home amidst much celebration.

   e. Marriage and Reception. The couple makes their vows and attends a wedding dinner where they are the center of attention.

   f. Morning After: The bride prepares breakfast for her new in-laws, who in turn do the same for the new couple.

4. Death. The dead person's family and friends mourn loudly while wearing coarse clothing. Certain foods and objects special to the deceased are put into the coffin. Relatives take willow branches, which represent the spirit of the deceased, to the cemetery; later these branches are used to ensure that the spirit completes its passage to the next world. Typically, a Taoist or Buddhist priest officiates at the funeral.

Chart 83

Timeline of Sikhism

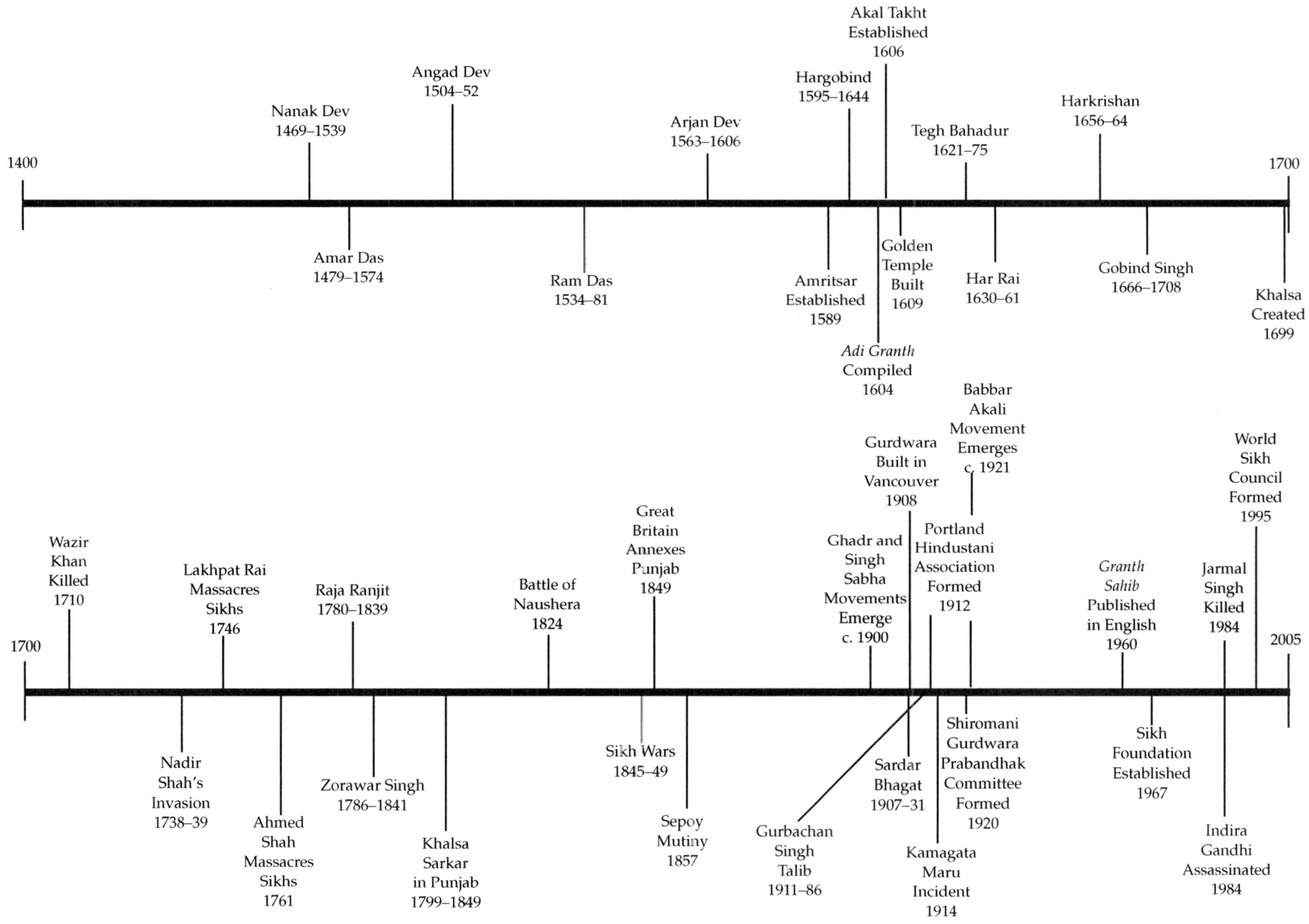

Nanak Dev
1469–1539

Angad Dev
1504–52

Amar Das
1479–1574

Ram Das
1534–81

Arjan Dev
1563–1606

Hargobind
1595–1644

Akal Takht
Established
1606

Tegh Bahadur
1621–75

Amritsar
Established
1589

Golden
Temple
Built
1609

Adi Granth
Compiled
1604

Har Rai
1630–61

Harkrishan
1656–64

Gobind Singh
1666–1708

Khalsa
Created
1699

1400

1700

Wazir
Khan
Killed
1710

Nadir
Shah's
Invasion
1738–39

Lakhpat Rai
Massacres
Sikhs
1746

Ahmed
Shah
Massacres
Sikhs
1761

Raja Ranjit
1780–1839

Zorawar Singh
1786–1841

Khalsa
Sarkar
in Punjab
1799–1849

Battle of
Naushera
1824

Great
Britain
Annexes
Punjab
1849

Sikh Wars
1845–49

Sepoy
Mutiny
1857

Ghadr and
Singh
Sabha
Movements
Emerge
c. 1900

Gurdwara
Built in
Vancouver
1908

Sardar
Bhagat
1907–31

Portland
Hindustani
Association
Formed
1912

Gurbachan
Singh Talib
1911–86

Kamagata
Maru
Incident
1914

Shiromani
Gurdwara
Prabandhak
Committee
Formed
1920

Babbar
Akali
Movement
Emerges
c. 1921

*Granth
Sahib*
Published
in English
1960

Sikh
Foundation
Established
1967

Jarmal
Singh
Killed
1984

Indira
Gandhi
Assassinated
1984

World
Sikh
Council
Formed
1995

1700

2005

Chart 84

Sikhism

Topic	Facts
Current Data	There are approximately 20 million devotees worldwide, 80 percent of which live in India (mainly in the Punjab area). Sikhism has three main sects: Udasis, Sahajdharis, and the Singhs. Prominent organizations include the World Sikh Council and the Sikh Foundation.
History	The founder of Sikhism, Guru Nanak Dev (1469–1538), was born into a Hindu family in India and remained a Hindu until he was in his 20s. At that time he concluded that Hinduism did not have the final answers to ultimate religious questions, and he undertook a study of several other religions. At the age of 28 he said that God (True Name) had spoken to him, commissioning him to spread the unifying message "There is no Hindu, there is no Muslim." Nanak then spent the bulk of the next 40 years teaching his unconventional doctrines throughout the Punjab area. Nanak had amassed a sizable following by the time he died, at which point Guru Angad Dev (1504–1552) became the Sikh movement's new leader. This line of succession continued through the ministries of eight subsequent gurus: Amar Das (1479–1574), Ram Das (1534–1581), Arjan Dev (1563–1606), Har Gobind (1595–1644), Har Rai (1630–1661), Har Krishan (1656–1664), Tegh Bahadur (1621–1675), and Gobind Singh (1666–1708). Arjan Dev, the fifth guru, gathered his writings and those of the first four gurus and entitled the compilation *Adi Granth* (True Book). After the death of Gobind Singh, this holy book became the final guru of Sikhism.
	The Sikh homeland (all of which formerly was in India) was divided in 1947 with the formation of Pakistan, an Islamic nation whose eastern border with India now ran through that homeland. Fearful of Muslim persecution, many Sikhs relocated to places within the boundaries of the "new" India. For the past 60 years, there has been ongoing friction in India between Hindus, Muslims, and Sikhs. This conflict reached a boiling point in 1984, when the (largely Hindu) Indian army besieged a Sikh temple in Amritsar, killing or wounding nearly 600 Sikhs. Prime Minister Indira Ghandi (1917–1984), who had authorized the attack, was later assassinated by her two Sikh bodyguards. Today, an effort is under way on the part of many Sikhs to create an independent Sikh nation to be named Khalistan (Land of the Pure).
Summary of Beliefs	The word *Sikh* means "learner" or "disciple," referring specifically to one who follows the divine call given by Nanak Dev, the first Sikh guru, during his ministry on earth. Though some scholars of Indian religion maintain otherwise, adherents insist that Sikhism is not a merger of Hindu and Islamic beliefs, but a unique religion that happens to share some ideas with both Hinduism and Islam. Nanak asserted that Hinduism and Islam were corrupt religions that prevented their respective adherents from seeing the true religion of God. He taught that all persons should be on a quest for truth in the midst of the distorting influences of Hindu and Muslim culture. Sikhism extols a strict monotheism summarized by the Mool Mantra, which declares that there is but one eternal, self-existent God who created all things. It further asserts that God fears nothing, has no enmity toward anything, and has been made known to men by the grace of the guru.

Chart 85

Sikhism (continued)

Topic	Summary of View
Creation	True Name (Karta Purukh as Creator) created the universe by means of a divine decree (*hukam*) that established a cosmic order. True Name also created an infinite number of other worlds, each containing its own set of sentient creatures, prophets, and sacred scriptures. The entire universe is sustained by God's loving power and is governed by both his justice (*nian*) and his grace (*nadar*). Though True Name is transcendent over his creation, the universe is divine in the sense that God controls it in much the same way that the spirit of a human being controls the body.
Scripture and Authority	Members of the Sikh religion are divided regarding their scripture. Some believe that the *Guru Granth Sahib*, compiled by Gobind Singh, the tenth guru, is the sole holy book of Sikhism. Others contend that the true holy book is the *Adi Granth*, compiled by Arjan Dev, the fifth guru, and that the *Granth Sahib* is not truly authoritative. It is argued that the *Granth Sahib* does not subtract from or contradict the *Adi Granth*, but supplements it with additional material. Copies of the *Granth Sahib* are objects of worship in Sikh temples (*gurdwaras*), often covered with a special canopy (*chandoa*). Some Sikhs keep a copy of the *Granth Sahib* in their home, though it is required that they build a room just for the book, where it rests on an altar (*manji*) of sacred pillows. Although the caretakers of the *Granth Sahib* provide some measure of leadership, Sikh worship (*diwan*) may be led by any member of the religious community (*panth*).
God	True Name is one God who possesses two distinct natures within the totality of his divine being. The personal nature is called Saguna, and the impersonal nature is called Nirguna. Saguna is material in form (it is the created universe) and thus has material (though nonetheless perfect) properties. Pious Sikhs can visualize True Name with respect to this nature, though he cannot take on human form. Nirguna is immaterial, without attributes, and incomprehensible. Pantheism is firmly rejected. True Name exercises meticulous providence over all events in the world. His Sikh followers call him True Name because referring to God by any other name invariably results in a confused concept of God. Although such people are not aware of it, True Name is the God of the adherents of all other religions.
Mankind	People are intrinsically good, and adherents of disparate religions are equal in the eyes of God. Each human soul contains a spark of the Divine Light, but a coating of human flaws and frailties covers this light. It is not true that some groups of people are more valuable than others, whatever the basis for making the distinction. In particular, the full equality of women with men is affirmed, especially in matters pertaining to the practice of the Sikh religion.
Sin	Sikh morality consists of pursuing righteousness (*dharmsal*) and avoiding vices. The five principal vices are worldly attachment (*moh*), pride (*ahankar*), anger (*krodh*), lust (*kam*), and greed (*lobh*). Sharing with others (*vand chakna*) and community service (*seva*) are vitally important to spiritual growth. People ought to be concerned less with themselves and more with loving others in a pure manner. A Khalsa is someone who is completely committed to following Sikh doctrine and practice. Traditional Hindu practices like female infanticide and wife burning (*sati*) are evil, as is the religious intolerance that characterizes Islam.

Chart 85

Sikhism (continued)

Topic	Summary of View
Salvation	Achieved by breaking the cycle of death and rebirth (*awagaun*) and merging with True Name (God). This process of liberation, which is rarely completed in a single lifetime, has three stages: 1. penetrating the Wall of Falsehood, which involves peeling layers of evil off the soul, 2. praising God and developing compassion for other people by means of meditation, and 3. one's soul being absorbed into the divine essence (Sach Khand). Liberation does not require austere practices like fasting, celibacy, yoga, or pilgrimages. Instead, it should be undertaken amidst the ordinary responsibilities of everyday life, along with studying the *Granth Sahib*, meditation, and daily remembrance of God (*nam simran*). A Gurmukh is a person who has achieved liberation (*mukhti*) and thus is totally God-centered.
Afterlife	All souls are reincarnated many times before they merge with True Name (God). Eventually, every soul will be absorbed into the divine essence. Because it is necessary to die in order to achieve liberation, the death of loved ones should not be mourned or seen as a grievous loss because death provides a means for the departed soul to become one with True Name.

Distinctive Beliefs and Practices	
Khalsa	Khalsa refers to a volunteer Sikh army that exists to protect and serve the larger Sikh community. Members take an oath to abide by a higher moral standard than is imposed on other Sikhs. They also are distinguished by their uncut hair (*kesh*), the wooden comb (*kangha*) they carry with them, the steel bracelet (*kara*) they wear, the short sword (*kirpan*) they use during Sikh ceremonies, and the shorts (*kachha*) they wear under their street clothes. When they undergo initiation (*amritsanskar*) into the group, male members receive the surname Singh (lion), while female members receive the surname Kaur (princess).
Amrit	*Amrit* means "nectar" and is holy sugar water used during the Khalsa initiation ritual. After pouring fresh water into a large iron bowl, five Khalsa members stir in sugar using a double-edged dagger while prayers are recited. When the prayers are completed, the *amrit* is given to each initiate in a special manner. Five sips of *amrit* are put into the palm of each initiate's right hand for him to drink, then *amrit* is sprinkled into the eyes and on the head of each initiate. Finally, each initiate drinks a small amount from the bowl until the bowl is empty.
Gurdwaras and Worship	Temples (*gurdwaras*) serve as the center of Sikh worship. Services are conducted on Sunday and last for hours. Worship includes singing, meditation, and readings from the *Granth Sahib*. The most important temple is the Golden Temple (Harmiandir Sahib) at Amritsar in the Punjab region of India.

Chart 85

Sikhism (continued)

Topic	Summary of View
Diwali	Diwali, a festival of lights established by Guru Amar Das, is held around October 25, when Sikhs assemble to receive the blessings of gurus.
Maghi	Sikhs visit their temples (*gurdwaras*) and listen to hymns (*kirtan*) to remember the martyrdom of the Forty Immortals (40 Sikhs killed in the battle of Muktsar in 1705), with the largest gathering at the battlefield of Muktsar. Maghi is held on the first day of Maghar Sangrant (about January 14).
Nitnem	*Nitnem* are daily prayers that adherents to Sikhism are to read at different times of the day. These include *Japji* of Guru Nanak, *Jap* and *Ten Swayyas* of Guru Gobind Singh (read in the morning), the *Guru Amar Das* and *Guru Arjun* (read at sunset), and *Kirtan Sohila* (five hymns composed by gurus), to be read at bedtime.
The Five Takhts (Thrones of Authority)	The Five *Takhts* are seats of authority that are to deal with religious matters and religious interpretations of secular matters since it was thought the Sikh temples should be solely used for worship. The first and the most important Takht stood opposite the gate of Harmandar Sahib at the Golden Temple in Amritsar.

Chart 85

PART 6
INDIGENOUS
RELIGIONS

Historical Relationships of Indigenous Religions

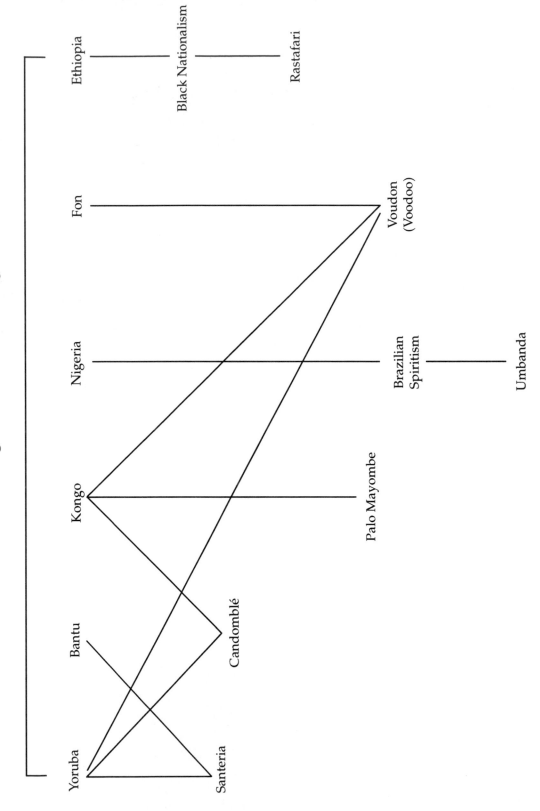

African Traditional Religion and Caribbean Religions

Ethiopia — Black Nationalism — Rastafari

Fon — Voudon (Voodoo)

Nigeria — Brazilian Spiritism — Umbanda

Kongo — Palo Mayombe

Bantu

Candomblé

Yoruba

Santeria

Chart 86

Historical Relationships of Indigenous Religions (continued)

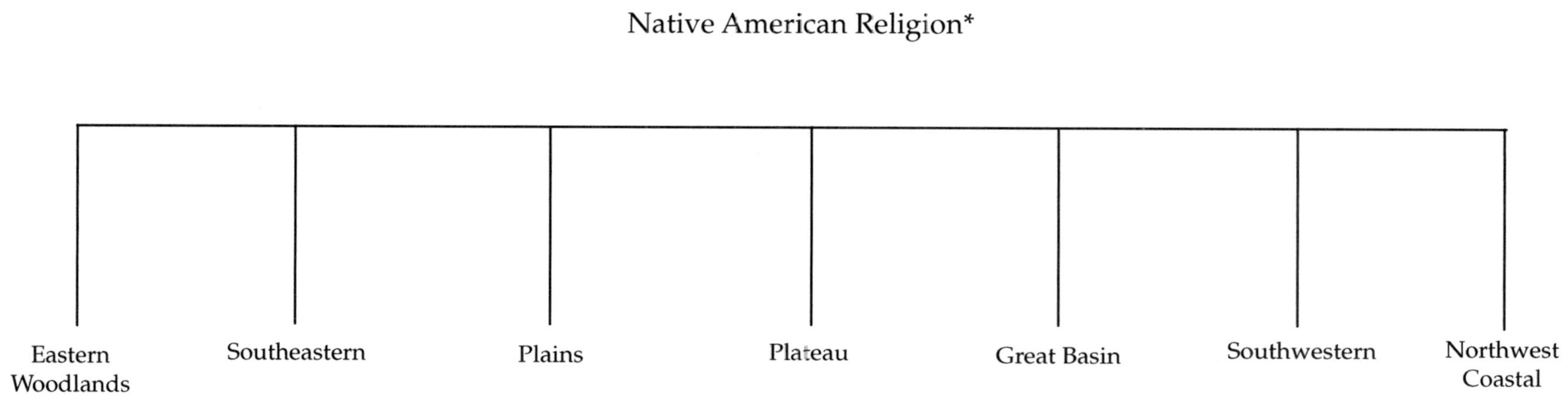

Native American Religion*

```
                          Native American Religion*
   ┌──────────┬──────────┬──────────┬──────────┬──────────┬──────────┐
Eastern   Southeastern  Plains    Plateau  Great Basin  Southwestern  Northwest
Woodlands                                                              Coastal
```

* Migration patterns, chronology, and development of beliefs and practices among tribes are extremely difficult to determine. Various subcultures and geographical groupings have been suggested, but all are subject to various limitations. Each of the groupings shown above included dozens of tribes, among which were the Algonquin, Apache, Arapaho, Blackfoot, Cherokee, Cheyenne, Chickasaw, Chinook, Chippewa, Comanche, Crow, Dakota, Delaware, Hopi, Huron, Illini, Iroquois, Lakota, Mohawk, Mohican, Mojave, Navajo, Osage, Ottawa, Pueblo, Seminole, Shawnee, Shoshone, Sioux, Spokane, Tonkawa, Tutuni, Ute, Yakima, and Zuni.

Chart 86

Comparison of Indigenous Religions

	Scripture and Authority*	God	Mankind
Caribbean (Imported)	Group beliefs and experience are primary, though the Bible and Roman Catholic tradition often play a subservient role in both doctrine and practice. Most have no religious writings. Distinct traditions are carefully guarded and are divulged mostly, if not exclusively, to initiates.	A supreme God is affirmed, though he is remote and inaccessible. Lesser deities and spirits are the ones with whom humans have regular contact. In Rastafari, God is immanent.	Mankind is a creation of God and has a spiritual dimension. Humans are closely linked to the spiritual world and depend on it for many things.
Traditional African	No holy book regulates beliefs and practices. The traditions of each tribe are transmitted orally and give an account of the tribe's relationship to the larger world.	Affirms a supreme creator God, unique and transcendent, who exercises control over the created world and the events of human life.	Humans are created by God, though they do not bear the divine image. Human life has great dignity, far exceeding in value and importance that of animals and other forms of life.
Native American	There are no sacred texts that serve as the basis for beliefs and practices. The worldview of each tribe is communicated through story-telling and myths that preserve a distinct tribal identity.	God is a Master Spirit and almighty Creator from which all life issues forth. His Spirit is ubiquitous.	A human being has two souls and the whole person is penetrated by the all-pervading Spirit. Mankind exists in a relationship of mystical interdependence with the land and all that lives in it.

* Generalizations about indigenous religions are difficult and necessarily imprecise due to the tremendous variety within these broader categories.

Chart 87

Comparison of Indigenous Religions (continued)

	Sin	Salvation	Afterlife
Caribbean (Imported)	Not adhering to particular standards of behavior and/or not performing prescribed rituals. Spirits inhabit the abode of the dead and cause trouble for those who do not perform the required rituals.	Obtained through magic, special ceremonies, sacrifices, and/or summoning and being possessed by spirits. Sometimes returning to Africa is viewed as a journey that brings salvation to the traveler.	Some groups believe in reincarnation, others maintain that departed spirits remain in the spirit world. Some also believe that witch doctors can turn dead people into zombies.
Traditional African	Violating certain ethical precepts and failing to uphold and cultivate the right kind of relationship with others in the tribe, ancestor spirits, and the natural environment. Evil is the result of offended spirits or practitioners of black magic.	Obtaining and maintaining tribal strength, security, and protection from injury and destruction. Aids to acquiring this goal include placating spirits, divination, talismans, libations, and tribal medicine.	When people die, they join their ancestors in the world of the spirits. However, in an important sense the whole person passes into the spirit-world, not just the person's spirit.
Native American	Attitudes and ways of life that wreak havoc on the harmony of creation and the integrity of land and life. Death is seen as a natural occurrence and is not feared.	Living in harmony with creation and the Spirit who pervades all things. Upholding the sacred order of things and the honor of the tribe.	Some believe in reincarnation, wherein people are reborn either as a human being or as an animal. Others think that humans return as ghosts or go on to another world in spirit form. Yet others hold that the spirits of the dead remain on their tribal homeland.

Chart 87

Timeline of African Traditional Religion

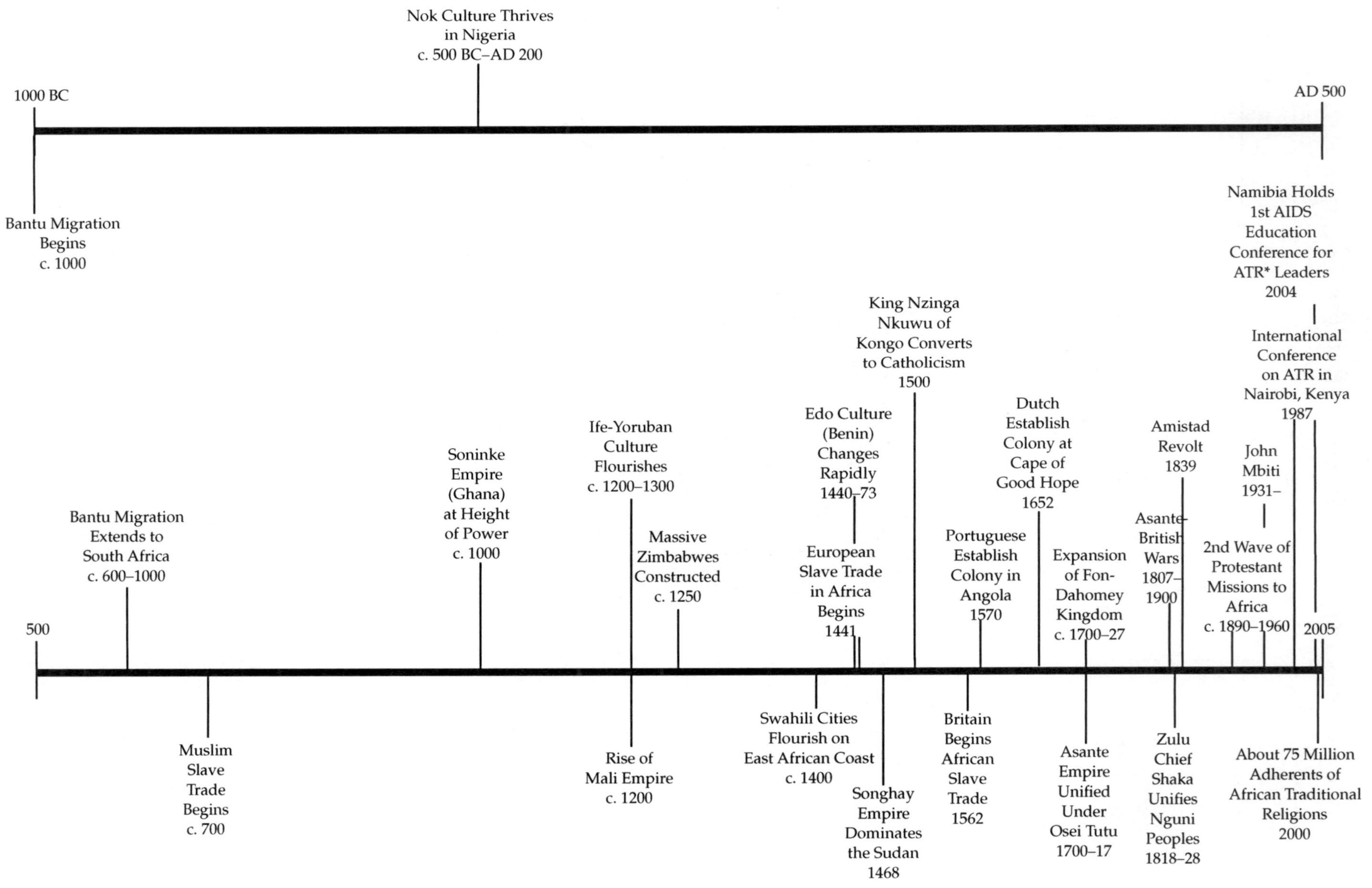

1000 BC

AD 500

Nok Culture Thrives
in Nigeria
c. 500 BC–AD 200

Bantu Migration
Begins
c. 1000

Namibia Holds
1st AIDS
Education
Conference for
ATR* Leaders
2004

International
Conference
on ATR in
Nairobi, Kenya
1987

John
Mbiti
1931–

2nd Wave of
Protestant
Missions to
Africa
c. 1890–1960

2005

About 75 Million
Adherents of
African Traditional
Religions
2000

Amistad
Revolt
1839

Asante-
British
Wars
1807–
1900

Zulu
Chief
Shaka
Unifies
Nguni
Peoples
1818–28

Dutch
Establish
Colony at
Cape of
Good Hope
1652

Expansion
of Fon-
Dahomey
Kingdom
c. 1700–27

Asante
Empire
Unified
Under
Osei Tutu
1700–17

King Nzinga
Nkuwu of
Kongo Converts
to Catholicism
1500

Portuguese
Establish
Colony in
Angola
1570

Britain
Begins
African
Slave
Trade
1562

Edo Culture
(Benin)
Changes
Rapidly
1440–73

European
Slave Trade
in Africa
Begins
1441

Songhay
Empire
Dominates
the Sudan
1468

Swahili Cities
Flourish on
East African Coast
c. 1400

Ife-Yoruban
Culture
Flourishes
c. 1200–1300

Massive
Zimbabwes
Constructed
c. 1250

Rise of
Mali Empire
c. 1200

Soninke
Empire
(Ghana)
at Height
of Power
c. 1000

Muslim
Slave
Trade
Begins
c. 700

Bantu Migration
Extends to
South Africa
c. 600–1000

500

Chart 88

* African Traditional Religion

African Traditional Religion

Topic	Facts
Current Data	Social and political conditions across Africa have acted to reshape and in some cases to bring about the disintegration of tribal life and local religious practices. However, many indigenous groups have synthesized traditional beliefs with those of Islam and/or Christianity. Roughly 75 million people throughout the African continent adhere to some form of African traditional religion. Prominent organizations include the Yoruba Alliance-USA and the Mami Wata Healers Society of North America.
History	Little is known about the religious beliefs or practices of African tribes before 1500. There is virtually no evidence regarding tribes in the southern portion of the continent. The sketchy accounts of tribal activities provided by anthropologists and missionaries are the basis for most scholarly theories concerning African religion prior to the 16th century, though a limited amount of evidence from archaeological digs and analysis of African languages also have played a role in formation of these theories. Many scholars who study African traditional religion are convinced that the Bantu people of ancient West Africa were monotheists and believed in an all-powerful creator God who was associated with the sun and sky.

It is believed that during the roughly 1,500 years stretching from the first century BC to the beginning of the 16th century AD, Bantu culture extended throughout most of Africa south of the equator, including the Kongo, Mwememutapa, and Luba kingdoms. In northern Africa, due to the combined impact of Roman colonization and Christian missions, by the early 6th century Christianity had more adherents than did indigenous religions.

In the late 7th century Islam entered Egypt, quickly spreading across a large portion of the continent. By the 8th century it had proceeded all the way to the northwest coast of Africa, by the 9th century to the west-central coast, and by the 14th century it extended as far south as the sub-Saharan grasslands of central Africa and along the east African coast as far south as Mozambique.

The 15th century witnessed the beginning of European colonization of Africa—mainly along the coasts—starting with Portugal. Holland, England, France, and other European nations quickly followed suit. The trans-Atlantic African slave trade soon was under way, which caused tremendous displacement and fracturing of traditional African religions. During the 18th century European colonialism intensified and penetrated nearly all regions of Africa. By 1912 every area of Africa except Ethiopia and Liberia was subject to one of several European nations.

By the 1950s and 1960s, the anger of these colonies toward their imperialist oppressors had mounted to the point where most European nations ruling over African territories decided to grant them independence. The decades following the withdrawal of the colonial powers brought a host of problems to the newly independent African nations, including widespread poverty, inadequate education, civil wars, damaging political alliances with nations outside of Africa, and the underdevelopment of natural resources. The social upheaval of this postcolonial period, along with the increasing encroachment of American consumer culture, has had an enormous impact on traditional African religion and culture. At the same time, a number of Christian missionary organizations have been engaged in an ongoing work to translate the Bible into the various native languages and dialects of Africa. |

Chart 89

African Traditional Religion (continued)

Topic	Facts
Summary of Beliefs	Although there is great variation among the beliefs and practices of the hundreds of tribes that adhere to African traditional religion, there also are a number of commonalities. 1. Belief in a supreme God, qualitatively different from lesser deities, who created the world and rules over it. 2. Belief in a world of ancestors and spirits that, though not visible, is present in the life of the tribe and with which one can interact. 3. Belief that the sacred permeates every area of life, which results in an attitude of reverence toward sacred objects, persons, places, and times. 4. Tribal traditions are passed down by means of a number of mediums: stories, songs, maxims, riddles, and artwork. 5. Belief that every crisis has a specific cause that can be ascertained by the tribe, and evil forces outside the control of the tribe always (or nearly always) cause the calamitous event. 6. Tribal rites are part of everyday life and are performed in conjunction with life passages, consecrations, initiations, purification, sacrifices, changing seasons, and the healing of illness. 7. Worship is a serious matter for which the whole tribe is responsible. Preparing the place of worship and dressing properly for worship are very important. 8. Belief in an afterlife that is described in the myths and funeral ceremonies of the tribe. 9. There is a deep respect for human life.

Topic	Summary of View
Creation	Despite significant variations among tribes, African creation accounts are united in relating that a supreme, mighty God is the creator and sustainer of all life. Myths in which God creates everything out of nothing (*ex nihilo*) exist, but are very uncommon. Often God is associated with the sun, moon, and/or rain. Some accounts begin with the creation of human beings, simply assuming that the world is in place. Most state that heaven was created before the earth. In some tribes, such as the Akan of Ghana, creation is deemed good. In others, like the Yoruba of southwest Nigeria and Benin, the world comes into being by mistake. Another common type of creation account involves a cosmic egg from which the world is made. For example, the Mande of southern Mali describe how Mangala used the round energy within himself to fashion the world. Many creation accounts relate that human beings originated with a divine or primeval mother. According to the Akposso of Togo, Uwolowu (God) sired the first human being through a woman he had created (apparently not a human herself). The Ibibio of Nigeria tell a story in which Obumo, the son of the mother goddess Eka-Abassi, made the first humans. The Tutsi of Rwanda narrate that the first created couple were unable to conceive children. In response to this unfortunate situation, God provided the woman with a small humanoid shape made of clay, from which she proceeded to make a human child.

Chart 89

African Traditional Religion (continued)

Topic	Summary of View
Creation (continued)	All tribes believe that a mystical force permeates the world of matter. Some, like the Bantu people, so strongly associate this force with existence itself that the two concepts are virtually indistinguishable. Many tribes view natural phenomena like thunder and raging rivers with awe, since they are believed to be manifestations of God's power.
Scripture and Authority	There are no sacred writings. Teachings are transmitted orally in a variety of forms, including myths, proverbs, prayers, ritual incantations, and the names of people and places. Other sources of teaching include symbols, ceremonies, art, dances, festivals, and magical objects. Chief-kings are living symbols of the tribe and serve as the point of contact between the tribe and its ancestors. Priests and priestesses have authority over the shrines and altars they help to maintain. Witch doctors determine the cause of sickness and prescribe cures. Diviners use magic to predict future events, often interpreting certain features of shells or nuts as a means of foretelling the future. Among the Ndembu of Zambia, spirits who are closely associated with the tribe chooses diviners.
God	Monotheism of some sort, in which God is the eternal transcendent creator and sustainer of all things, is universally affirmed. God is supremely wise, almighty, holy, loving, just, and merciful. Nevertheless, traditional religion in East Africa tends to be more strictly monotheistic than is the case in West Africa. God is unique in that he is the ground of his own being; the Zulu call God uZivelele, which means "The Self-existent One." God is a sovereign ruler, controlling human destiny and the forces of nature, and is far-removed from day-to-day affairs. God is an invisible spirit, and thus depictions of him are shunned. God is classified as neither male nor female, though some tribes, such as the Igbo of southeastern Nigeria, honor a mother goddess. In some cases it is thought that God is unknowable. For example, the name the Maasai of Kenya and Tanzania say for God is Engai, which means "The Unknown One." The Tenda of Guinea use the name Hounounga (The Unknown).

Every known people-group in Africa has a name for God. In regions of eastern Africa, God is commonly referred to as Mulungu. In much of south-central Africa, the name for God is Leza. Another regional divine name is Nyambe, used in southwestern Africa from Botswana to Cameroon. In West Africa, names for God include Ngewo (the Mende of Sierra Leone), Amma (the Dogon of Mali), and Tangba You (Lobi of the Ivory Coast).

Often it is thought that God dwells in a very distant region of the sky and that he can be approached only through intermediaries. Belief in the existence of such mediating spiritual beings (called *orisha*) is widespread; more than 400 have been documented. Though under God's authority, it is these *orisha* who are venerated. Moreover, *orisha* are often classified into sky spirits and earthly spirits. The former are associated with "heavenly" things like the sun, the stars, and rainstorms. The latter are further divided into two types: (1) those associated with objects (or phenomena) like mountains, lakes, forests, and earthquakes, and (2) the spirits of tribal ancestors. |

Chart 89

African Traditional Religion (continued)

Topic	Summary of View
Mankind	Human beings are endowed with great dignity. They have both material and spiritual aspects. God's decision to create humans shows that he cares about them, yet humans are not made in the "image of God." Most African creation myths do not instruct the first humans to take dominion over the natural world, though there are exceptions to this, like the account given by the Fang of Gabon, which states that human beings should create civilization, in contrast to the wilderness of the bush. Many tribes, such as the Hausa of northern Nigeria and southern Niger, declare that human beings are superior to all other aspects of the created world; any comparisons between human beings and animals are met with hostility. Human beings ought to seek protection from harm, security, and membership in tribal communities. It is important to maintain good relations with living family members and ancestral spirits. Head of families and tribal authorities are afforded deep respect.
Sin	An all-encompassing moral order has been set in place by God, designed to promote human flourishing and the preservation of nature. The laws, customs, rules, and taboos within this ethical framework serve to strengthen interpersonal relationships of all kinds, especially those of the clan. There is no such thing as private sin; all misconduct harms the whole community. Moral offenses include murder, kidnapping, malevolent sorcery, causing deliberate harm to the body or property of another, theft, lying, breach of covenant, sexual wrongdoing (including adultery, rape, sexual abuse of children, incest, and homosexuality), and being rude to the elderly. Virtues include protecting children, orphans, and widows; caring and showing respect for elderly people (especially parents), the sick, the infirm, and the mentally handicapped; kindness; truthfulness; friendliness; hospitality; hard work; and generosity. Witchcraft or angry spirits cause all instances of evil and death.
Salvation	African traditional religion is driven by an intense desire on the part of adherents for safety, power, and the well-being of the community. Tribes seek protection from misfortunes like defeat in war, attacks by savage animals, failed crops, drought, and extended illness. A great diversity of practices designed to procure these things exist, including consulting spirits, offering libations to ancestors, animal sacrifice, wearing magical amulets, and herbal medicine. Many adherents obtain the services of someone trained in divination (acquiring information from spiritual sources) in order to find out why they have been afflicted with certain problems. The Zulu people sometimes approach Inkosi Yezulu (Chief of the Sky) for assistance in prevailing over adversity, but only in cases when other remedies have been tried and failed.
Afterlife	After death, the entire person, not just the spirit, goes to the spirit world (though in a form that is invisible). Among the Bantu, this invisible person, who prior to the death of the body was hidden, is known as "the little man" (*muntu*). The "vital force" of the tribe, which must be maintained in order for the tribe to be preserved and prosper, can be boosted by means of prayers, sacrifices, and prescribed rituals. People sometimes petition departed spirits or mention their names when taking oaths. Death rituals are carefully performed to ensure that the spirits of the dead are content in the next world so that they will not return to wreak havoc for the tribe.

Chart 89

African Traditional Religion (continued)

Topic	Summary of View
Afterlife (continued)	There are few beliefs about the precise nature of the afterlife. The LoDagaa of Ghana speak of a river between the land of the living and the realm of the dead. Zulus believe that persons killed by lightning are taken directly to heaven by Unvelingqangi (God) and hence do not live under the earth as ancestors of the tribe.

Distinctive Beliefs and Practices

Topic	Summary of View
"Force"	Adherents of African traditional religion believe in a divine energy, or mystical force, that fills the world. They employ a variety of practices to tap into the power of this force and draw on it in the course of many activities that are common to the tribe, such as healing, protecting persons and property, finding lost items, divination, exorcism, and witchcraft. Despite being widespread, the practice of magic arouses considerable anxiety in many tribal communities, in many cases resulting in accusations and quarrels. At the same time, the benevolent use of this force is cherished for the many benefits it brings the tribe.
Rites of Passage	Various rites are performed at key junctures in life: birth, puberty, marriage, and death. Some tribes, such as the Ashanti of Ghana, wait until a week after birth to give their children names; they do this because it is distressingly common for infants to die soon after birth. Puberty rites involve preparation for particular social roles, temporary separation from the tribe, and in some cases circumcision of girls. It is common for marriage to involve making a covenant and the exchange of valuable items. For example, as part of Zulu marriage customs, the bride is given choice cattle.
Cleanliness	Traditional Zulu religion places a premium on cleanliness. Members of the community take as many as three baths each day. Different kinds of food are eaten with different sets of plates and utensils.
Veneration of Ancestors	Veneration of ancestors is practiced among the majority of tribal groups in Africa, but these practices are not uniform. Among those who practice veneration, there is the belief that the spirits of ancestors continue only as long as they are not forgotten, so the living often communicate with their dead ancestors through prayers and various ritual offerings. The benefit is not one-sided because the ancestors are expected to use superhuman powers to help the relatives who are alive. Ancestors also are viewed as mediators between human family members and God. Though ancestors are considered to be benign, they may also punish or harm family members who have ignored them.
Nature Spirits	Though commonly used in connection with African traditional religion, the term "animism" does not accurately describe the beliefs of that religion in the vast majority of cases. This is because nearly all adherents of African traditional religion do not believe that spirits reside in everything in the natural world, but rather that only certain caves, waterfalls, groves, stones, etc., are inhabited by spirits. Thus only specific places and objects are viewed as being sacred. In fact, some tribes do not believe that spirits inhabit particular things. Some sacred places and objects are thought to be the dwelling place of ancestors. The Basongye of Mali believe that the spiritual forces contained in artifacts (like pots, masks, and drums) can be used to bring success or harm to the tribe.

Chart 89

African Traditional Religion (continued)

Distinctive Beliefs and Practices

Origin of Evil and Death	In African creation myths, the first humans usually are portrayed as having lived in a paradise where God took care of them; in some cases it is said that God dwelt with them on earth or that they lived in the sky with God. Many African creation myths recount that God bestowed immortality, resurrection, or rejuvenation on the first human beings. Some myths tell how the first people failed a test of obedience given them by God, resulting in their separation from him. Others allege that human wretchedness originated with animals like the hyena, which ate the rope that formerly had kept heaven and earth together. In one common account, the original paradise was forfeited and heaven and earth became separated. God went to live in heaven while human beings continued to live on the earth. The three gifts (rejuvenation, resurrection, and immortality) were lost and replaced by disease, suffering, and death.

Chart 89

Caribbean Religions

Topic	Facts
Current Data	The number of adherents of all forms of Caribbean religion mentioned in this volume is difficult to ascertain, given the structure of most of them. An extremely rough estimate would put the worldwide total at 65 million.
History	With the exception of Palo Mayombe, which began in Africa, these various religions originated in the Caribbean as a result of the Spanish and Portuguese trans-Atlantic slave trade and/or its social aftermath. The events that led to the spawning of Caribbean religions began in the early 1500s when Santeria emerged in Cuba and continued until the early 1900s with the advent of Rastafari. Since the origin and development of these religions was highly influenced by the existence and perpetuation of the slave trade in the Caribbean, some of the most important events in their histories were the initiation, expansion, and eventual abolition of human slavery by the various European colonial powers of that period. Other significant events include major political decisions that either improved or worsened the situations for these religions' practitioners and cultural transformations that led to greater social acceptance of these religions.
Summary of Beliefs	Although it is difficult to make useful generalizations about these Caribbean religions, given the many unique elements of each, a few generalizations seem relatively unproblematic. However, most of these are methodological or sociological in nature rather than strictly doctrinal. 1. They arose out of conditions of subjugation or disenfranchisement, are tightly linked to the racism and social marginalization experienced by their adherents, and embody counter-cultural forms of group identity. 2. Their fundamental beliefs are rooted in African traditional religions, but many of their practices were formed as practical ways of dealing with the harsh realities of slavery and/or cultural imperialism. 3. They comprise a synthesis of some form of African traditional religion and select components of Christianity (though the influence of Christianity is substantially less in the case of Rastafari). 4. Their distinctive practices typically made use of whatever materials and conditions were available at the time and place of their origin and were freely modified (within limits) to fit the particular circumstances their practitioners faced. These practices are part of a larger, complex system of rituals and symbols. 5. They sanction politically subversive activities designed as a means of maintaining an African-tribal identity (somewhat modified) in the face of colonial oppression as well as other forms of resistance to the powers they perceive as domineering and enslaving. 6. They look back to a primordial past of some kind when things were better and cling to hope for a better future. Given the great diversity of "doctrinal views" among these religions, it is impossible to make any helpful generalizations concerning the topical categories (Creation, Scripture and Authority, God, Man, Sin, Salvation, and Afterlife) used in the other overview charts in this volume.

Chart 90

Comparison of Caribbean Religions

	Scripture and Authority	God	Mankind
Rastafari	Main source of revelation is personal experience of God. Knowledge is often gained during group religious activities. Ganja marijuana is a source of spiritual insight. To be properly understood, the Bible must be seen from the perspective of disenfranchised black people. Sacred books include the *Holy Piby* and the *Kebra Negast*.	God is black and is named Jah. He disclosed himself in Moses, then Elijah, then Jesus Christ, and finally in Ras Tafari (aka Haile Selassie), who was the savior of blacks suffering under white oppression. Some Rastafarians think Selassie is still alive; most believe that since his death he has possessed a spiritual body. As emperor of Ethiopia, Selassie was a direct descendant of King David.	Africans are closely identified with the ancient Israelites, who were God's chosen people and black. The experience of slavery by blacks in the southern United States parallels the suffering of the Jews in ancient Egypt. Whites are generally inferior to blacks, though each white person should be evaluated on personal merit.
Santeria	No sacred texts are used. Instead, traditions are transmitted orally. There is a twelve-level hierarchy of positions within the religion, which includes high priests and those who have undergone various initiation rites.	Olorun is the one supreme God, remote, austere, and difficult to approach. He interacts with the world and makes his will known via spiritual emissaries called *orisha*, who are manifestations of his knowable aspects. The *orisha* represent the forces of nature. They function as sacred patrons to adherents, ruling over the forces of nature and human life in its every aspect. Servants of Olorun, they play an important role in everyday affairs, though they must receive continual nourishment (primarily in the form of animal sacrifices) to survive.	Human beings are formed by an *orisha* called Obatala, though each person receives the "breath of life" from Olorun. All people have a pattern of energy that grounds their individual consciousness and shapes their personality and character. Humans can summon the *orisha* to perform services for them. Humans are at the center of creation, controlling and directing its energy flows, yet are interdependent on every other part of the world.
Umbanda	W. W. da Matta e Silva's *The Secret Doctrine of Umbanda* and *The Tight Fundamentals of Umbanda* by Silva's disciple Rivas Neto are the two main writings that function as sacred scripture. Within limits, each temple is free to devise its own approach to the performance of sacred rituals.	According to many adherents, the primary god is Ogun, though there are many other important deities, known as the Spirits of the Cosmic Brotherhood of Umbanda. Groups of lesser deities work under higher ones. These spirit beings have manifested themselves in many forms, including that of native Brazilians.	The original ancestors of mankind are spirit beings who revealed the religious mysteries to people on earth, specifically to the Red Race of the Tupy lineage in ancient Brazil. Humans are these spirits in perishable bodies (but with an immortal essence) that progress in their spiritual evolution dependent on karma.

Chart 91

Comparison of Caribbean Religions (continued)

	Scripture and Authority	God	Mankind
Voudon (Voodoo)	Rather than Voudon being grounded in a holy book or books, priests and priestesses have the most basic religious authority. These men and women act as confessors, doctors, magicians, advisers, prophets, and fortune-tellers; they also perform rites of initiation, cast spells, and concoct magic potions.	The ultimate God is Bondye, who orders the cosmos but is distant from mundane affairs. A pantheon of spirit-ambassadors known as *loa* accomplish his work on earth. The *loa* exert a profound influence on every sphere of life. Ogou and Loco Atisou are two of the most significant ones.	Humans are comprised of five parts: the mortal flesh, the spirit of the flesh, the star of destiny, the "big good angel" (roughly, the soul), and the "little good angel" (roughly, the conscience).

	Sin	Salvation	Afterlife
Rastafari	Human misbehavior is due to a lack of divine consciousness, and is not the result of estrangement between God and man. Moral code includes the following precepts: shaving and tattoos are forbidden, near-vegetarianism, worship of Rastafari alone, loving all people and especially blacks, working to achieve a global brotherhood, and following the laws of ancient Ethiopia.	Realizing personal oneness with God and the return of blacks to Africa are the major components in the matter of salvation. Some understand the return to Africa as literal, while others believe the return is symbolic of the growth of African culture and the liberation of Jamaica. Land grants given to African immigrants in 1955 have been viewed as a fulfillment of prophecy. When all blacks return to Africa, the Western nations will collapse, thus paving the way for black rule.	Ethiopia is heaven on earth and Jamaica is hell on earth. There is no life after death, and thus neither heaven nor hell exist in the traditional sense.

Chart 91

	Sin	Salvation	Afterlife
Santeria	Olorun has communicated 11 commandments through Obatala; these rules help people to live in harmony with the *orisha*. Humans are entrusted with the task of keeping the *ashe* of the universe (life-force that runs through all things, living and inanimate) flowing through all kinds of created entities.	Once initiated, practitioners receive godparents who oversee their spiritual progress. Magic is based on knowledge of the *orisha* and how to interact with them. Basic spells require such items as plants, herbs, stones, flowers, fruits, and animals; herbs are considered to have very powerful properties. An *orisha* may ask that an adherent give up a bad habit or wear certain jewelry. Animal sacrifices are essential to winning favor with the *orisha*. Trance possession is common; during ceremonies *orisha* enter the bodies of priests if properly persuaded.	Only this world exists, though it contains both visible and invisible dimensions. After death, the human soul can be transformed into an ancestral spirit.
Umbanda	During ancient times the fundamental body of spiritual teaching was badly corrupted. After this the Tupy lineage divided into Tupy-Nambá and Tupy-Guarany. Although these groups later returned to their original path of spiritual development, the consequences of this division persist in human mental life as the dilemma between spirit and matter.	Consists in procuring personal knowledge of the laws that rule the cosmos. This occurs when spirit beings in the astral planes reveal the laws to humans through certain prescribed channels. Enlightenment is not possible for selfish, vain, or proud persons. The path to enlightenment is extremely difficult, requiring assistance from the spirit beings.	All people will eventually achieve cosmic awareness in an immortal, disembodied state. This will come to pass by means of the work of the spirit beings who guide the planetary evolution of earth via the propagation and practice of Umbanda.
Voudon (Voodoo)	The *loa* largely determine the behavior of practitioners, and thus a kind of spiritual fatalism is invoked in resolving disputes. Personal moral responsibility is deemed impossible.	Rituals to beckon the *loa* involve dancing, drumming, chanting, trance states, and animal sacrifices. Legba, the *loa* of the gate and crossroads, is invoked to begin such ceremonies. *Loas* are summoned via a priest pounding a special drawing. The life force of the sacrificed animal becomes part of the *loa*, which then shares its divine energy with participants.	Upon death a person's two spiritual aspects are released. If the proper rituals are performed correctly, part of the person goes to the world of the dead and becomes a *loa*. Without these rituals, the person can become trapped in the earth or even be made into a zombie. People come before God for judgment and attempt to argue their case.

Chart 91

Timeline of Rastafari

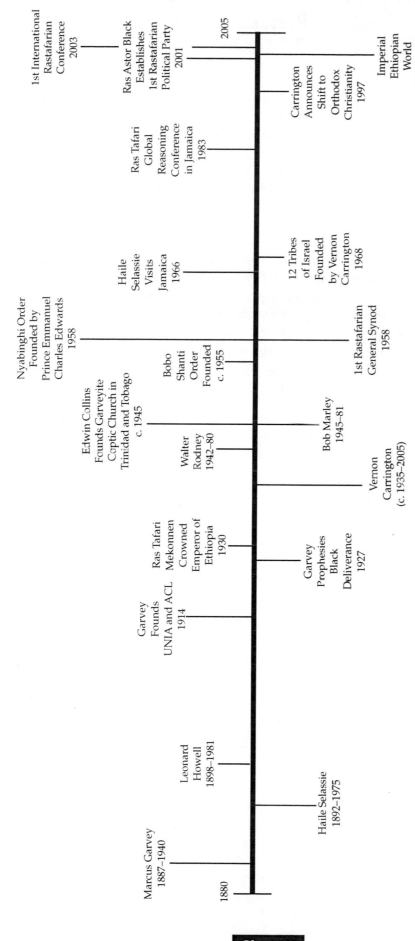

Chart 92

Rastafari

Topic	Facts
Current Data	It is estimated that there are between 3,000 and 5,000 Rastafarians in the United States. The exact number is difficult to establish since many people have adopted the dress and hairstyle of Rastafarianism, though they may not share its beliefs. Global numbers for Rastafarianism are believed to be about 1 million. Some smaller branches of Rastafarianism are The Twelve Tribes of Israel, the Ethiopian Nation Congress, the Ethiopian World Federation, and the Nyhabinghi Theocracy Government.
History	Rastafari originated from Ethiopianism and Black Nationalism, with the first Rastafarians adhering to the teachings of Jamaican Marcus Mosiah Garvey (1887–1940). Garvey was promoting within blacks an appreciation for their history and a sense of purpose and self-esteem. He contended that the European colonial nations had fragmented the African continent by dispersing African blacks throughout the world, and by this act had caused blacks to lose the ability to succeed in expressing themselves socially and to organize themselves politically. To Garvey, blacks had been made to view themselves as inferiors and had been stunted intellectually due to the manner in which the white race had labeled and treated blacks. Attempts at integration were without value; the only way for the black race to achieve dignity was to sever all associations with the white world. In light of these beliefs, Garvey founded the Universal Negro Improvement Association and the African Communities League. The major goal of these organizations was to encourage blacks to strive for self-reliance and to return to their homeland of Africa. Garvey, who led this movement until 1940, supposedly prophesied that a black king would arise in Africa, resulting in deliverance of the black people.
	As if in fulfillment of the prophecy of Marcus Garvey that "a king" would be crowned in Africa, Prince Ras Tafari Makonnen was crowned emperor of Ethiopia in 1930. The emperor then took the title of Emperor Haile Selassie (Power of the Trinity). This event marked the beginning of the Rastafari religion, as Rastafarianism quickly gained a large following.
	The religion, almost from its inception, developed into three groups (the leaders of which were Joseph Hibbert, Archibald Dunkley, and Robert Hinds). These groups were unified in the belief that Haile Selassie was the messiah of the black people. They also were united in the view that blacks should return to Africa to escape white oppression. They emphasized the use of nonviolence to achieve political ends. They also opposed Jamaica's colonial status.
	The Rastafari movement, particularly its claims regarding Haile Selassie as the black messiah, was undermined in 1935 when the Italian army under Mussolini invaded Ethiopia and found the people uneducated and impoverished, and the country economically in shambles and ill-prepared militarily.
	During the 1940s and 1950s, Rastafari became far more political in Jamaica at the expense of its religious dimension, with political demonstrations and frequent conflicts with police as they demonstrated against poverty, segregation, and the colonial status of the island. Due to these conflicts, Rastafari gained an unfavorable public image in Jamaica, with its members viewed as uncouth, cultic, and anti-white. During the 1960s Rastafarianism was severely suppressed, with hundreds arrested and a number of its members killed.

Chart 93

Rastafari (continued)

Topic	Facts
History (continued)	An important political event that benefited Rastafari occured in 1958, when Prince Edward Emmanuel of Jamaica created a Rastafari group, convened a general synod, and established a large Rastafari church. In 1961 an important Rastafarian spokesman, Ras Sam Brown, became an independent candidate for the Jamaican parliament on the Black Man's Party ticket. Although he lost, getting fewer than 100 votes, his 21 Points formed the political basis of the Rastafarian movement. On April 21, 1966, Haile Selassie visited Jamaica, convincing Rastafari leaders there not to relocate to Ethiopia until the black people of Jamaica had been liberated. In honor of his visit, April 21 became a special holy day to the Rastafari movement.
Summary of Beliefs	At first Rastafari was undefined in its core beliefs, but early in its development Leonard Howell set forth six basic principles as pivotal for Rastafari: 1. the superiority of the black race, 2. hatred of whites (with some exceptions),* 3. exacting revenge on whites because of the evil perpetrated against blacks, 4. opposing and exposing the oppression of blacks in Jamaica, 5. the need for blacks to return to Africa, and 6. the recognition of Haile Selassie as the messiah and the only legitimate ruler of the black people. In addition to these foundational principles are three other beliefs necessary to be a true follower of the religion: 1. the white race is "Babylon" and has held down blacks' political power, first by slavery, and then through poverty, inequality, and "white trickery"; 2. acceptance of a kind of monism, in which humans and God are one reality, the "I and I" (or I-n-I); and 3. the name of God is Jah, and the presence of Jah in his people helps them to overcome difficulties in life.

Topic	Summary of View
Creation	Rastafari embraces a view of the world in which the person and the Creator are not seen as being separate from each other. Understanding this helps to explain the excessive use of the personal "I" in Rastafari and also the unusual usage of "I-n-I" rather than we. This terminology is to emphasize the unity of the individual and the Creator, who is said to be in each person.
Scripture and Authority	Personal experience serves as the primary authority in Rastafari, though the Bible is viewed as a holy book. The reason for this is that the internal witness of God within the individual is the final arbiter of truth, and the Bible, though important, is often incorrect due to corrupted translations that differ from the original texts written in the Amharic language of Ethiopia. The internal truth that comes from the indwelling of God and cosmic union of the individual and God is achieved individually

*This changed during the course of Rastafari history. See "Mankind" and "Sin."

Chart 93

Rastafari (continued)

Topic	Summary of View
Scripture and Authority (continued)	and corporately during "reasoning sessions," (religious services). This religious experience is enhanced by the use of marijuana, bringing both revelation and healing. Other than religious experience and the Bible, Rastafari accepts the *Holy Piby*, a commonly used "black man's Bible," and *Kebra Negast*, an Ethiopian holy book.
God	The Rastafari God is black and is immanent in his children and in the world. He revealed himself to Moses, the first savior, as Jah. Three avatars, or saviors, are believed to have appeared before the advent of Ras Tafari (Haile Selassie): Moses, Elijah, and Jesus Christ. Haile Sellassie, the last avatar, however, is the black Messiah. He came in the flesh to redeem all blacks who have been oppressed by whites. Rastafarians differ as to the nature and importance of Haile Selassie, with some considering him still alive, and most believing him to be present only in memory and spirit. He is viewed as the direct descendent of the biblical King David, with an unbroken line of Ethiopian kings from the time of Solomon and Sheba. He died in August 1975.
Mankind	The African peoples are closely identified with the ancient nation of Israel. God's chosen people were black, hence modern black people are their descendants. A historical parallel to the book of Exodus is seen in the black experience of slavery in the South prior to the American Civil War. The black race, like the Jews of antiquity, suffered oppression under unjust rulers because of their sin, yet the humiliation of this slavery is part of the divine plan of redemption. Some view the black race as a living reincarnation of biblical Israel. White people are generally inferior to blacks, having emerged from an ancient, wicked civilization devoid of a spiritual dimension to their corporate life. The white race is seen as unnatural. Still, each white person is to be accepted on the basis of individual merit and should not be rejected unless proven guilty of racism.
Sin	Problems in human conduct result from inadequacies of divine consciousness, not from any kind of rift between creature and Creator, whether moral or metaphysical. Moral code includes the following precepts: eschewing shaving, tattoos, and cutting one's flesh; virtual vegetarianism; worship of Rastafari exclusively, yet respecting other objects and forms of worship; loving all mankind, but especially black people; disapproval of hate, jealousy, envy, deceit, guile, and treachery; nonparticipation in the pleasures and evils of modern society; striving toward the creation of a world brotherhood; practicing charity to those in distress; and following the laws of ancient Ethiopia.
Salvation	The meaning of salvation varies among adherents of Rastafari, with some believing that blacks will return to Africa, or to Ethiopia specifically, while others believe the salvation is more symbolic, a return to African cultural values and the commitment of the liberation of Jamaica. Some within the movement consider the land grants given to African immigrants in 1955 to be a fulfillment of this hope. There is a perception for those who view the return to Africa literally, that when blacks return to Africa, the white West will collapse, providing the impetus for the proper rule by blacks.

Chart 93

Rastafari (continued)

Topic	Summary of View
Afterlife	Ethiopia is heaven on earth, while Jamaica is hell on earth. There is no afterlife or literal heaven and hell.

Distinctive Beliefs and Practices	
Dietary and Consumption Practices	The diet of the Rastafari is patterned after, as they understand it, the dietary laws of the Hebrew scriptures, excluding the eating of pork, dead flesh, alcohol, tobacco, and food that is prepared by anyone who is not Rastafarian. This is because they presume to be in the lineage of the ancient Hebrews. Many Rastafarians do not use eating utensils or plates.
Dreadlocks	What attracts the attention of the average non-Rastafarian is the way in which members of Rastafari wear their hair—in "dreadlocks." This practice is based on their understanding of Numbers 6:5–6, "No razor must be used on his head.... he must let the hair of his head grow long." Dreadlocks are produced by tightly curling one's hair without combing or brushing it, and washing it only with water. There are a number of reasons why adherents of Rastafari wear dreadlocks. One is to cause "dread" among whites because of the fearful appearance of the locks. Another is to imitate the appearance of a lion, relating to the fact that a title of Haile Selassie was the Lion of the Tribe of Judah. Third, the dreadlocks are believed to collect and distribute mental energy, so that shaking the dreadlocks releases energy that will destroy the white power structure.
Reggae Music	Possibly the most positive public expression of Rastafari is what is known as reggae music. Not known to the non-initiate is that this entertaining music is replete with Rastafarian symbolism, readily understood in Jamaican society. Reggae was largely unknown in the general public until the rise of Jamaican musician Bob Marley (1945–81), who popularized the reggae sound, identifying it with Rastafari.
Symbolic Colors	Red: Blood of the martyrs of Jamaican history Black: African skin color Green: Jamaican vegetations; hope of victory over oppression

Chart 93

Timeline of Santeria and Palo Mayombe

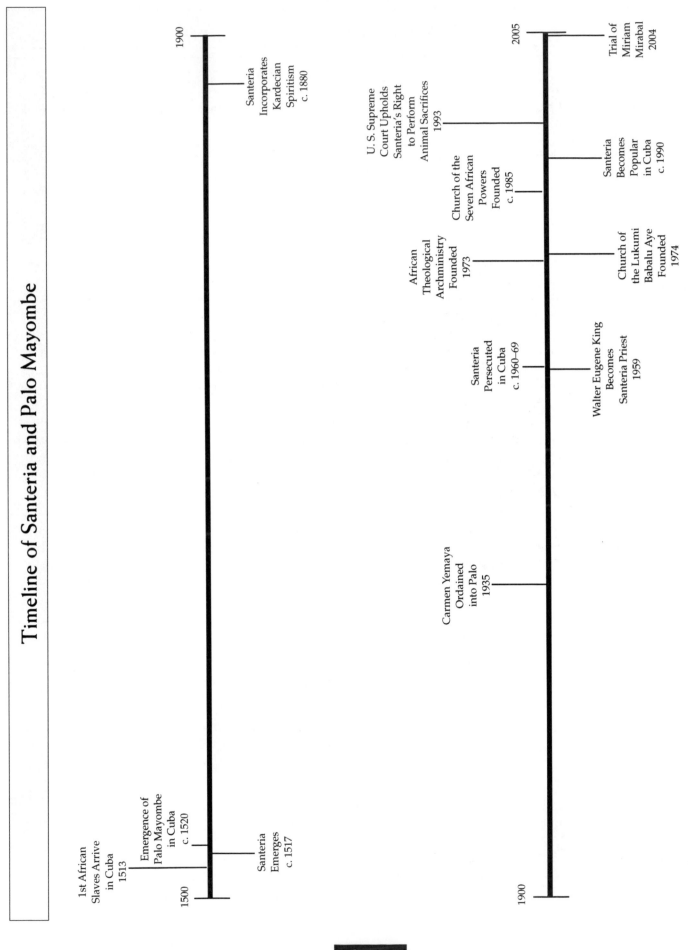

1st African Slaves Arrive in Cuba
1513

Emergence of Palo Mayombe in Cuba
c. 1520

Santeria Emerges
c. 1517

1500

Santeria Incorporates Kardecian Spiritism
c. 1880

1900

Carmen Yemaya Ordained into Palo
1935

Santeria Persecuted in Cuba
c. 1960–69

Walter Eugene King Becomes Santeria Priest
1959

African Theological Archministry Founded
1973

Church of the Lukumi Babalu Aye Founded
1974

Church of the Seven African Powers Founded
c. 1985

Santeria Becomes Popular in Cuba
c. 1990

U. S. Supreme Court Upholds Santeria's Right to Perform Animal Sacrifices
1993

Trial of Miriam Mirabal
2004

1900

2005

Chart 94

Santeria

Topic*	Facts
Current Data	Santeria is not a global religion. Most of its adherents reside in the Caribbean islands of Cuba and Haiti. It's also found in Hispanic communities in the United States (in Florida, New Jersey, and the cities of New York and Los Angeles), in South America (Argentina, Brazil, Colombia, and Venezuela), and in Mexico. France and the Netherlands are the only European countries with members. Other names for the religion are Regla de Ocha (The Rule of the Orisha) and Lukumi.
History	Santeria was started in the Caribbean islands, mainly Cuba and Haiti, by African slaves. These slaves brought with them their tribal religions, such as those of the Yoruba and Bantu peoples, but these beliefs and practices were discouraged, if not forbidden, by their slave owners. Instead, the slaves were baptized into the Roman Catholic faith. They secretly kept their tribal faiths by associating each of their spirits, called *orisha*, with a particular Roman Catholic saint.

Throughout its history Santeria has largely been a secret religion. The obvious reason for the secrecy was to avoid punishment from "Christian" slavemasters. The worship practices remained secret even after the abolition of slavery in Cuba and Haiti because of public disapproval. After the rise of Communism in Cuba in the 1960s until the 1990s, Santeria again came under considerable suppression. But since the 1990s membership in Santeria has exploded. In the United States, some Santeria churches have become known to the public. The Church of the Lukumi Babalu Aye, which began in the early 1970s in Hialeah, Florida, went public when it appealed to the U.S. Supreme Court regarding a city ordinance forbidding animal sacrifices as part of a religious ritual. The Supreme Court sided with the church. Another Santeria church that has gained prominence is The African Theological Archministry, founded by Walter Eugene King. This South Carolina congregation boasts 10,000 members. |
| **Summary of Beliefs** | The term "Santeria" comes from a Spanish word *santo*, meaning "worship of saints," though sometimes it is translated "The Way of the Saints." Since Santeria is a secret religion, in most instances, little is known outside the religion as to its beliefs and practices. However, it is possible to discern some aspects of the religion from a variety of sources.

Santeria is based on the concepts of *ashe* and *ebo*. *Ashe* is a Yoruba word meaning "so be it." It is a symbol of the divine power that Olorun (God) employed in creating the universe. All the spells and rituals of Santeria are performed so as to acquire *ashe* from the *orisha* (emissaries of Olorun). *Ebo* is the Santerian concept of sacrifice. By means of special sacrifices, *orisha* are propitiated so that they will give more *ashe* to those who offer the sacrifices.

The practices of the Santerian religion, being a secret religion generally known only to is devotees, are carefully guarded, and its traditions are carefully preserved. Additionally, participation in the various rituals are taken very seriously since the worshipers are judged by Olorun and the *orisha* for the manner of their participation. |

* The Brazilian name for Santeria is Condomble Jege-Nago.

Chart 95

Topic	Summary of View
Creation	Olorun is the creator and owner of the universe and the supreme source of *ashe*, the spiritual energy that permeates the universe. Reality consists of five descending levels of power: Olorun, the *orisha*, human beings, human ancestors, and everything else. Even the lowest level of the created order—the animate and inanimate creation—is necessary to the universe and may be used by humans to benefit the entire universe of spirit and matter. There is a symbiotic relationship between these two worlds, an interdependency of the spirit (invisible) world and physical (visible) world. Even as the spirits are unable to receive *ashe* without humans, so in turn the lower powers are unable to ascend to a higher plane without humans. Humans are the connection between these two realms and may be inhabited by spirits from the invisible world.
Scripture and Authority	Has no written scriptures; its traditions are passed down orally to initiates. Extant written records either are direct transcriptions of initiates' descriptions concerning the oral tradition done by researchers or come from the notebooks of the godmother or godfather of someone involved in the religion. There is a twelve-level hierarchy within the religion (listed here in descending order from the highest rank to the lowest): (1) *Omokolobas* (a rank held by few), (2) *Cunaldo/Wanaldo* (*babalawos*, or high priests, who have been consecrated to *Ifa* and obtained the consecrated knife), (3) *Oluwos* (men consecrated to *Ifa* during an *asiento* ceremony), (4) *Babalawos* (men consecrated to *Ifa* without undergoing an *asiento* ceremony), (5) *Santeros* (men and women who have received the initiation known as *Pinaldo*), (6) *Santeros* (men and women who have received the *asiento*, or *kariorocha*, initiation), (7) *Aleyos* (those who have received the initiation *Abo-faca* (for men) or *Ico-fa* (for women), (8) *Aleyos* (those who have received the initiation *Los Guerreros*), (9) *Aleyos* (those who have received the Necklaces initiation), (10) *Aleyos* (those who have received an *osain* amulet), (11) those who believe in Santeria but have not undergone any initiation or received any amulets, and (12) those who do not believe in *orisha* or Santeria (unbelievers).
God	There exists one supreme God, Olorun (also known as Olodumare, "the Head Guardian"), who is perceived by Santerians as remote and unapproachable. Followers of Santeria make no attempt to worship or associate with this deity in any way. This does not mean, in Santerian thought, that Olorun is inactive. In fact, he is viewed as involved in the universe and is experienced through *orisha*—spirits who work in the universe and rule over the forces of nature—who reveal different aspects of the nature of Olorun. Knowledge of Olorun would be unknown except for the *orisha*. They also work in followers of Santeria, sustaining and leading worshipers. These *orisha*, though powerful, are nonetheless finite beings and must receive sustenance from humans in the form of both food and praise, which occurs during the ritual of an animal sacrifice. Unlike Olorun, the *orisha* are approachable through prayer, ritual offerings, or in a trance. They often have been associated with saints in the Roman Catholic religion because of the secrecy that occurred early in the historical development of Santeria.

Chart 95

Santeria (continued)

Topic	Summary of View
Mankind	Humans were created by the action of the *orisha* by means of the "breath of life" which comes from Olorun, and each person possesses a distinctive energy pattern that is basic to the person's consciousness and personality. The *orisha* assist humans to tap into their energy source and develop their powers. Through a reciprocal relationship, humans feed and praise the *orisha* and the *orisha* possess and aid the humans. One's ancestors, called Ara Orun (People of Heaven) are venerated and entreated for moral guidance; their names are recited at family ceremonies.
Sin	The God Olorun gave 11 commandments to the *orisha* Obatala in order to keep humans from surrendering to evil and so that they might live in harmony with the *orisha* and have success in life. The commandments are: 1. Do not steal. 2. Do not kill except in self-defense or for obtaining food. 3. Do not eat human flesh. 4. Live in peace with other human beings. 5. Do not covet the property of others. 6. Do not curse the name of Olorun, or Olodumare. 7. Honor your father and mother. 8. Do not ask for more than can be provided for you, and you will be content with your fate. 9. Do not fear death or commit suicide. 10. Teach Olorun's commandments to your children. 11. Respect and obey Olorun's laws. Humans are also required to keep the *ashe* of the universe flowing through all types of created beings.
Salvation	Santeria does not include an idea of salvation in which a person is liberated from a spiritual condition that relates to an afterlife, as is found in most Eastern and Western religions. For the adherent of Santeria, worship of the *orisha* through various rituals brings the person into association with the *orisha* and one's ancestors. This provides the ongoing help to increase the person's spiritual energy. Persons communicate with the *orisha* through different magic spells that are cast through the use of herbs, plants, stones, and other physical objects. As part of the relationship with the *orisha*, the devotee may be asked by the *orisha* to change behavior that the *orisha* considers harmful or even to wear certain articles of clothing or jewelry. Or the worshiper may be required to make an animal sacrifice (performed by a priest, *babalochas*) in times of severe trial or sickness in order to solicit the help of the *orisha*. Another practice of great significance in Santeria is called *hembe*, in which an *orisha* may be convinced to enter the body of a priest, a desirable act because it is a means of bringing *ashe*, spiritual energy.

Chart 95

Santeria (continued)

Topic	Summary of View
Afterlife	Adherents of Santeria believe in a physical world and a spiritual world. *Orisha* and ancestors live in the spirit world, while humans and lower creation (animate and inanimate) exist in the physical world. At death the human spirit can be changed into an ancestral spirit (*egun*) and live in the spirit world.
Distinctive Beliefs and Practices	
Ceremony of the Knife (*Cuchillo*)	Only *santeros* (priests) can undergo this initiation. The knife they receive is thought to bring prestige and self-assurance to the *santero*, because they can use it during major ceremonies. The initiation costs around $4,000.
Babalu-Aye	Anyone can undergo this initiation, even non-priests. During the ceremony, *santeros* (priests) make predictions about the initiate's future, and cleansing rituals are performed that are thought to transfer the person's problems and sickness onto the special ritual objects used for the occasion. Expenses run about $2,000.
Botanicas	Botanicas are stores dedicated to the Santerian religion, selling various items used in the worship and practice of the religion. These stores stock charms, herbs, potions, and other similar items.
Agogo	A ritual bell that can be used to summon an *orisha* in time of need.
Coconut Divination	All the ceremonies and initiations of Santeria require the use of coconuts. Coconut divination is the most commonly used type and the only kind used by both *santeros* (priests) and *babalawos* (high priests). The purpose of this practice is to determine whether or not the *orisha* (spiritual emissaries) are satisfied with their offerings and what must be done with the offerings when the ceremony is over.
Seashell Divination (*Caracoles*)	Seashells function as mouthpieces of the *orisha* (spiritual emissaries) in this divination system. Each *orisha* possesses his or her own set of 21 cowrie shells, which are kept with ritual stones in a tureen. If a person wishes to speak to an *orisha*, the person must ask a *santero* to read that *orisha's* shells, because one cannot read the shells of one's own saint.
Ritual Stones	The spiritual essence of the *orisha* is gathered in groups of ritual stones representing them. If an animal is sacrificed, its blood is poured directly on these stones; after the ceremony the stones are rinsed off. The contents of the tureen, which holds these stones, must never be photographed or seen by an uninitiated person.

Chart 95

Appendix: Palo Mayombe

History, Basic Beliefs and Practices	Slaves who were forcibly removed from the Congo region of Africa were taken to the Americas (specifically Brazil, Venezuela, Colombia, and Cuba), and they brought with them a religion known as Palo Mayombe (Palo Monte in Cuba). Though it is similar to Santeria, Palo Mayombe is said to be more involved with evil spirits and to manifest a darker side of the religion. The primary beliefs of this religion are that humans can communicate with spirits who are viewed as able to animate physical things. This in turn empowers the humans who worship them. In Palo Mayombe the most important spirits are the spirits of the dead, or darkness (called *endoki*), the spirits of natural objects, and those who reveal themselves in nature and in humans. One distinction among practitioners of Palo is that some believe that lower spirits are in subjection to a High God of Light called Ensambi; others do not. The primary ritual of Palo Mayombe involves the *nganga*, a consecrated cauldron that is filled with various sacred objects such as sticks, bones, and earth.
	To be initiated into Palo one must undergo a ceremony called Rayamiento (scratching), wherein the new devotee has special marks traced on the skin and makes a pact with the spirit who lives in the cauldron. After this ceremony, the initiate is protected by the *nkisi* (spirit) who rules the *nganga* of the initiate's godfather.
	A divination method called *kujamputu* is practiced in Palo, which is very similar to that found in Santeria divination. Special symbols, each with a sacred character, play a key role in identifying spirits. Permission must be obtained from these spirits before holding important ceremonies. By drawing these symbols, believers are granted supernatural powers. The influence of Roman Catholicism on Palo Mayombe is seen in the worship of the Holy Ghost, the use of crucifixes, and the utterance of certain Catholic prayers.

Chart 95

Timeline of Umbanda and Candomblé

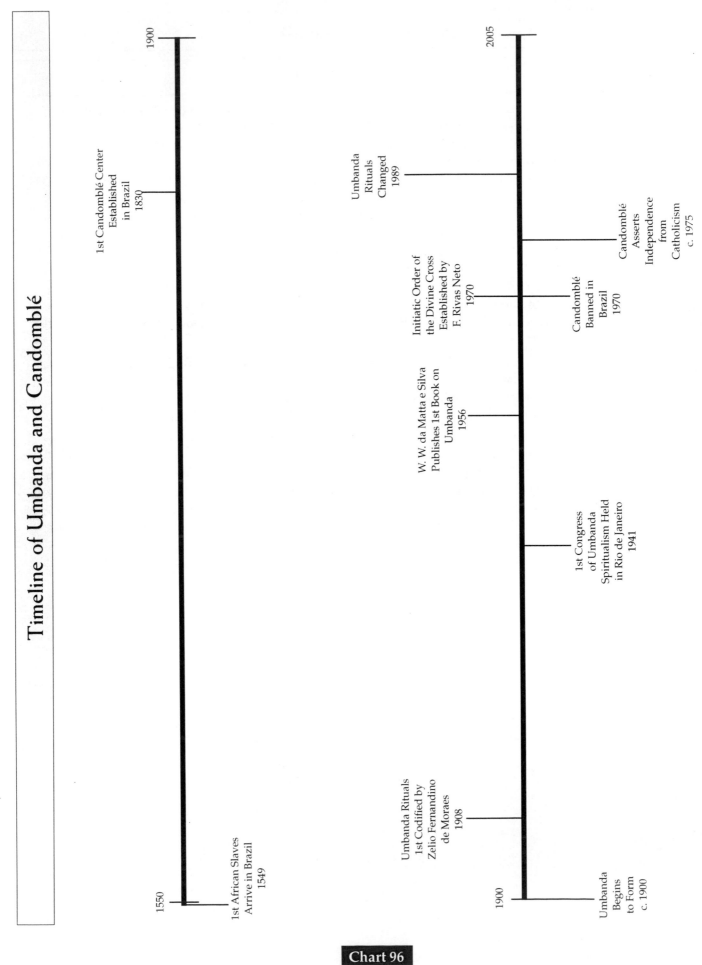

1550

1st African Slaves
Arrive in Brazil
1549

1830
1st Candomblé Center
Established
in Brazil

1900

1900

Umbanda
Begins
to Form
c. 1900

Umbanda Rituals
1st Codified by
Zelio Fernandino
de Moraes
1908

1st Congress
of Umbanda
Spiritualism Held
in Rio de Janeiro
1941

W. W. da Matta e Silva
Publishes 1st Book on
Umbanda
1956

Initiatic Order of
the Divine Cross
Established by
F. Rivas Neto
1970

Candomblé
Banned in
Brazil
1970

Candomblé
Asserts
Independence
from
Catholicism
c. 1975

Umbanda
Rituals
Changed
1989

2005

Chart 96

Umbanda

Topic	Facts
Current Data	Umbanda has approximately 70 million adherents and sympathizers, mainly in Brazil, but numbers are difficult to determine since its organizational structure prevents this. Most of its temple rituals have been altered since 1989 as it has moved beyond Brazil to other parts of the world.
History	In late 19th century Brazil, Umbanda was born from a syncretism of Nigerian religion and indigenous Brazilian spiritism, occultism, Eastern religions, and Roman Catholicism. Organizationally it came into existence in 1908 through the work of Zélio Fernandino de Moraes. Known originally as Alabanda, the name was changed to Umbanda. The famous medium W. W. da Matta e Silva introduced its esoteric teaching to the public in his 1956 book *Umbanda de Todos Nós*. Most of Umbanda's rituals occur within temples, practices that incorporate many divergent beliefs, a fact that has helped Umbanda to attract people with divergent religious beliefs.
Summary of Beliefs	In view of its highly syncretistic nature from spiritism, the occult, Eastern religion, and Roman Catholicism, Umbanda has a cacophony of beliefs, and due to the mysterious manner in which its practices occur within the private temples (*terreiros*) of the religion, much about it is unknown. These beliefs include the acceptance of spiritual beings (of the Umbanda Astral Chain) who manifest themselves and reveal secret information to participants in the rituals. They are able to lead the worshiper to express faith and to understand matters such as reincarnation and karma. These spiritual beings are viewed as being the first ones to take human form on the earth and have complete knowledge and understanding of all philosophy, religion, art, and science, which they have imparted to humans throughout human history. The reason that there are so many different religions is that this revealed knowledge has been distorted and misused by humans. Mediums of Umbanda assist people to learn and embrace this ancient knowledge.

Topic	Summary of View
Creation	The cause for the origin of the universe is a group of divine laws known as the Cosmic Proto-Synthesis. In turn, these "generating principles of the universe" are the basis for the four pillars of human knowledge, namely, religion, philosophy, science, and art.
Scripture and Authority	Umbanda has several important texts. The first was written by W. W. da Mata e Silva, entitled *Doutrina Secreta de Umbanda* (The Secret Doctrine of Umbanda) and the second by his disciple Rivas Neto, called *Fundamentos Herméticos de Umbanda* (The Tight Fundamentals of Umbanda). Another book, entitled the *Revelation of the Hexagramatic Cross*, contains information on how to receive spiritual protection and how to properly serve the Masters of Karma and to help other people (known as the Doctrine of the Three Paths). Additionally, spiritual beings (Spirits of the Cosmic Brotherhood of Umbanda) reveal knowledge to spiritual communities who are receptive, which helps mankind to develop spiritually.

Chart 97

Umbanda (continued)

Topic	Summary of View
God	The major God is Ogun, the God of War, Energy, and Metal (versions differ on this). He is also the God who controls life and death, keeps matter in motion, and controls gravity. After Ogun are numerous deities and spirit beings who are organized into various groups and sub-groups (called lines and phalanges). Lesser deities, called lines, are under a higher deity (*orixa*). Under the lines are deities called phalanges. The number, names, and types of deities vary from temple to temple.
Mankind	The original ancestors of mankind are spirit beings who were the first to take human form on the earth and to convey information to humans. It is believed that the Red race of the Tupy Lineage in ancient Brazil was the first to be taught the Umbanda religion during Lemuroid times (according to Umbanda, a period in ancient history). Human beings are really incarnate spirits in perishable human bodies. The spirit development of the person follows the laws of karma.
Sin	The conflict between spirit and matter is due to the Original Tradition taught by the spirit beings who originally came to earth. Because of this distortion, the Tupy Lineage divided into the Tupy-Mambá and Tupy-Guarany groups. The Tupy-Mambá group followed the Spiritual Principle; the Tupy-Guarany followed the Nature Principle. Though eventually there was a return to the Original Tradition, there remains a struggle in humans between spirit and matter.
Salvation	The spiritual beings who occupy the Superior Astral Planes impart laws to humans, which then may be used to help others and to achieve enlightenment. Enlightenment requires that persons do away with selfishness, vanity, and pride, and instead practice simplicity, humility, and purity. In order to develop these virtues, these spirit beings come to the temples of Umbanda to assist humans by means of mediums.
Afterlife	All persons will eventually come to an understanding of cosmic awareness. The continuing work of the *orixas* in directing the evolution of the earth's peoples will bring this about through the spread and practice of Umbanda.

Distinctive Beliefs and Practices

Yantric Doctrine	Cosmic codes have existed at the Astral Level since the beginning of creation. They vibrate constantly to the rhythm and cycles of the *oxala* (divine spirits). These codes are written using small pieces of chalk called *pemba*, made from African clay. By means of the sacred writing, worshipers can control the forces of nature, call on the spirit beings in the Astral Level, and get spirits to do their bidding.
Tantric Doctrine	This is the Doctrine of the Spiritual Light in which creation is relived and the spirit of the person passes into the Kingdom of Matter. In this event the spiritual conscience is experienced in the physical body.
Gira	A word that refers to the different rituals of Umbanda, particularly festive *gira*, development *gira*, and charity *gira*.

Chart 97

Umbanda (continued)

Distinctive Beliefs and Practices

Amaci	A liquid obtained by macerating particular herbs in water. This liquid is then used to wash the heads of Umbanda adherents in a pre-initiation ceremony.
Feitura-De-Cabeca	A liquid made from herbs that is used in a pre-initiation rite to wash the heads of the Umbanda worshiper.

Appendix: Candomblé*

History	In 1549 the first African slaves arrived in Brazil, the majority being from modern-day Congo, Angola, and Mozambique. These slaves brought their African religions with them, including belief in their ancestral spirits. Some of the slaves who escaped from slavery joined with native Brazilian witch doctors and religious leaders, and a syncretism occurred with the religious practices they retained from their Roman Catholic masters, their African beliefs and practices, and the native Brazilian religious views. The actual beliefs and practices of the followers of Candomblé were hidden from public view because of how Roman Catholic terms, names, and practices were used to mask their true religion. Prohibited by the Brazilian government until 1970, today Candomblé is one of the fastest-growing religious movements in Brazil.
Basic Beliefs	Candomblé borrows from and parallels Roman Catholic beliefs to which early adherents were exposed as slaves in Brazil. For example, there is one all-powerful God, Olodumare. Spirits who communicate with humans through the spirit messenger Esu serve this God. These servant spirits are patterned after the saints of the Roman Catholic Church. This adaptation allowed the slaves to continue worshiping their own deities without alerting their Catholic masters. The spirits (*orixa*) have different attributes for which they are worshiped. The Candomblé priests and priestesses use cowrie shells to help devotees know what to do and to reveal information about a person's *orixas*.
Sacred Space	In the early 19th century, the first Candomblé temple was built in Salvador, the capital of Bahia, in eastern Brazil. Candomblé temples have sanctuaries within them dedicated to the *orixas* who assist worshipers to achieve a spiritual rebirth by entering them. Usually a temple is under the authority of a black woman who uses divination to contact the *orixas*.
Rituals	Candomblé rites are conducted in the Yoruba language of West Africa. They occur at night, usually continuing all night. Ceremonies are composed of dancing in which spirits are summoned to enter the bodies of the worshipers. After hours of dancing, the spirits enter the worshipers' bodies. Each worshiper then changes clothes to signify an association with the spirit that has entered the body.

There are three main branches of Candomblé: Gege-Nago (the most African), Angola-Congo (more mixed), and Caboclo (the most syncretic). The African-based religions Macumba and Quimbanda are also found in Brazil.

Chart 97

Timeline of Voudon (Voodoo)

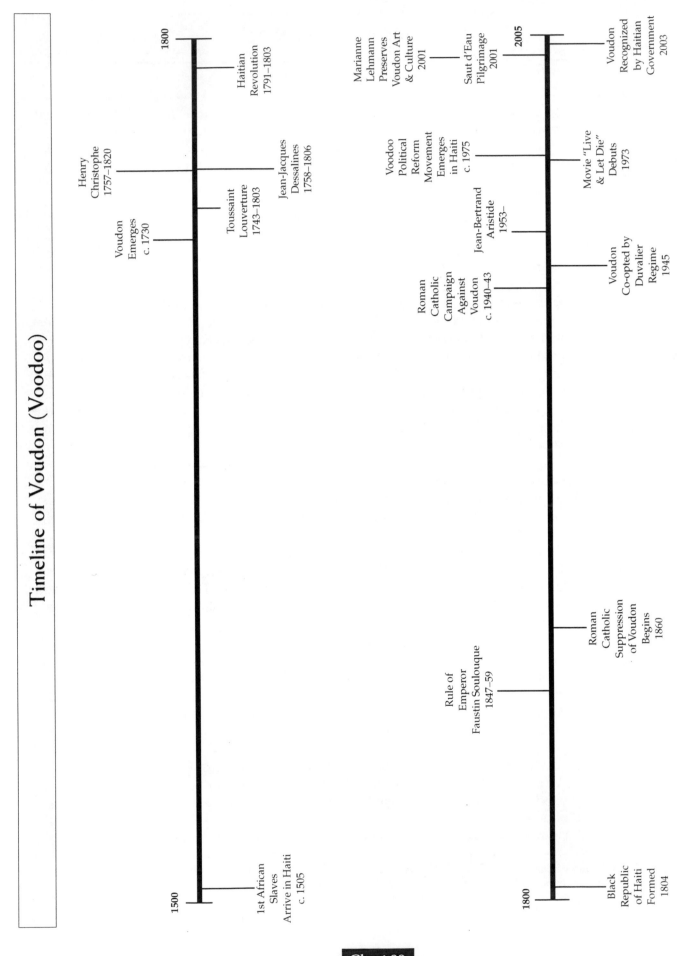

1500

1st African Slaves Arrive in Haiti c. 1505

Voudon Emerges c. 1730

Toussaint Louverture 1743–1803

Henry Christophe 1757–1820

Jean-Jacques Dessalines 1758–1806

Haitian Revolution 1791–1803

1800

Black Republic of Haiti Formed 1804

Rule of Emperor Faustin Soulouque 1847–59

Roman Catholic Suppression of Voudon Begins 1860

Roman Catholic Campaign Against Voudon c. 1940–43

Voudon Co-opted by Duvalier Regime 1945

Jean-Bertrand Aristide 1953–

Voodoo Political Reform Movement Emerges in Haiti c. 1975

Movie "Live & Let Die" Debuts 1973

Marianne Lehmann Preserves Voudon Art & Culture 2001

Saut d'Eau Pilgrimage 2001

Voudon Recognized by Haitian Government 2003

2005

Chart 98

Voudon (Voodoo)

Topic	Facts
Current Data*	Popularly known as "voodoo." By far, the greatest concentration of followers is in Haiti, where some estimate that 80 to 90 percent of the adult population practices the religion. As Haitians have migrated to other parts of the world, they have taken their religion with them. Today Voudon communities exist in the Dominican Republic, Ghana, and in the United States in New Orleans, Miami, and New York City. Worldwide as many as 50 million people practice Voudon in some form.
History	The Voudon religion had its origins in West Africa, most probably with the Fon peoples of Dahomey (parts of present-day Benin, Togo, and Nigeria). After being sold into slavery and transported to the New World (Haiti in particular), many Africans blended their traditional religious beliefs with elements of Roman Catholicism as a means of keeping their religion alive. By appropriating these Roman Catholic ideas and attending Mass regularly, slave communities were able to practice their religion in a manner that was largely covert and thus acceptable to their Catholic owners. Voudon gradually emerged during the period 1730–90. The three African groups which appear to have the strongest influence on Voudon are the Yoruba of present-day Nigeria, the Fon of Dahomey, and the Kongo of present-day Zaire and Angola. Because of how Voudon developed, reliable information about its formative years is scarce.
	During 1790–1800, Voudon experienced a considerable degree of growth and cohesion in Haiti. From 1800 to 1815, Voudon was suppressed by three Haitian rulers: Toussaint Louverture, Jean-Jacques Dessalines, and Henry Christophe. The next 35 years saw a quiet, steady spread of Voudon. Under Emperor Soulouque (1847–59), Voudon became politically acceptable and emerged publicly. Intermittent periods of Roman Catholic suppression occurred during the years 1860–1945, culminating in a strident campaign against Voudon in the 1940s. Since this time the Roman Catholic Church has greatly limited its suppression of Voudon in Haiti. Beginning in 1945, Voudon was co-opted by the Duvalier regime (Francois Duvalier ruled 1957–71 and Jean-Claude Duvalier ruled 1971–86) as a way of tricking the populace into thinking that their dictator had supernatural powers. There has been a reemergence of Voudon in recent decades, especially as a driving force in the peasant movement toward social reform in Haiti.
Summary of Beliefs	Voudon centers around an array of elaborate rituals intended to summon, control, and appease various spirits (*loa*), of which there are hundreds, though some are only aspects of other *loa*. Gran Maitre, the High God, is too remote to be approached directly or worshiped in a personal way, so devotees emphasize serving the *loa*. Devotees are encouraged to let the *loa* teach them. Voudon is a religion with very little dogma; there exists a great variety of both theory and practice. What is common to all manifestations of Voudon is the belief in *loa* and the desire to serve them, be filled with them, and be controlled by them. The *loa* act as intermediaries between human beings and God, similar in some respects to the way in which

* "Voodoo" is a Creole French term, deriving from the religion's original name, "Vodun," which is marked by belief in a pantheon of gods known as *loa*. Also called "Hoodoo."

Chart 99

Voudon (Voodoo) (continued)

Topic	Facts
Summary of Beliefs (continued)	Roman Catholics view their saints. Voudon tends to be experiential and its development is based on local needs and the particular *loa* being dealt with. Many Voudon practitioners think of themselves as Roman Catholic, attend Mass regularly, and participate in the sacraments of the Roman Catholic Church. They combine aspects of these rituals and beliefs with Voudon. An example is the connection of worship of the snake deity Damballah and St. Patrick, or identification of the spirit Ogou and St. James the Elder. Two types of Voudon are practiced, each with its own *loa*. The *loa* Rada is peaceful and happy (associated with Africa), while the *loa* Petro is angry and mean (associated with Haiti). Petro is associated with black magic, curses, the making of zombies, and sexual orgies. Adherents to Rada make up approximately 95 percent of Voudon. Despite these differences, there are many points in common. All Voudon is concerned with healing of people, for which they use herbs, the assistance of their *loa*, and, recently, Western medicine.

Topic	Summary of View
Creation	The serpent god Damballah created the waters of the earth, according to Voudon accounts, and by moving his coils he formed the earth's hills and valleys as well as the planets and stars. When the sun shone through the waters of the earth, a rainbow appeared. Damballah was so taken with the rainbow that he made her his wife, Aida-Wedo.
Scripture and Authority	Voudon has no sacred writings. Rather, religious authority is vested in priests (*houngan*) and priestesses (*mambo*). These religious leaders are both community and religious leaders and perform many secular and religious tasks within the community, including confessor, physician, magician, counselor, and fortune-teller. They also perform rites of initiation, cast spells, and concoct magic potions.
God	There is only one ultimate God (Gran Maitre, meaning Great Master, or Bondye, meaning Good God), who is concerned mainly with the grand scheme of the plan and order of the universe. However, he has brought together a large number of spirit beings who represent him and his interests on earth and who make sure that humans do not feel themselves abandoned by him. These beings are called *loa*. They have specific duties given to them by Gran Maitre. They control the major forces of the universe and communicate with humans on a daily basis. They are also largely in control of all events, good and bad, in the lives of humans. Followers of Voudon do not believe themselves to be responsible for what occurs since all is ultimately caused by the *loa*. In addition to the *loa*, ancestral spirits are involved with those still living in the physical world. Well-known *loa* include Ogou and Loco Atisou. Ogou, as a warrior, represents stability, order, and authority; he is expressed by believers through the symbols of fire, lightning, and the phallus. Loco Atisou, the gate between the spirit world and the physical world, is the *loa* of wisdom and medicine, depicted by the sun and ritual waters.

Chart 99

Voudon (Voodoo) (continued)

Topic	Summary of View
Mankind	Humans are composed of five parts, namely the mortal flesh, the spirit of the flesh, the star of destiny, the soul (big good angel), and the conscience (little good angel). The soul and the conscience are the most important in Voudon religion and upon death leave for the world of the dead. At death the soul, or *gros-bon-ange*, presents the person to God and argues that person's case.
Sin	A kind of spiritual fatalism dominates ethical considerations insofar as the *loa* determine the actions of devotees to a tremendous degree. The reality of personal moral responsibility is denied, since most of what happens in the realm of human behavior is caused by the *loa*.
Salvation	Salvation is thought to be more temporal than eternal and concerns the acquiring of health and wealth in this world. It is achieved by joining together elements of the African past and select worship practices of Roman Catholicism. Worshipers observe two ceremonies (*rada* and *petro*), both involving the activities of drumming, dancing, chanting, and entering into trances, all of which are for the purpose of summoning the *loa*. The place of these ceremonies tends to be near trees in which some *loa* are said to reside; the trees are respected as divine. Along with these practices, Roman Catholic prayers are recited, often followed by ecstatic utterances. Presided over by a *houngan*, a *mambo* (male assistant) uses a ritual sword (*la place*) to divide the material from the immaterial world, allowing the *loa* to enter the worship site. These ceremonies regularly involve the sacrifice of various animals. It is thought that the animal in this sacrifice becomes part of the *loa*, so that the blood of the animal is consumed by the worshipers in order for them to share in the divine energy of the *loa*.
Afterlife	For the Voudon believer, death is not considered the end of life. Rather, this is when a person's spiritual aspects are released (the *gros-bon-ange* and *ti-bon-ange*). Assisted by Voudon death rituals (*dessounin*), the spirit returns to what is known as Ginen (world of the dead). There the person's spirit becomes a *loa*. At the time of death, the spirit hovers around the dead body for nine days, and is not permitted to leave due to Nine Nights rituals performed by a Voudon priest. The components of this ritual are to stuff cotton in the ears and nostrils of the corpse, to tie the mouth shut, and to tie the knees and big toes. The priest dances around the body, whispering into the ears the deceased person's name. After this, the *gros-bon-ange* possesses the priest as it leaves for Ginen. If more than nine days have passed since death, the *ti-bon-ange* can be raised from the grave in a ceremony in which rum and pennies are thrown on the grave. Unless a person goes through proper death rituals, the spirit can become trapped on earth. A departing spirit may be captured by a *bokor* (one who practices black magic) and used for evil purposes. A *bokor* might turn the spirit into a *zombi astral* (soul without a body; different from a zombie, a body without a soul), doomed to wander the earth. Two ways to keep a *bokor* from capturing a person's spirit are to drive a stake through the heart of the dead person or to decapitate the dead.

Chart 99

Voudon (Voodoo) (continued)

Distinctive Beliefs and Practices

Pe	A stone altar where ritual tools are kept. This stone is covered in offerings such as candles, food, money, amulets, ceremonial rattles and flags (*drapeaux*), beads, drums, and sacred stones.
Djevo	A small ceremonial room representing a tomb where the initiate undergoes a ritual death and rebirth into Voudon.
Laver Tete	A baptism of sorts in which devotees wear a white robe and have water poured over their head while chanting particular incantations. Its purpose is to invoke the blessings of the major *loa*, Damballah.
Govi	A container that the *loa* are called into where they are asked questions about the concerns of Voudon adherents.
Zombies	The depiction in many people's minds of zombies has been created by Hollywood, in which zombies are the "walking dead." In Voudon, zombies (bodies without souls) are created by *bokors* (those who practice black magic), who give a magic concoction to living persons, which causes the organs of the body to slow to such an extent that the person appears to be dead. The person is buried, and a couple of days later is dug up and given an antidote that revives the person. However, the person's brain has sustained permanent damage, leaving the person unable to remember the past or to speak, thus becoming a slave of the *bokor*.
Baka	An evil spirit that roams at night, often taking the form of an animal. These spirits can be called on to perform evil deeds, but may exact revenge on the family of the person who summons them.
Wanga	Those who practice Voudon believe that supernatural forces may be captured and enclosed in bottles or packets, what they call *wanga*. The purpose is to cause sickness or difficulties for a specific individual, who is the target of the spell that is cast.
Voodoo Dolls	The mental picture often formed at the mention of Voodoo is that of a witch doctor sticking pins into a voodoo doll. This depiction of Voudon, however, is one largely created by Hollywood and not practiced in Haiti or in other places where Voudon is prominent. Only in New Orleans, in the early 1900s, is there a record of dolls being used by Voudon believers. The purpose was to cast a spell on the person symbolized by the doll; the spell could be for either good or ill.

Chart 99

Timeline of Native American Religion

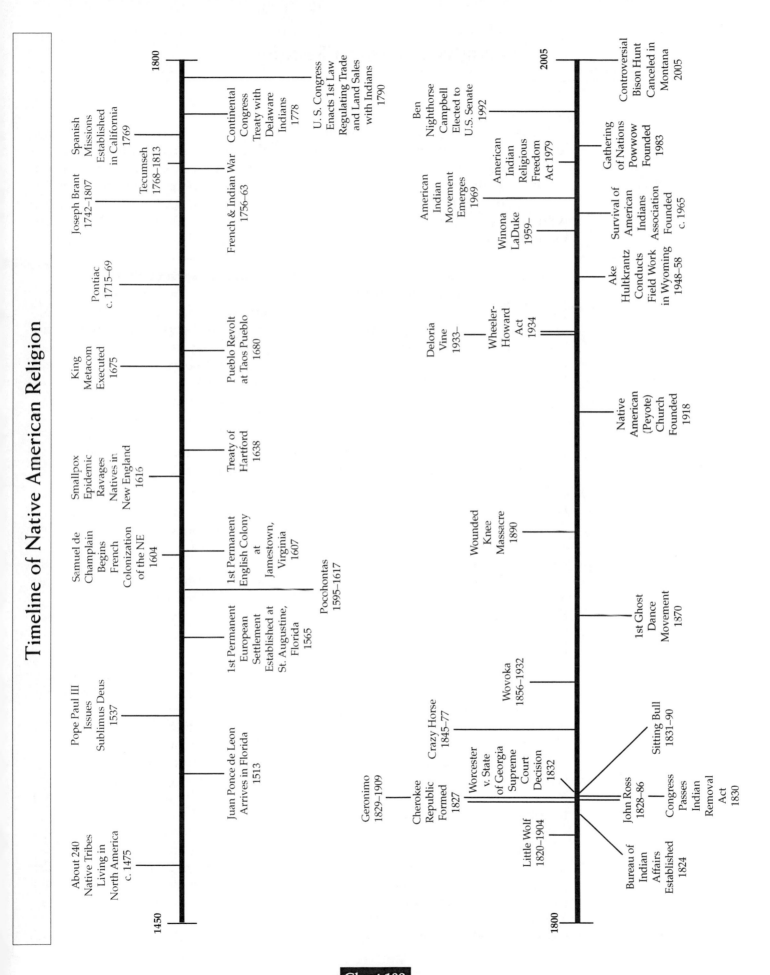

About 240 Native Tribes Living in North America c. 1475

Pope Paul III Issues Sublimus Deus 1537

Juan Ponce de Leon Arrives in Florida 1513

1st Permanent European Settlement Established at St. Augustine, Florida 1565

Samuel de Champlain Begins French Colonization of the NE 1604

1st Permanent English Colony at Jamestown, Virginia 1607

Pocohontas 1595–1617

Smallpox Epidemic Ravages Natives in New England 1616

Treaty of Hartford 1638

King Metacom Executed 1675

Pueblo Revolt at Taos Pueblo 1680

Pontiac c. 1715–69

Joseph Brant 1742–1807

Tecumseh 1768–1813

French & Indian War 1756–63

Spanish Missions Established in California 1769

Continental Congress Treaty with Delaware Indians 1778

U. S. Congress Enacts 1st Law Regulating Trade and Land Sales with Indians 1790

1450 — 1800

Geronimo 1829–1909

Cherokee Republic Formed 1827

Little Wolf 1820–1904

Worcester v. State of Georgia Supreme Court Decision 1832

Crazy Horse 1845–77

Bureau of Indian Affairs Established 1824

John Ross 1828–86

Congress Passes Indian Removal Act 1830

Sitting Bull 1831–90

Wovoka 1856–1932

1st Ghost Dance Movement 1870

Wounded Knee Massacre 1890

Native American (Peyote) Church Founded 1918

Deloria Vine 1933–

Wheeler-Howard Act 1934

Ake Hultkrantz Conducts Field Work in Wyoming 1948–58

Winona LaDuke 1959–

American Indian Movement Emerges 1969

American Indian Religious Freedom Act 1979

Ben Nighthorse Campbell Elected to U.S. Senate 1992

Survival of American Indians Association Founded c. 1965

Gathering of Nations Powwow Founded 1983

Controversial Bison Hunt Canceled in Montana 2005

1800 — 2005

Chart 100

Native American Religion

Topic	Facts
Current Data	In the 2000 United States census, 4.1 million residents reported themselves as American Indian (or Alaskan Native) alone or in combination with one or more other racial groups, comprising 1.5 percent of the population. Of this group, 2.5 million reported themselves as American Indian or Alaskan Native only (0.9 percent of the population). California, Oklahoma, New Mexico, and South Dakota are the states with the highest percentages of Native American residents. Only two tribes number more than 200,000: Cherokee (approximately 370,000) and Navajo (about 225,000).
History	Scholars differ considerably as to the origin of Native American culture and religion. The most common theory, until recently, was that the Western Hemisphere was covered in ice and lacked human civilization until about 11,000 years ago (9200 BC). The first humans in the Americas, according to this theory, were hunters from Asia who walked on dry land (now underwater) along the Bering Strait from Siberia to Alaska. Various early hunting expeditions traveled southward into the Great Plains and the Southwest. Some traveled all the way to the southernmost part of South America. But recent archaeological discoveries indicate that the first humans arrived much earlier and may have entered the Western Hemisphere from a variety of other routes, including Australia, southern Asia, and Europe. Both theories are disputed by Native Americans, whose oral traditions state that Native American tribes did not originate elsewhere, but have always lived in the Americas.
	Much remains unknown concerning the emergence of Native American religions because until the late 19th century, all such knowledge was contained solely within the oral traditions of the Native American tribes. This began to change early in the 20th century with development of written tribal languages. The diversity among these religions is due to the difference in the geographical and environmental situations of the tribes; each Native American religion included references to the plants and animals associated with the tribe. These native religions were weakened by the westward expansion of settlements in the Americas (particularly in the United States), the forced location of tribes onto reservations, and the work of Christian missionaries among them.
	Struggles continue between the Native American people and the United States government over issues relating to the practice of their religion and their entitlement to land taken from their ancestors in military conquests. Various tribes have filed lawsuits against the government over federal use of lands they claim. Certain tribes (the Navajo, Hopi, and Zuni in the Southwest) have been permitted to keep portions of their ancient lands, making it possible for them to continue many of their traditions. The Native American Church (in the tradition of the original Peyote religion) was established in 1918 and continues the use of peyote, a hallucinogenic drug from the peyote cactus, in its worship, a use not sanctioned by the federal government.
Summary of Beliefs	Sweeping generalizations about Native American religions are impossible because there is no single expression of religion common to the more than 250 distinct tribal groups (anthropologists commonly divide these into seven major groupings) that exist today. The tribal traditions, which molded the Native American religious perspectives, were preserved by the elders within each tribe. This does not mean that tradition ruled supreme over changing circumstances, however. Native Americans

Chart 101

Native American Religion (continued)

Topic	Facts
Summary of Beliefs (continued)	in the past altered religious views based on dreams, visions, and changed circumstances. Within Native American religious communities, there were a number of religious practitioners thought to possess a variety of powers, including contact with the spirit world, healing, and foretelling the future. Religious leaders bore various titles such as medicine man, shaman, and diviner. A person who was struck by lightning was considered a candidate for such a position.

Topic	Summary of View
Creation	Creation stories vary from tribe to tribe. Usually a tribe's version of creation explained how benevolent spirits or deities put the tribe's people on the land where they lived, a homeland that served as the center of the world and around which all creation revolved. Beyond this common theme, accounts varied greatly. Some tribes believed that the land was originally inhabited by humans who later were transformed into animals. Other legends described the world as having different layers, with the natural physical world being the middle segment. These layers were linked by the "World Tree" that had its roots in the underground, its trunk going through the world of the tribe, and its top in the sky layer. Other tribes thought their ancestors had originally been under the earth and came into this world through a hole in the earth's surface. The Shawnee believed that their ancestors were created in another world (balanced on the back of a giant turtle) and traveled to this world. The creation myth of the Blackfoot has Old Man traveling from the north to the south, creating the earth's landscape and humans as he travels. Along the journey he mixed red dye in the ground, from which he fashioned the first woman and her baby boy.
Scripture and Authority	The sacred stories of Native Americans were passed down from generation to generation by oral tradition. These stories served to preserve tribal identity and provided an important means for Native Americans to understand matters of life and death and to become aware of their obligations to the world and how those obligations affected their daily life. These stories also gave them a sense of their relationship with the creation.
God	Native American tribes hold in common a belief that there is a Supreme Creator or Master Spirit who is the source of all life, and that he pervades the universe. The nature of this Spirit is considered a mysterious power that cannot be sufficiently described in human language. In addition to the Great Spirit that created the world, it is generally believed that there is also a hero or trickster who teaches the tribe how to live and who provides for its needs. Lesser spirits control the weather and relate to the tribe. Among some tribes, the Creator and the spirits are thought to be a unified entity, such as Wakan-Tanka (Great Spirit) of the Lakota. In this view, God is both transcendent (beyond any limits or understanding) and immanent (within human experience), is neither singular nor plural, and has both personal and impersonal features.

Chart 101

Native American Religion (continued)

Topic	Summary of View
Mankind	According to the beliefs of many tribes, humans possess two souls. One is the person's breath, which lives inside the person and dies when the body dies. The other is a "free soul," which departs from the body and wanders around when the person is ill and during dreams. A characteristic of Native American tribes, when speaking of themselves, is to name themselves "the people," but when speaking of other tribes, whom they view as being of lesser importance, to use the name of the respective tribe. The Creator did not place humans over creation, but instead expects humans to be spiritual companions with all other created things (some tribes exclude dogs), including inanimate things.
Sin	Human beings have moral obligations toward all other parts of the creation. If these obligations are kept, harmony and balance are preserved (the Navajo word *hozho* captures this idea). Right actions are those that promote harmony in the creation; wrong actions are those that diminish this harmony. For example, Cherokee ethics dictated that things of opposing kinds should only be allowed to interact within carefully prescribed boundaries. No tribe has an account of a fall into sin wherein the first humans rebelled against God and thus were expelled from their homeland. However, several tribes tell stories about the origin of death. According to the Alsea, the only reason the first death was permanent was that the cousin of the father whose child died didn't want the child to return to the land of the living until the father was no longer sick; this made permanent the nature of death.
Salvation	Salvation consisted of maintaining a closeness between spirit and nature, and the tribe being in a proper relationship with the world. Consequently, there was little separation between the sacred and the ordinary. The worlds of spirit and nature were so mingled that it was difficult to determine where one began and the other ended. For example, shamans went into trance states during which their souls would roam freely to search for lost items. Medicine men and women contacted spirits for the purpose of learning how to cure ills. Some persons would take peyote to produce an altered state of consciousness in which they would receive a vision that guided their future life. Some were trying to meet their personal guardian spirit. Special dances were performed to influence the course of nature and the future. For example, the Arapaho and Cheyenne did a Sun Dance to renew and sustain the earth, and the well-known Ghost Dance was performed to bring about the defeat of white settlers and the resurgence of the buffalo.
Afterlife	Native Americans differed on their beliefs regarding the afterlife. Some tribes believed that people are reincarnated either as a human being or as an animal, others believed that humans return to this world as ghosts or go on to another world, and some believed little could be known about the afterlife. Most tribes believed that the spirits of tribal ancestors remain alive on the tribal homelands and must be properly honored there. Death was viewed as natural, since every person is a part of creation. Both good and evil people were thought to inhabit the same world after death. No reports have been found of any native peoples affirming the existence of heaven or hell prior to the arrival of European settlers. However, some tribes believed that the world would end at a future time.

Chart 101

Native American Religion (continued)

Distinctive Beliefs and Practices

Time	There are two types of time: mythic time, which is a time before the establishment of the tribe in its homeland, and historical time. In mythic time, the spirits and the material world are closely interconnected and have no barriers, so different parts of the creation have little difficulty communicating with each other. This is the kind of time understood when recounting tribal accounts of creation, early migrations, and a tribe's heroes. Historical time is time as we know it, which includes stories of good harvests and difficult winters.
Sacred Landscapes	Specific landscapes signified important aspects of a tribe's way of life and were viewed as sacred. Native American tribes regularly used objects, such as certain rocks or trees, in rituals. Rites of initiation often took place, for example, in remote forests or on the top of mountains. Native Americans didn't believe the land belonged to them, but that they and the land were spiritually connected.
Animals	Most tribes viewed animals as related to them since, according to their creation legends, animals once were changed into humans. Many tribes performed elaborate ceremonies in which tribesmen displayed behavior similar to animals that were deemed important by that tribe. Certain animals occupied positions of dominance over others in their species. For example, the eagle was believed to be the "chief" of all flying creatures. Many animals were viewed as having great wisdom and power and were thought to serve as mediators between human beings and spiritual forces.
Buffalo	The buffalo played a very important role in the lives and stories of many tribes in North America. In fact, the lives of many tribes revolved around the buffalo. The tongues of buffalo, which sometimes were eaten during ceremonies, were considered the animal's most sacred part. For some tribes, buffalo skulls represented rebirth. Although necessary for the survival of the tribe, killing a buffalo disturbed the natural kinship between animals and human beings, so tribes sought reconciliation with the buffalo through prescribed rituals such as the Sun Dance.
Hunting Ceremonies	Hunting ceremonies were designed to appease the spirit of the animal that had been killed during the hunt and to persuade living animals to allow themselves to be hunted for food, clothing, and implements. Shamans performed this "sympathetic magic," and, in some cases, hunters whispered ritual apologies and blessings to the spirits of dying animals.
Totemism	A totem is an object (bird, animal, or plant) that serves as an emblem for a clan or family. Totems are represented on big wooden poles carved with various totem symbols that have special significance to the tribe that made the pole. Totemism—the beliefs and practices surrounding totems—is characterized by the following: (1) the totem is viewed as a companion, protector, or helper with superhuman powers and is respected, in some cases becoming an object of awe; (2) special names and emblems are used to refer to the totem; (3) practitioners partially identify with the totem; (4) killing, eating, touching, or shunning the totem is prohibited; and (5) totemistic rituals are performed. Contrary to popular understanding, the most important symbols are at the bottom of the totem pole, not the top.

Chart 101

Glossary

acculturation. A cultural change in people due to exposure, usually prolonged, to a different cultural style.

advent. In Christianity, the coming of Christ, first at his birth, again at the second coming.

agnostic. One who withholds judgment on whether God exists, or believes we cannot know whether God or gods exist.

agnosticism. 1. The belief that it is impossible to know whether God or gods exist. 2. The state of being uncertain as to whether God or gods exist.

Al-Qadr. The unchangeable decree of Allah.

amalozi. The word for "ancestors" in African traditional religion.

anathema. A curse; a fervent denunciation.

animism. 1. The attribution of conscious life to objects in and phenomena of nature and to inanimate objects. 2. The belief that spirits of some kind inhabit and affect most objects in the world.

annihilationism. The belief that after death, unrepentant sinners will be destroyed rather than suffer eternal punishment.

anthropomorphic deities. Gods who have taken human form or appear to be human.

apocalypse. The events or a revelation relating to the end of all things, the end times, and the destruction of the universe.

apologetic works. Writings that set forth reasons for particular beliefs.

apostate churches. Christian churches that have departed from the historical orthodox doctrines of Christianity.

apostasy. Renunciation of a religious faith; defection; abandonment of a previous loyalty.

apostolic church. 1. A church that dates back to the time of the apostles of Jesus Christ or claims to have an unbroken line of succession to that time. 2. A church that follows the teachings of the apostles.

asceticism. Strict self-denial as a measure of personal and spiritual discipline or holiness.

aseity. Self-existence; the absolute self-sufficiency, autonomy, and independence of God.

ashe. In Santeria, a symbol of divine power or spiritual energy that permeates the universe.

astral plane. In Umbanda, a spiritual realm beyond the material world in which higher beings reside; another dimension of the universe.

atheism. The belief that God or gods do not exist.

atheist. One who believes that God does not exist.

Atman. In Hinduism, (1) the Universal Spirit, or (2) the immortal soul in every person.

atonement. The ancient Jewish view that God covered the sins of the Jewish people when they offered a sacrifice on the Day of Atonement, not looking at the sins so as to punish the people but (provisionally) reconciling with them. According to Christian theology, the sins that were covered were finally forgiven at the death of Jesus on the cross. The term "atonement" is often used incorrectly to refer to the forgiveness of sins, that is, redemption.

atonement, substitutionary. See *substitutionary atonement.*

avatar. In Hindusim, a manifestation of Brahman who descends into the realm of mortals, usually when there is widespread ignorance about the path to enlightenment.

avidya. In Hinduism, ignorance concerning the true nature of existence or reality.

awagaun. The cycle of death and rebirth in Sikhism.

bardo. In Buddhism, an intermediate state of the soul; the stage after death and prior to rebirth.

bhakti. A word meaning "devotion to a god or gods," which in turn has become the name of a Hindu devotional movement.

Big Bang. A scientific theory that the universe originated in an explosion from a single dense point about 8–14 billion years ago. Also referred to as the "expanding universe theory."

bodhi. In Buddhism, awakening; enlightenment.

bodhisattva. In Buddhism, a highly powerful being striving toward enlightenment; a compassionate person who delays the realization of enlightenment in order to assist others in that same quest.

Brahma. Hindu creator God and member of the Hindu "trinity" that also includes Vishnu and Shiva.

Brahman. In Hinduism, the unchanging, endless, ubiquitous ground of all being; often identified as being everything.

canon. A sanctioned collection of writings, often religious in nature.

canon of scripture. The books recognized by Jews and/or Christians as being inspired by God and thus authoritative in matters of faith and life.

cognate. Related by derivation or descent.

communicable attributes. Those divine attributes that God shares (to some finite degree) with human beings, such as love, mercy, and righteousness. Incommunicable divine attributes are those that belong to God alone, such as eternality, infinity, omnipotence, and omniscience.

consecrated. Dedicated to a sacred purpose.

cosmic. Of, relating to, or concerned with abstract spiritual or metaphysical ideas.

cosmogony. An account of the origin and evolution of the universe.

cosmology. A theory dealing with structure of the universe as a whole.

cosmos. The universe viewed as an orderly, harmonious whole.

crucicentrism. A central focus on the redemptive sacrifice of Jesus Christ on the cross.

cultural pluralism. See *pluralism, cultural.*

deification. 1. Making something into a god, or becoming a god or godlike. 2. In Eastern Orthodoxy, participating in a mystical way in the very essence of God without becoming God.

deism. The belief that God created the universe and established its natural laws, but then ceased to be involved in its operation or in human affairs.

dependent origination. The Buddhist metaphysical view that all the phenomena of experience arise together as a mutually interdependent whole.

devekut. In Hasidic Judaism, constant devotion and unceasing consciousness of God's presence; communion between God and humankind.

dharma. In various Eastern religions, (1) the act of fulfilling one's duty by adhering to customs and/or divine law, and (2) the principles or laws of existence and reality.

dharmakaya. The Truth Body of the Buddha, often said to be "empty" and beyond description.

dichotomy. Division into two (often contradictory) groups or sets.

discursive thinking. Reliance on analysis and reasoning rather than intuition.

divination. Foretelling the future or discovering hidden knowledge with the aid of supernatural powers or interpretation of omens.

diviner. Someone who engages in divination.

divinity. A divine being, or the state or quality of being divine.

dogma. A tenaciously held belief that is viewed as firmly established; an authoritative tenet or doctrine.

dogmatism. An arrogant, stubborn assertion of belief.

dukkha. In Buddhism, suffering that results from ignorance of one's true nature.

dynamic inspiration. In Christianity, the view that the essential meaning or basic idea of a sentence or section in the Bible is inspired, though not every particular word.

ecclesial. Of or relating to a church or the government of that church.

ecumenical. Concerned with establishing or promoting unity among churches or religions.

empirical science. A method of studying the natural world based on observation, experience, and repeatable testing.

Enlightenment, the. A European intellectual and cultural movement of the 18th century that advocated the autonomy and sufficiency of human reason; also called the Age of Reason.

epistemic. Of or relating to knowledge or knowing.

epistemology. A branch of philosophy examining the nature and grounds of knowledge, especially its justification and limits.

eschatology. The branch of theology that deals with ultimate or final things, like the end of the world, the afterlife and the resurrection of the dead, the destiny of humanity, the second coming of Christ, the last judgment.

esoteric. Knowledge that is restricted to a small group; not publicly disclosed; confidential.

eternality. The state of existing outside of time.

eugenics. The study of hereditary improvement of a group of people by controlled selective breeding.

ex nihilo. Latin for "out of nothing."

exorcism. A ritual in which spirits or demons are cast out of a person who is possessed by them.

expiation. The act of forgiving someone's sins. This is different from "atonement," which refers to covering or paying for someone's sins. The Christian Scriptures add another element, that of propitiation, or satisfying the wrath of God against sin.

filial piety. An important aspect of Confucianism, involving respecting and honoring one's parents and other elders.

filioque clause. A disputed phrase in the Nicene Creed meaning "and the Son." The Western Church argued that the Holy Spirit proceeds eternally from the Father and the Son, whereas the Eastern Church said that the Holy Spirit proceeds only from the Father. This was a contributing factor in the split between the Western and Eastern churches in 1054.

finitude, human. The state of being limited in various ways that is endemic to all human beings.

fravashis. In Zoroastrianism, preexistent souls created by Ahura Mazda.

gnostic gospels. Accounts of the life of Jesus attributed to various apostles (such as Thomas) that portray Jesus as a dispenser of hidden wisdom concerning how the soul can escape its entrapment in this evil, material world. These gospels are from the late 2nd century and early 3rd century AD. They are largely made up of alleged sayings of Jesus and were propagated by the Gnostics who argued against the orthodox church.

Gnosticism. An ancient religion that contends that the god of the Old Testament is an evil deity who desires to keep human souls trapped in their evil physical bodies, and that the God revealed by Jesus Christ is a higher and good deity. Beginning elements of Gnosticism were present in the 1st century AD but it did not become a mature religion until the 2nd and 3rd centuries. Its arguments were refuted by a number of the late 2nd century fathers of the Eastern Church. Gnosticism was a syncretism of Jewish, Neoplatonic, and Zoroastrianism philosophies, though it expressed its ideas using Christian symbols and stories.

grace, justifying. 1. In Roman Catholicism, supernatural aid from God in response to salutary acts of sinners, granted in consideration of the merits of Christ. 2. In classical Protestantism (Reformed theology), the unmerited favor of God whereby he provides forgiveness and mercy to sinners.

guru. A teacher or guide in matters of religion or spirituality.

Halakha. The corpus of rabbinic law, custom, and tradition in Judaism.

henotheism. The belief that there are multiple gods, but only one is supreme and hence most worthy of worship.

heretic. A person who holds doctrines or theological views that are at variance with the orthodox beliefs of the community of faith of which he or she is a part; someone whose views deviate from a widely accepted standard of religious belief.

hermeneutics. The theory and methods for interpretation of text, especially the Bible.

holiness. 1. The state or quality of being set apart for a special use. 2. The state or quality of being morally pure.

Holy Eucharist. In Roman Catholicism, the sacrament in which the body and blood of Jesus Christ (who is divine and human) is said to be present in visible form in the bread and wine and is shared with the communicant.

iconoclast. One who destroys religious images or opposes their veneration.

idiosyncratic. Unusual or eccentric; odd; distinct from all others of its kind.

imago dei. Latin for "the image of God."

immanence. God's presence in the world, in contrast to the view that God and the world are indistinct.

immanent. God as present, within; indwelling; near.

immutable. Incapable of undergoing change.

incantation. Words used in reciting a charm or spell in an attempt to achieve a specific result.

incarnation. The visible physical or quasi-physical form of a soul or deity.

incorporeal. Without any material body or form; a spirit.

ineffable. Incapable of being described.

inerrant. Without error; free of misstatements of fact.

infallible. Incapable of being incorrect.

infinite. Without end or boundary; unlimited.

Intelligent Design. A scientific theory that certain features of the universe and of living organisms exhibit characteristics that are best explained by positing an intelligent agent as their cause.

Judaism, Rabbinical. See *Rabbinical Judaism.*

justification. 1. In Roman Catholicism, a process wherein a sinner is progressively made righteous through being infused with God's righteousness. 2. In Reformed theology, an act of God whereby a sinner is declared righteous in view of Jesus Christ's death, resurrection, and perfect righteousness being imputed to the sinner.

justifying grace. See *grace, justifying.*

kami. In Shinto, spirits venerated by devotees, taking various forms: as natural objects and forms of life, as guardians of clans and their territories, as family ancestors or souls of the deceased, as national leaders, or as abstract creative forces.

libation. Pouring of a liquid offering in a religious ritual; the liquid so poured.

liturgy. Prescribed ritual forms or a series of ritual acts used for a religious ceremony or service.

Logos. 1. The divine wisdom manifest in the creation, government, and redemption of the world and often identified with the second person of the Trinity. 2. Reason, which in ancient Greek philosophy is the controlling principle of the universe.

mantra. In various Eastern religions, a sacred verbal formula repeated in prayer, meditation, or incantation; a chant.

Masoretic text. The Hebrew text of the Tanakh approved by most groups within Judaism which comes from the Masoretes, Jewish scribes who lived about 1,100 years ago. The Dead Sea Scrolls, which date to about a thousand years earlier than the Masoretic text, are very close to that text, demonstrating the carefulness of the scribes.

materialism. The philosophical view that all of reality consists of, and can be fully explained in terms of, physical matter.

maya. In Hinduism, the illusion that persons are real.

matrilineal. Relating to, based on, or tracing ancestral descent through the maternal line.

metaphysical dualism. A philosophical view that reality consists of two fundamental kinds of things, usually thought to be spirit and matter.

metaphysical properties. Properties that cannot be described or investigated by empirical means.

metaphysics. The branch of philosophy that examines the nature of reality, especially the most basic things that exist in the world.

modalism. A view in theology in which God is said to be one in person and nature, manifesting himself in different forms (modes) at various times and places.

moksha. In Hinduism and Jainism, release from suffering and the cycle of death and rebirth.

monasticism. Refraining from worldly endeavors in order to pursue spiritual goals, often in community with others who have vowed to do the same.

monism. A philosophical view that reality is composed of only one kind of substance. The nature of this substance can vary, depending on the type of monism.

monotheism. The belief that there is only one God.

moral relativism. A theory in ethics that claims that concepts like good and evil, right and wrong are not defined from an objective standard but are relative to the individuals or cultures that employ them.

mortal sin. In Roman Catholicism, a sin that concerns a grave matter and is committed with full knowledge of its seriousness and with deliberate and complete consent. Such a sin results in loss of justifying grace.

mystery religions. Religion that are centered on a body of wisdom in which the core of beliefs and practices are secrets, revealed only to initiates.

mythic time. A time before or outside of historical time.

naturalism. A philosophical view which maintains that there are no supernatural entities of any kind and all phenomena can be explained in terms of natural causes and laws. Not to be mistaken for materialism, since naturalists believe in the existence of things that are neither material nor supernatural, like numbers and abstract objects.

Neoplatonism. A philosophical system developed at Alexandria, Egypt, in the 3rd century AD by Plotinus (205–70) and his successors. It is a mixture of the philosophy of Plato, mysticism, Judaism, and Christianity. It posits a single source from which all existence emanates and with which individual souls can be mystically united.

nirvana. 1. In philosophical Buddhism, the extinction of the self at liberation, with neither a place nor a state of consciousness. 2. In popular Buddhism, a state of indescribable bliss, the ultimate goal of existence.

normative. Of, relating to, or prescribing an objective norm or standard.

obeisance. A bodily gesture or movement that expresses deference or homage; an attitude of deference or homage.

occultism. A belief in or use of magical powers that are available to human beings.

omnibenevolence. The state of being perfectly loving.

omniperfection. The state of possessing all possible perfections.

omnipotence. The state of being all-powerful.

omnipresenc. The state of being present everywhere.

omniscience. All-knowing; the state of knowing everything: past, present, and future, actual and contingent.

ontological dichotomy. A sharp metaphysical distinction between two different kinds of things.

ontology. The branch of philosophy that examines the nature and structure of being in general and of particular objects.

oracle. 1. A person who consults a deity to receive an answer to a specific question. 2. The response given by an oracle after the consultation. 3. A shrine erected for the worship and consultation of a particular deity.

orisha. In African traditional religion and Santeria, spiritual emissaries of Olorun (God) who mediate between the spiritual and material worlds, and who are worshiped and propitiated. (The term can be used as either singular or plural.)

ossuary. A container or receptacle, such as an urn or vault, used for holding the bones of dead persons.

panentheism (process theism). The view that God is related to the world in a way similar to the way in which the human mind is related to the human body; thus the world is part of God, but God is more than the world, and they are dependent on each other.

pantheism. 1. The belief that God and the universe are one and the same thing. 2. The belief that God is somehow diffused throughout the universe as its animating principle.

pantheon. The ensemble of gods associated with a particular religion.

Pentateuch. The first five books of the Hebrew Scriptures.

perdition. Eternal damnation.

phenomenal world. The world of appearances; the world as perceived by human beings.

pluralism, cultural. 1. A condition in which elements of diverse culture coexist within a larger society. 2. The belief that such a state of affairs is good and desirable.

pluralism, religious. 1. The state of affairs in which numerous distinct religious groups are present and tolerated within a society or organization. 2. The belief that such a state of affairs is desirable or beneficial in some way.

polytheism. The belief that more than one god exists. Often these multiple deities are great in number and display limited abilities.

process theism. See *panentheism.*

prolegomena. A preliminary discussion in which foundational issues are discussed before moving on to other matters; prefatory remarks or observations.

propitiate. To procure or regain the favor or goodwill of a person or a deity; to appease or mollify.

propitiation. A conciliatory offering to a god that turns away its wrath against those who somehow offended the deity. In Christian theology, the death of Christ turns away the wrath of God against sin.

Protestant Reformation, the. A movement that emerged in 16th-century Europe as a series of attempts to reform the Roman Catholic Church. It led to the modification or rejection of a number of Roman Catholic doctrines and practices and the establishment of various Protestant church groups.

providence, divine. The care, management, and control exercised by God as he superintends the events of the universe, especially those of human history.

Rabbinical Judaism. The majority position within Judaism, which states that both the written Torah and the traditions of Jewish rabbis are legitimate sources of authority for beliefs and practices. Distinguished from Karaite Judaism, which asserts that only the written Torah possesses religious authority.

Reformation, the. See *Protestant Reformation.*

reincarnation. A process in which the disembodied soul is "reborn" into a body different from the one in which it previously resided.

religious pluralism. See *pluralism, religious.*

ritual. A ceremonial act or series of acts, often done for specific religious purposes.

samsara. The cycle of death and rebirth in Hinduism and Buddhism.

satori. A spiritual awakening sought by practitioners of Zen Buddhism that often occurs suddenly.

schismatic. Someone who advocates or participates in the division of a group, often one connected to a religion.

seer. 1. Someone with the power of clairvoyance. 2. A prophet.

sentient. Having sense perceptions.

shamanism. A set of practices which involve communication between the visible and spirit worlds by intermediaries called shamans.

sovereignty, divine. The supremacy of authority possessed by God as he rules over his creation.

spiritism. The beliefs and practices of people who believe that the dead can communicate with the living by means of certain techniques or protocols.

substitutionary atonement. In Christian theology, a doctrine asserting that Jesus Christ paid the penalty for the sins of his people when he died on the cross, enabling them to be forgiven without God compromising his just and holy character.

sunyata. In Buddhism, the emptiness of all seemingly real things.

Syncretism, religious. Combining or fusing diverse religious beliefs or practices.

talisman. A sacred object, worn on the body, that is believed to confer spiritual powers or protection on its bearer; a magical amulet.

Talmud. The collection of ancient rabbinic writings consisting of the Mishnah and the Gemara and considered authoritative in Orthodox Judaism.

tantra. 1. A Hindu or Buddhist scripture dealing with various ritual acts and techniques, sometimes including sexual practices. 2. The rituals and practices outlined in the tantra.

Tao, the. A ubiquitous force that permeates the cosmos, regulating and upholding the natural order of things. The Tao must be in proper balance to maintain harmony and equilibrium in society.

tawfiq. In Islam, divine favor shown toward one or more of Allah's creatures.

Tawheed. The Oneness of Allah, a central concept in Islam.

theism, classical. Belief that there is one God who created the world and possesses attributes such as omnipotence, omniscience, omnipresence, perfect love, immutability, impassibility, and aseity.

theistic evolution. The belief that God created all living creatures, including human beings, through a lengthy process of biological evolution.

theophany. A visible manifestation of God to human beings, often for the purpose of conveying an important message.

Tirthankara. In Jainism, a human who achieved enlightenment and subsequently became an immortal being.

Torah. 1. The first five books of the Hebrew Scriptures; the Pentateuch. 2. The entire body of Jewish law and commentaries, including both the Hebrew Bible and rabbinic tradition.

transcendent. To be above, beyond, distinct, or independent of the material universe.

Transmigration of the soul. The passage of the soul from one body into another after death.

ubiquitous. The state of being everywhere at the same time; omnipresent.

Unitarianism. The belief that God is one in person and nature.

universalism. The belief that eventually all human beings will be saved from the wrath of God and reconcile with him.

veneration. An act or attitude of great respect, honor, or reverence toward a person or thing; worship. In Roman Catholicism veneration is distinguished from worship, the former involving lesser reverence toward certain exalted creatures (such as the Virgin Mary and departed saints), the latter involving the highest reverence toward God.

venial sin. In Roman Catholicism, a sin that does not meet one or more of the conditions for being a mortal sin. Such a sin results in the perpetrator having to spend time in purgatory in order to pay its penalty.

verbal inspiration. A doctrine that God intended each and every word in the text of Scripture to be precisely what it is, though the biblical authors wrote without any sense of coercion or intrusion on their personality or writing style.

vicarious atonement. See *substitutionary atonement.*

Sources

PART 1. PROLEGOMENA TO WORLD RELIGIONS

Chart 1. What Is Religion?

Berger, Peter. *The Sacred Canopy: Elements of a Sociological Theory of Religion.* 2nd ed. New York: Doubleday, 1990.

Bradley, F. H. *The Collected Works of F. H. Bradley.* Vol. 6. Chicago: University of Chicago Press, 1998.

Clouser, Roy A. *The Myth of Religious Neutrality: An Essay on the Hidden Role of Religious Beliefs in Theories.* Notre Dame, Ind.: University of Notre Dame Press, 1991.

Durkheim, Emile. *The Elementary Forms of the Religious Life.* Reprint ed. New York: Free Press, 1995.

Frazier, James. *The Golden Bough.* Abridged, Reprint ed. New York: Penguin Classics, 1998.

Hick, John. *An Interpretation of Religion: Human Responses to the Transcendent.* New York: Palgrave Macmillan, 2004.

Livingston, James C. *Anatomy of the Sacred: An Introduction to Religion.* New York: Macmillan, 1989.

Martineau, James. *The Study of Religion: Its Sources and Contents.* Part One. Reprint ed. Whitefish, Mont.: Kessinger, 2003.

Otto, Rudolf. *The Idea of the Holy: An Inquiry into the Non-Rational Factor in the Idea of the Divine and Its Relation to the Rational.* Reprint ed. New York: Oxford University Press, 1976.

Robertson, Roland. *The Sociological Interpretation of Religion.* Oxford: Blackwell, 1972.

Schleiermacher, Friedrich. *On Religion: Speeches to Its Cultured Despisers.* Reprint ed. Cambridge: Cambridge University Press, 1996.

Smart, Ninian. *The Religious Experience.* 5th ed. Upper Saddle River, N.J.: Prentice Hall, 1996.

Tiele, Cornelius P. *Elements of the Science of Religion.* Reprint ed. New York: AMS, 1979.

Tillich, Paul. *The Dynamics of Faith.* New York: Harper, 1985.

Yinger, J. Milton. *Religion, Society and the Individual.* New York: Macmillan, 1965.

Chart 2. Four Functional Modes of Religion

Bishop, Peter D., and Michael Darnton, eds. "The Nature of Religion." In *The Encyclopedia of World Faiths: An Illustrated Survey of the World's Living Religions.* New York: Facts on File, 1988, 13.

Chart 3. Three Basic Views on Faith and Reason

Gellman, Jerome I. *The Experience of God and the Rationality of Theistic Belief.* Ithaca, N.Y.: Cornell University Press, 1997.

Helm, Paul, ed. *Faith and Reason.* New York: Oxford University Press, 1999.

Chart 4. Terms Relating to Religion

Geivett, R. Douglas, and Gary R. Habermas, eds. *In Defense of Miracles: A Comprehensive Case for God's Actions in History.* Downers Grove, Ill.: InterVarsity, 1997.

Yandell, Keith E. *The Epistemology of Religious Experience.* Cambridge: Cambridge University Press, 1995.

Chart 5. Six Dimensions of Religion

Bishop, Peter D., and Michael Darnton, eds. "The Nature of Religion." In *The Encyclopedia of World Faiths: An Illustrated Survey of the World's Living Religions.* New York: Facts on File, 1988, 7.

Chart 6. Do All Religions Lead to God?

Netland, Harold A. *Encountering Religious Pluralism: The Challenge to Christian Faith and Mission.* Downers Grove, Ill.: InterVarsity, 2001.

Zacharias, Ravi. *Jesus Among Other Gods: The Absolute Claims of the Christian Message.* Nashville: Thomas Nelson, 2000.

Chart 7. Comparison of Foundational Religious Worldviews

Geisler, Norman L., and William D. Watkins. *Worlds Apart: A Handbook on World Views.* 2nd ed. Eugene, Ore.: Wipf and Stock, 2003.

Sire, James W. *The Universe Next Door: A Basic Worldview Catalog.* Downers Grove, Ill.: InterVarsity, 1997.

PART 2. COMPARISON OF WORLD RELIGIONS

Chart 8. Major World Religions in Order of Founding

Smith, Huston. *The Illustrated World's Religions: A Guide to Our Wisdom Traditions.* San Francisco: Harper San Francisco, 1995.

Chart 9. Comparison of Beliefs Among Religions

Corduan, Winfried. *Neighboring Faiths: A Christian Introduction to World Religions.* Downers Grove, Ill.: InterVarsity, 1998.

Breuilly, Elizabeth, Joanne O'Brien, Martin E. Marty, and Martin Palmer, eds. *Religions of the World: The Illustrated Guide to Origins, Beliefs, Traditions, and Festivals.* New York: Facts on File, 1997.

Chart 10. Holy Books of World Religions

Smart, Ninian. *The World's Religions.* 2nd ed. Cambridge, UK: Cambridge University Press, 1998.

PART 3. ANCIENT MEDITERRANEAN RELIGIONS

Chart 11. Religions of the Ancient Mediterranean World

Beaver, R. Pierce, ed. *Eerdmans' Handbook to the World's Religions.* Grand Rapids, Mich.: Eerdmans, 1994.

Bottero, Jean. *Religion in Ancient Mesopotamia.* Chicago: University of Chicago Press, 2004.

Chart 12. Ancient Near Eastern Deities (Excluding Egypt)

Black, Jeremy A., and Anthony Green. *Gods, Demons and Symbols of Ancient Mesopotamia: An Illustrated Dictionary.* Austin, Texas: University of Texas Press, 1992.

Turner, Patricia, and Charles Russell Coulter. *Dictionary of Ancient Deities.* New York: Oxford University Press, 2001.

Chart 13. Egyptian Paganism

Budge, Ernest Alfred Thompson Wallis. *The Dwellers on the Nile: The Life, History, Religion, and Literature of the Ancient Egyptians.* New York: Dover, 1977.

Frankfort, Henri. *Ancient Egyptian Religion: An Interpretation.* Reprint ed. Mineola, N.Y.: Dover, 2000.

Morenz, Siegfried. *Egyptian Religion.* Ithaca, N.Y.: Cornell University Press, 1992.

Shaw, Ian, ed. *The Oxford History of Ancient Egypt.* Rev. ed. New York: Oxford University Press, 2002.

Taylor, John H. *Death and the Afterlife in Ancient Egypt.* Chicago: University of Chicago Press, 2001.

Chart 14. Gods of the Egyptian Pantheon

Hart, George. *The Routledge Dictionary of Egyptian Gods and Goddesses.* 2nd ed. New York: Routledge, 2005.

Wilkinson, Richard H. *The Complete Gods and Goddesses of Ancient Egypt.* New York: Thames & Hudson, 2003.

Chart 15. Greek Paganism

Burkert, Walter. *Greek Religion.* Reprint ed. Cambridge, Mass.: Harvard University Press, 1987.

Easterling P. E., and J. V. Muir, eds. *Greek Religion and Society.* Cambridge: Cambridge University Press, 1985.

Mikalson, Jon D. *Ancient Greek Religion.* Oxford: Blackwell, 2004.

Price, Simon. *Religions of the Ancient Greeks.* Cambridge: Cambridge University Press, 1999.

Chart 16. Roman Paganism

Ando, Clifford. *Roman Religion.* Edinburgh: Edinburgh University Press, 2004.

Forman, Margaret, and Werner Lyttelton. *The Romans: Their Gods and Their Beliefs.* New York: Harper Collins, 1985.

Scheid, John. *An Introduction to Roman Religion.* Bloomington, Ind.: Indiana University Press, 2003.

Turcan, Robert. *The Gods of Ancient Rome: Religion in Everyday Life from Archaic to Imperial Times.* New York: Routledge, 2001.

Chart 17. Graeco-Roman Deities

Adkins, Leslie and Roy A. *Dictionary of Roman Religion*. New York: Oxford University Press, 2001.

Houtzager, Guus. *The Complete Encyclopedia of Greek Mythology*. Lisse, Netherlands: Rebo, 2003.

Price, Simon, and Emily Kearns, eds. *Oxford Dictionary of Classical Myth and Religion*. New York: Oxford University Press, 2003.

PART 4. WESTERN RELIGIONS

Chart 18. Historical Relationships of Western Religions

Loftin, John D. *The Big Picture: A Short World History of Religions*. Jefferson, N.C.: McFarland & Co., 1999.

Noss, David S. *A History of the World's Religions*. 11th ed. Upper Saddle River, N.J.: Prentice-Hall, 2002.

Chart 19. Comparison of Western Religions

Fisher, Mary Pat. *Living Religions: Western Traditions*. Upper Saddle River, N.J.: Pearson, 2003.

Oxtoby, Willard Gurdon. *World Religions: Western Traditions*. New York: Oxford University Press, 1996.

JUDAISM

Chart 20. Timeline of Judaism

Davies, W. D., Louis Finkelstein, William Horbury, and John Sturdy, eds. *The Cambridge History of Judaism*. Vols. 1–3. Cambridge: Cambridge University Press, 2000.

Chart 21. Judaism

Baeck, Leo. *The Essence of Judaism*. Rev. ed. New York: Schocken, 1987.

Bamberger, Bernard J. *The Story of Judaism*. 3rd ed. New York: Schocken, 1971.

De Lange, Nicholas. *An Introduction to Judaism*. Cambridge: Cambridge University Press, 2000.

Neusner, Jacob. *The Way of Torah: An Introduction to Judaism*. 7th ed. Belmont, Calif.: Wadsworth, 2003.

"Judaism 101." *www.jewfaq.org*.

Chart 22. Comparison of Beliefs within Judaism

Raphael, Marc Lee. *Profiles in American Judaism: The Reform, Conservative, Orthodox, and Reconstructionist Traditions in Historical Perspective*. New York: Harper & Row, 1984.

Rosenthal, Gilbert S. *The Many Faces of Judaism: Orthodox, Conservative, Reconstructionist and Reform*. New York: Behrman, 1979.

Sonsino, Rifat, and Daniel B. Syme. *What Happens After I Die?: Jewish Views of Life After Death*. New York: United American Hebrew Congregations, 1990.

Chart 23. Orthodox Judaism

Freundel, Barry. *Contemporary Orthodox Judaism's Response to Modernity*. Jersey City, N.J.: Ktav, 2003.

Heschel, Abraham Joshua. *God in Search of Man: A Philosophy of Judaism,* Reprint ed. New York: Farrar, Straus & Giroux, 1997.

Sarna, Jonathan. *American Judaism: A History*. New Haven, Conn.: Yale University Press, 2004.

Schlossberg, Eli W. *The World of Orthodox Judaism*. Northvale, N.J.: Jason Aronson, 1997.

Wouk, Herman. *This Is My God*. Reprint ed. New York: Back Bay, 1992.

"Eliezer Segal's Home Page." *www.ucalgary.ca/~elsegal*.

Chart 24. Conservative Judaism

Dorff, Elliot N. *Conservative Judaism: From Our Ancestors to Our Descendants*. Rev. ed. New York: United Synagogue of Conservative Judaism, 1996.

Gordis, Robert, and Max Gelb. *Understanding Conservative Judaism*. Jersey City, N.J.: Ktav, 1979.

Nadell, Pamela S. *Conservative Judaism in America: A Biographical Dictionary and Sourcebook*. Westport, Conn.: Greenwood, 1988.

Sklare, Marshall. *Conservative Judaism: An American Religious Movement.* Reprint ed. Lanham, Md.: University Press of America, 1985.

"Jewish Virtual Library." *www.us-israel.org/jsource/Judaism/conservatives.html.*

Chart 25. Reform Judaism

Borowitz, Eugene B., and Naomi Patz. *Explaining Reform Judaism.* Springfield, N.J.: Behrman House, 1985.

Kaplan, Dana Evan. *American Reform Judaism: An Introduction.* New Brunswick, N.J.: Rutgers University Press, 2003.

Kohler, Kaufmann, Emil G. Hirsch, and David Philipson. "Reform Judaism from the Point of View of the Reform Jew." Online *Jewish Encyclopedia. www.jewishencyclopedia.com/view.jsp?artid=170&letter=R#470.*

Meyer, Michael A. *Response to Modernity: A History of the Reform Movement in Judaism.* Detroit: Wayne State University Press, 1995.

Syme, Daniel B. *An Overview of Reform Judaism.* New York: Union of American Hebrew Congregations, 1983.

Chart 26. Hasidic Judaism

Boteach, Shmuel. *Wisdom, Understanding, and Knowledge: Basic Concepts of Hasidic Thought.* Northvale, N.J.: Jason Aronson, 1995.

Buber, Martin. *The Way of Man According to the Teaching of Hasidism.* Reprint ed. New York: Citadel, 1995.

Dan, Joseph. *The Teachings of Hasidism.* Springfield, N.J.: Behrman House, 1996.

Rabinowicz, Tzvi M. *The World of Hasidism.* Portland, Ore.: Vallentine-Mitchell, 1970.

Schneersohn, Shalom Dovber, and Eliyahu Touger. *To Know G-D.* New York: Merkos Linyonei Chinuch, 1998.

"Breslov Research Institute." *www.breslov.org.*

Chart 27. Jewish Scriptures According to Rabbinic Tradition

Bruce, F. F. *The Canon of Scripture.* Downers Grove, Ill.: InterVarsity, 1988.

Chart 28. Jewish Holy Days

Meron, Michal. *The Jewish Festivals and Holy Days.* Hewlett, N.Y.: Gefen, 1996.

Chart 29. The Jewish Calendar

Brand, Chad, Trent C. Butler, Charles Draper, and Archie England, eds. *Holman Illustrated Bible Dictionary.* Nashville: Broadman & Holman, 2003.

Chart 30. The Jewish Covenants

Price, Randall. *Islam and Israel.* Salem, Ore.: Earl Radmacher Lectureship, 2003.

CHRISTIANITY

Chart 31. Timeline of Christianity

Curtis, A. Kenneth, J. Stephen Lang, and Randy Petersen. *The 100 Most Important Events in Christian History.* Grand Rapids, Mich.: Revell, 1998.

Gonzales, Justo L. *The Story of Christianity: Reformation to the Present Day.* San Francisco: Harper San Francisco, 1985.

"African Christianity: A History of the Christian Church in Africa." *www.bethel.edu/~letnie/AfricanChristianity/index.html.*

Kim, Andrew E. "History of Christianity in Korea: From Its Troubled Beginning to Its Contemporary Success." *www.kimsoft.com/1997/xhist.htm.*

"Underground Church in China." *www.worldserveusa.org/christmas/underground.*

Chart 32. Christianity

Erickson, Millard J. *Introducing Christian Doctrine.* 2nd ed. Grand Rapids, Mich.: Baker Academic, 2001.

Leith, John Haddon. *Basic Christian Doctrine.* Louisville, Ky.: Westminster John Knox, 1993.

McGrath, Alister E. *Christian Theology: An Introduction.* 3rd ed. Oxford: Blackwell, 2001.

McManners, John. *Oxford Illustrated History of Christianity.* New York: Oxford University Press, 1990.

Chart 33. Comparison of Beliefs within Christianity

Badham, Roger A., ed. *Introduction to Christian Theology: Contemporary North American Perspectives*. Louisville, Ky.: Westminster John Knox, 1998.

Lacoste, Jean-Yves, ed. *Encyclopedia of Christian Theology*. New York: Routledge, 2004.

McGrath, Alister E., ed. *The Blackwell Encyclopedia of Modern Christian Thought*. Reprint ed. Oxford: Blackwell, 1995.

Smith, David L. *A Handbook of Contemporary Theology: Tracing Trends and Discerning Directions in Today's Theological Landscape*. Grand Rapids, Mich.: Baker Academic, 2000.

Chart 34. Roman Catholicism

Burns, Robert A. *Roman Catholicism after Vatican II*. Washington, D.C.: Georgetown University Press, 2001.

———. *Roman Catholicism Yesterday and Today*. Chicago: Loyola University Press, 1992.

Catechism of the Catholic Church. New York: Bantam-Dell, 1995.

Crocker III, H. W. *Triumph—The Power and the Glory of the Catholic Church: A 2,000-Year History*. New York: Prima, 2001.

Cunningham, Lawrence S. *The Catholic Faith: An Introduction*. Mahway, N.J.: Paulist, 1986.

Stravinskas, Peter M. J., ed. *Our Sunday Visitor's Catholic Encyclopedia*. Rev. ed. Huntington, Ind.: Our Sunday Visitor, 1998.

Chart 35. Eastern Orthodoxy

Binns, John. *An Introduction to the Christian Orthodox Churches*. Cambridge: Cambridge University Press, 2002.

Lossky, Vladimir. *Orthodox Theology: An Introduction*. Crestwood, N.Y.: St. Vladimir's Seminary Press, 1997.

Neale, John Mason. *A History of the Holy Eastern Church: The Patriarchate of Antioch*. Reprint ed. Piscataway, N.J.: Gorgias, 2003.

Pelikan, Jaroslav. *The Spirit of Eastern Christendom*. Chicago: University of Chicago Press, 1977.

Ware, Kallistos. *The Orthodox Way*. Rev. ed. Crestwood, N.Y.: St. Vladimir's Seminary Press, 1995.

Chart 36. Liberal Protestantism

Dorrien, Gary J. *The Making of American Liberal Theology: Idealism, Realism, and Modernity, 1900–1950*. Louisville, Ky.: Westminster John Knox, 2003.

Hutchinson, William R., ed. *American Protestant Thought in the Liberal Era*. Lanham, Md.: University Press of America, 1984.

Reardon, Bernard M. G. *Liberal Protestantism*. Stanford, Calif.: Stanford University Press, 1968.

Roof, Wade Clark, and William McKinney. *American Mainline Religion: Its Changing Shape and Future*. New Brunswick, N.J.: Rutgers University Press, 1987.

Spong, John Shelby. *A New Christianity for a New World: Why Traditional Faith Is Dying and How a New Faith Is Being Born*. San Francisco: Harper San Francisco, 2002.

Diamond, Etan, Kevin Mickey, and David J. Bodenhamer. "The Decline of Mainline Protestantism." Electronic Cultural Atlas Initiative's Polis Center. *www.ecai.org/nara/nara_article.html*.

Chart 37. Evangelical Protestantism

Balmer, Randall. *Blessed Assurance: A History of Evangelicalism in America*. Boston: Beacon, 1999.

Bebbington, David W. *The Dominance of Evangelicalism: The Age of Spurgeon and Moody*. Downers Grove, Ill.: InterVarsity, 2005.

Kantzer, Kenneth S., and Carl F. H. Henry. *Evangelical Affirmations*. Grand Rapids, Mich.: Zondervan, 1990.

Noll, Mark A. *American Evangelical Christianity: An Introduction*. Oxford: Blackwell, 2000.

———. *The Rise of Evangelicalism: The Age of Edwards, Whitefield, and the Wesleys*. Downers Grove, Ill.: InterVarsity, 2004.

Ross, Hugh, Mark Van Bebber, and Paul S. Taylor. *Creation and Time: A Report on the Progressive Creationist Book*. 2nd ed. Gilbert, Ariz.: Eden, 1996.

"Institute for the Study of American Evangelicals." *www.wheaton.edu/isae*.

Chart 38. Fundamentalist Protestantism

Couch, Mal, ed. *The Fundamentals for the Twenty-First Century: Examining the Crucial Issues of the Christian Faith*. Grand Rapids, Mich.: Kregel, 2000.

Marsden, George M. *Fundamentalism and American Culture: The Shaping of Twentieth-Century Evangelicalism, 1870-1925.* New York: Oxford University Press, 1980.

Melling, Philip H. *Fundamentalism in America.* Edinburgh: Edinburgh University Press, 2001.

Torrey, R. A., and Charles L. Feinberg, eds. *The Fundamentals: The Famous Sourcebook of Foundational Biblical Truths.* Rev. ed. Grand Rapids, Mich.: Kregel, 1990.

"Institute for the Study of American Evangelicals." *www.wheaton.edu/isae.*

Chart 39. Pentecostal-Charismatic Protestantism

Anderson, Allan. *An Introduction to Pentecostalism: Global Charismatic Christianity.* Cambridge: Cambridge University Press, 2004.

Anderson, Robert Mapes. *Vision of the Disinherited: The Making of American Pentecostalism.* New York: Oxford University Press, 1979.

Arrington, French L. *Christian Doctrine, Volume 3: A Pentecostal Perspective.* Cleveland, Tenn.: Pathway, 1994.

Burgess, Stanley M., and Eduard M. Van der Maas, eds. *The New International Dictionary of Pentecostal and Charismatic Movements.* Rev. ed. Grand Rapids, Mich.: Zondervan, 2002.

Synan, Vinson. *The Holiness-Pentecostal Tradition: Charismatic Movements in the Twentieth Century.* 2nd ed. Grand Rapids, Mich.: Eerdmans, 1997.

Williams, J. Rodman. *Renewal Theology.* 3 vols. Grand Rapids, Mich.: Zondervan, 1988–92.

"Lewis Wilson Institute for Pentecostal Studies." *www.vanguard.edu/wilsoninstitute/index.aspx.*

Chart 40. Christian Creeds and Councils

Hoezee, Scott. *Speaking As One: A Look at the Ecumenical Creeds.* Grand Rapids, Mich.: Faith Alive Christian Resources, 1997.

"Church History." *www.goarch.org/en/ourfaith/history.*

"Historic Church Documents." *www.reformed.org/documents.*

Chart 41. Christian Holy Days

Self, David. *High Days and Holidays: Celebrating the Christian Year.* Oxford: Lion, 1993.

"Catholic Encyclopedia." *www.newadvent.org/cathen.*

Chart 42. Christian Scriptures

New American Standard Bible. Anaheim, Calif.: Foundation, 2001.

ISLAM

Chart 43. Timeline of Islam

Lewis, Bernard. *Islam in History: Ideas, People, and Events in the Middle East.* Rev. ed. Chicago: Open Court, 2001.

Rahman, H. U. *A Chronology of Islamic History, 570–1000 C.E.* London: Ta-Ha, 1995.

"A Brief Chronology of Muslim History." *www.usc.edu/dept/MSA/history/chronology.*

Chart 44. Islam

Bowker, John Westerdale. *What Muslims Believe.* Oxford: Oneworld, 1999.

Esposito, John L., ed. *The Oxford History of Islam.* New York: Oxford University Press, 2000.

Lewis, Bernard, ed. *The World of Islam: Faith, People, Culture.* New York: Thames & Hudson, 1991.

Rippin, Andrew. *Muslims: Their Religious Beliefs and Practices,* 2nd ed. London: Routledge, 2001.

Halsall, Paul. "Islamic History Sourcebook." *www.fordham.edu/halsall/islam/islamsbook.html.*

Chart 45. Comparison of Beliefs within Islam

Bosworth, C. E., ed. *The Encyclopedia of Islam.* New York: Brill, 2004.

Kabbani, Muhammad Hisham. *Encyclopedia of Islamic Doctrine: Beliefs.* Vol. 1. Chicago: Kazi, 1998.

Nigosian, S. A. *Islam: Its History, Teaching, and Practices*. Bloomington, Ind.: Indiana University Press, 2004.

Chart 46. Sunni Islam

Endress, Gerhard. *An Introduction to Islam*. New York: Columbia University Press, 1988.

Robinson, Neal. *Islam: A Concise Introduction*. Washington, D.C.: Georgetown University Press, 1999.

Waines, David. *An Introduction to Islam*. 2nd ed. Cambridge: Cambridge University Press, 2003.

Watt, William Montgomery. *Islam: A Short History*. Oxford: Oneworld, 1999.

"Dar es Salaam Tabligh." *www.dartabligh.org*.

Chart 47. Shi'ite Islam

Al-Tabatabai, Muhammed H. *Shi'ite Islam*. 2nd ed. Albany: State University of New York Press, 1979.

Halm, Heinz. *Shi'ism*. 2nd ed. New York: Columbia University Press, 2004.

Momen, Moojan. *An Introduction to Shi'i Islam: The History and Doctrines of Twelver Shi'ism*. New Haven, Conn.: Yale University Press, 1987.

Sachedina, Abdulaziz Abdulhussein. *The Just Ruler. Al-Sultan Al-Adil in Shi'ite Islam: The Comprehensive Authority of the Jurist in Imamite Jurisprudence*. New York: Oxford University Press, 1998.

Sobhani, Ayatollah Ja'far. *Doctrines of Shi'i Islam: A Compendium of Imami Beliefs and Practices*. London: I. B. Tauris and The Institute of Ismaili Studies, 2001.

Chart 48. Sufi Islam

Arberry, Arthur John. *The Doctrine of the Sufis*. Cambridge: Cambridge University Press, 1977.

Baldick, Julian. *Mystical Islam: An Introduction to Sufism*. New York: New York University Press, 1989.

Chittick, William C. *Sufism: A Short Introduction*. Oxford: Oneworld, 2000.

Schimmel, Annemarie. *Mystical Dimensions of Islam*. Raleigh, N.C.: University of North Carolina Press, 1975.

Sonn, Tamara. *A Brief History of Islam*. Oxford: Blackwell, 2004.

Godlas, Alan. "Sufism's Many Paths." *www.uga.edu/islam/Sufism.html*.

Chart 49. Nation of Islam

Decaro, Louis A. *Malcolm and the Cross: The Nation of Islam, Malcolm X, and Christianity*. New York: New York University Press, 1998.

Gardell, Mattias. *In the Name of Elijah Muhammad: Louis Farrakhan and the Nation of Islam*. Durham, N.C.: Duke University Press, 1996.

Lincoln, C. Eric. *The Black Muslims in America*. 3rd ed. Grand Rapids, Mich.: Eerdmans, 1994.

Malcolm X and Alex Haley. *The Autobiography of Malcolm X*. New York: Ballantine, 1992.

Marsh, Clifton. *The Lost-Found Nation of Islam in America*. Blue Ridge Summit, Penn.: Scarecrow, 2000.

Chart 50. Islamic Calendar and Holy Days

Gulevich, Tanya. *Understanding Islam and Muslim Traditions: An Introduction to the Religious Practices, Celebrations, Festivals, Observances, Beliefs, Folklore, Customs, and Calendar System of the World's Muslim Communities, Including an Overview of Islamic History and Geography*. Detroit: Omnigraphics, 2004.

BAHA'I

Chart 51. Timeline of Baha'i

Smith, Peter. *The Baha'i Faith: A Short History*. Oxford: Oneworld, 1999.

"The Baha'i World." *www.bahai.org*.

Chart 52. Baha'i

Cole, Juan R. I. *Modernity and the Millennium: The Genesis of the Baha'i Faith in the Nineteenth-Century Middle East*. New York: Columbia University Press, 1998.

Esslemont, J. E. *Baha'u'llah and the New Era: An Introduction to the Baha'i Faith.* 5th ed. Wilmette, Ill.: Baha'i Publishing Trust, 1980.

Hatcher, William S., and J. Douglas Martin. *The Baha'i Faith: The Emerging Global Religion.* San Francisco: Harper & Row, 1985.

Momen, Moojan. *The Baha'i Faith: A Short Introduction.* Oxford: Oneworld, 1999.

SECULAR HUMANISM

Chart 53. Timeline of Secular Humanism

Jacoby, Susan. *Freethinkers: A History of American Secularism.* New York: Metropolitan Books, 2004.

Chart 54. Secular Humanism

Flew, Antony. *Atheistic Humanism.* Amherst, N.Y.: Prometheus, 1993.

Jacoby, Susan. *Freethinkers: A History of American Secularism.* New York: Metropolitan Books, 2004.

Kurtz, Paul. *In Defense of Secular Humanism.* Amherst, N.Y.: Prometheus, 1983.

Lamont, Corliss. *The Philosophy of Humanism.* Amherst, N.Y.: Humanist Press, 1997.

Norman, Richard. *On Humanism.* New York: Routledge, 2004.

Radest, Howard B. *The Devil and Secular Humanism: The Children of the Enlightenment.* Westport, Conn.: Praeger, 1990.

Vaughn, Lewis. *The Case for Humanism: An Introduction.* Lanham, Md.: Rowman & Littlefield, 2003.

PART 5. EASTERN RELIGIONS

Chart 55. Historical Relationships of Eastern Religions

Bowker, John, ed. *The Cambridge Illustrated History of Religions.* Cambridge: Cambridge University Press, 2002.

Kitagawa, Joseph M., ed. *Religious Traditions of Asia: Religion, History, and Culture.* New York: Curzon, 2002.

Chart 56. Comparison of Eastern Religions

Baird, Robert D., and Alfred Bloom. *Religion and Man: Indian and Far Eastern Religious Traditions.* New York: McGraw-Hill, 1998.

Fisher, Mary Pat. *Living Religions: Eastern Traditions.* Upper Saddle River, N.J.: Pearson, 2003.

Oxtoby, Willard Gurdon. *World Religions: Eastern Traditions.* New York: Oxford University Press, 2001.

HINDUISM

Chart 57. Timeline of Hinduism

Metcalf, Barbara D., and Thomas R. Metcalf. *A Concise History of India.* Cambridge: Cambridge University Press, 2001.

Wolpert, Stanley. *A New History of India.* 6th ed. New York: Oxford University Press, 1999.

"A Tribute to Hinduism." *www.atributetohinduism.com.*

Chart 58. Hinduism

Flood, Gavin D. *Introduction to Hinduism.* Cambridge: Cambridge University Press, 1996.

Herman, A. L. *A Brief Introduction to Hinduism: Religion, Philosophy, and Ways of Liberation.* Boulder, Colo.: Westview, 1991.

Klostermaier, Klaus K. *A Short Introduction to Hinduism.* Oxford: Oneworld, 1998.

Knott, Kim. *Hinduism: A Very Short Introduction.* New York: Oxford University Press, 2000.

Shattuck, Cybelle. *Hinduism.* New York: Routledge, 1999.

Chart 59. Comparison of Beliefs within Hinduism

Michaels, Axel. *Hinduism: Past and Present.* Princeton, N.J.: Princeton University Press, 2003.

Narayananm, Vasudha. *Hinduism: Origins, Beliefs, Practices, Holy Texts, Sacred Places.* New York: Oxford Univ. Press, 2004.

O'Flaherty, Wendy P. *Karma and Rebirth in Classical Indian Traditions.* Berkeley: University of California Press, 1980.

Chart 60. Brahmanism

Arya, Raj Narain. *Brahmin and Brahminism: A Historical Survey*. New Delhi, India: Blumoon, 2001.

Basham, A. L., and Kenneth G. Zysk. *The Origins and Development of Classical Hinduism*. New York: Oxford University Press, 1991.

Heesterman, Jan C. "Vedism and Brahmanism." In Lindsay Jones, gen. ed. *Encyclopedia of Religion*. 2nd ed. Vol. 14. Farmington Hills, Mich.: Thomson-Gale, 2005.

Myers, Michael Warren. *Brahman: A Comparative Theology*. New York: Curzon, 2001.

Chart 61. Advaita Vedanta

Deutsch, Eliot. *Advaita Vedanta: A Philosophical Reconstruction*. Honolulu: University of Hawaii Press, 1980.

Potter, Karl H., Austin B. Creel, and Edwin Gerow. *Guide to Indian Philosophy*. Boston: G. K. Hall, 1988.

Ram-Prasad, Chakravarthi. *Advaita Epistemology and Metaphysics: An Outline of Indian Non-Realism*. New York: Curzon, 2003.

Satchidanandendra, Swami. *The Method of the Vedanta: A Critical Account of the Advaita Tradition*. New York: Columbia University Press, 1990.

Chart 62. Bhakti

Anand, Subhash. *The Way of Love: The Bhagavata Doctrine of Bhakti*. Columbia, Mo.: South Asia Books, 1996.

Bhattacharya, B. *Bhakti: The Religion of Love*. Kolkata, India: UBS, 2003.

Eck, Diana L., and Francoise Mallison, eds. *Devotion Divine: Bhakti Traditions from the Regions of India*. Groningen, The Netherlands: University of Groningen Press, 1991.

Werner, Karel, ed. *Love Divine: Studies in Bhakti and Devotional Mysticism*. New York: Curzon, 1993.

Chart 63. Self-Realization Fellowship, Appendix on Transcendental Meditation

Ghosh, Sananda Lal. *Mejda: The Family and the Early Life of Paramahansa Yogananda*. Los Angeles: Self-Realization Fellowship, 1980.

Russell, Peter. *The TM Technique: An Introduction to Transcendental Meditation and the Teachings of Maharishi Mahesh Yogi*. New York: Penguin, 1990.

Walters, J. Donald. *Essence of Self-Realization: The Wisdom of Paramahansa Yogananda*. Nevada City, Calif.: Crystal Clarity, 1990.

Yogananda, Paramahansa. *Journey into Self-Realization: Discovering the Gifts of the Soul*. Los Angeles: Self-Realization Fellowship, 1997.

Yogi, Maharishi Mahesh. *Science of Being and Art of Living: Transcendental Meditation*. Rev. ed. Fairfield, Iowa: Maharishi University Press, 2001.

Yukteswar, Swami Sri. *The Holy Science*. Los Angeles: Self-Realization Fellowship, 1984.

Chart 64. Ananda Marga Yoga Society

Acarya, Avadhutika Ananda Mitra. *The Spiritual Philosophy of Shrii Shrii Anandamurti*. Calcutta: Ananda Marga Publications, 2002.

Anandamurti, Shrii Shrii. *Discourses on Tanta*. Calcutta: Ananda Marga Publications, 1993.

Avadhuta, Acarya Vedaprajinananda. *The Wisdom of Yoga*. Calcutta: Ananda Marga Publications, 1990.

Sarkar, Prabhat Rainjan. *Yoga Psychology*. Calcutta: Ananda Marga Publications, 1990.

"Ananda Marga Yoga Society." *http://religiousmovements.lib.virginia.edu/nrms/anan.html*.

Chart 65. Hare Krishna

Barker, Eileen. *Of Gods and Men: New Religious Movements in the West*. Macon, Ga.: Mercer University Press, 1983.

Bryand, Edwin F., and Maria L. Ekstrand. *The Hare Krishna Movement: The Postcharismatic Fate of a Religious Transplant*. New York: Columbia University Press, 2004.

Miller, Timothy. *America's Alternative Religions*. Albany: State University of New York Press, 1995.

Prabhupada, Swami. *The Science of Self-Realization*. Los Angeles: Bhaktivedanta Book Trust, 1994.

Rochford, E. Burke. *Hare Krishna in America*. New Brunswick, N.J.: Rutgers University Press, 1985.

Chart 66. Timeline of Buddhism

Skilton, Andrew. *A Concise History of Buddhism*. Birmingham, U.K.: Windhorse, 1997.

"Timeline of Buddhist History." *www.simhas.org/timeline.html*.

"Timelines of Buddhist History." *www.buddhanet.net/e-learning/history/b_chron-txt.htm*.

Chart 67. Buddhism

Berry, Thomas. *Buddhism*. New York: Columbia University Press, 1989.

Conze, Edward. *Buddhism: A Short History*. Oxford: Oneworld, 2000.

Gethin, Rupert. *The Foundations of Buddhism*. New York: Oxford University Press, 1998.

Gombrich, Richard Francis. *How Buddhism Began: The Conditioned Genesis of the Early Teachings*. London: Athlone, 1996.

Harvey, Peter. *An Introduction to Buddhism: Teachings, History and Practices*. Cambridge: Cambridge University Press, 1990.

Keown, Damien. *Buddhism: A Very Short Introduction*. New York: Oxford University Press, 2000.

Chart 68. Comparison of Beliefs within Buddhism

Buswell, Robert E. *Encyclopedia of Buddhism*. New York: Macmillan, 2004.

Olson, Carl. *The Different Paths of Buddhism: A Narrative-Historical Introduction*. New Brunswick, N.J.: Rutgers University Press, 2005.

Robinson, Richard H., Willard L. Johnson, and Thanissaro Bhikkhu. *Buddhist Religions: A Historical Introduction*. 5th ed. Belmont, Calif.: Wadsworth, 2004.

Chart 69. Mahayana Buddhism, Appendix on Pure Land Buddhism

Asvaghosa. *The Awakening of Faith: The Classic Exposition of Mahayana Buddhism*. Reprint ed. Mineola, N.Y.: Dover, 2003.

Blum, Mark L. *The Origins and Development of Pure Land Buddhism*. New York: Oxford University Press, 2002.

Gyatso, Geshe Kelsang. *The Bodhisattva Vow: The Essential Practices of Mahayana Buddhism*. 2nd ed. Glen Spey, N.Y.: Tharpa, 1995.

Suzuki, Daisetz Teitaro. *Outlines of Mahayana Buddhism*. Reprint ed. New Delhi, India: Munshiram Manoharlal, 2000.

Williams, Paul. *Mahayana Buddhism: The Doctrinal Foundations*. 2nd ed. New York: Routledge, 2005.

Chart 70. Theravada Buddhism

Collins, Steven. *Selfless Persons: Imagery and Thought in Theravada Buddhism*. Cambridge: Cambridge University Press, 1990.

Van Gorkom, Nina. *The Buddha's Path: An Introduction to Theravada Buddhism*. Essex, U.K.: Triple Gem, 1995.

Williams, Paul, and Anthony Tribe. *Buddhist Thought: A Complete Introduction to the Indian Tradition*. New York: Routledge, 2000.

"Readings in Theravada Buddhism." *www.accesstoinsight.org*.

Chart 71. Vajrayana Buddhism

Gyatso, Geshe Kelsang. *Essence of Vajrayana: The Highest Yoga Tantra Practice of Heruka Body Mandala*. Glen Spey, N.Y.: Tharpa, 1997.

Gyatso, Tenzin. *The Way to Freedom: Core Teachings of Tibetan Buddhism*. San Francisco: Harper San Francisco, 1994.

Novick, Rebecca McClen. *Fundamentals of Tibetan Buddhism*. Freedom, Calif.: Crossing, 1999.

Powers, John. *Introduction to Tibetan Buddhism*. Ithaca, N.Y.: Snow Lion, 1995.

Chart 72. Zen Buddhism

Dumoulin, Heinrich. *Zen Buddhism: A History*. Reprint ed. New York: Macmillan, 1994.

Kapleua, Roshi Philip. *The Three Pillars of Zen: Teaching, Practice, and Enlightenment*. Rev. ed. Boston: Beacon, 1993.

Radcliff, Benjamin, and Amy Radcliff. *Understanding Zen*. Boston: Charles E. Tuttle, 1993.

Suzuki, Daisetz Teitaro. *An Introduction to Zen Buddhism*. Santa Barbara, Calif.: Grove, 1991.

Chart 73. Nichiren Shoshu Buddhism

Causton, Richard. *Nichiren Shoshu Buddhism*. New York: Harper Collins, 1989.

Hurst, Jane D. *Nichiren Shoshu Buddhism and the Soka Gakkai in America: The Ethos of a New Religious Movement*. New York: Garland, 1992.

Ikeda, Daisaku. *Unlocking the Mysteries of Birth and Death … and Everything in Between: A Buddhist View of Life*. 2nd ed. Santa Monica, Calif.: Middleway, 2004.

Kirimura, Yasuji. *Buddhism and the Nichiren Shoshu Tradition*. Tokyo: Nichiren Shoshu International Center, 1986.

Snow, David A. *Shakubuku: A Study of the Nichiren Shoshu Buddhist Movement in America*. New York: Garland, 1993.

TAOISM

Chart 74. Timeline of Taoism

Yu, David C. *History of Chinese Daoism*. Vol. 1. Lanham, Md.: University Press of America, 2000.

Kirkland, Russell. "The Taoist Tradition: A Historical Outline." *www.arches.uga.edu/~kirkland/rk/pdf/guides/TMGID.pdf*.

Chart 75. Taoism, Appendix on Religious Taoism

Kirkland, Russell. *Taoism: The Enduring Tradition*. New York: Routledge, 2004.

Kohn, Livia. *Daoism and Chinese Culture*. Cambridge, Mass.: Three Pines, 2001.

Maspero, Henri. *Taoism and Chinese Religion*. Amherst, Mass.: University of Massachusetts Press, 1981.

Oldstone-Moore, Jennifer. *Taoism: Origins, Beliefs, Practices, Holy Texts, Sacred Places*. New York: Oxford University Press, 2003.

Robinet, Isabelle. *Taoism: Growth of a Religion*. Stanford, Calif.: Stanford University Press, 1997.

Hansen, Chad. "The Metaphysics of Tao." *www.hku.hk/philodep/ch/Metaphysics%20of%20Dao%20doc.htm*.

JAINISM

Chart 76. Timeline of Jainism

Chatterjee, Asim Kumar. *Comprehensive History of Jainism*. 2nd ed. 2 vols. New Delhi: Munshiram Manoharlal, 2000.

"An Outline of Jain History." *http://www.cs.colostate.edu/~malaiya/jainhout1.html*.

Chart 77. Jainism

Chapple, Christopher Key. *Jainism and Ecology: Nonviolence in the Web of Life*. Cambridge, Mass.: Harvard University Press, 2002.

Dundas, Paul. *The Jains*. New York: Routledge, 2002.

Jaini, Padmanabh S. *The Jaina Path of Purification*. Berkeley, Calif.: University of California Press, 1979.

Shah, Natubhai. *Jainism: The World of Conquerors*. Brighton, UK: Sussex Academic Press, 1998.

Sharma, V. K. *History of Jainism*. New Delhi: D. K. Print World, 2002.

ZOROASTRIANISM

Chart 78. Timeline of Zoroastrianism

Boyce, Mary. *A History of Zoroastrianism*. New York: Brill, 1991.

"Zoroastrian Archives." *www.avesta.org*.

Chart 79. Zoroastrianism

Boyce, Mary. *Zoroastrians: Their Religious Beliefs and Practices*. New York: Routledge, 2001.

Clark, Peter. *Zoroastrianism: An Introduction to an Ancient Faith*. Brighton. UK: Sussex Academic Press, 1999.

Kotwal, F. M., and J. W. Boyd. *A Guide to the Zoroastrian Religion*. Chico, Calif.: Scholars, 1982.

Zaehner, R. C. *The Dawn and Twilight of Zoroastrianism*. Rev. ed. London: Phoenix, 2003.

"Ancient Iranian Cultural and Religious Research and Development Center." *www.ancientiran.com*.

SHINTOISM

Chart 80. Timeline of Shinto

Picken, Stuart D. B. *Historical Dictionary of Shinto*. Blue Ridge Summit, Penn.: Scarecrow, 2002.

"Japanese History." *www.kotobuki-p.co.jp/nenpyo.htm*.

Chart 81. Shinto

Breen, John, and Mark Teeuwen, eds. *Shinto in History: Ways of the Kami.* Honolulu: University of Hawaii Press, 2000.

Inoue, Nobutaka, and Ito Satoshi. *Shinto: A Short History.* New York: Routledge, 2003.

Kallen, Stuart A. *Shinto.* San Diego: Greenhaven, 2001.

Kitagawa, Joseph Mitsuo. *Religion in Japanese History.* New York: Columbia University Press, 1966.

Littleton, C. Scott. *Shinto: Origins, Rituals, Festivals, Spirits, Sacred Places.* New York: Oxford University Press, 2002.

Hines, Richard. "Shinto Creation Stories." *www.wsu.edu/~dee/ANCJAPAN/CREAT.HTM.*

CONFUCIANISM

Chart 82. Timeline of Confucianism

Yao, Xinzhong. *The Encyclopedia of Confucianism.* New York: Routledge, 2003.

"Chinese Philosophy." *www.rep.routledge.com/article-related/G001.*

Chart 83. Confucianism

Nagai, John H., and Evelyn Nagai. *Confucianism.* Oxford: Oneworld, 2000.

Taylor, Rodney Leon. *The Religious Dimensions of Confucianism.* Albany, N.Y.: State University of New York Press, 1990.

Tucker, Mary Evelyn. "Confucianism." In Bron Raymond Taylor, gen. ed. *Encyclopedia of Religion and Nature.* New York: Continuum, 2004.

Wright, Arthur. *Confucianism and Chinese Civilization.* Stanford, Calif.: Stanford University Press, 1975.

Xun, Zhou, and T. H. Barrett. *An Introduction to Confucianism.* Cambridge: Cambridge University Press, 2000.

"Confucius." *http://plato.stanford.edu/entries/confucius.*

SIKHISM

Chart 84. Timeline of Sikhism

"Major Historical Events." *www.sikh-history.com/sikhhist/events/index.html.*

"Sikh History Timeline." *www.allaboutsikhs.com/history.*

Chart 85. Sikhism

Ajitsingh, Charanjit. *The Wisdom Of Sikhism.* Oxford: Oneworld, 2001.

McLeod, W. H. *The Sikhs: History, Religion, and Society.* New York: Columbia University Press, 1989.

Singh, Gopal. *A History of the Sikh People: 1469–1978.* New Delhi: World Sikh University Press, 1979.

Singh, Patwant. *The Sikhs.* New York: Knopf, 2000.

Singh, Sirdar Kapur. *Sikhism: An Ecumenical Religion.* Chandigarh, India: Institute of Sikh Studies, 1993.

PART 6. INDIGENOUS RELIGIONS

Chart 86. Historical Relationships of Indigenous Religions

Josephy Jr., Alvin M. *500 Nations: An Illustrated History of North American Indians.* New York: Gramercy-Random House, 2002.

Thornton, John, Michael Adas, Edmund Burke III, and Philip D. Curtin. *Africa and Africans in the Making of the Atlantic World, 1400–1800.* 2nd ed. Cambridge: Cambridge University Press, 1998.

Chart 87. Comparison of Indigenous Religions

Chevannes, Barry. *Rastafari and Other African-Caribbean Worldviews.* New Brunswick, N.J.: Rutgers University Press, 1998.

Harvey, Graham, ed. *Indigenous Religions: A Companion.* New York: Continuum, 2000.

Simpson, George Eaton. *Black Religions in the New World.* New York: Columbia University Press, 1978.

AFRICAN

Chart 88. Timeline of African Traditional Religion

Shillington, Kevin. *History of Africa*. Rev. ed. New York: Macmillan, 1995.

"African Timelines." *http://web.cocc.edu/cagatucci/classes/hum211/timelines*.

"World History Archives: Africa." *www.hartford-hwp.com/archives/30*.

Chart 89. African Traditional Religion

Curtin, Philip. *African History*. 2nd ed. Boston: Addison-Wesley, 1995.

King, Noel Q. *African Cosmos: An Introduction to Religion in Africa*. Belmont, Calif.: Wadsworth, 1986.

Mbiti, John S. *Introduction to African Religion*. 2nd ed. Portsmouth, N.H.: Heinemann, 1991.

Parrinder, Edward Geoffrey. *African Traditional Religion*. 3rd ed. Westport, Conn.: Greenwood, 1970.

Zahan, Dominique. *The Religion, Spirituality, and Thought of Traditional Africa*. Chicago: University of Chicago Press, 1983.

"African Creation Stories." *http://dickinsg.intrasun.tcnj.edu/diaspora/creation.html*.

"African Traditional Religion." *www.afrikaworld.net/afrel*.

CARIBBEAN

Chart 90. Caribbean Religions

Bisnauth, Dale. *History of Religions in the Caribbean*. Trenton, N.J.: Africa World Press, 1996.

Gossai, Hemchand, and Nathaniel Samuel Murrell, eds. *Religion, Culture and Tradition in the Caribbean*. New York: Palgrave Macmillan, 2000.

Chart 91. Comparison of Caribbean Religions

Olmos, Margarite Fernandez, and Lizabeth Paravisini-Gebert. *Creole Religions of the Caribbean: An Introduction from Vodou and Santeria, to Obeah and Espiritismo*. New York: New York University Press, 2003.

Sweet, James H. *Recreating Africa: Culture, Kinship, and Religion in the Portuguese World, 1441–1770*. Raleigh: University of North Carolina Press, 2003.

Chart 92. Timeline of Rastafari

Mack, Douglas R. A. *From Babylon to Rastifari: Origin and History of the Rastafarian Movement*. Lake Havasu City, Ariz.: Frontline, 1999.

Redington, Norman Hugh. "A Sketch of Rastafari History." *www.cc.utah.edu/~jmr08860/rasta1.html*.

Chart 93. Rastafari

Chevannes, Barry. *Rastafari: Roots and Ideology*. Syracuse, N.Y.: Syracuse University Press, 1994.

Edmonds, Ennis Barrington. *Rastafari: From Outcasts to Culture Bearers*. New York: Oxford University Press, 2003.

Erskine, Noel Leo. *From Garvey to Marley: Rastafari Theology*. Gainesville, Fla.: University of Florida Press, 2005.

Forsythe, Dennis. *Rastafari: For the Healing of the Nations*. Reprint ed. New York: One Drop, 1996.

Johnson-Hill, Jack A. *I-Sight: The World of Rastafari*. Lanham, Md.: Rowman & Littlefield, 1995.

Lee, Helene. *The First Rasta: Leonard Howell and the Rise of Rastafarianism*. Chicago: Lawrence Hill, 2003.

Chart 94. Timeline of Santeria and Palo Mayombe

"Cuba: History, Part 2." *www.kwabs.com/cuba_history__2.html*.

"Santeria." *http://religiousmovements.lib.virginia.edu/nrms/santeria.html*.

Chart 95. Santeria, Appendix on Palo Mayombe

Brandon, George. *Santeria from Africa to the New World: The Dead Sell Memories*. Bloomington, Ind.: Indiana University Press, 1993.

Canizares, Raul. *The Book on Palo*. Emeryville, Calif.: Original, 2002.

De La Torre, Miguel A. *Santeria: The Beliefs and Rituals of a Growing Religion in America*. Grand Rapids, Mich.: Eerdmans, 2004.

Hagedorn, Katherine J. *Divine Utterances: The Performance of Afro-Cuban Santeria*. Washington, D.C.: Smithsonian Institution Press, 2001.

Murphy, Joseph M. *Santeria: An African Religion in America*. Boston: Beacon, 1993.

Clark, Mary Ann. "Santeria." *http://sparta.rice.edu/~maryc/Santeria*.

Chart 96. Timeline of Umbanda and Candomblé

"History of the Umbanda Movement in Brazil." *www.umbanda.org/histo_e.htm*.

"Macumba/Candomble." *http://religiousmovements.lib.virginia.edu/nrms/macu.html*.

Chart 97. Umbanda, Appendix on Candomblé

De Osa, Veronica. *Umbanda: Brazil's Old and New Spiritism*. East Rutherford, N.J.: New Horizon, 1984.

Hess, David J. *Spirits and Scientists: Ideology, Spiritism, and Brazilian Culture*. Philadelphia.: Pennsylvania State University Press, 1991.

Langguth, A. J. *Macumba: White and Black Magic in Brazil*. New York: Harper & Row, 1975.

Voeks, Robert A. *Sacred Leaves of Candomblé: African Magic, Medicine, and Religion in Brazil*. Austin, Texas: University of Texas Press, 1997.

Wafer, James William. *The Taste of Blood: Spirit Possession in Brazilian Candomblé*. Philadelphia: University of Pennsylvania Press, 1991.

"Umbanda." *www.umbanda.org/abert_e.htm*.

Chart 98. Timeline of Voudon (Voodoo)

Antippas, Andy P. *A Brief History of Voodoo: Slavery and Survival of the African Gods*. New Orleans: Hembco, 1988.

"History of Vodun in the West." *http://religioustolerance.org/voodoo.htm*.

Hounon, Mamaissii Vivian Odelelasi Dansi. "Voodoo: A History of Religious Persecution and Suppression." *www.mamiwata.com/history1.html*.

Chart 99. Voudon (Voodoo)

Desmangles, Leslie G. *The Faces of the Gods: Voodoo and Roman Catholicism in Haiti*. Raleigh, N.C.: University of North Carolina Press, 1993.

Leyburn, James Graham. *The Haitian People*. New Haven, Conn.: Yale University Press, 1966.

Metraux, Alfred. *Voodoo in Haiti*. New York: Pantheon, 1989.

Rigaud, Milo. *Secrets of Voodoo*. San Francisco: City Lights, 1985.

Wand, Kelly. *Voodoo: Fact or Fiction?* San Diego: Greenhaven, 2004.

NATIVE AMERICAN

Chart 100. Timeline of Native American Religion

Debo, Angie. *The History of the Indians of the United States*. London: Pimlico, 1995.

Nichols, Roger L. *American Indians in U.S. History*. Norman, Okla.: University of Oklahoma Press, 2004.

"Native Times.com." *http://nativetimes.com*.

Chart 101. Native American Religion

Erdoes, Richard, and Alfonso Ortiz, eds. *American Indian Myths and Legends*. Magnolia, Mass.: Peter Smith, 1997.

Gill, Sam D. *Native American Religions: An Introduction*. 2nd ed. Belmont, Calif.: Wadsworth, 2004.

Hultkrantz, Ake. *Shamanic Healing and Ritual Drama: Health and Medicine in Native North American Religious Traditions*. New York: Crossroad/Herder & Herder, 1997.

Leeming, David Adams, and Jake Page. *The Mythology of Native North America*. Norman, Okla.: University of Oklahoma Press, 1998.

Martin, Joel W. *The Land Looks After Us: A History of Native American Religion*. New York: Oxford University Press, 2001.

Vecsey, Christopher, ed. *Religion in Native North America*. Moscow, Idaho: University of Idaho Press, 1990.

Wilson, James. *Native American Religion*. New York: Oxford University Press, 1999.

"Native American Statistics." *www.nativevillage.org/Messages%20from%20the%20People/Population%20statistics.htm*.

Note: Statistics on many of the religions in this volume are found at *www.adherents.com*.

Recommended Reading List

Bowker, John Westerdale. *World Religions: The Great Faiths Explored and Explained*. New York: Dorling Kindersley, 1997.

Braswell Jr., George W. *Understanding World Religions*. Nashville: Broadman & Holman, 1994.

Coogan, Michael D., ed. *The Illustrated Guide to World Religions*. New York: Oxford University Press, 2003.

Corduan, Winfried. *Neighboring Faiths: A Christian Introduction to World Religions*. Downers Grove, Ill.: InterVarsity Press, 1998.

Crim, Keith, ed. *The Perennial Dictionary of World Religions*. Reprint ed. San Francisco: Harper Collins, 1989.

Hexham, Irving. *Concise Dictionary of Religion*. 2nd ed. Vancouver: Regent College Press, 1999.

Hopfe, Lewis M., and Mark R. Woodward. *Religions of the World*. 9th ed. Upper Saddle River, N.J.: Prentice-Hall, 2003.

Lewis, James F., and William G. Travis. *Religious Traditions of the World*. Grand Rapids, Mich.: Zondervan, 1991.

Masuzawa, Tomoko. *The Invention of World Religions: Or, How European Universalism Was Preserved in the Language of Pluralism*. Chicago: University of Chicago Press, 2005.

Melton, Gordon J., ed. *The Encyclopedia of American Religions: A Comprehensive Study of the Major Religious Groups in the United States*. 7th ed. Farmington Hills, Mich.: Gale, 2002.

Miethe, Terry L. *The Compact Dictionary of Doctrinal Words*. Minneapolis: Bethany House, 1988.

Young, William. *The World's Religions: Worldviews and Contemporary Issues*. Upper Saddle River, N.J.: Prentice-Hall, 1995.

Zaretsky, Irving, and Mark P. Leone. *Religious Movements in Contemporary America*. Princeton, N.J.: Princeton University Press, 1974.

"Philosophy, Theology & Religion." St. Martin's College. *http://philtar.ucsm.ac.uk.*

"Virtual Religion Index." Rutgers University. *http://virtualreligion.net/vri.*

CPSIA information can be obtained at www.ICGtesting.com
Printed in the USA
LVOW091411070613

337442LV00004B/6/P